In the Footsteps of Dante

Mimesis

―
Romanische Literaturen der Welt

Herausgegeben von
Ottmar Ette

Band 99

In the Footsteps of Dante

Crossroads of European Humanism

Edited by
Teresa Bartolomei and João R. Figueiredo

DE GRUYTER

The publication of this volume was made possible with the support of the Italian Cultural Institute of Lisbon and the Research Center for Communication and Culture (CECC) [funded by the Fundação para a Ciência e Tecnologia (FCT), Portugal, under the reference UIDP/00126/2020].

ISBN 978-3-11-162742-7
e-ISBN (PDF) 978-3-11-079604-9
e-ISBN (EPUB) 978-3-11-079609-4
ISSN 0178-7489

Library of Congress Control Number: 2022945740

Bibliographic information published by the Deutsche Nationalbibliothek
The Deutsche Nationalbibliothek lists this publication in the Deutsche Nationalbibliografie; detailed bibliographic data are available on the internet at http://dnb.dnb.de.

© 2024 Walter de Gruyter GmbH, Berlin/Boston
This volume is text- and page-identical with the hardback published in 2023.
Typesetting: Integra Software Services Pvt. Ltd.

www.degruyter.com

Acknowledgments

This book collects the contributions presented on occasion of *Dias de Dante* 2021, held in Lisbon from September to November 2021 to celebrate the 700th anniversary of Dante's death. The programme was organized around four foci: an exhibition of early editions and manuscripts of Dante's work and relative to it, accompanied by two drawings by Sandro Botticelli graciously lent by the Vatican Apostolic Library (*Visions of Dante: Botticelli's Inferno*, Calouste Gulbenkian Foundation, Lisbon, 24 September – 29 November 2021); an international conference (*Dante: a poet of our time*, 25 September); a series of "Lectures on Dante" (September – November); a cycle of conversations and events around the exhibition ("Around Dante"), organized by the Calouste Gulbenkian Foundation (September–November).

Bringing this ambitiously broad and diversified project into existence was possible thanks to the cooperation of various international institutions, both public and private, which supported the commemoration of Dante with their indispensable organisational and financial efforts.

The editors of this book, who were also the curators of the project, would like warmly to thank all the involved institutions for their commitment and support: CECC (Research Centre for Communication and Culture, Catholic University of Portugal); CITER (Research Centre for Theology and Religious Studies, Catholic University of Portugal); the Embassy of Italy in Portugal; School of Arts and Humanities, University of Lisbon; Calouste Gulbenkian Foundation; IIC (Italian Cultural Institute of Lisbon); Vatican Apostolic Library.

Institutional involvement is built on people's commitment and goodwill. All our gratitude is therefore due to those who have participated in various ways in the decision-making and operational process, generously providing the significant human and financial resources necessary for the realisation of the events: Alexandra Ambrósio Lopes (CECC|UCP, Director); Maria Helena Borges and João Carvalho Dias (Calouste Gulbenkian Foundation); Paola D'Agostino (Embassy of Italy in Portugal); Arnaldo do Espírito Santo (ADFLUL, President); Carlo Formosa (Italian Ambassador in Portugal); José Tolentino de Mendonça (BAV, Librarian and Archivist); Alexandre Palma (CITER | UCP, Director); Stefano Scaramuzzino (IIC Lisbon, Director); Miguel Tamen (School of Humanities, University of Lisbon, Dean); Silvana Urzini (IIC Lisbon); Luisa Violo (IIC Lisbon, former Director).

The final stage of this journey, with the publication of the conference and lectures on Dante, has been made materially possible through the financial support of the IIC and CECC. Our gratitude goes to Dr. Scaramuzzino and Dr. Violo of the IIC, and to Professor Alexandra Ambrósio Lopes of the CECC, who have helped make this publication possible.

https://doi.org/10.1515/9783110796049-202

It has been a real pleasure to cooperate with de Gruyter publishing house, in the person of our editorial manager, Maxim Karagodin. To his untiring kindness and constructive helpfulness, we owe our final thanks.

Contents

Acknowledgments —— V

Teresa Bartolomei and João R. Figueiredo
Foreword —— 1

Prologue

José Tolentino De Mendonça
We Are All Called upon to Build Visions: The *Divine Comedy* as a Pedagogy of the Gaze —— 11

Section I: Dante. A Poet of Our Time

Carlo Ossola
"Supra te et non subter": The Biblical Humanism of the *Comedy* —— 31

Paola Nasti
Biblical *Signa* and Dante's Words: For a Taxonomy of Biblical Intertextuality in the *Comedy* —— 45

Albert Russell Ascoli
Dante and the Faith of the Reader —— 81

Teresa Bartolomei
Dante: Talking to the Dead – Giving a Voice to Silence —— 109

Lina Bolzoni
Dante: Memory Matters in the *Comedy* —— 149

Giulio Ferroni
Dante, Poet of a Europe to Come —— 167

Section II: Dante in Portugal

Isabel Almeida
Dante in the Century of Camões —— 179

João R. Figueiredo
Dante and Camões: Epic and the Portrayal of Humanity —— 203

Arnaldo do Espírito Santo
Dante and the Fifth Empire —— 215

Rita Marnoto
Dante in Portugal: An Ethereal Gaze —— 243

Jorge Vaz de Carvalho
Dante: Poetry and Translation —— 257

Epilogue

Alberto Manguel
Dante the Geographer —— 269

Editions and Translations —— 277

Notes on Contributors —— 279

General Index —— 287

Teresa Bartolomei and João R. Figueiredo
Foreword

2021 marked the 700 years of Dante Alighieri's death. The vast oeuvre of this poet and thinker of encyclopaedic erudition and dazzling artistic power is inscribed in the collective memory of the West and beyond, to such a wide extent that the task of contemporary criticism is to transform into hermeneutic insight the intuition that claims Dante as a 'classic of humanity'.

This critical challenge starts from a paradox: what is it that makes Dante universal and relevant to the present-day reader, if everything in his writing exhibits, on the contrary, a strong contextualism, a passionate identification with his own condition of a man of the *Trecento*, a Catholic and a Florentine? In fact, the self of his poetry is robust and omnipresent, but only liminally does it dissolve into the lyrical abstraction of an inner experience devoid of spatial and temporal coordinates: it is increasingly impregnated, on the contrary, with historical, political, and religious references, performing as a witness, interpreter, and judge, one severe and polemical, of his own era. The lyrical writing of the *Vita nuova* expands into an encyclopaedic review of human knowledge in the *Convivio* and into a passionate political utopia in the *De Monarchia*. The author's self-consciousness transcends itself into a revolutionary perspective of historical linguistics in *De vulgari eloquentia*. All these different intellectual and literary paths converge in the *Divine Comedy*, an inexhaustible collection of reality and imagination, of dreams and memory, of visions and concepts, of immanent and transcendent experiences, of factual data and abstractions.

Everything in Dante is a laboratory of contradictions, and in them his greatness is manifested: the author of sublime visions of the afterlife nourished by eschatological mysticism, Alighieri also brings into poetry the daily chronicle of his own city and ongoing political conflicts, the evocation of crimes of passion (such as the murder of Paolo and Francesca, an adulterous couple of unforgettable gracefulness) and sordid political events. Conversations of exquisite spiritual finesse alternate with lurid tavern brawls; the repulsive and the grotesque are interspersed with the tragic hieraticism of magnanimous souls greater than their condemnation. Arduous theological discussions are grafted onto the most partisan political pamphletism. Evocations of incomparable lyrical delicacy are knotted to powerful dramatic sequences. Dante is a prodigious author who plays all the instruments of the literary orchestra because he gives voice to all the registers of the human condition. The strength of his writing springs from their irreducible complexity, which does not pretend to heal existential and stylistic dissonances and contrasts, but explores them to the core, to release their power of meaning and truth.

To recognise Dante's greatness, what makes him a classic of humanity, it is therefore necessary to acknowledge the contradictions in his work, explore them, understand what makes them so fruitful. Not to harmonise Dante, in his inexhaustible complexity, but to leave him free in his formidable capacity for perspective vision, is the task of the scholar who tackles his works, not claiming to objectify him in a sterile philological univocity but opening the treasure chest of his writing to contemporary readers. Different points of view, possibly incompatible sensibilities, mutually alien approaches, must therefore converge around the poet.

It is in this spirit of critical freedom and unprejudiced questioning of the poet's topicality that Italian, American and Portuguese scholars came to Lisbon in the autumn of 2021, to gather around Dante's work, not with the simple intention of exposing the results of their own research but with the broader ambition of activating specific hermeneutical scenarios that may help the academic public to free itself from sterile specialisms and ordinary readers to rediscover the expressive and cognitive riches of Dante's writing. Dante was a great linguistic, cultural and poetic ferryman. His work is an incessant dialogue between pagan classicism and Christian theology, Latin and the vernacular, everyday experience and mysticism, political and religious passion; the frontiers of genre, style and content dissolve, broken down by the irresistible breath of the poetic word and the ethical and cognitive passion. It is a magnificent, unique complexity, which makes of Dante's work a crossroad of Western humanism.

This spirit of fruitful transversality is reflected in the decision to open and close the cycle of celebrations and the selection of texts in this book with two writers: the poet Cardinal, Librarian and Archivist of the Holy Roman Church, José Tolentino de Mendonça, and the Argentinean-Canadian erudite essayist and fictionist Alberto Manguel. In the radical diversity of their geographical origins and cultural backgrounds, both authors identify Dante as an essential point of reference in their literary universe.

José Tolentino de Mendonça elaborates an evocative reinterpretation of the travel chronicle that is the *Divine Comedy*, reading it as a path of re-education of the gaze, from blindness to the perception of the invisible. Dante makes his pilgrimage, as he explicitly declares, to be able to see again: "Quinci sù vo per non esser più cieco" ("That I be blind no longer, through this place I pass", Pg XXVI, 58). His otherworldly journey is, in other words, a path of learning a truthful relationship with reality, which is articulated in three precise gnoseological stages, corresponding to the three spheres of experience he passes through. In order to learn to see, it is first necessary to reconstruct one's relationship with the object, secondly to become aware of the intersubjective dimension of the gaze, and finally to re-establish a loving relationship with the world and beings: one does not really see what one does not love. Nothing is further from the intent and spirit of the *Comedy*, the Portuguese poet therefore warns, than to read it as a formidable archive of beautiful images to interpose between our contemplation and the world. Picking up on a dazzling intuition by Osip Mandel'štam, for whom Dante's poem is, on the contrary, "a machine for the disintegration of images, of visual substitutes, of made visions", de Mendonça invites us to read the *Comedy* as an exercise in detoxification from the media proliferation of images, from the visual inflation promoted by digital devices. Dante teaches the reader to strip himself of received and instantaneous images in order to slowly, patiently and creatively construct his own visions.

Alberto Manguel also places the theme of the *Divine Comedy* as a journey at the centre of his reflection, highlighting, however, not the dynamics of vision, but that of the construction of a space. Dante is a geographer, who draws a cartography of that "Great Beyond" that we present outside the "here" of our sensitive experience, of the "dark forest" of the human condition, in its tragic load of error and suffering, guilt and vulnerable innocence. In order not to feel lost in the here and now of earthly life, Dante teaches, it is necessary to 'think' of the beyond as the space of what we desire: of what we can be, do and know. In Manguel's reading, according to Dante, master of the "trasumanar" ("Passing beyond the human", Pd I, 70), man's vocation is to be the goal of himself, the point of arrival of a journey that constructs its own destination as it unfolds in the articulation of ever new frontiers: limits surpassed in the moment they are traced, coordinates of an imaginary geography that is not a fanciful invention but a condition of reality in its capacity to concretely model human existence.

If the two writers summoned in the volume poetically transfigure their own reception of Dante into a universal image – the journey as a school of the gaze and as a cartography of human self-transcendence – and show us once again how literature can always be a source and object of new literature, the approach of the scholars who accompany them is evidently different. They are divided into two sections, reflecting the two main objectives, convergent but not entirely assimilable, pursued in the construction of the programme of commemorations of the seventh centenary of Dante's death in Lisbon.

On the one hand, the intention was to present to the Portuguese public some of the most significant voices of the contemporary Dante studies, privileging a 'universalising' point of view, capable of highlighting the permanent poetic, cultural, and spiritual topicality of Dante's work ("Dante: A Poet of Our Time" was the title of the inaugural colloquium).

On the other hand, it seemed timely to develop an updated and as complete as possible overview of the reception of Dante's works in Portugal, which appears singularly intermittent, in a karstic continuity, never entirely extinguished, but at times silenced by the clear prevalence of the Petrarchan model.

The first section opens with an essay by **Carlo Ossola** reconstructing in a dizzying intertextual filigree the patristic texture that filters and conveys the scriptural sources of the Comedy. The author takes a clear and surprising position in the age-old debate on whether Dante belongs to the autumn of the Middle Ages or to the dawn of modernity. In recognizing in Dante one of the precursors of Humanism, Ossola does not appeal, as usual, to his sophisticated and unprejudiced recovery of classical culture, but precisely to the peculiar elaboration of the medieval matrix of departure, essentially biblical and theological, which is brightly oriented by the poet to a vision of human dignity characterised by "self-sovereignty", the capacity for self-transcendence (dilatation, *latitudo animi*) and enhancement of the experience of reality. "The entire adventure of believing, of seeing, of writing lies within this *making man capable of the world*: in this aspiration there is a perfect continuity between Saint Benedict and Saint Francis, and between them and Dante and Italian humanism, as far as Giovanni Pico della Mirandola's *De hominis dignitate* of at the end of the fifteenth century" writes Ossola. Dante's is a 'biblical humanism' that euphorically transfigures creaturality into transhumanity ("passing beyond the human"), *delectatio* into *dilatatio*, expiation into redemption. Dante's man is placed by God "always at the top, never at the bottom". He is a man called to ascend "above himself", greater than his earthly limits, pregnant with infinity.

In close counterpoint to Carlo Ossola's essay, **Paola Nasti**'s contribution also examines the scriptural sources of the *Comedy*. Besides the important philological value of the precise analysis of the biblical matrix of three key words ("Eli", "beloved", "worms") used by Dante in the *Comedy*, Paola Nasti's essay is of outstanding methodological interest. It is a paradigmatic start to a new way of recognising the biblical intertextuality that weaves Dante's poem. The prevailing tendency among researchers up to now has been to identify the direct or indirect scriptural quotations that crop up in the *Comedy* (mediated by the patristic and theological tradition), in a reading grid that favours commentary, without adequately taking into account two other techniques of study and dissemination of the sacred text that were very widespread in the Middle Ages: *concordantiae* and *distinctiones*, classificatory-comparatist hardware of the occurrences of key terms in all the biblical books. Nasti therefore proposes a lexical analysis that identifies the poet's precise use of biblical terms and organises the occurrences into a taxonomy based on a tripartite typology, consisting of "quote-words", "pericope-words", and finally "monad-words". The application of the general model to three specific examples analysed in the essay opens extremely promising and innovative research scenarios.

The religious horizon of Dante's poetry, highlighted in its biblical sources by Ossola and Nasti, is analysed by **Albert Russell Ascoli** in its specific literary value according to the hermeneutical hypothesis that the *Comedy*'s fundamental authorial strategy is that of an interpellation of the reader's faith. Taking up and developing with some innovative passages his now classic research work on the construction of a modern notion of authorship in Dante's work, Ascoli points out that this ambition of revolutionary self-determination on the part of the writer is counterbalanced by the creation of an equally unprecedented device of readership: the authority and autonomy of the emissary writer can in fact be affirmed only if it is matched by a similar freedom on the part of the recipient reader, who must choose whether, how much and what to "believe" in what is said in the work. By systematically disarming every hermeneutic automatism, Dante structures his text as a critical space in which the reception of meaning is also inseparably an evaluation of its truth and of the credibility of its author. The hermeneutic paradox of the necessity and impossibility of dissociating the reader's faith from that of the author (according to Gadamer, only those who believe in it understand the message) is converted in Dante into a highly refined textual strategy, in which the author's explication of the demand for credibility enhances rather than reduces the reader's freedom, confronting him with epistemic challenges that broaden the conceptual horizon of the notion of reality.

The issue of the author's credibility is also at the centre of **Teresa Bartolomei**'s essay, which attributes the genesis of the *Comedy* as a poem of the afterlife to the autobiographical need, robustly self-rehabilitating, to guarantee the truthfulness of one's own representation of the facts (the status of "exul immeritus"), structurally problematised by the *self-testimonial fallacy*. Through the Christian and theological resemantisation of the poetic and pagan *topos*, both epic and orphic, of the *catabasis*, the descent to the underworld of the hero chosen by the god or the poet who wants to recover his beloved, Dante integrates the lyrical-confessional device of prosopopoeia with the hermeneutic-theological device of typological-figural metalepsis, implemented as a mechanism of truth certification of the individual point of view. By assigning the biographical and autobiographical narrative to deceased witnesses and actors, who see temporal events *sub specie aeternitatis*, the poet factually corroborates and figuratively interprets his own existence and his own vision of history as a significantly authentic *littera* of a prophetic message of salvation valid on a moral, allegorical, and anagogical level.

In a fascinating journey through the history of the art of memory, **Lina Bolzoni** identifies the structural architecture of the *Comedy* as an integral part of an ancient mnemotechnical tradition that was particularly flourishing in the Middle Ages, placing itself at the service of a parenetic and catechetical strategy of spreading the Christian code of vices and virtues, in a rigorous taxonomic mapping of divine law and human behaviour. Words and images are inextricably linked in the construction of a metaphysical universe with an ethical matrix, in which the difference between good and evil traces insuperable boundaries or gradual contiguities, vertiginous hierarchies and irreversible directions. The *loci*, sculpted by the pilgrimage as shifting landscapes of eternal or transitory punishments and ecstatic gradations of rarefied abstractness, are populated by *imagines agentes*: souls that figuratively exemplify their own moral condition as eschatologically definitive meaning. In the prodigious machine of Dante's writing, the arid conceptuality of moral taxonomy takes on the flesh of image, intelligence, and affection, taking shape in a "visibile parlare" ("the speech made visible", Pg X, 95), in an inextricable interdependence of vision and word, which is indelibly inscribed in the reader's memory.

Dante is a poet who thought of Europe and helped Europe to think of itself, as **Giulio Ferroni** observes in a contribution that combines philology and cultural history in a refined way. The statute of Dante as a European poet, clearly formulated by Ernst Robert Curtius, has first solid literary reasons: Dante proposed and imposed a self-understanding of the artist and a notion of the character as "final object" that are decisive in shaping the vision of the dignity of the individual subject that constitutes the greatest legacy of Western humanism. However, it is also on the level of the historical, political, and spiritual ideals professed by Dante, presented not only in the *Comedy*, but also in speculative works such as the *De Monarchia* and in militant writings such as some of the *Epistles*, that the Florentine poet stands out as a passionate witness to an idea of Europe as a political community, which places him at the centre of the continent's self-awareness. Unity and governmental subsidiarity are compatible and necessary, in the utopian fresco drawn by Dante, to guarantee the peoples of Europe peace, justice and the conditions for a flourishing civil development. According to Ferroni: "The unity of the human race and the necessity of the monarch who rules over it and guides it to the power of knowledge does not preclude the autonomy of individual communities and political institutions, within the broader arrangement of the universe" is the central idea of Dante's political thought, a visionary witness of a Europe still *in fieri*, still to come, but possible.

The section dedicated to "Dante in Portugal" opens with the essay by **Isabel Almeida**. Fully aware of the distinction between alluding to an author and really knowing his works, she surveys Portuguese literature of the 16th and 17th centuries in search of Dante. Unlike the Spanish case, where the *Comedy* was read and much admired, the presence of the Italian poet turns out to be rather elusive, in the same way as the information about the presence of his books in Portuguese libraries is scarce, but several quotations emerge here and there, mainly *via* Spanish translation, in works by some of the major poets and writers: Gil Vicente, Bernardim Ribeiro, Jorge Ferreira de Vasconcelos, Francisco de Sá de Miranda. The latter however, albeit having travelled in Italy and enlivened the Portuguese letters with fruitful Italian influences, seems to have been impervious to Dante.

In face of the evidence, the silence is telling: in Renaissance Portugal, Dante is more referred to and mentioned in metaliterary texts as a sign of erudition and high culture, than actually engaged with. As far as influence and intertextuality, Petrarca clearly triumphs over his immediate precursor.

If Dante is not explicitly referred to by Camões in his epic *The Lusiads*, arguably the most influent poem written in Portuguese, it is the overall political attitude of the Florentine poet, the structure of the *Comedy* and some of its most characteristic locutory modes that can be fruitfully used to assess the achievements of *The Lusiads*. Thus **João R. Figueiredo** explores several parallels between the two epic poems, beyond the limits of the usual comparison, a touchstone of Portuguese literary criticism (and Camões' studies in particular). The giant Adamastor emerges as a sublime hyperbole of the many damned souls Dante comes across in the Inferno: the form of address, the prophetic capacity, the irate state of mind, are common to, e. g. Farinata. Furthermore, the giant is immobile at the southmost tip of the African continent, in the very same way Satan is frozen at the centre of the Earth. Africa can be therefore envisaged as a kind of Inferno, the bottom of the physical world to which one is forced to descend in order spiritually to ascend afterwards. A major difference arises between the *Comedy* and *The Lusiads* in the guise of a pessimistic twist introduced by Camões: the paradise to which Vasco da Gama is inducted is no more than a fiction, a prosthetic idyll more apt to console the reader than actually to reward the nominal hero, Vasco da Gama, whose bloodthirsty career Camões openly upbraids.

The Jesuit António Vieira, arguably the finest prose stylist in the Portuguese language, wrote extensively about Portugal's providential destiny as the ruler of the Fifth Empire, a spiritual realm under one king only, a utopia that blended politics and religion at a time when Portugal was struggling to free itself from the Spanish rule and regain its independence. Having just translated Dante's *De Monarchia*, and having translated Vieira's *Clavis Prophetarum* in the past, **Arnaldo do Espírito Santo** was challenged to write about Vieira's and Dante's concept of empire, and came to the conclusion that, other than similarities in form, that were to be expected, António Vieira clearly drew on Dante's views and arguments to achieve his baroque extravaganza. This is a major breakthrough both in the scholarship of António Vieira, as no association to Dante had previously been suggested, and in the scholarship of Dante, whose poetry did not have much impact on Portuguese literature, but whose concepts of "law", "predestination", "universal empire" and "universal peace" as construed in *De Monarchia* were at the basis of Vieira's political and spiritual views.

Rita Marnoto completes the survey of Dante's reception in Portuguese culture and literature as far as the 19th century is concerned. This was the time when the bonds between Italy and Portugal were strengthened for political reasons (capped with a Royal wedding). Literary concerns followed them closely: as Dante was seen as a sort of national icon, a moral representative of the ideals of the Risorgimento, so Camões became a symbol of uncompromising national pride, beginning with the Peninsular wars and emerging Romantic sensibility, and ending with the *ultimatum* and turmoil caused by British colonial ambitions that collided with Portuguese interests in Africa. This was also the time when the first translations of the *Comedy* (or parts thereof) were published. The close parallel Dante-Camões was duly emphasised by several authors, foremost among them Teófilo Braga, the late-Romantic, Republican, historian of Portuguese literature; and by the arts, that produced a prolific iconography.

Only recently were Portuguese verse translations of the full text of the *Comedy* published. **Jorge Vaz de Carvalho** is the author of the latest (2021). In his chapter, a personal testimony of his cyclopic work, he describes his task as an essay in loyalty, not treason, contrary to what the saying goes, and presents the criteria for his translation, that will likely become the standard version of Dante's poem for the Portuguese-speaking world.

Lisbon, June 2022

Prologue

José Tolentino De Mendonça
We Are All Called upon to Build Visions
The *Divine Comedy* as a Pedagogy of the Gaze

> Ma ficca li occhi per l'aere ben fiso,
> e vedrai [. . .].
> Allora più che prima li occhi apersi;
> guarda'mi innanzi, e vidi
>
> But let your eyes be fixed attentively
> and, through the air, you will see [. . .].
> I opened – wider than before – my eyes;
> I looked ahead of me, and I saw
>
> Purgatorio XIII, 43–44, 46–47

Premise

If a classic is a piece of work whose interpretation can never be complete, then the *Divine Comedy* is the quintessential classic, since it has been the source of countless, contrasting and, in some cases, tempestuously irreconcilable hermeneutic viewpoints over the past seven centuries. As noted by the Russian poet Osip Mandelstam, who arrived at Dante very much out of the beaten way in the 1930s, and relied on Dante to literally survive Stalin's terror, the greatness of the *Comedy* lies precisely in the tension that pervades it, and which renders it a battlefield of registers, instances, languages and visions. As Mandelstam explains, to read Dante is to refuse to remain fettered to a particular present, since his intricately constructed poetry "shakes us awake" to remind us, to assure us that we are "on the way," "forever on the road." In effect, Dante's writing does not mean to set itself (or us, as readers) into a rigid pattern, a closed rationality, or a fixed style. On the contrary, the senses intervene in the writing, much as athletes about to go "into the decisive fight"[1]: the truth in the text (and, likewise, the truth in the reading) lies in the engendered fray, in the tension, in the supreme heightening it demands; in a complementary, rather than permutational, logic.

---

[1] Osip Mandelstam: *Selected Essays*. Sidney Monas (ed.), Clarence Brown & Robert Hughes (tr.). Austin, Texas: University of Texas Press 1977, p. 4.

Note: Translated from the Portuguese by Cassilda Alcobia-Murphy.

Some read the *Divine Comedy* as the tale of a sinner's pilgrimage in search for redemption (for himself and, prophetically, for the reader), as claimed in the *Epistle to Can Grande*; while others view it as a settling of scores by a banished politician seeking rehabilitation in the tribunal of history. For others still, it is a paean to a woman loved but never attained, an exploit of love, hidden or sublimated within its dense eschatological figuration (C. S. Singleton). Others identify a mystical, contemplative *journey* in the poem, a sort of *itinerarium mentis in Deum* (C. Ossola), while others still emphasise the literary and rhetorical artistry consciously woven into the writing, thus downplaying any theological ambitions when measured against its artistic virtuosity (T. Barolini). Others yet read the *Divine Comedy* as a fascinating *Trésor* of human knowledge in literary form: the *Comedy* as an encyclopaedia of 14th-century religious, philosophical, political and scientific knowledge, a conventional model passed down by his mentor, Brunetto Latini, to Dante, who went on to recast it as a universal literary creation (from B. Nardi to E. Gilson). Others, in turn, tend to dispense with the information contained within, to focus instead on the purely aesthetic experience of a text unparalleled in its lyrical, dramatic, and imagic power (B. Croce). Non-Christian readings tend to value it as a crucial step in Western realism, a foundational locus for the self-representation of European culture (E. Auerbach), while Christian readings identify in the poem an artistically commanding expression of faith itself, an indelible mark of Christian truth in the blazing experience of mankind (T. S. Eliot).

As an example, in his Apostolic Letter *Candor Lucis Aeternae*, which recently marked the seventh centenary of the death of Dante Alighieri, Pope Francis stated: "Dante reads the depths of the human heart. In everyone, even in the most abject and disturbing figures, he can discern a spark of the desire to attain [...] fulfilment. [...] Dante becomes the interpreter of the universal human desire to follow the journey of life to its ultimate destination, when the fullness of truth [...] will be revealed. [...] Dante's journey, especially as it appears in the *Divine Comedy*, was truly a journey of desire."[2]

The volume I have been given the honour of introducing is, to this extent, a prime example of this plurality, where difference is valued as an asset rather than a hindrance, and interpretative paths intersect without necessarily 're-covering.' The occasion that elicited the texts in the present volume, namely the commemoration, in Lisbon, of the seventh centenary of the death of Dante Alighieri, aimed essentially to open new paths, rather than to cross through familiar landscapes,

---

[2] Francis, Pope: Apostolic Letter *Candor Lucis aeternae* on the VII Centenary of the death of Dante Alighieri, 25.03.2021, §4 (Online: https://press.vatican.va/content/salastampa/en/bollettino/pubblico/2021/03/25/210325a.html, accessed 14.09.2021).

and to privilege a culturally diverse approach, faithful to the encyclopaedic ethos of an author who distinguished himself not only as a poet, but also as a philologist (in *De vulgari eloquentia*), as a theorist of the politics and reformation of the Church (in *De monarchia* and the *Epistulae*), and as a moral philosopher and nuanced hermeneutist (in the *Convivio*). The writer Alberto Manguel thus joins some of today's most renowned Dante scholars (Albert Russell Ascoli, Lina Bolzoni Giulio Ferroni, Paola Nasti and Carlo Ossola), alongside five Portuguese researchers (Isabel Almeida, Arnaldo do Espírito Santo, João R. Figueiredo, Rita Marnoto and Jorge Vaz de Carvalho) who explore the little-studied field of the reception of the poetry and ideas of Dante in Portugal, including issues of translation and literary tradition, intertextual crisscrossings and poetic models.

Intended as an initial, rather than a final, word on these topics, this anthology invites us to return to Dante, and to acknowledge his work as an intellectual challenge for the present moment, while reminding us that this return cannot be reduced to an indifferent technicism. To come back to Dante is to smash the boundaries of the literary sphere in the strictest sense, in order to inscribe literature onto a broader anthropological plane, while attaining, in the process, proof of his magnitude, not only in cultural and artistic terms, but also in terms of his human and spiritual value. To return to Dante is to unseat hoary dualisms, and to acknowledge that the natural and the supernatural are not alternative worlds, but complementary forms of being in the world; that time and eternity are two conditions of the self in search of meaning; that good and evil are choices whereby the subject defines itself conspicuously, but which are not, in absolute terms, defined by the subject. To return to Dante is to explore our inherited universe of Western humanism, in all its contradictory facets, unfulfilled promises, and burgeoning intuitions. To return to Dante is to rediscover that art has everything to do with morality, even as both gainsay this relationship and turn their backs on each other. It is the realisation that true spirituality is not indifferent to politics, that religion is a driving force of history, and that literature is a place for the self-construction of rationality. To return to Dante is, in short, to ask ourselves who we are, and to acknowledge that it is by asking this very question that Man becomes who he is; not necessarily through the production of answers and conclusions, but through the actual journeys of discovery and new beginnings. As attested to by the contributions to this volume, we leave this experience not with conclusions, but with internal openings, crevices that project the gaze, journeys unafraid of what glimmers in the distance. Accordingly, desire has been enhanced, the boundaries of our pilgrimage expanded, and whether we name it as such or not, the impulse that moves us has been intensified. In this sense, we all partake in Mandelstam's aspiration at the end of his "Conversation about Dante," which he expressed thus: "It is my hope that the object of Dante scholarship will become the coordination of the impulse and the text."[3]

That I Be Blind No Longer, through This Place I Pass

For my myself, I take part in this dialogue on Dante simply as a daily visitor of poetry, who finds in this author a limpid outpouring of aesthetic and spiritual experience, and many of those "things new and old" (Mt 13:52) that Christ states, in the parable, to be the treasure of every scribe who begins his path towards knowledge. And it is my intention precisely to share one of these "things" – I do not know exactly whether new or old – which I have noticed ever more deeply within the endless portmanteau of the *Divine Comedy*, and which is perhaps pertinent to the aim that brought us together and that found a moment of singular power in the exhibition *Visions of Dante: The* Inferno *according to Botticelli*. In effect, it is my conviction that this poem, without prejudice to the multiple interpretative possibilities itemised above, can also be read as a poetic and spiritual pedagogy of the gaze, as an itinerary of the learning of vision. It is certainly not by happenstance, but for a reason consubstantial to this poetic writing, that Dante's work has been the object of sweeping interest from preeminent artists such as Botticelli, Blake, Doré, Bouguereau, Rodin, and Rauschenberg, among many others. It is as if painters, engravers, and sculptors of different eras and traditions felt called upon by Dante to see with him, through him, beyond him. The historical profusion of visual glosses on the *Comedy* asserts the visionary force of a text that does not dictate a perspective or an imagic pattern, but unequivocally *sets the gaze in motion*. It does not impose a representation of the real, but asks of each of us to construct our own gaze, to contribute to its activation and maturation.

The *Divine Comedy* is therefore a true pedagogy of the gaze for its readers, because it delineates a patient path for the schooling of vision, which the poem's protagonist performs in the first person, under the guidance of several masters, and during which he undergoes exacting optical tests, shores up unexpected visual talents, encounters extreme situations that lift sleep from his eyes, hitherto captive (like those of the reader) to the vices of habit, the entropy of indifference, and the manacles of sloth and evil.

Dante encounters us, as if to rouse us to this crucial enterprise, when he textually declares to the souls of the seventh circle of Purgatory, that "to see again," to "be blind no more" is the central aim of his pilgrimage while he lives among the dead:

---

[3] Osip Mandelstam: *Selected Essays*, p. 44.

Quinci sù vo per non esser più cieco;	That I be blind no more, through this place
donna è di sopra che m'acquista grazia,	I pass; above a lady has gained grace
per che 'l mortal per vostro mondo reco.	for me; therefore I bear my mortal body across
	[your world.
	Purgatorio XXVI 58–60

In the reflection to follow, I shall attempt to briefly reconstruct the three stages of this schooling of vision during Dante-the-pilgrim's journey through the great beyond, in a path of progressive refinement of his (and I daresay, our) ability to see. This pedagogical process entails, at a first stage – that of the Inferno – a reconstruction of the relationship between the gaze and its object, in a meticulous re-education of attention, of the focus on contents, and of the quandary of light. To look into the pitch-black of deepest night, to see the heart of darkness, is not only possible but indispensable, as the guide tells his disciple. This is, in fact, the key to exiting the human condition as a radical inferno of sorts and to entering the next stage: that of the light-dark of Purgatory, where suffering is redeemed through hope, where limits are acknowledged as being forgiven and healed, in a plausible process of approximation to plenitude.

In this second stage – the stage of Purgatory – there is a deepening of the training of the gaze, as it becomes reconciled with its object, in an exercise of cleansing of the pathologies of vision which are rooted in the failures of the subject, namely that of narcissistic isolation. While, in the first stage, the pilgrim is taught that the seeing is a matter of the right relationship with object, space, situation and light, the next phase reveals that the gaze is rooted in the relationship with others, a practice that is constructed and validated intersubjectively, woven dialogically in the interdependence of different gazes.

The awareness of the relational nature of the gaze does not reach its peak, however, until the third and final stage of the Dantean journey. Namely, in the revelation that love is the matrix underlying the great mystery of humanity. In other words: the intellectual and moral relationship that produces vision as an intersubjective exercise is only ever fully realised as a relationship of love. Only when understood and enacted as a mode of love does the gaze reach the fullness of its powers. Paradise celebrates the liberation of the gaze, reconstructed at last, healed at last, enabled with the kind of vision that re-establishes the full harmony of the subject with being; transcending, in proximity and communion, that distance and separation that seemed to us inescapable in the human act of seeing.

First Stage of the Journey. Reconstructing the Gaze as Relationship with the Object. Attention, Direction, Context, Light

One of the central breakthroughs of Tolstoy's realism, later taken up by Russian formalists such as Viktor Shklovsky, is the intuition that one of the primary functions of art is to activate the recipient's attention, stimulating their ability to take in the world and, as such, to construct reality itself. Art is, from this standpoint, an indispensable instrument of knowledge, both moral and theoretical, since it sets up the subject in a new cognitive stance. If truth, both practical and epistemic, may only be achieved through a precise relationship between experience and its contents, both subjective and objective, internal and external, then to competently enter into this relationship is a prerequisite to reaching the truth. If one cannot look, one cannot see. If one cannot hear, one cannot listen. If one cannot touch, one cannot feel. This 19th-century notion finds its precursor in Dante, who constructs the entire poem around explicating this principle, valid at the sensory, intellectual and spiritual levels:

> Allora più che prima li occhi apersi; I opened – wider than before – my eyes;
> guarda'mi innanzi, e vidi I looked ahead of me, and saw
>
> *Purgatorio* XIII, 46–47

In order to see, it is necessary to open one's eyes further, to risk gaping them wide, to direct one's gaze in the right direction, to allow oneself enough time for the gaze to settle ("let your eyes be fixed attentively"), to learn to use the vital resource of light. The *Divine Comedy* is, to a great extent, an account of failed attempts to see, the written admission to a professed and slowly healed blindness; of a self-aware, and subsequently mended myopia; of an obscurity that becomes progressively enlightened, in a systematic deconstruction of the idea that seeing is a purely passive exercise, an inert reception of an unmodulated exteriority through the triggering of the ascetic game that constitutes the gaze. Dante teaches us that seeing is not simply a matter of opening one's eyes, but rather to open them as never before, and to choose in which direction to train them, to find a source of light. It is to become aware of what we do when we look (to contemplate is to concentrate on seeing, to make one's vision an object of reflection; it is to make it resonate internally). Seeing concerns the gaze and the light, it is something we must actively devise, a task that we learn from others, from mistakes made, from repeated experience, from the successes that become points of reference. Dante's long perambulation in the *Comedy* is a chronicle of this learning process. Therefore, the last verse of the poem ("The Love that moves the sun and the other stars" *Paradiso* XXXIII, 145) deliberately reverses the darkness invoked in the opening tercet ("I found myself within a shadowed forest", *Inferno* I, 2), thus turning this optical parable into a crucial textual key.

In effect, the attentive reader may decipher it from the outset, when the guide – a poet – who offers his assistance to the lost voyager in the prologue to the poem qualifies his rescue mission as a journey whose primary objective is to hear and, above all, to see:

e io sarò tua guida,	and I shall guide you, taking
e trarrotti di qui per loco etterno;	you from this place to an eternal place,
ove *udirai* le disperate strida,	where you shall *hear* the howls of desperation
vedrai li antichi spiriti dolenti,	and *see* the ancient spirits in their pain,
ch'a la seconda morte ciascun grida;	as each of them laments their second death;
e *vederai* color che son contenti	and you shall *see* those souls that are content
nel foco,	within the fire,

Inferno I, 113–118 (m.e.)

The awkward traveller of the beginning of the poem coherently grasps the meaning of this proposal, welcoming it as a process of acquisition of a level of vision they would not have otherwise attained by themselves:

E io a lui: 'Poeta, io ti richeggio	And I replied: 'O poet – by that God
per quello Dio che tu non conoscesti,	whom you had never come to know – I beg you,
a ciò ch'io fugga questo male e peggio,	that I may flee this evil and worse evils,
che tu mi meni là dov' or dicesti,	to lead me to the place of which you spoke,
sì ch'io veggia la porta di san Pietro	that I may see the gateway of Saint Peter
e color cui tu fai cotanto mesti.'	and those whom you describe as sorrowful.'
Allor si mosse, e io li tenni dietro.	Then he set out, and I moved on behind him.

Inferno I, 130,133–136

The 'I' that pounds these tercets (five times within the space of seven lines) is the "I" of the blind man who realises he must be guided in order to recover his vision. The "I" of one who does not see because he has lost both the ability to look and light itself. He describes his extreme condition as follows: "tal mi fece la bestia senza pace / che, venendomi 'ncontro, a poco a poco / mi ripigneva là dove 'l sole tace"; "so was I when I faced that restless beast, / which even as he stalked me, step by step / had thrust me back to where the sun is speechless" (*Inferno* I, 58–60). That the intercessor of his salvation is Lucia, the patron saint of vision (*Inferno* II, 97–108), is therefore something more than a quaint allusion to the author's veneration in the throes of an eye malady. Rather, it signals a deeper hermeneutic necessity: the conversion of the lost man, his reunion with the truth, entailing the regeneration of his ability to look and to attain the light, through the patient guidance of the poet who, by showing, by accompanying, teaches the wanderer to see, and urges him to move beyond conventional appearance, beyond the unquestioned and the unthought. Speaking poet to poet, Virgil summarises thus his mission as companion and master:

l'anima sua, ch'è tua e mia serocchia,	his soul, the sister of your soul and mine,
venendo sù, non potea venir sola,	in its ascent, could not – alone – have climbed
però ch'al nostro modo non adocchia.	here, for it does not see the way we see.
Ond' io fui tratto fuor de l'ampia gola	Therefore, I was brought forth from Hell's broad jaws
d'inferno per mostrarli, e mosterrolli	to guide him in his going; I shall lead
oltre, quanto 'l potrà menar mia scola.	him just as far as where I teach can reach

Purgatorio XXI, 28–33

"To show",[4] to teach one with a deficient or distorted vision to see, is what Virgil does throughout the *Inferno* and *Purgatorio*, in a delicately differentiated pedagogy, full of indication and censure: of a propositional indication of the object and of a way of seeing, on the one hand; and, on the other, of a censure of the blindness of the apprentice, lost in the twists and turns of the labyrinth of his own loneliness. To *direct* and *to correct* the disciple's attention is the work of the tireless Latin poet along the way, repeating anew, the inaugural "Look" which is both a promise and an opening up to a new experience, while alerting, without discouraging, to the deviations and errors of the "false gaze" committed by the learner:

sì che d'onrata impresa lo rivolve,	distracting him from honorable trials –
come falso veder bestia quand'ombra.	as phantoms frighten beasts when shadows fall

Inferno II, 47

Worse than not seeing is to convince oneself of the perfection of one's vision. This is self-deception; it is to be caught in the trap of self-delusion. Blindness is not merely the inability to see. It is a form of seeing distorted by the unilateralism of a gaze that discards what it does not want to take in; it is conditioning by a pre-formatting that becomes a barrier; an imposing obstacle that impedes the perception of the real.

In this regard, a scene from Canto XXI of the *Inferno* is a formidable lesson in visual learning:

---

[4] "E 'l duca disse: 'I' son un che discendo / con questo vivo giù di balzo in balzo, / e di mostrar lo 'nferno a lui intendo'." ("My guide replied: 'From circle down to circle, / together with this living man, I am / one who descends; I mean to show him Hell.'") (*Inferno* XXIX, 94–96).

I' vedea lei, ma non vedëa in essa	*I saw it, but I could not see within it;*
mai che le bolle che 'l bollor levava,	no thing was visible but boiling bubbles,
e gonfiar tutta, e riseder compressa.	the swelling of the pitch; and then it settled.
Mentr'io là giù fisamente mirava,	And while I watched below attentively,
lo duca mio, *dicendo 'Guarda, guarda!'*,	My guide called out to me: *'Look! Look!'*,[5]
mi trasse a sé del loco dov' io stava.	and then, from where I stood, he drew me near.
Allor mi volsi come l'uom cui *tarda*	*I turned around* as one who *is keen to see*
di veder quel che li convien fuggire	*a sight* from which it would be wise to flee,
e cui paura sùbita sgagliarda,	and then is horror-stricken suddenly –
che, *per veder, non indugia 'l partire*:	who *does not stop* his flight and yet *looks back*
e vidi dietro a noi un diavol nero	and then – *behind us there* – *I saw* a black
correndo su per lo scoglio venire.	demon as he came racing up the crags.

Inferno XXI, 19–30 (m.e.)

At this stage, the pilgrim looks, without yet seeing what is hidden in what he looks upon, without seeing what the seen actually is ("I saw it, but I could not see within it"). The pilgrim sees the real only as an undecipherable surface, a veil that hides an assumed, but inaccessible content. What he sees is merely a symptom ("boiling bubbles") that intimates something deeper, which his gaze cannot penetrate. In this case, concentration ("I watched . . . attentively") is not only fruitless, but harmful, since it diverts attention from something more relevant yet to be seen. It ensnares the pilgrim in the setting, in the context. On the contrary, to truly see implies not only a spatial inherency, but also a temporal inherency, a cleaving to what is about to happen, about to become present. To truly see, therefore, is achieved only by those who learn to temporally configure space into situation, event and presence.

The guide promptly intervenes to correct the pupil's relational error. "Look, look!": you look, but you do not see! Open your eyes properly! – he seems to be saying. This warning entails a spatial relocation ("from where I stood, he drew me near"; "I turned around") caused by the temporal redirecting of attention ("who does not stop . . . and yet looks back"). Only one able to combine spatial and temporal inherency can truly see the situation in which they find themselves, can see themselves as presence, as cleaving to the self and to the real ("I saw," where "I had not thought to look": "behind us there").

To see is to enter into communion with the world, with others, with the happening of time (it is to know how to read "the signals of time"); it is to perceive reality in the complexity of its different temporal, spatial, and factual aspects, as

---

[5] The Italian takes on the dual meaning of "Take care!" and "Look!" (T / n)

they mature their variances and interdependence. This is not a passive exercise, quite the contrary. It requires the highly flexible skill of connecting the inside to the outside, of abandoning oneself in order to resituate oneself in a world that is not stasis, but exodus and wandering; that is not homogeneity, but discontinuity; that is not solitude, but community. To see is a matter of attention, but also of receptiveness, adaptation, suitability of light, training and verification. Vision is verified only in hospitality and partaking, at that dotted line that joins seeing with what is seen.

Second Stage of the Journey. Reconstructing the Gaze as Intersubjective Relationship. The Blindness of Solitude

From what has been so far illustrated, it can be understood that one does not recover one's vision alone. We need guides, educators, spiritual forbears, counsellors, visionaries, poets, and interlocutors to show, correct, amplify, differentiate, and teach. To see once more, to leave behind the "shadowed forest" with its paltry light and with the gaze distorted by inner phantoms (the beasts that haunt and impede progress, pulling one towards the darkness), the blind man must follow one who *shows*, and who represents a feature of light, a *flame*.[6] Seeing is not the product of a purely solipsistic dynamic between subject and object; between the self and the world, but implies, at all times, a *you*, a dialogic dimension that constructs the gaze as a transitive exercise. Only in interlocution does the gaze become vision, a bridge to the world, a device for leaving behind the solitude of the self in order to establish its inherency in the *real* which, as posited in the contemporary world by Wittgenstein, is the place inhabited by all, *the place where the desert of the I becomes the city of the we.*

---

6 Beatrice is the "light between . . . mind and truth" (*Purgatorio* VI, 45), as Dante is told by Virgil who, in turn (cf. below, *Purgatorio* IV, 30) is characterised by his disciple as the "gentle light" (*Purgatorio* XIII, 16), through which he can finally see clearly:

Ond' io: 'Maestro, il mio veder s'avviva sì nel tuo lume, ch'io discerno chiaro quanto la tua ragion parta o descriva.'	At which I said: 'Master, my sight is so illuminated by your light – I recognise all that your words declare or analyze.'

Purgatorio XVIII, 10–12

This communal dimension of vision emerges progressively in the learner's awareness of the gaze along his journey, becoming explicit practice and destiny in the second stage, that of Purgatory.

In the first stretch of the journey, the Inferno, obscurity is paired with isolation. Evil is the realm of the radical separation of the subject, enclosed within himself, bereft of the light of truth, of good, and of the other. The first pedagogical concern of the guide, at that stage of the journey was, therefore, not only to show (to promote through the exhortation: *Look!*) and to correct visual errors,[7] but also to teach how to move forward, how to find one's bearings, even in darkness, and to develop mechanisms to make up for the lack of vision dictated by the radical fracture of one's communion with the world. Evil is not to choose the world above God, but to break this communion with the world and with others that is bestowed in God, in order to make oneself absolute. Evil is a form of blindness, because it isolates man within himself, renders him unable to see beyond himself; it impels him into an abyssal and impenetrable unavailability towards the other:

---

7 *See* how, in Canto X of the *Inferno*, Virgil reproaches Dante's inattention, who is slow to see that Farinata has risen from his fiery grave and is addressing him:

Ed el mi disse: 'Volgiti! Che fai?	But he told me: 'Turn round! What are you doing?
Vedi là Farinata che s'è dritto:	That's Farinata who has risen there –
da la cintola in sù tutto 'l vedrai.'	you will see all of him from the waist up.'
	Inferno X, 31–33

Censure (expressed in the question: Fool, "What are you doing?") is a pedagogical act that articulates the command ("Turn around!") in a deictic cue ("see there"), which expands from the present to the future, foreshadowing the fact that there is more to see (a "you will see" inflected in a description: "from the waist up").

See how the reproach of the inertia of the gaze, frozen into what has already been seen, is pedagogically substantiated as temporal diagnosis and promise:

Ma Virgilio mi disse: 'Che pur guate?	But Virgil said to me: 'Why are you staring so insistently
perché la vista tua pur si soffolge	Why does your vision linger there below
là giù tra l'ombre triste smozzicate? . . .	among the lost and mutilated shadows? . . .
E già la luna è sotto i nostri piedi;	The moon already is beneath our feet;
lo tempo è poco omai che n'è concesso,	the time allotted to us now is short,
e altro è da veder che tu non vedi.'	and there is more to see than you see here.'
	Inferno XXIX, 4–6, 10–12

Oscura e profonda era e nebulosa	dark and deep and filled with mist,
tanto che, per ficcar lo viso a fondo,	is such that, though I gazed into its pit,
io non vi discernea alcuna cosa.	I was unable to discern a thing.
'Or discendiam qua giù nel cieco mondo'	'Let us descend into the blind world now'

Inferno IV, 10–13

From this radical sightlessness, from the *abyss* of this "melancholy valley" (IV 8), from this "starless air" (*Inferno* III, 23), this "part where no thing gleams" (*Inferno* IV, 151), escape is both necessary and possible, but only by following Ariadne's thread, made up of the "immense desire" for good, truth and "hope of ... climbing up" (*Inferno* I, 54), translated into a surrender to another, into putting one's trust in a relationship that is both premise and precondition for redemption:

... ma qui convien ch'om voli;	... but here
dico con l'ale snelle e con le piume	I had to fly: I mean with rapid wings
del gran disio, di retro a quel condotto	and pinions of immense desire, behind
che speranza mi dava e facea lume.	the guide who gave me hope and was my light.

Purgatorio IV 27–30

To trust another is to individuate an exit path from the *dark and deep obscurity* of evil; it is the crucial step to abandoning the Inferno, to return to the caress of light. In this sense, to see is also akin to a gift, a freely given offering we are bestowed, as opposed to a mere skill, or an ability or power. Educating one's gaze paradoxically involves the willingness to relinquish it, to close one's eyes. Not coincidentally, two of the terraces of *Purgatorio* (described in cantos XIII through to XV) articulate this process of re-education as a transient, but utter, abrogation of vision: the Envious and the Wrathful have their eyes neutralised, either sewn shut or rendered sightless by a thick fog. To see in detriment of the other, to see against the other, is a distortion of the gaze that can only be corrected by a powerlessness that leaves one completely at the mercy of the other,[8] that teaches us that *one cannot see without the other*:

8
e l'un sofferia l'altro con la spalla,	another's shoulder served each shade as prop
e tutti da la ripa eran sofferti.	and all of them were bolstered by the rocks:
Così li ciechi a cui la roba falla,	so do the blind who have to beg appear
stanno a' perdoni a chieder lor bisogna,	on pardon days to plead for what they need,
e l'uno il capo sopra l'altro avvalla	each bending his head back and toward the other

Purgatorio XIII, 59–63

quel fummo ch'ivi ci coperse,	nor covered them with such rough textured stuff
che l'occhio stare aperto non sofferse;	my eyes could not endure remaining open;
onde la scorta mia saputa e fida	so that my faithful, knowledgeable escort
mi s'accostò e l'omero m'offerse.	drew closer as he offered me his shoulder.
Sì come cieco va dietro a sua guida	Just as a blind man moves behind his guide,
per non smarrirsi e per non dar di cozzo	that he not stray or strike against some thing
in cosa che 'l molesti, o forse ancida,	that may do damage to – or even kill – him,
m'andava io per l'aere amaro e sozzo	so I moved through the bitter, filthy air,
ascoltando il mio duca che diceva	while listening to my guide, who kept repeating:
pur: 'Guarda che da me tu non sia mozzo.'	'Take care that you are not cut off from me.'

Purgatorio XVI, 5, 7–15

To lose one's sight and to be forced to defer to someone else's vision, to walk beside them, to cling to them, thus becomes the only way to "heal" a gaze contaminated by the alienating violence of a self overcome by the death drive and the phantoms of one's narcissism. To listen ("while listening to my guide, who kept repeating") thus becomes essential to the process of re-educating one's vision. Seeing also involves words, which construct sensory perception as a communally-coded, communally-produced experience of knowledge. There can be no looking without listening, no vision without words. There is no "I" without "we." To not envisage this is to not see at all.

Third Stage of the Journey. Reconstructing the Gaze as a Relationship of Love. To See Is to Love

This intersubjective dimension of the gaze, learned during the second part of the journey away from blindness, is not, however, solely rational and moral. At the top of the Purgatory, Virgil, the poet who embodies the light of natural reason, cedes his place as guide and educator to Beatrice, the woman whom Dante loves, a figure of reason enhanced by faith: intellect alone does not suffice to see, to arrive at the vision in which the subject finds the fullness of his own desire, and leaves behind the drawn-out yearning for novelty[9] in order to finally feel fulfilled,

---

9 The gaze is curious by nature, eager for novelty, as the poet reminds us when he describes his own contentment when faced with the multitude of sights in the first terrace of Purgatory:

Li occhi miei, ch'a mirare eran contenti	My eyes, which had been satisfied in seeking
per veder novitadi ond' e' son vaghi,	new sights – a thing for which they long –

Purgatorio X, 103–104

fully sated, fully in communion with his very being, truly "seen" in all that is truth, beauty, and goodness.[10]

At the edge of Purgatory, on that threshold between earth and heaven, between nature and eternity, that earthly paradise, the reunion with his beloved regenerates the pilgrim's vision, endowing him with an unconditional ability to welcome good. If crossing through the night of the Hell had allowed him to "see – once more – the stars", the ascent through Purgatory enables him to *climb unto them*, to place himself in the very midst of light:

Io ritornai da la santissima onda rifatto sì come piante novelle rinovellate di novella fronda,	From that most holy wave I now returned ... remade, as new trees are renewed when they bring forth new boughs, I was
puro e disposto a salire a le stelle	pure and prepared to climb unto the stars. *Purgatorio* XXXIII, 142–145

The utter darkness of the first part of the journey is overcome, in the second part, by the variation between light and shadow that characterises Purgatory as an earthly condition in endless flight from itself. The attention, now healed, the focus, now calibrated, the recovery of one's bearings are, nonetheless, still being hindered by the discontinuity of light, by the inexorable return of nightfall, which blocks the path, the ascension, the joy of purification. In the third and final part of the journey, conversely, there is light alone: love reigns and vision triumphs, now finally free, assured and replete, in a surge of intensity and joy in which the gaze and love are as one. To see and to love are synonymous, they manifest themselves as two sides of the sole relationship of the subject with the self, in which the deep communion of the "I" with the other becomes a life-force, eternity, an exuberance that transfigures identity-as-process:

---

10 | | |
|---|---|
| Così la mente mia, tutta sospesa,
mirava fissa, immobile e attenta,
e sempre di mirar faceasi accesa. | So was my mind – completely rapt, intent,
steadfast, and motionless – gazing; and it
grew ever more enkindled as it watched. |
| A quella luce cotal si diventa,
che volgersi da lei per altro aspetto
è impossibil che mai si consenta; | Whoever sees that Light is soon made such
that it would be impossible for him
to set that Light aside for other sight; |
| però che 'l ben, ch'è del volere obietto,
tutto s'accoglie in lei, e fuor di quella
è defettivo ciò ch'è lì perfetto. | because the good, the object of the will,
is fully gathered in that Light; outside
that Light, what there is perfect is defective
Paradiso XXXIII, 97–105. |

> Trasumanar significar per verba
> non si poria; però l'essemplo basti
> a cui esperïenza grazia serba.
>
> Passing beyond the human cannot be
> worded; let Glaucus serve as simile –
> until grace grant you the experience.
> *Paradiso* I, 70–72

Language, that most fundamental of resources – even the words of Dante himself – fall short of the power of vision-as-love, that renders man more than man, enables him "pass beyond the human," in the joy of the union with oneself's other, a gift offered and received, in which the exchange – both visual and amorous – is not distributive but multiplicative, and one in which there is no simple reciprocity, but a sharing that is transformative. The act of seeing, heightened through love, is the self transformed through the content of vision:

> ma per la vista che s'avvalorava
> in me guardando, una sola parvenza,
> mutandom' io, a me si travagliava.
>
> but through my sight, which as I gazed grew stronger,
> that sole appearance, even as I altered,
> seemed to be changing.
> *Paradiso* XXXIII 112–114

Through the act of seeing exercised as love, the subject enters into a communion with the object that fulfils his desire, and is not arrested in a stasis that precludes all else, but rather is introduced to the ecstasy that generates more besides. Not to have more, but to be more, together; to become untrammelled newness: such is the condition of the "strange sight" (*Paradiso* XXXIII, 136) where all desires are consummated ("And I, who was now nearing Him who is / the end of all desires, as I ought", *Paradiso* XXXIII, 46–47) as a manifestation of the joy of mutual love that unlocks the limits of the finite being in the infinity of love.

The "I", which in the first two stages of the journey was an afflicted burden and a site of temptation to be purified, finally reclaims, under the light of Paradise, the absolute dignity attendant on being loved and being able to love. The "I" is no longer a quandary to be contended with or reconfigured in its epistemic and moral pathologies, but becomes a welcome and welcoming richness; it engages in more than dialogue: it is *dia-logos*, a process of union with oneself's other, a shared regeneration:

> così de li occhi miei ogne quisquilia
> fugò Beatrice col raggio d'i suoi,
> che rifulgea da più di mille milia:
>
> onde mei che dinanzi vidi poi;
>
> even so
> did Beatrice dispel, with her eyes' rays,
> which shone more than a thousand miles, the chaff
> from my eyes:
>
> I saw better than I had before;
> *Paradiso* XXVI, 76–79

Once again, the pilgrim does not arrive at this final revelation on his own. After guiding him to the discovery of the loving matrix of the gaze, Beatrice hands the disciple over to the mystical command of a new guide, Saint Bernard, so he may take him to the highest destination of learning: "And he replied: 'That all your longings may be satisfied, / Beatrice urged me from my place'" (*Paradiso* XXXI, 65–66). Saint Bernard's role is to mediate Dante's desire unto Mary, the universal intercessor of the desires of men unto the Son, who in turn is the eschatological intercessor of human desire unto the Father. This chain of transitive mediations, rendered increasingly absolute, clarifies that the gaze that is truly recognised as love is not an appropriation of the object, an "immediate" gratification of the "I", but a relationship of reciprocity, a loving union generated as a process of meaning-making, a choice made out of freedom, and not the result of mere mechanical causality. Ecstatic vision, as the joy of infinite communion, is not the nullification of history, of differences, of processes, or of the mediations involved therein. It is not an absolute decontextualization, but rather the reiteration of difference as union:

Nel suo profondo vidi che s'interna,	In its profundity I saw – ingathered
legato con amore in un volume,	and bound by love into one single volume –
ciò che per l'universo si squaderna:	what, in the universe, seems separate, scattered:
sustanze e accidenti e lor costume	substances, accidents, and dispositions
quasi conflati insieme, per tal modo	as if conjoined – and in such a way that what I tell
che ciò ch'i' dico è un semplice lume.	is only rudimentary.

Paradiso XXXIII, 85–90

Just as the heterogeneity of the universe is not nullified, but reiterated in the consummate unity of love's primacy, so is the finite self not erased in the union with infinite love, but regenerated, in a path that keeps him intact in his subjectivity and in the full consciousness of himself; in the notion of the exteriority of the world as difference and not as separation; in the memory of a shared path; in the gratitude for the gift bestowed by all who accompanied him on his moral, cognitive and spiritual reconstruction.

Conclusion

The fact that words are insufficient to express the fullness of the experience in which love and vision are manifested as one does not make them any less necessary. The fact that mediations are surmounted in the final moment does not make them expendable. Nothing along the journey to the final destination is deemed worthless, or discarded. None of the lessons learned, none of the guides who followed along, are forgotten in the record of this journey of construction of a healed, joyful and loving gaze that is offered in the *Divine Comedy*.

To see is not merely to open one's eyes, nor is it simply to accumulate images, but to create a vision out of patience, humility and love. The difference is crucial, but it is clear how often, how increasingly, this has been ignored.

We live in an age saturated with images: we engage with a surfeit of technological devices and are weighed down by their continuous onslaught. The real risk is that, instead of intensifying our gaze, these overflowing images in fact erase it, by taking on the role of its mechanical and repetitive substitutes. It is easy to relinquish the attempt to mature one's own vision by importing prefabricated visual products that in effect become barriers between oneself and the world. The school of the gaze imparted by the *Divine Comedy*, a poem full of "things new and old", enjoins us to free ourselves from this illusion, to become aware of this peril, to begin our journey and to activate, to train, to purify our own gaze. What a pity it would be, if one were to read the *Divine Comedy* merely as a repository of beautiful, terrifying, powerful, extravagant and unforgettable images. And let us recall once again Osip Mandelstam, when he observed that this poem, while training the reader's gaze, is also a mechanism for the disintegration of images, of visual substitutes, and ready-made sights.[11] Let us therefore allow the *Divine Comedy* to destroy the images that blind us and to help us build our own visions – new, free, joyful, because they are generated by love and engender love in turn. Dante has the truth of it. We are all called upon to build visions.

Bibliographical References

Francis, Pope: Apostolic Letter *Candor Lucis aeternae* on the VII Centenary of the death of Dante Alighieri, 25.03.2021. Online: https://press.vatican.va/content/salastampa/en/bollettino/pubblico/2021/03/25/210325a.html.

Mandelstam, Osip: *Selected Essays*. Edited and translated by Sidney Monas, Clarence Brown & Robert Hughes. Austin, Texas: University of Texas Press 1977.

---

11 "By his very nature Dante shakes the sense and violates the integrity of the image." (Ossip Mandelstam: *Selected Essays*, p. 21). And yet one "cannot fail to note the conditioning of vision for the apperception of new things. This conditioning is developed into a genuine dissection: Dante divines the layered structure of the retina: *di gonna in gonna . . .*" (*Ibidem*, p. 29). Here, Mandelstam is quoting a tercet from the *Paradiso*:

E come a lume acuto si disonna	And just as a sharp light will startle us
per lo spirto visivo che ricorre	from sleep because the spirit of eyesight
a lo splendor che va di gonna in gonna,	races to meet the brightness that proceeds from
	layer to layer in the eye.

Paradiso XXVI, 70–73

Section I: Dante. A Poet of Our Time

Carlo Ossola
"Supra te et non subter": The Biblical Humanism of the *Comedy*

1 "Et eris semper supra, et non subter"

In order to illustrate which aspects of the *Comedy* may be defined in terms of 'biblical humanism', I believe it is sufficient to evoke, alongside the verses of the highest *dignitas hominis* in the entire poem:

Non aspettar mio dir più né mio cenno;	Await no further word or sign from me:
libero, dritto e sano è tuo arbitrio,	your will is free, erect, and whole – to act
e fallo fora non fare a suo senno:	against that will would be to err: therefore
per ch'io te sovra te corono e mitrio.	I crown and miter you over yourself.

(*Purgatorio* XXVII, 139–142)

their biblical source, the "constituet te Dominus in caput, [...] eris semper supra et non subter" of Deuteronomy 28:13–14:

> The Lord will make you the head, not the tail. If you pay attention to the commands of the Lord your God that I give you this day and carefully follow them, you will always be at the top, never at the bottom. Do not turn aside from any of the commands I give you today, to the right or to the left, following other gods and serving them.[1]

We may thus observe that this humanistic 'sovereignty' over the self (it is no coincidence that Félicité de Lamennais translated these verses "c'est pourquoi, *souverain de toi-même*, je te couronne et te mitre") has sound biblical roots, further augmented by Dante's echoing of the concept of 'rectitude' (and 'justice'), which stems from verse 14 and is particularly marked in *Monarchia*, I, xi, 3:

> *iustitia, de se et in propria natura considerata, est quedam rectitudo sive regula* obliquum hinc inde abiciens (*justice, considered in itself and in its own nature, is a kind of rectitude or rule* which spurns deviation from the straight path to either side; and thus it does not admit of a more and a less – just like whiteness considered in the abstract),

equal to the cited precept: "do not turn to the right or to the left" (also Proverbs 4: 27)

---

[1] "[13] Constituet te Dominus in caput, et non in caudam: et eris semper supra, et non subter: si tamen audieris mandata Domini Dei tui quae ego praecipio tibi hodie, et custodieris et feceris, [14] ac non declinaveris ab eis nec ad dexteram, nec ad sinistram, nec secutus fueris deos alienos, neque colueris eos".

Note: Translated from the Italian by Matthew Coneys Wainwright.

https://doi.org/10.1515/9783110796049-003

The commentary of Ambrosius, Jerome and other Church Fathers (Rabanus Maurus, Rupert of Deutz, etc.) on this passage follows similar lines, and is consistent in underlining the pre-eminence that man acquires by respecting the order of creation:

> faciet te Dominus Deus tuus excelsiorem cunctis gentibus, quae versantur in terra. Venientque super te universae" (Deu: 28:1–2) (*PL*, 28, 449D)

Nor does the New Testament deviate from this message, for in the Parable of the Talents Matthew reaffirms: "'Euge, serve bone et fidelis. Super pauca fuisti fidelis; supra multa te constituam: intra in gaudium domini tui'" (25:21 and 23).[2]

Dante explains this condition in further detail later in the same canto. The poet-pilgrim is preparing to fulfil and exceed his own condition of *viator*: "My *will on will* to climb above was such / that at each step I took I felt the force / within my wings was growing for the flight" (121–123). It is precisely this Bonaventuran *supra nos* that Virgil will consecrate at the end of the canto: "therefore I crown and miter you over yourself" (142). And it is a "supra nos" that Bonaventure exquisitely explains in the *Itinerarium mentis in Deum* I, 2:

> oportet nos intrare ad mentem nostram, quae est imago Dei aeviterna, spiritualis et intra nos, et hoc est ingredi in veritate Dei; oportet nos transcendere ad aeternum, spiritualissimum, et supra nos, aspiciendo ad primum principium, et hoc est laetari in Dei notitia et reverentia Maiestatis.[3]

Such an elevation therefore does not exacerbate desire (even if Ambrosius himself acknowledges that "humanum tamen est desideria supra nos extendere" (*Expositio in psalmum David* CXVIII, in *PL* 15, 1449D); nor does it represent mere transcendence through contemplation: "Contemplatio est mentis in Deum suspensae quaedam elevatio, aeternae dulcedinis gaudia degustans" (*Scala Paradisi*, ch. I: *Descriptio quatuor graduum exercitationum spiritualium. Lectio. Meditatio. Oratio. Contemplatio*).[4] Rather, it is a 'reaching beyond', because "passing beyond the human ("transumanare") is not within our grasp:

---

[2] "His master replied, 'Well done, good and faithful servant! You have been faithful with a few things; I will put you in charge of many things. Come and share your master's happiness!'"

[3] "Then we must return to ourselves, to our *mens*, which is the eternal image of God, and this means walking in the truth of God. Finally, *it is necessary that we transcend ourselves towards the eternal*, which is the most spiritual entity, *turning our gaze above us towards* the First Principle: this means to rejoice in the knowledge of God and in awe of His majesty" (Online: http://www.documentacatholicaomnia.eu/03d/1221-1274,_Bonaventura,_Itinerarium_Mentis_in_Deum,_LT.pdf, accessed 26.07.2022) (m.e.).

[4] John Climacus: *Scala Paradisi*. In: *Patrologiæ Græcæ*. Edited by Jacques Paul Migne (Vol. 88). Paris 1860. (Online: https://www.mlat.uzh.ch/browser?path=7360&text=7360, accessed 26.07.2022).

Trasumanar significar *per verba*	Passing beyond the human cannot be
non si poria; però l'essemplo basti	worded; let Glaucus serve as simile –
a cui esperïenza grazia serba.	until grace grant you the experience.
S'i' era sol di me quel che creasti	Whether I only was the part of me
novellamente, amor che 'l ciel governi,	that You created last, You – governing
tu 'l sai, che col tuo lume mi levasti.	the heavens – know: it was Your light that raised me.

(*Paradiso* I, 70–75)

In his *De tripartito tabernaculo* (*PL* 198, 776B), Adam Scotus refers to this concept using the verses of Ovid's *Heroides* (IV, 91–92: *Phaedra to Hippolytus*): "arcus – et arma tuae tibi sunt imitanda Dianae – / si numquam cesses tendere, mollis erit".[5] Reaching beyond, and receiving forgiveness: a "supra nos", albeit in the knowledge that we cannot "pass beyond the human",

2 Delectasti / Dilatasti

In order to understand the roots of medieval biblical humanism, we must recall the dawn of civilisation that revived the industrious *dignitas* of the West from the ashes of the Roman Empire through the prayerful diligence of monastic work, thanks to Saint Benedict (Nursia, c. 480 – monastery of Montecassino, c. 547)[6] and the Benedictine order. Benedict's Hesiodic and Christian rule – "ora, lege et labora" – trusts in the redemptive ability of human activity to act as a seed of 'culture', infusing creation so that it bears fruit and serves the needs of man. Gregory the Great (c. 540 – 604) recalls how Benedict saw a vision in which the whole world appeared to him as though gathered in a single beam of sunlight:

> The man of God, Benedict, being diligent in watching, rose early before the time of matins (his monks being yet at rest) and came to the window of his chamber where he offered up his prayers to almighty God. Standing there, all of a sudden in the dead of the night, as

---

[5] "The bow – and you should imitate the weapons of your Diana – if you never cease to bend it, will grow slack" (Latin – Online: http://www.thelatinlibrary.com/ovid/ovid.her4.shtml, accessed 26.07.2022. English Translation by Grant Showerman [1931 Loeb] – Online: https://www.theoi.com/Text/OvidHeroides1.html#4, accessed: 26.07.2022).
[6] Ezra Pound traces the "dawn of romance" to St Benedict and his *Rule*. It is with this remark that he begins the first page of his *Spirit of Romance*, and – much earlier than the Oaths of Strasbourg (842 AD) or Provencal poets – gearlds the new civilisation of the West (see: The Phantom Dawn, chapter I of *The Spirit of Romance*, 1910; Italian translation: *Lo spirito romanzo*, Milan: SE, 1991, p. 19).

he looked forth, he saw a light that banished away the darkness of the night and glittered with such brightness that the light which shone in the midst of darkness was far more clear than the light of the day. During this vision a marvellously strange thing followed, for, as he himself afterward reported, the whole world, gathered together, as it were, under one beam of the sun, was presented before his eyes. [. . .]

Although we say that the world was gathered together before his eyes, yet it is not that heaven and earth were drawn into any lesser room than they are of themselves. The soul of the beholder was more enlarged, rapt in God, so that it might see without difficulty that which is under God.[7]

The entire adventure of believing, of seeing, of writing lies within this *making man capable of the world*: in this aspiration there is a perfect continuity between Saint Benedict and Saint Francis, and between them and Dante and Italian humanism, as far as Giovanni Pico della Mirandola's *De hominis dignitate* of at the end of the fifteenth century.

The relationship with the divine is, from Saint Benedict to Dante, one of "dilation", the expansion of human faculties beyond the limits of man's terrestrial nature. Saint Gregory's expression "sed videntis animus est dilatatus" itself recalls Psalm 17 (18): "et dedisti mihi protectionem salutis tuae et dextera tua suscepit me et disciplina tua correxit me in finem et disciplina tua ipsa me docebit / *dilatasti gressus meos*".[8] In the *Divine Comedy*, Dante will recall the ancient formula and situate it at the culmination of his ascent of Mount Purgatory, now in close proximity to the Earthly Paradise. No sooner than she has appeared,

---

[7] Gregory the Great, *Dialogues*, book II, ch. 35: "Cumque vir Dei Benedictus, quiescentibus adhuc fratribus, instans vigiliis, nocturnae orationis tempore praevenisset, ad fenestam stans et omnipotentem Deum deprecans; subito inytempesta noctis hora respiciens, vidit fusam lucem desuper, cunctas noctis tenebras effugasse, tantoque splendore clarescere, ut diem vinceret lux illa, quae in tenebris radiasset. Mira autem res valde in hac speculatione secuta est: quia, sicut post ipse narravit, omnis etiam mundus, velut sub uno solis radio collectus, ante oculos eius adductus est. [. . .] Quod autem collectus mundus ante eius oculos dicitur, non coelum et terra contracta est, sed videntis animus est dilatatus: qui in Deo raptus, videre sine difficultate potuit omne, quod infra Deum est. In illa ergo luce, quae exterioribus oculis fulsit, lux interior in mente fuit" [see Grégoire le Grand: *Dialogues. Texte, critique et notes par Adalbert de Vogüé*. Paris: Cerf 1978–1980. "Sources chrétiennes", no. 251, 260, 265]. I owe this precious quotation to Father Cesare Falletti, *lumen viatorum*, who I thank wholeheartedly.

[8] Psalm 17 (18):36–37: "You make your saving help my shield, and your right hand sustains me; your help has made me great. You provide a broad path for my feet".

Matelda explains to the pilgrims why it is so difficult to pass beyond the river that separates them, and which Dante has already crossed with his desire:[9]

"Voi siete nuovi, e forse perch' io rido",   [. . .] She began:
cominciò ella, "in questo luogo eletto   "You are new here and may – because I smile
a l'umana natura per suo nido,   in this place, chosen to be mankind's nest –

maravigliando tienvi alcun sospetto;   wonder, perplexed, unable to detect
ma luce rende il salmo *Delectasti*,   the cause; but light to clear your intellect
    is in the psalm beginning *Delectasti*.
                                           (*Purgatorio* XXVIII, 76–80)

Though widely accepted, the 'Vulgate' proposed by Giorgio Petrocchi for verse 80 ("but light [. . .] is in the psalm beginning 'Delectasti'")[10] is not attested by any of the oldest and most authoritative witnesses of the *Comedy*: the Landiano, Urbinate Latino and Cortonese codices[11] all agree on "*dilatasti*" ("but light is in the psalm beginning '*Dilatasti*'"), following a reading substantiated by Benvenuto da Imola, one of the most perceptive of the early commentators:

Quod autem ista sit intentio literae videtur patere ex praecedentibus, quia dixit: vos estis novi; et ex sequentibus, quia aliqui textus habent, *dilatasti*: et hic est versiculus alterius psalmi, ubi propheta tendens ad perfectionem virtutis, quae in paradiso deliciarum typice designatur, dicit: *Dilatasti, Domine, gressus meos*, etc.[12]

Having presented the two possible readings of the verse, Benvenuto opts decisively for the second, *Dilatasti* ("Potest etiam aliter exponi litera ista, et non minus bene . . . ", "Quod autem ista sit intentio literae videtur patere [. . .] ex sequentibus, quia aliqui textus habent: dilatasti"), precisely because it indicates man "tendens ad perfectionem virtutis, quae in paradiso deliciarum typice designatur".

---

9 "I halted, and I set my eyes upon / the farther bank, to look at the abundant / variety of newly-flowered boughs" (*Purgatorio* XXVIII, 34–36).
10 Psalm 91 (92):5: "Quia delectasti me Domine in factura tua: et in operibus manuum tuarum exultabo" ["For you make me glad by your deeds, Lord; I sing for joy at what your hands have done"].
11 Respectively, Piacenza, Biblioteca Comunale Passerini Landi MS 190 (the Landiano Codex, dating from 1336); Biblioteca Apostolica Vaticana, codice Urbinate latino 366 (the Urbinate Codex of 1352); and Cortona, Biblioteca Comunale Codice Cortonese 88 (completed by 1340). On the history of the *Comedy's* early manuscript tradition, see Giorgio Petrocchi's Nota introduttiva to Dante Alighieri: *La Divina Commedia*. Turin: Einaudi 1975, pp. VII–XXII.
12 Benevenuti de Rambaldis de Imola Comentum super Dantis Aldigherij Comoediam, nunc primum integre in lucem editum sumptibus Guilielmi Warren Vernon, curante Jacobo Philippo Lacaita. Florentiae, G. Barbèra, 1887. (Online: https://dante.dartmouth.edu/biblio.php?comm_id=13755, accessed 15.12.2021).

The same reading of *Dilatasti* is adopted in the edition of the *Comedy* prepared by Federico Sanguineti[13] and was suggested as early as 1967 in a sensitive reading by Antonio Enzo Quaglio.[14] At the summit of the *Purgatorio*, Dante is doubtful (in the previous verse, Matelda observes "you may [. . .] wonder, perplexed, unable to detect the cause") and there is no reason for his 'understanding' to spring forth from "diletto" (a premature and unjustified delight, since Dante has not yet cleansed and renewed himself in the waters of the Lethe, Canto XXXI, and the Eunoe, Canto XXXIII).[15] Rather, it emerges in a manner consistent with the progression of the canto;[16] from the opening ("dilatasti") of a way – according to Psalms 4 and 17 (18)[17] – which leads from tribulation to freedom and breadth of vision. From Augustine to Aquinas, "dilatasti" signals the growing "latitudo animi". Man is a *viator*, a pilgrim, and passes through the "dolores inferni" (Psalm 17[18]:6) in order to acquire more 'capable' insight, to "open" the way towards perfection ("Qui perfecit pedes meos tanquam cervorum, et super excelsa statuens me": again Psalm 17 [18]:34), almost an outline of Dante's journey and his ascent.

Thomas Aquinas exquisitely summarises this tradition, leading from tribulation to liberation, from anguish to 'open air' (indeed, shortly afterwards Beatrice

---

[13] *Dantis Alagherii Comedia, edizione critica per cura di FEDERICO SANGUINETI*. Florence: Edizioni del Galluzzo, 2001, ad locum. Also by Federico Sanguineti, see *Dantis Alagherii Comedia. Appendice bibliografica 1988–2000*. Florence: Edizioni del Galluzzo per la Fondazione Ezio Franceschini 2005.

[14] Antonio E. Quaglio: Il canto XXVIII. In: *Lectura Dantis Scaligera. Purgatorio*. Florence: Le Monnier 1967, p. 1057–1058. The suggestion has also been discussed by Vincent Truijen in the *Enciclopedia Dantesca*, under *Delectasti*, Online: https://www.treccani.it/enciclopedia/delectasti_%28Enciclopedia-Dantesca%29/ and brought into question – albeit without retracing the 'reasons' for Dante's choice – by Concetto Del Popolo: Matelda. In: *Letture classensi*. 8, Ravenna: Longo 1979, pp. 125–126 .

[15] Dante is extremely precise on this point, and shortly after specifies that there is no improvement over earthly perception unless the "memory of sin" has already been purged in the Lethe and regenerated in the Eunoe: "To one side, it is Lethe; on the other, / Eunoe; *neither stream is efficacious* / unless the other's waters have been tasted" (*Purgatorio* XXVIII, 130–132, m.e.).

[16] A canto that is entirely one of walking, stepping, journeying towards fulfilment: "and took the plain, advancing slowly, slowly" (5); "Now, though my steps were slow, I'd gone so far / into the ancient forest that I could / no longer see where I had made my entry" (22–24: a description that recalls the *incipit* of the poem itself); "I halted, and I set my eyes upon" (34); "the flowers that colored all of her pathway" (42); "and scarcely lets one foot precede the other" (54); "The river kept us just three steps apart" (70). These formulae precede the "*Dilatasti* (gressus meos)" of verse 80.

[17] See Psalm 4:2: "in tribulatione dilatasti mihi" ["give me relief from my distress"]; and Psalm 17 (18): 35: "Dilatasti gressus meos subtus me: et non sunt infirmata vestigia mea" ["You provide a broad path for my feet, so that my ankles do not give way"].

will be "seen through the air, unveiled completely"; XXXI, 145), in his commentary on Psalm 4:

> For he [the Psalmist] says: *in tribulatione dilatasti mihi*, for it is *dilatasti* rather than *liberasti*; as if he were saying: not only have you freed me, but in the tribulation itself you have enlarged my heart, according to *Psalm XVII: dilatasti gressus meos subtus me, et non sunt infirmata vestigia mea*; or also: you have granted me greatness of mind to bear patiently, or again: amplitude in posterity, of which Gen. IX testifies: *dilatet Deus Japhet*.[18]

In the *Summa theologiae*, the author had even more explicitly opposed "delectare" and "dilatare". In an article from which Dante seems quite literally to draw inspiration, he observes that "pleasure" (*delectatio*) belongs to the emotions and "dilation" (*dilatatio*) to the desire that is fulfilled in "praeceptum caritatis", in love:

> It would seem that expansion is not an effect of pleasure. For expansion seems to pertain more to love, according to the Apostle (2 Cor. 6:11): "Our heart is enlarged." [. . .]

> Further, when a thing expands it is enabled to receive more. But receiving pertains to desire, which is for something not yet possessed. Therefore expansion seems to belong to desire rather than to pleasure.[19]

From Saint Benedict to Aquinas and Dante, the 'vision' is to *dilate* understanding: to open the way to the infinite, to an understanding of a way *nondum habita*. This infinite breadth brims over in the *Paradiso*: "By now you see the height, you see the breadth, / of the Eternal Goodness" (XXIX, 142); and Dante one final time *dilates* in a perfume of elation, a "fragrance of praise", the sweetest and most heartfelt gift that Beatrice bestows on Dante and us:

---

18 Thomas Aquinas, *In psalmos Davidis expositio* [*Ps.* IV, 1](Parma: Typis Petri Fiaccadori 1863): "Dicit autem *in tribulatione dilatasti mihi*, quia plus est *dilatasti* quam *liberasti*; quasi dicat: non solum liberasti, sed in ipsa tribulatione cordis latitudinem tribuisti: *Ps. XVII: dilatasti gressus meos subtus me, et non sunt infirmata vestigia mea*; vel latitudinem animi ad patienter sustinendum, vel latitudinem potestatis de qua dicitur *Gen.* IX: *dilatet Deus Japhet*".

19 Thomas Aquinas: *Summa theologiae, Prima secundae,* Quaestio XXXIII, art. 1, 1–2 (Alba / Roma: Editiones Paulinae 1962, p. 697): "Videtur quod dilatatio non sit effectus delectationis. Dilatatio enim videtur ad amorem magis pertinere, secundum quod dicit apostolus, II ad Cor. VI, cor nostrum dilatatum est. [. . .] Praeterea, ex hoc quod aliquid dilatatur, efficitur capacius ad recipiendum. Sed receptio pertinet ad desiderium, quod est rei nondum habitae. Ergo dilatatio magis videtur pertinere ad desiderium quam ad delectationem. » (Engl. Trans. Online: http://www.documentacatholicaomnia.eu/03d/1225-1274,_Thomas_Aquinas,_Summa_Theologiae_%5B1%5D,_EN.pdf, accessed 15.12.2021).

> Nel giallo de la rosa sempiterna,
> che si digrada e dilata e redole
> odor di lode al sol che sempre verna,
>
> qual è colui che tace e dicer vole,
> mi trasse Bëatrice, e disse: "Mira
> quanto è 'l convento de le bianche stole!
>
> Vedi nostra città quant' ella gira;

> Into the yellow of the eternal Rose
> that slopes and stretches and diffuses fragrance
> of praise unto the Sun of endless spring,
>
> now Beatrice drew me as one who, though
> he would speak out, is silent. And she said:
> "See how great is this council of white robes!
>
> See how much space our city's circuit spans!
> (*Paradiso* XXX, 124–130)

Indeed, it is Benedict – almost as if Dante remembers the vision described by Gregory the Great and returns it to its author – who will cause faith to dilate in the celestial pilgrim, the same faith which, with a fitting image of the 'opening' of the rose, we shall encounter again in the words of Beatrice:

> E io a lui: "L'affetto che dimostri
> meco parlando, e la buona sembianza
> ch'io veggio e noto in tutti li ardor vostri,
>
> *così m'ha dilatata mia fidanza,*
> *come 'l sol fa la rosa quando aperta*
> tanto divien quant' ell' ha di possanza".

> I answered: "The affection that you show
> in speech to me, and kindness that I see
> and note within the flaming of your lights,
>
> *have given me so much more confidence*
> *just like the sun that makes the rose expand*
> and reach the fullest flowering it can".[20]
> (*Paradiso* XXII, 52–57) (m.e.)

Paradiso XXIII is the canto richest in images of *impossibilitas dicendi* on the part of the poet,[21] and also the canto which to the greatest extent celebrates the *excessus mentis* not as a 'decline' but rather an 'uncontainable overflowing' of vision and understanding, *dilating* all that is human beyond the human:

---

[20] It should be remembered that St Benedict, together with St Francis and St Augustine, will appear at the summit of the "throne in glory" of the blessed in Paradise (*Paradiso* XXXII, 35).
[21] "I am compelled to leave it undescribed" (XXIII, 24); "I was as one who, waking from a dream / he has forgotten, tries in vain to bring / that vision back into his memory" (XXIII, 49–51); "If all the tongues that Polyhymnia / together with her sisters made most rich / with sweetest milk, should come now to assist / my singing of the holy smile that lit / the holy face of Beatrice, the truth / would not be reached – not its one – thousandth part" (XXIII, 55–60); "And thus, in representing Paradise, / the sacred poem has to leap across, / as does a man who finds his path cut off" (XXIII, 61–63).

Come foco di nube si diserra	Even as lightning breaking from a cloud,
per dilatarsi sì che non vi cape,	expanding [*dilatarsi*] so that it cannot be pent,
e fuor di sua natura in giù s'atterra,	against its nature, down to earth, descends,
la mente mia così, tra quelle dape	so did my mind, confronted by that feast,
fatta più grande, di sé stessa uscìo,	expand; and it was carried past itself –
e che si fesse rimembrar non sape.	what it became, it cannot recollect.
	(*Paradiso* XXIII, 40–45) (m.e.)

The mind made to "expand", "carried past itself": in Dante, the *excessus* attributed to the mystical vision is the fulfilment and summit of humanity – that of the "glowing Substance" of Christ[22] – and the *dilation* of the knowledge which Benvenuto da Imola had, referring to *Dilatasti* in his commentary, assigned to the "accedentibus ad apicem virtutis perfectae".

3 "Asperges me"

There is much to be reflected on and learned in relation to 'Dante's biblical humanism' when the poem examines itself in its many penitential passages (particularly in *Purgatorio*). I wish to underline that its vision *is more redemptive than expiatory*; and it seems to me that this is shown in exemplary fashion by one possible reading of the "Asperges me" of *Purgatorio* XXXI.

In his immersion in the Lethe, Dante succeeds in removing any trace of 'memory of sin'. The rite of purification, signalled by the citation from the *Miserere*, "Asperges me" (verse 98), had two distinct exegetical traditions. One of these emphasised ablution from sin: thus, Rupert of Deutz (*De divinis officiis*, PL 170, 177C) noted that according to the Law lepers were cleaned with a hyssop branch (Leviticus 14:3–7). The other, meanwhile, was wholly focused on celebrating the *renovatio* of cleansing, as in Bruno di Segni: "'Qui dat nivem sicut lanam, nebulam velut cinerem spargit' [. . .] Dat Dominus fidelibus suis nivem, quando baptizantur: dat lanam, De hac nive alibi dicitur: 'Asperges me hyssopo et mundabor, lavabis me et super nivem dealbabor' (Psalm 50 [51]:8). Dat ergo Dominus nivem, id est candorem et pulchritudinem nivis" (*Expositio in Psalmos*, PL 164, 1221A). This thriving second exegetical tradition is drawn on by a Dante full of sweetness and love: "The lovely woman opened wide her arms; / she clasped my head, and then she thrust me under" (100–101). No expiatory or initiation rite was richer in *jouissance* than the oozing humility encapsulated in the dance – as in a

---

22 *Paradiso* XXIII, 32.

fontaine de Jouvence – of the four nymph-stars that Dante encounters, and who restore in him the true "vita nova".

4 "Science and Experience"

In the criticism, what generally separates Dante's world from that of humanism lies in the cleft between the philosophy of 'universals' that drives the world of Scholasticism and the individual 'experience' that inspires and justifies humanism. The boundary, however, is not quite this clear. It is sufficient to recall one of the maxims of that prince among humanist experimenters, Leonardo: "It is an easy matter for a man who is well versed in the principles of his art, to become universal in the practice of it, since all animals have a similarity of members, that is, muscles, tendons, bones, &c. These only vary in length or thickness, as will be demonstrated in the Anatomy" (*Treatise on Painting*, §76|28 "Of Being Universal").[23] Certainly, there is anatomy; but – as observed by a keen reader of Dante – the need for 'universality' remains.

Again: it is observed that Dante's poem belongs to the great medieval genre of 'visions', while the humanism of Alberti, and above all of Leonardo, is centre on experimental knowledge of *realia*.

If we consider Canto XV of Purgatorio (85–93), which lies at the very heart of the poem, we certainly encounter an exemplification of the vision:

Ivi mi parve in una visïone estatica di sùbito esser tratto, e vedere in un tempio più persone;	There I seemed, suddenly, to be caught up in an ecstatic vision and to see some people in a temple; and a woman
e una donna, in su l'entrar, con atto dolce di madre dicer: "Figliuol mio, perché hai tu così verso noi fatto?	just at the threshold, in the gentle manner that mothers use, was saying: "O my son, why have you done this to us? You can see
Ecco, dolenti, lo tuo padre e io	how we have sought you – sorrowing, your father
ti cercavamo". E come qui si tacque, ciò che pareva prima, dispario.	and I". And at this point, as she fell still, what had appeared at first now disappeared.

---

[23] "Dell'essere universale": recorded as §76 in the Italian edition (*Trattato della Pittura di Leonardo da Vinci, condotto sul cod. Vaticano Urbinate 1270, con prefazione 1452–1519*. Edited by Gaetano Milanesi with texts by Giorgio Vasari and Marco Tabarrini, according to Manuscript. Urb. Lat. 1270 | Biblioteca Apostolica Vaticana. Roma: Unione Cooperativa Editrice 1890, p. 45), and as §28 in the English translation (*Treatise on Painting*. Transl. by John Francis Rigaud, R.A. London: George Bell & Sons 1877, p. 11).

Yet we are also met with "science and experience" (21):[24] a hendiadys that anticipates the humanist trajectory, from Leonardo to Galileo, of experimentation and testing, following a path that Thomas Aquinas inherits from Aristotle: "and says [the philosopher] that in men science and art arise from experience") (*Sententia libri Metaphysicae*, 1, 1, 18; 1).[25] It is useful here to remember that "esperienza" is among the most significant terms within the *Comedy*, appearing at the 'highest' points of the poem; it is repeated around a dozen times and marks the conception, the very root of Dante's humanism, beginning from the "brief address" of Ulysses:

"O frati", dissi, "che per cento milia perigli siete giunti a l'occidente, a questa tanto picciola vigilia	'Brothers,' I said, 'o you, who having crossed a hundred thousand dangers, reach the west, to this brief waking – time that still is left
d'i nostri sensi ch'è del rimanente *non vogliate negar l'esperïenza*, di retro al sol, del mondo sanza gente.	unto your senses, *you must not deny experience* of that which lies beyond the sun, and of the world that is unpeopled.
Considerate la vostra semenza: fatti non foste a viver come bruti, ma per seguir virtute e canoscenza".	Consider well the seed that gave you birth: you were not made to live your lives as brutes, but to be followers of worth and knowledge.'
	(*Inferno* XXVI, 112–120) (m.e.)

While the proud challenge of Ulysses fails, other 'experience' proves to be precious and providential, beginning with the very purposes and nature of the journey: "but that he may gain *full experience*, / I, who am dead, must guide him here below, / to circle after circle, throughout Hell" (*Inferno* XXVIII, 48–50). Indeed, for the pilgrim Dante the entire journey is 'experience', culminating in the summit of Paradise:

---

24 This paragraph takes into consideration Il poema degli universali, my Introduction to Dante Alighieri: *Divina Commedia* (Edited by C. Ossola. Venice: Marsilio 2021, pp. IX–LXII). The lexical choice here diverges from Mandelbaum's rendering of Purgatorio XV, 21, where 'experience' is translated as 'experiment' (n.Tr.).

25 "[E]t dicit, quod ex experientia in hominibus fit scientia et ars" (Online: https://www.corpusthomisticum.org/cmp0101.html, accessed 15.12.2021).

> Dei cinque che mi fan cerchio per ciglio,
> colui che più al becco mi s'accosta,
> la vedovella consolò del figlio:
>
> ora conosce quanto caro costa
> non seguir Cristo, per l'esperïenza
> di questa dolce vita e de l'opposta.
>
> Of those five flames that, arching, form my brow,
> he who is nearest to my beak is one
> who comforted the widow for her son;
>
> now he has learned the price one pays for not
> following Christ, through his experience
> of this sweet life and of its opposite.
>
> *(Paradiso* XX, 43–48)[26]

It is entirely true that the point of equilibrium in Dante – insofar as knowledge is concerned – is the situation of experience within the flowing of grace, as recalled in the famous tercet we have already evoked here:

> Trasumanar significar per verba
> non si poria; però l'essemplo basti
> *a cui esperïenza grazia serba.*
>
> Passing beyond the human cannot be
> worded; let Glaucus serve as simile –
> *until grace grant you the experience.*
>
> *(Paradiso* I, 70–72) (m.e.)

And yet, in Dante 'experience' is already a certainty: it is 'baggage' that coalesces, accumulates, a rich well of tested experimentation, as embodied in exemplary fashion by the Guinizelli of *Purgatorio* XXVI (67–75):

> Non altrimenti stupido si turba
> lo montanaro, e rimirando ammuta,
> quando rozzo e salvatico s'inurba,
>
> che ciascun' ombra fece in sua paruta;
> ma poi che furon di stupore scarche,
> lo qual ne li alti cuor tosto s'attuta,
>
> "Beato te, che de le nostre marche",
> ricominciò colei che pria m'inchiese,
> *"per morir meglio, esperïenza imbarche!"*
>
> Each shade displayed no less astonishment
> or less confusion than a mountaineer,
> who, even as he stares about, falls silent
>
> when, rough and rustic, he comes to the city;
> but when they'd set aside astonishment –
> that's soon subdued in noble hearts – he who
>
> had questioned me before, began again:
> "Blessed are you who would, *in order to
> die better, store experience of our lands!"*
>
> (m.e.)

In the language of the Florentine "traders", who he so detested, and with the experience of modernity ("store experience!"), Dante declares the meaning of his own journey.

Trade in the merchandise of experience, even before that of grace. Humanism was born.

---

[26] The reference here is to Trajan, who is spoken of *Purgatorio* X, 73–93.

Bibliographical References

Primary Literature and Early Authors

The following editions and translations are used throughout.

Adam Scotus (Adam of Dryburgh): *De tripartito tabernaculo*. PL, 198, 776B.
Ambrosius, Saint: *Expositio in psalmum David CXVIII*. PL, 15, 1449D.
Aquinas Thomas: *In psalmos Davidis expositio* [Ps. IV, 1]. *Parma*: Typis Petri Fiaccadori 1863.
Aquinas, Thomas: *Sententia libri Metaphysicae*. Online: https://www.corpusthomisticum.org.
Aquinas, Thomas: *Summa theologiae*. Alba/Roma, Editiones Paulinae 1962 (Engl. Trans. Online: http://www.documentacatholicaomnia.eu/03d/1225-1274,_Thomas_Aquinas,_Summa_Theologiae_%5B1%5D,_EN.pdf).
Benvenuto da Imola: Commentary on the *Comedy* (Benevenuti de Rambaldis de Imola Comentum super Dantis Aldigherij Comoediam, nunc primum integre in lucem editum sumptibus Guilielmi Warren Vernon, curante Jacobo Philippo Lacaita. Florentiae, G. Barbèra, 1887). Online: https://dante.dartmouth.edu/biblio.php?comm_id=13755.
Bonaventure, Saint: *Itinerarium mentis in Deum*. Online: http://www.documentacatholicaomnia.eu/03d/1221-1274,_Bonaventura,_Itinerarium_Mentis_in_Deum,_LT.pdf.
Bruno di Segni: *Expositio in Psalmos*. PL 164, 1221A.
Gregory the Great (Pope Gregory I), Saint: *Dialogues*. Edited by Adalbert de Vogüé. Paris: Cerf 1978–1980 ("Sources chrétiennes", no. 251, 260, 265).
John Climacus (Ioannes Climacus), Saint: *Scala Paradisi*. In: *Patrologiæ Græcæ*. Edited by Jacques Paul Migne (Vol. 88). Paris 1860. Online: https://www.mlat.uzh.ch/browser?path=7360&text=7360.
Leonardo da Vinci: *Trattato della pittura di Leonardo da Vinci, condotto sul cod. Vaticano Urbinate 1270, con prefazione 1452–1519*. Edited by Gaetano Milanesi, with texts by Giorgio Vasari and Marco Tabarrini, according to Manuscript. Urb. Lat. 1270 | Biblioteca Apostolica Vaticana. Roma: Unione Cooperativa Editrice 1890 (*Treatise on Painting*. Engl. Transl. by John Francis Rigaud, R.A. London: George Bell & Sons 1877).
Ovid (Publius Ovidius Naso): Ovid's *Heroides*. Online: http://www.thelatinlibrary.com/ovid.html (English translation, online: theoi.com).
Rupert of Deutz: *De divinis officiis*. PL 170, 177C.

Secondary Literature

Del Popolo, Concetto: Matelda. In: *Letture classensi*. 8, Ravenna: Longo 1979, pp. 125–126.
Ossola, Carlo: Il poema degli universali. Introduction to Dante Alighieri: *Divina Commedia*. Edited by Carlo Ossola. Venice: Marsilio 2021, pp. IX–LXII.
Petrocchi, Giorgio: Nota introduttiva to Dante Alighieri: *La Divina Commedia*. Turin: Einaudi 1975, pp. VII–XXII.
Pound, Ezra: *Lo spirito romanzo* (1910). Milano: SE 1991.
Quaglio, Antonio E.: Il canto XXVIII. In: *Lectura Dantis Scaligera. Purgatorio*. Florence: Le Monnier 1967, pp. 1057–1058.

Sanguineti, Federico (ed.): *Dantis Alagherii Comedia*. Florence: Edizioni del Galluzzo 2001.
Sanguineti, Federico: *Dantis Alagherii Comedia. Appendice bibliografica 1988–2000*. Florence: Edizioni del Galluzzo per la Fondazione Ezio Franceschini 2005.
Truijen, Vincent: Delectasti. In: *Enciclopedia Dantesca*. Online: https://www.treccani.it/enciclopedia/delectasti_%28Enciclopedia-Dantesca%29/.

Paola Nasti
Biblical *Signa* and Dante's Words: For a Taxonomy of Biblical Intertextuality in the *Comedy*

1 Biblical Intertextuality

In the Middle Ages, studying, reading and living out the Bible meant above all memorising its *lectio* through a deep process of *meditatio* and *ruminatio*.[1] By slowly 'digesting' what they learned from the Bible and the Church's multiple traditions associated with it, the faithful Christians transformed the doctrine, stories and language of the book of God into a cultural and spiritual 'tempering' that saturated them to the point of becoming almost muscle memory. Reproducing or reinventing the word of God, in a more or less conscious manner, was thus part of their experience of life. In a context so profoundly permeated by the divine word, it can be limiting, if not misguided, to search for traces of the Bible as a citational source. Study of the phenomena of biblical intertextuality in the Middle Ages cannot be reduced

---

[1] According to Jean Leclercq, *ruminatio* was the contemplative and creative reading of the Bible practised by monks: "The word meditatio, borrowed from the military vocabulary of ancient Latin, is equivalent to a word in the Hebrew Bible meaning 'to repeat'. The activity to which it refers consists in applying oneself attentively to the practice of complete memorization. It causes the text that has been read to penetrate, as it were, one's entire being, body and soul. The text thus comes, to some extent, to be a part of the reader who has assimilated it to himself by holding it in his mouth. To evoke this complex phenomenon, many authors liked to compare the reader to a ruminant, an animal that digests its food twice and was considered to be among the 'clean' animals in the Old Testament (cf. Leviticus 11). Such authors apply to the spiritual activities of reading and meditation the vocabulary that serves to designate the different phases of *ruminatio*: chewing, the perception of flavour, digestion, and the assimilation of the food to the organism. After it has been read, one perceives the sense of a text on the *palatum cordis* (palate of the heart) or in ore cordis (in the mouth of the heart). Throughout this process and thereafter, one responds in the presence of God – this is prayer, *oratio*." Jean Leclercq: Commentary on Biblical and Ecclesiastical Literature from Latin Antiquity to the Twelfth Century (trans. A. Kraebel). In: *The Mediaeval Journal*, 2.2 (2012), p. 27–53, p. 31. For Bede's use of this term, see André Crépin: Bede and the Vernacular. In: *Famulus Christi: Essays in Commemoration of the Thirteenth Centenary of the Birth of the Venerable Bede*. Edited by Gerald Bonner. London: S.P.C.K. 1976, p. 170–192, p. 172. On memory in the Middle Ages: M. J Carruthers: *The Book of Memory: A Study of Memory in Medieval Culture*. Cambridge: Cambridge University Press 1990.

Note: Translated from the Italian by Matthew Coneys Wainwright.

to the retrieval of citations, repetitions, direct or possible echoes. This is above all due to the fluidity of textual *limina* and the intermingling of *littera* and *commentum*. Indeed, in the Middle Ages the words of *scribae Dei* were rarely presented without commentary, on the contrary they were always accompanied by a dense apparatus of glosses which interpreted and enriched them, often modifying their sense.[2] Perhaps more problematically, the difficulty of intertextual 'archaeology' also results from the fact that biblical memory is often concealed within the repetition of a single word – a word which can unlock an entire textual and spiritual universe.

In the work of Dante, citations, references, and relatively clear echoes of the Bible are, as we know, extremely frequent.[3] As Dante himself repeatedly declares,

---

[2] On biblical exegesis and commentary: Gilbert Dahan: *L'exégèse chrétienne de la Bible en occident médiéval XIIe–XIVe siècle. Patrimoines, christianisme*. Paris: Cerf 1999; Henri de Lubac: *Exégèse médiévale: les quatre sens de l'écriture*, 4 vols. Paris: Aubier 1959-1964; *La Bibbia del XIII secolo. Storia del testo, storia dell'esegesi. Convegno della Società Internazionale per lo studio del Medioevo Latino (SISMEL) Firenze, 1–2 giugno 2001*. Edited by Giuuseppe Cremascoli and Francesco Santi. Florence: SISMEL, Edizioni del Galluzzo 2004; *Le Moyen Âge et la Bible*. Edited by Pierre Riché and Guy Lobrichon. Paris: Beauchesne 1984; *The Bible in the Medieval World: Essays in Honour of Beryl Smalley*. Edited by by Katherine Walsh and Diana Wood. Studies in Church History Subsidia 4. Oxford: Blackwell 1985; *The Early Medieval Bible: Its Production, Decoration, and Use*. Edited by Richard Gameson. Cambridge| New York: Cambridge University Press 1994; *The Practice of the Bible in the Middle Ages: Production, Reception, and Performance in Western Christianity*. Edited by Susan Boynton and Diane J. Reilly. New York: Columbia University Press 2011; *The New Cambridge History of the Bible, ii: From 600 to 1450*. Edited by Richard Marsden and E. Ann Matter. Cambridge: Cambridge University Press 2012. On the senses of the Bible: Beryl Smalley: Use of the Spiritual Senses of Scripture in Persuasion and Argument by Scholars in the Middle Ages. In: *Recherches de Théologie et Philosophie Médiévales*, 52 (1985), p. 44–63; Alastair J. Minnis: Quadruplex Sensus, Multiplex Modus: Scriptural Sense and Mode in Medieval Scholastic Exegesis. In: *Interpretation and Allegory*. Leiden, The Netherlands: Brill 2000, and Ian Christopher Levy: The Literal Sense of Scripture and the Search for Truth in the Late Middle Ages. In: *Revue d'Histoire Ecclesiastique*, 104, 3–4 (2009), p. 783–827. See also: Frans Van Liere: *An Introduction to the Medieval Bible*. Cambridge: Cambridge University Press 2014, p. 230–233.

[3] There is a burgeoning literature on the Bible in the *Comedy*. Here, I note only some general studies: Giovanni Barblan: *Dante e la Bibbia. Atti del Convegno internazionale promosso da "Biblia" (Firenze, 26–28 settembre 1986)*. Florence: Olschki 1988; V. Stanley Benfell: *The Biblical Dante*. Toronto: University of Toronto Press 2011; Peter S. Hawkins: *Dante's Testaments: Essays in Scriptural Imagination*. Stanford: Stanford University Press 1999; Sergio Cristaldi: Dalle beatitudini all'"Apocalisse". Il Nuovo Testamento nella "Commedia". In: *Letture classensi* 17, series Edited by Nicolò Mineo. Ravenna: Longo 1988, p. 23–67; *La Bibbia di Dante. Esperienza mistica, profezia e teologia biblica in Dante. Atti del Convegno Internazionale di Studi (Ravenna: 7 novembre 2009)*. Edited by Giuseppe Ledda. Ravenna: Centro Dantesco dei Frati Minori Conventuali 2011; Giuseppe Ledda: *La Bibbia di Dante*. Turin / Bologna,:Claudiana – EMI, 2015; Lino Pertile:

the Bible is his book, the alpha and omega of all writing. And yet, despite the pervasiveness of biblical intertextuality in the Florentine's work, even today we not only lack a complete list of all possible biblical references in Dante, but also – and perhaps more concerningly – a taxonomy of the different ways in which the poet engaged with the scriptural tradition.[4] In order to be truly exhaustive, such a classification would have to consider not only the critical categories known to scholars of literary intertextuality but also the taxonomic criteria discussed by scholars of the Bible and its ancient tradition.[5] Indeed, the challenge of such a classification will not only consist in measuring the degree of 'distance' from the cited text, but also and more crucially the means and aims of its reuse and the nature of the paratexts involved. In my opinion, this desired taxonomy of biblical references in Dante should include an important 'citational' category rarely employed in criticism yet significant for those who are concerned with the Bible in the Middle

---

La puttana e il gigante. Dal Cantico dei Cantici al Paradiso Terrestre di Dante. Ravenna: Longo 1998; Gianfranco Ravasi: *I salmi nella "Divina Commedia"*. Foreword by Enrico Malato. Rome: Salerno 2013; Paola Rigo: *Memoria classica e memoria biblica in Dante*. Florence: Olschki, 1994. I will also take the liberty of referring to my own studies: *Favole d'amore e 'saver profondo': La tradizione salomonica in* Dante. Ravenna: Longo, 2007, and Dante e la tradizione scritturale. In: *Dante*. Edited by Robert Rea and Justin Steinberg. Rome: Carocci 2020, p. 267–285.

4 On the phenomenon of Biblical intertextuality in the classical sense: Christopher Kleinhenz: The Poetics of Citation: Dante's "Divina Commedia" and the "Bible". In: *Dante: The Critical Complex. Vol. 4. Dante and Theology: The Biblical Tradition and Christian Allegory*. Edited by Richard Lansing. New York & London: Routledge 2003, p. 301–321. Closer to a religious sense of intertextuality is Carolynn Lund-Mead: The "Vulgata" in the "Commedia": Self-Interpreting Texts. In: *Dantean Dialogues: Engaging with the Legacy of Amilcare Iannucci*. Edited by Maggie Kilgour and Elena Lombardi. Toronto: University of Toronto Press 2013, p. 155–173.

5 Gérard Genette: *The Architext: An Introduction*. Berkeley: University of California Press 1992, p. 83–84; Idem: *Palimpsests: Literature in the Second Degree*. Lincoln NE and London: University of Nebraska Press 1997; Idem: *Paratexts: Thresholds of Interpretation*. Lincoln NE and London: University of Nebraska Press 1997. On intertextuality in the Bible: *Intertextuality in Biblical Writings*. Edited by by Sipke Draisma. Kampen: Kok 1989; *Reading between Texts: Intertextuality and the Hebrew Bible*. Edited by Danna N. Fewell. Louisville: Westminster / John Knox Press 1992; Jeffery M. Leonard: Inner-Biblical Interpretation and Intertextuality. In: *Literary Approaches to the Bible*. Edited by Douglas Mangum and Douglas Estes. Bellingham, WA: Lexham Press 2017, p. 97–141; Steve Moyise: Intertextuality and the Study of the Old Testament in the New Testament. In: *The Old Testament in the New Testament*. Edited by S. Moyise. Sheffield: Sheffield Academic Press 2000, p. 14–41; Idem: Intertextuality and Biblical Studies: A Review. In: *Verbum et Ecclesia*, 23, 2 (2002), p. 418–431; Idem: Dialogical Intertextuality. In: *Exploring Intertextuality: Diverse Strategies for New Testament Interpretation of Texts*. Edited by B. J. Oropeza and Steve Moyise. Eugene, OR: Cascade Books 2016, p. 3–15. See also: Richard B. Hays: *Echoes of Scripture in the Gospels*. Waco, TX: Baylor University Press 2016; Idem: *Echoes of Scripture in the Letters of Paul*. New Haven: Yale University Press 1989.

Ages: the use of key words, a technique of textual referencing that is fundamental to understanding one of the most important kinds of biblical intertextuality, as this was perceived by medieval students and readers of the holy book.

The 'invention' of biblical concordances originated in the thirteenth century with the work of Hugh of Saint-Cher, who composed his *Concordantiae sacrorum bibliorum* by gathering together all the occurrences of a single word (or a fragment of a verse), indicating its place in the text with a brief citation of the chapter.[6] *Concordantiae* swiftly developed into a fundamental tool for preachers, who could use the verbal concordance to expand on a subject by pivoting to other Biblical *loci* through a key word.[7] In his *De Modo Componendi Sermones*, Thomas Waleys noted the remarkable value of verbal concordances for identifying the "auctoritates" which were crucial for paraenetic discourse:

> Utitur autem praedicator concordantia vocali quando adducit auctoritates quae non solum in sententia concordant cum verbis thematis [. . .] sed etiam concordant in verbis [. . .] Facile est auctoritates habere, ex eo quod factae sunt Concordantiae super Bibliam et super originalia sanctorum, secundum ordinem alphabeti, ut auctoritates possint faciliter inveniri [. . .] ita quod cuidam, ad habendum auctoritates ad libitum, non est magna difficultas.[8]

Concordantiae represented the natural evolution of other works that sought to classify biblical vocabulary and imagery, and which were often included in thirteenth- and fourteenth-century bibles. Such works were clearly aimed at facilitating both swift consultation and interpretation; they vary in nature and length, ranging from Jerome's *Interpretationes nominum hebraicorum* to thematic concordances, from glossaries to lists of topics for sermons.[9] It is also

---

[6] Bert Roest: Mendicant School Exegesis. In: *The Practice of the Bible in the Middle Ages*, p. 179–204, p. 181.

[7] On late medieval sermons: Nicole Bériou: Les Sermons latins après 1200. In: *The Sermon*. Edited by Beverly Kienzle.Turnhout: Brepols 2000, p. 363–447.

[8] De modo componendi sermones. In: *Artes Praedicandi: Contribution à l'Histoire de la Rhétorique au Moyen Age*. Edited by Thomas-Marie Charland. Ottawa: Institut D'Études Médiévales 1936, p. 345, pp. 390–391. On the use of concordances in preaching: Marian Michele Mulchahey: *First the Bow is Bent in Study: Dominican Education Before 1350*. Toronto: Pontifical Institute of Mediaeval Studies 1998, p. 509–513; Richard H. and Mary A. Rouse: The Verbal Concordance to the Scriptures. In: *Archivum Fratrum Praedicatorum*, 44 (1974), p. 5–30. The first concordance completed at St Jacques probably dates from 1235 (*ante quem* 1247): Richard H. and Mary A. Rouse: The Development of Research Tools in the Thirteenth Century. In: *Authentic Witness. Approaches to Medieval Texts and Manuscripts*. Notre Dame IN: University of Notre Dame Press 1991, p. 221–255, p. 203.

[9] In addition to R. H. and M. A. Rouse's The Development of Research Tools in the Thirteenth Century (cited above), see also Emmanuelle Kuhry: Dictionnaires, distinctions, recueils de propriétés en milieu cistercien: outils pour la prédication, sources pour l'étude de la nature. In: *Les Cisterciens*

not unusual to encounter works like the *Summarium bibliae*, in which the entire Bible "is summarised (metrically), with one word per chapter; the key word is amplified by a few additional words, usually copied above the line in a smaller script (some copies include only the one, key word, rendering the text almost incomprehensible)."[10]

As a halfway point between such tools for study and commentary, the genre of *distinctiones* also enjoyed significant dissemination in the twelfth and thirteenth centuries and continued to gain ground throughout the fourteenth.[11] *Distinctiones* were "répertoires dans lesquels sont classé, le plus souvent par ordre alphabétique – parfois dans un ordre méthodique – les divers mots et vocables de l'Écriture, pour chacun desquels sont distingués, d'où le titre de Distinctiones, les sens symboliques, illustrés chacun par quelque textes scripturaires".[12] This kind of tool for biblical study and exegesis became essential to help preachers 'distinguish' the meanings of the various biblical themes and terms they discussed in their sermons. Among the most widespread *distinctiones* were certainly those of Peter Cantor, known as the *Distinctiones Abel*, and of Alan of Lille.[13]

---

et la transmission des textes (XIIe–XVIIIe siècles). Edited by Thomas Falmagne, Dominique Stutzmann, Anne-Marie Turcan-Verkerk. Turnhout: Brepols 2018, p. 286–337; Laura Light: Non-Biblical Texts in Thirteenth-Century Bibles. In: *Medieval Manuscripts, Their Makers and Users*. A Special Issue of Viator in Honor of Richard and Mary Rouse. Los Angeles University of California: Center for Medieval and Renaissance Studies. Brepols, Turnhout 2011, p. 169–83. On the *ars praedicandi*: Phyllis B. Roberts: The *Ars Praedicandi* and the Medieval Sermon. In: *Preacher, Sermon and Audience in the Middle Ages*, Edited by by Carolyn Muessig. Leiden: Brill 2002, p. 39–62. For an example of topical concordances: Thomson, S. Harrison: Grosseteste's Topical Concordance of the Bible and the Fathers. In: *Speculum*, 9, 2 (1934), p. 139–144. Among these tools, William Brito's *Expositiones vocabulorum Biblie* and *Expositio prologorum Biblie* were also widely read.

10 Laura Light: Non-Biblical Texts, p. 181.

11 Louis J. Bataillon: Intermédiaires entre les traités de morale pratique et les sermons: les distinctiones bibliques alphabétiques. In: *Les genres littéraires dans les sources théologiques et philosophiques médiévales. Définition, critique et exploitation* (Actes du colloque de Louvain-la-Neuve, 25–27 mai 1981). Louvain-la-Neuve: Université catholique de Louvain 1982, p. 213–226; Richard H. and Mary A. Rouse: Biblical Distinctiones in the Thirteenth Century. In: *Archives d'histoire doctrinale et littéraire du moyen âge*, 41 (1975), p. 27–37.

12 Marie Dominique Chenu: *La théologie au XIIe siècle*. Paris: Vrin 1975, p. 19. For the evolution of the genre: Geneviève Hasenohr: Un recueil de 'Distinctiones' bilingue du début du XIVe siècle: Le Manuscrit 99 de la Bibliothèque Municipale De Charleville. In: *Romania*, 99, no. 393 (1) (1978), p. 47–96.

13 Stephen A. Barney: Peter the Chanter's Distinctiones Abel. In: *Allegory, Myth, and Symbol*. Edited by Morton W. Bloomfield. Cambridge, MA: Harvard University Press 1981, p. 87–107.

There can be no doubt that Dante was familiar with the 'easy' use of tools used by preachers to simplify their parenetic tasks. He himself complains of their limitations in his brief invective against them in *Paradiso* XXIX:

Ora si va con motti e con iscede	But now men go to preach with jests and jeers,
a predicare, e pur che ben si rida,	and just as long as they can raise a laugh,
gonfia il cappuccio e più non si richiede.	the cowl puffs up, and nothing more is asked.

(*Paradiso* XXIX, 115–117)

For the poet, the use of *iscede*[14] risks allowing the word of God to be drowned out amid the babble of the preachers and their "inventions":[15]

Per apparer ciascun s'ingegna e face	Each one strives for display, elaborates
sue invenzioni; e quelle son trascorse	his own inventions; preachers speak at length
da' predicanti e 'l Vangelio si tace.	of these – meanwhile the Gospels do not speak.

(*Paradiso* XXIX, 94–96)

This criticism should not, however, lead us to assume that these forms of medieval biblical 're-use' were disregarded by Dante himself. On the contrary, knowledge of study and composition tools was essential to those who like Dante sought to call the faithful and their preachers to integrated study of the biblical word, and thus strove to re-establish correct biblical exegesis on the basis of careful consideration of the literal meaning of the Bible, as demonstrated by his observations in the third book of the *Monarchia*.[16] Moreover (as is well known), the poet

---

[14] I am aware that the common interpretation of the term "iscede" refers to 'jeers' on the basis of medieval readings (Mandelbaum also translates it this way). However the OVI dictionary also includes other meaning of the term that in my view might be more apt to understand the text: 'Redazione primitiva di un testo'; '[o]ggetto usato come termine di riferimento per la realizzazione di oggetti identici per dimensioni e forma; modello' (http://tlio.ovi.cnr.it/TLIO/, accessed 26.07.2022); Dante himself uses the latin term 'cedula' to describe his *Quaestio de acqua et terra* (I, 3). On this use of the term in the *Quaestio* see the forthcoming article by Zygmunt Baranski: 'Questio quedam exorta est': Dante's *Questio de aqua et terra* between *questio disputata* and *tractatus*, between rhetoric and *reportatio*, between fact and fiction, between Verona and Ravenna.

[15] On Dante and preaching: Carlo Delcorno: Cadenze e figure della predicazione nel viaggio dantesco. In: Lettere Italiane, 37, 3 (1985), p. 299–320; Idem: Schede su Dante e la retorica della predicazione. In: *Miscellanea di studi danteschi in memoria di Silvio Pasquazi*. Edited by Alfonso Paolella, Vincenzo Placella, Giovanni Turco. Naples: Federico & Ardia, I, 1993, p. 301–312; George Ferzoco: Dante and the Context of Medieval Preaching. In: *Reviewing Dante's theology*. Edited by Claire E. Honess and Matthew Treherne. Bern: Peter Lang, II, 2013, p. 187–210; Nicolò Maldina: *In Pro del Mondo: Dante, la Predicazione e i Generi della Letteratura Religiosa Medievale*: Rome: Salerno 2018.

[16] P. Nasti, "Dante and Ecclesiology", in *Reviewing Dante's Theology*, ed. by C. E. Honess, M. Treherne, Oxford/Bern/Berlin, Lang, II, 2013, pp. 43–88.

exploits biblical 'particulas' at several points in the poem, knowing that he can rely on the memory of his readers to complete quotations or the incipits of famous lines of scripture or liturgical texts.

The present study considers three of these *key-words* in order to illustrate not only how biblical intertextuality infuses the *Comedy* by permeating even its most tightly-knit wording, but also how Dante often sought to bring order to the confusion caused by perfunctory interpretations and uses of the Bible, which distracted from their literal meaning or from a correct moral or allegorical exegesis of the biblical word.

In order to move towards a taxonomy, three categories of 'key words' shall be analysed: citations, which directly or indirectly echo a passage of the Bible in its entirety; pericopes, which recall a biblical book or episode and apply its narrative or ideological knowledge to the target text; and monads, simple and isolated words that nevertheless function as the key to understanding a theological or spiritual question, beginning from the wording of the Bible. All these examples have a 'Christological' dimension and are thus words that illuminate how Dante constructs his Christology *per verba*.

2 Citations: "Eli"

The pilgrim's journey begins precisely with a citation when, fleeing the three beasts of the dark forest, the *agens* sees Virgil and, citing Psalm 50 (51), pleads "Have mercy on me" (*Inferno* I, 65). As centuries of commentary on this passage have demonstrated, recourse to this citation serves to establish the narrative situation as well as the identity of Dante as character and author.[17] The exegetic, liturgical and theological tradition associated with Psalm 50 (51) had endowed the verb "miserere" ("have mercy") with the entire penitential history of man, who recognises his own sin and calls on God's mercy. Dante's "miserere" is thus not only a request for grace, but also a recognition of guilt. Moreover, since the biblical singer of the "miserere" is David, the author whom Dante

---

[17] Robert Hollander: Dante's Use of the Fifth Psalm. A Note on *Purg*. XXX, 84. In: *Dante Studies*, XCIX, 1973, p. 145–150; Theresa Federici: Dante's Davidic Journey: From Sinner to God's scribe. In: *Dante's "Commedia": Theology as Poetry*. Introduced and edited by Vittorio Montemaggi and Matthew Treherne: Notre Dame IN: Notre Dame University Press 2010, p. 180–209; Nicolò Maldina: "Per poenitentiam factum prophetam". Filigrane davidiche nel prologo della "Commedia". In: *Poesia e profezia nell'opera di Dante*. Edited by Giuseppe Ledda. Ravenna: Centro Dantesco dei Frati Minori Conventuali 2019, p. 163–17; Alessandro Vettori: *Dante's Prayerful Pilgrimage: Typologies of Prayer in the Comedy*. Leiden-Boston: Brill 2019, p. 67–80.

characterises as "the singer of the Holy Spirit", the pilgrim's plea places Dante on the right path of Davidic *imitatio*: a shadowing that is every bit as moral as it is authorial.

Beyond the "miserere", which has been widely discussed in criticism, the majority of biblical citations, though many, are very brief. One citation that has only rarely been considered is the "Eli" of *Purgatorio* XXIII, 74. Interest in this biblical 'cameo' is linked to its theological and religious significance, but also to its intrinsically citational nature. According to Mark and Matthew, "Elôï, élôï, lama sabacthaneï" is the cry of Christ when he calls out to the Father from the cross: "My God, my God, why have your foresaken me?" (Mark 15:34; Matthew 27: 46). Yet, in the Gospels, "Elôï, élôï" is in fact a quotation from Psalm 21 (22):2. At the most dramatic moment of his Passion, Christ cites a Davidic passage to confirm a tenet of his entire preaching: his incarnation is the fulfilment of the law, and his new word confirmation of the old. Through citations like "Elôï, élôï", Christ, or his evangelists, establish figurative reading of the Bible, the most deeply Christian reading of the word of God: everything written seeks to reveal the mysteries of the Messiah's Incarnation, Passion and Resurrection. Everything written is, therefore, a guide to bodily resurrection as the salvation made possible through the sacrifice of the Son of God.[18] Citing this passage also meant reflecting on biblical intertextuality as the mode of writing which is necessary to reveal the trajectory of the divine project, from creation to salvation.

The "Eli" citation is embedded in one of the most interesting and, arguably, dramatic allusions to the Passion of Christ in the entire *Comedy*.[19] In *Purgatorio*

---

[18] On Christ as fulfilment: Matthew Levering: *Christ's Fulfillment of Torah and Temple: Salvation According to Thomas Aquinas*. Notre Dame IN: University of Notre Dame Press 2002. On the Passion in the Middle Ages: Thomas H. Bestul: *Texts of the Passion: Latin Devotional Literature and Medieval Society*. Philadelphia: University of Pennsylvania Press 1996; Celia Chazelle: *The Crucified God in the Carolingian Era: Theology and Art of Christ's Passion*. Cambridge: Cambridge University Press 2001; William P. Loewe: *Lex Crucis: Soteriology and the Stages of Meaning*. Philadelphia: Fortress Press 2016; Henri Leclercq: Croix et crucifix. Edited by Fernand Cabrol and H. Leclercq: *Dictionnaire d'Archeologie Chretienne et de Liturgie*. Paries: Librairie Letouzey et Ané 1948, vol. 3, pt. 2, 3045–3131; Alasdair A. MacDonald, Bernhard Ridderbos, Rita M. Schlusemann (eds): *The Broken Body: Passion Devotion in Late Medieval Culture*. Groningen: Egbert Forsten 1998; Gerard R. Viladesau: *The Beauty of the Cross: The Passion of Christ in Theology and the Arts from the Catacombs to the Eve of the Renaissance*. Oxford: Oxford University Press 2006, Idem: *The Crucifixion of Jesus: History, Myth, Faith*. Minneapolis: Fortress Press 1995.

[19] For important observations on this citation, see George A. Trone: The Cry of Dereliction in *Purgatorio* XXIII. In: *Dante Studies*, 113 (1995), p. 111–129. On the Passion in the *Comedy*, I take the liberty of mentioning my own essay: Paola Nasti: Soteriologia e Passione nella 'Commedia'. In: *Theologus Dantes*. Edited by Luca Lombardo, Diego Parisi, Anna Pegoretti. Venice: Edizioni Ca' Foscari 2018, p. 103–138; see also: on Christ in Dante: Oliver Davies: Dante's *Commedia* and

XXIII,[20] Forese compares the desire of the gluttons who suffer for their sin to Christ's desire for the cross:

> E non pur una volta, questo spazzo   as we go round this space, our pain's renewed –
> girando, si rinfresca nostra pena: I speak of pain but I should speak of solace,
> io dico pena, e dovria dir sollazzo,   for we are guided to those trees by that
>
> ché quella voglia a li alberi ci mena   same longing that had guided Christ when He
> che menò Cristo lieto a dire 'Elì',   had come to free us through the blood He shed
> quando ne liberò con la sua vena.   and, in His joyousness, called out: 'Eli'.
>
> (*Purgatorio* XXIII, 70–75)

The comparison established by Dante points towards the penitent's identification with Christ through expiatory suffering.[21] This penitential dimension, closely linked

---

the Body of Christ. In: *Dante's Commedia: Theology as Poetry*. Edited by Vittorio Montemaggi and Matthew Treherne. Notre Dame IN: Notre Dame University Press 2010, p. 161–179; Adriano Lanza: Il 'sacrosanto segno' e il 'venerabil segno'. In: Idem: *Dante eterodosso. Una diversa lettura della Commedia*. Bergamo: Moretti Honegger 2004, p. 102–112; Claudio Gigante: 'Adam sive Christus'. Creazione, incarnazione, redenzione nel canto VII del *Paradiso*. In: *Rivista di Studi Danteschi*, 8, 2 (2008), p. 241–268; Alessandro Ghisalberti: *Paradiso*, canto VII. Dante risponde alla domanda: perché un Dio uomo?. Edited by Ennio Sandal: *Lectura Dantis Scaligera 2009–2015*. Rome / Padua: Antenore 2016, p. 141–158; Attilio Mellone: Il primato di Cristo secondo Dante. In: Idem: *Saggi e letture dantesche*. Salerno: Editrice Gaia 2005, p. 373–391; Christopher Ryan: Paradiso VII: Marking the Difference between Dante and Anselm. In: *Dante and the Middle Ages: Literary and Historical Essays*. Edited by John Barnes and Cormac Ó Cuilleanaín. Dublin: Irish Academic Press 1995, p. 117–137; Pasquale Sabbatino: La Croce nella *Divina Commedia*. In: *Critica letteraria*, 115–116 (2002), p. 275–298; Gennaro Sasso: . . . a far vendetta corse / della vendetta del peccato antico (Pd VI 92-3). In: *Bollettino di Italianistica. Rivista di critica, storia letteraria, filologia e linguistica*, 3, 1 (2006), p. 15–40; Jeffrey T. Schnapp: Unica spes hominum, crux, o venerabile signum. In: *The Transfiguration of History at the Center of Dante's Paradise*. Princeton: Princeton University Press 1986; Mary Alexandra Watt: *The Cross that Dante Bears: Pilgrimage, Crusade, and the Cruciform Church in the Divine Comedy*. Gainesville: University Press of Florida 2005. Fundamental for the study of pain in Dante, including in relation to the Passion, are: Manuele Gragnolati: *Experiencing the Afterlife: Soul and Body in Dante and Medieval Culture*. Notre Dame IN: University of Notre Dame Press 2005; Lino Pertile: Sul dolore nella Commedia. In *Letteratura e filologia tra Svizzera e Italia. Studi in onore di Guglielmo Gorni*. Edited by Maria Antonietta Terzoli, Alberto Asor Rosa, Giorgio Inglese. 3 vols. Rome: Edizioni di Storia e Letteratura 2010, I, p. 105–120.

20 On liturgical and biblical references in the Forese canto, see Ronald L. Martinez: Dante's Forese, the Book of Job, and the Office of the Dead: A Note on Purgatorio 23. In: *Dante Studies*, 120 (2002), p. 1–16.

21 For atonement and salvation, among others see: Anna Cerbo: Espiazione e recupero totale della libertà dal peccato (*Purgatorio* XXI, 58–78). In: *Dante oltre il medioevo. Atti dei Convegni in ricordo di Silvio Pasquazi* (Roma 16 e 30 novembre 2010). Edited by V. Placella. Rome: Pioda 2012, p. 39–57; Carlo Delcorno: 'Ma noi siam peregrin come voi siete'. Aspetti penitenziali del 'Purga-

to the Cross as a symbol of the punishment borne by Christ, is present – as one might imagine – throughout *Purgatorio,* a canticle that indeed begins and finishes in the name of the crucifixion (VI, 118–119; XXXIII, 61–63). In this sense, the cross is above all – according to the ancient reading of Athanasius, subsequently espoused by Augustine and Anselm – the instrument through which Christ takes the place of humanity to pay the price of Adam and Eve's sin with his blood ("through the blood he shed") and free the just from *damnatio*.[22] In *Purgatorio* XXXIII, through the repetition of "Eli" (Matthew 27:46), Dante's reference to the Gospel episode of the Passion seems to point the reader towards reflection on the penitential value of Christ's death. Moreover, as the *glossa ordinaria* summarises, "Heli Heli" is Christ's cry of humiliation as he weeps and dies for the sins of the world:

> *Heli Heli lamazabatani?* Hoc est: Deus meus, Deus meus ut quid dereliquisti me?
> [interl.] humana natura erat derelicta, sed non Dei Filius
> [marg.] *Heli Heli Lamazabatani Etc.* Quorum suscipit naturam eorundem plorat miseriam. In quo ostendit quantam ipsi flere debent qui peccant. Ne mireris verborum humilitatem et querimonias derelicti, cum formam servi sciens scandalum crucis videas.[23]

Read from a Christological perspective, the quotation from Psalm 21(22) in this New Testament passage could intensify the episode's penitential meaning, as the Church Fathers considered the psalm to be a prophecy of Christ's suffering as a man during the *via crucis*. Christ appears naked, scorned, even as vile as a worm: "Ego autem sum vermis, et non homo; opprobrium hominum, et abjectio plebis" (21 [22]:7). It is no coincidence, therefore, that for the celebration of Good Friday, Psalm 21 (22) was the most widely cited of the Psalms that figuratively narrate Christ's experience of suffering.[24]

---

torio '. In: *Da Dante a Montale. Studi di filologia e critica letteraria in onore di Emilio Pasquini*. Edited by Gian Mario Anselmi, Bruno Bentivogli, Alfredo Cottignoli, Fabio Marri, Vittorio Roda, Gino Ruozzi, and Paola Vecchi Galli. Bologna: Gedit 2005, p. 11–30; Giuseppe Ledda: Sulla soglia del Purgatorio: peccato, penitenza, resurrezione. Per una 'lectura' di *Purgatorio* IX. In: *Lettere Italiane*, 66 (2014) 1, p. 3–36.

22 J. Patout Burns: The Concept of Satisfaction in Medieval Redemption Theory. In: *Theological Studies*, 36, 2 (1975), p. 285–305. Brian Leftow: Anselm on the Cost of Salvation. In: *Medieval Philosophy and Theology*, 6 (1997), p. 73–92.

23 Here and subsequently, quotations from the *Glossa ordinaria* on the Song of Songs follow the online version referred to above: https://gloss-e.irht.cnrs.fr/php/editions_chapitre.php?livre=../sources/editions/GLOSS-liber30.xml&chapitre=30_2 (accessed 24.06.2022). Lesley Smith: *The Glossa Ordinaria: The Making of a Medieval Bible Commentary*. Leiden: Brill 2009, p. 145–153.

24 Yvonne Rokseth: La liturgie de la passion vers la fin du Xe siècle. In: *Revue de musicologie*, 31 (1949), p. 9–26 and *Ibidem*, 32 (1950), p. 1–58. For liturgy linked to the cross: Bernard Capelle: Aux origines du culte de la croix. In: *Questions liturgiques et paroissiales*, 27 (1946), p. 157–162.

However, this same Davidic text also helped exegetes to read Christ's evangelical cry as an announcement of the Father's kingdom rather than an indication of doubt in his love. Indeed, read through the filter of Psalm 21 (22), Christ's "derelinquisti" had no negative connotation, but was considered by exegetes as testament to the triumph of the divine over the human: through Christ, the flesh is abandoned in order to gain heaven. The reading of Augustine, who dedicated numerous sermons to Psalm 21 (22), is particularly well known in this regard:[25]

> Videte quanta passus est! Iam ut dicamus passionem et ad illam maiori gemitu veniamus, videte quanta modo patitur, et deinde videte quare! Quis enim fructus? Ecce speraverunt patres nostri, et eruti sunt de terra Aegypti. Et sicut dixi, tam multi invocaverunt, et statim ad tempus, non in futura vita, sed continuo liberati sunt. Ipse Iob diabolo petenti concessus est, putrescens vermibus; tamen in hac vita recuperavit salutem, duplo accepit quae perdiderat: Dominus autem flagellabatur, et nemo subveniebat; sputis deturpabatur, et nemo subveniebat; colaphis caedebatur, et nemo subveniebat; spinis coronabatur, nemo subveniebat; levabatur in ligno, nemo eruit; clamat; Deus meus, Deus meus, utquid me dereliquisti? Non subvenitur. Quare, fratres mei? quare? Qua mercede tanta passus est? Omnia ista quae passus est, pretium est. Cujus rei pretio tanta passus est, recitemus, videamus quae dicat. Primum quaeramus quae passus sit, deinde quare: et videamus quam sint hostes Christi, qui confitentur quia tanta passus est, et tollunt quare. Hinc audiamus totum in isto psalmo, et quae passus sit, et quare. (Psalm XXI, II. 8)[26]

It is in the sense attributed to it by Augustine that Psalm 21 (22) was taken up in sermons dedicated to the resurrection and in the Paschal liturgy. The *tractus* "Deus, Deus Meus", sung on Palm Sunday, is one example of a rewriting of the eschatological motif "Heli Heli": "Deus, Deus meus, respice in me: quare me dereliquisti? / Longe a salute mea verba delictorum meorum . . . / Annuntiabitur Domino generatio ventura, et annujntiabunt caeli iustitiam eius. Populo qui nascetur, quem fecit Dominus" (Psalm 21 [22]: 2–9, 18, 19, 22, 24, 32; cf. Matthew 27: 46).[26]

For the reader of Dante, then, the penitential context of the psalm is inescapable, but "Eli" also, and above all, refers to a vision of the crucifixion as ransom for and victory over eternal death.[27] Indeed, the psalm closes with an exaltation of divine glory, the source of life, the true food and manna, which is essential

---

[25] Augustine: *Enarrationes in Psalmos, I-L*. In: *Corpus Christianorum Series Latina*, vol. 38. Edited by D.Eligius Dekkers and Johannes Fraipont: Turnhout: Brepols, 1956; references to Psalm 21 (22): CCSL 38: 121–42; CCSL, 39: 1163; CCSL 40: 1494; CCSL 36: 138.

[26] The Liturgy and Time. Vol IV. In: *The Church at Prayer*. Edited by Ir.n. H. Dalmais, Pierre Jounel and A. Georges Martimort. Collegeville: The Liturgical Press 1985, p. 75.

[27] Of particular significance in this regard is Rabanus Maurus's *Opusculum de Passione Domini*. PL 112, coll. 1125–1430. See also Larry Ayres: An Italian Romanesque Manuscript of Hrabanus Maurus' *De Laudibus Sanctae Crucis* and the Gregorian Reform. In: *Dumbarton Oaks Papers*, 41 (1987), p. 13–27.

for anyone who, like Forese, must rediscover the true meaning of their corporeal desires:

> Edent pauperes, et saturabuntur, et laudabunt Dominum qui requirunt eum: vivent corda eorum in saeculum saeculi. Reminiscentur et convertentur ad Dominum universi fines terrae; et adorabunt in conspectu ejus universae familiae gentium: quoniam Domini est regnum, et ipse dominabitur gentium. Manducaverunt et adoraverunt omnes pingues terrae; in conspectu ejus cadent omnes qui descendunt in terram. Et anima mea illi vivet; et semen meum serviet ipsi. Annuntiabitur Domino generatio ventura; et annuntiabunt caeli justitiam ejus populo qui nascetur, quem fecit Dominus. (Psalm 21 [22]:27–32)

For Forese, citing "Eli" is thus not a ploy to exalt suffering, but a means of declaring obedience to and faith in the eternal freedom that, according to medieval spirituality, is earned by those who follow Christ on the cross by harmonising their own will with the divine will. The suffering of the souls in Dante's Purgatory is the will of God, but since divine *unio* is only reached through the correspondence of will ("voglia") between God and man, obedient penitents, like Christ, make God's will their own and thus enjoy ("sollazzo") the punishments that purify them. The poet's wording also, and indeed most crucially, underlines Christ's joy[28] rather than his suffering, since for Dante the cross is an act of the Trinity's will to which Christians must joyfully conform.[29] The willing participation of Christ (and the Trinity) in his Passion is one of the most revolutionary and innovative aspects of late medieval soteriology.[30] In this new theological perspective, God chooses to sacrifice himself in the Son out of love, and thus out of desire and will. This will is contentment, as Dante himself states in *Paradiso* VII:

---

[28] An important study on the joyful Christ is Romano Manescalchi: Il Cristo lieto (*Purg.* XXIII 74) a confronto con analoghe rappresentazioni. In: *Parola del testo: semestrale di filologia e letteratura italiana comparata*, 20, 1 / 2 (2016), p. 23–40. Interesting observations on the happiness of Christ are also given by Giulia Gaimari: La letizia di Cristo nel *Purgatorio*: un'ipotesi di lettura. In: *Studi Danteschi*, 82 (2016), p. 165–18.

[29] See: P. Nasti, "Sotereologia"; see also Christopher Ryan: *Paradiso* VII: Marking the Difference Between Dante and Anselm. In: *Dante and the Middle Ages*. Edited by John C. Barnes and Cormac O Cuilleana. Dublin: Irish Academic Press 1995.

[30] Robert Prentice: O. F. M.: The Voluntarism of Duns Scotus, as Seen in His Comparison of the Intellect and the Will. In: *Franciscan Studies*, 28 (1968), p. 63–103; Thomas M. Ward: Voluntarism, Atonement, and Duns Scotus. In: *Heythrop Journal*, 58 (2017), p. 37–43.

Ma perché l'ovra tanto è più gradita da l'operante, quanto più appresenta de la bontà del core ond' ell' è uscita,	[...] But since a deed pleases its doer more, the more it shows the goodness of the heart from which it springs, the Godly Goodness that imprints the world
la divina bontà che 'l mondo imprenta, di proceder per tutte le sue vie, a rilevarvi suso, fu contenta.	was happy to proceed through both Its ways to raise you up again.

(*Paradiso* VII, 106–111)

To summarise, then, the citation "Eli" allows Dante to recall the biblical text to illuminate the tropological and anagogical sense of his own vision: the condition of the penitent souls nearing and after death is one of joyful repentance. Yet this citation also permitted him to clarify his position concerning a highly controversial passage of the two testaments that apparently showed Christ in too human and desperate a light when confronted with death. Indeed, as Thomas Aquinas notes in his commentary on Matthew, misreading Psalm 21 (22) meant risking to commit Arius or Nestorius's heresy:

> Unde dicit Hieronymus quod impii sunt qui aliter Psalmum illum exponere volunt quam de passione Christi. Notate, quod quidam male intellexerunt. Unde debetis scire quod fuerunt duae haereses. Una quae in Christo non posuit verbum unitum, sed quod verbum fuit loco animae, et hoc posuit Arius. Alii vero, quod verbum non fuit unitum naturaliter, sed per gratiam, sicut in aliquo iusto; ut in prophetis, et sic Nestorius. Unde exponebant Deus, Deus meus, ut quid dereliquisti me? Dicunt quod hoc dicebat verbum Dei, et vocat eum Deum, quia creatura sua est, et conqueritur, quod hoc verbum fecit sibi uniri, et post dereliquit eum. Sed haec est expositio impia, quia semper cum eo est; unde divinitas non dimisit carnem, nec animam: unde in Io. VII, v. 29: qui me misit, mecum est. t; unde vult dicere: quare voluisti ut passioni traderer, et isti obtenebrarentur? Item signat admirationem, unde admirabilis est Dei caritas.[31]

Reading "Eli" correctly in the Gospels and Psalms was above all necessary to exalt the fulfilment of the divine will. Dante did not need to distance himself from Arius or Nestorius, but by associating "Eli" with the 'joyful' Christ he clarifies an aspect of his Christology which he may have deemed an impediment to defending himself from the accusation of having misinterpreted Scripture. This, however, was perhaps also a response to the culture of his time. The representation of the Christ-*patiens* that was beginning to dominate late medieval culture, and which was visually expressed in the creation of suffering crucifixes, focused on Christ

---

[31] Thomas Aquinas, *Super Evangelium S. Matthaei lectura*, caput 27, lectio I 2 (Online: https://www.corpusthomisticum.org/cml26.html, accessed 24.06.2022).

as man.[32] Dante's insistence on Christ's *gaudium* suggests that he might have considered these new forms of pity as narratives that obscured the true message of the cross as a symbol of the victory of divine charity, the victory of the divine over man, of light over darkness. In the *Comedy*, the citation "Eli" is thus an invitation to read the Bible correctly according to the intertextual connections established by Christ himself, and celebrating, with Psalm 21 (22), the certainty of future glory.

3 Pericopes: "Diletto"

What I intend with the term 'pericope' does not indicate simple biblical calques, which result from what Moore termed the scriptural phraseology of Dante (and of which Moore offers excellent examples). Neither are pericopes linked to the free translations of the Vulgate that appear so frequently in the *Comedy*. Rather, this label designates words which often appear in clusters with other key words and refer to pericopes, parables, or thematic or narrative groups, or even entire books of the Bible, in an essentially obvious but undeclared manner.

The case we shall examine is of particular interest because its semantic thread is woven into no fewer than four cantos of the *Paradiso* (X–XIV) without the biblical source ever being cited in a more direct way. The term in question is "diletto", used as a substantive adjective. Dante employs the lemma "diletto" on numerous occasions in his work, often with reference to Beatrice (his *diletto* in the sense that she is his beloved) or to the joys and pleasures of terrestrial and otherworldly life (55 references). Only on two occasions, both within the heaven of the Sun, "diletto" is employed as a substantive adjective to identify Christ, first in canto XI and subsequently in canto XIII:[33]

---

[32] Ewert Cousins: The Humanity and the Passion of Christ. In: *Christian Spirituality: High Middle Ages and Reformation*, Edited by Jill Raitt, Bernard McGinn and John Meyendorff. New York: Crossroad 1987, p. 375–39. On visual representations of the Passion: Hans Belting: *The Image and its Public in the Middle Ages: Form and Function of Early Paintings of the Passion*. New Rochelle, N.Y.: A.D. Caratzas 1990; Anne Derbes: *Picturing the Passion in Late Medieval Italy: Narrative Painting, Franciscan Ideologies, and the Levant*. Cambridge: Cambridge University Press 1996.
[33] I have discussed these verses and their relationship with the Bible and exegesis in Paola Nasti: 'Caritas' and Ecclesiology in Dante's Heaven of Sun. In: *Dante's "Commedia": Theology as Poetry*. Introduced and edited by Vittorio Montemaggi and Matthew Treherne. Notre Dame IN: Notre Dame University Press 2010, p. 210–244.

La provedenza, [...]	Providence [...]
però che andasse ver' lo suo diletto	so that the Bride of Him who, with loud cries, had
la sposa di colui ch'ad alte grida	wed her with His blessed blood, might meet her
disposò lei col sangue benedetto,	Love [*lo suo diletto*] with more fidelity and more
in sé sicura e anche a lui più fida,	assurance in herself, on her behalf
due principi ordinò in suo favore,	commanded that there be two princes, one
che quinci e quindi le fosser per guida.	on this side, one on that side, as her guides.
	(*Paradiso* XI, 28–36)

Con questa distinzion prendi 'l mio detto;	Take what I said with this distinction then;
e così puote star con quel che credi	in that way it accords with what you thought
del primo padre e del nostro Diletto.	of the first father and of our Beloved.
	[*nostro Diletto*]
	(*Paradiso* XIII, 109–111)

In both cases, as indicated by the voice of Thomas Aquinas, the "diletto" is Christ, the lover of the Church-sponsa (another key word of biblical origin, which, as we shall see, is closely connected – as a cluster – with the term "diletto").

Nuptial metaphors are frequently employed in the Old Testament and appear in the books of Hosea and Jeremiah, as well as in the Psalms. Indeed, this *topos* clarified one of the most important aspects of the teaching of the prophets: that the relationship between God and his people is a matrimonial bond based on love. Notwithstanding the prevalence of this metaphor within the Old Testament, throughout the Middle Ages the most beautiful, memorable and iconic bride of Scripture was the one praised by Solomon in the Song of Songs, a sensual poem that celebrates the love between a bride and her beloved in terms of desire and longing to such an extent that Christian exegetes were forced to read it exclusively as a prophecy, allegory, or a figurative depiction of the salvific promise established by God between Christ and the Church or the Christian soul.[34] In this Solo-

---

[34] On this exegetic tradition: Friedrich Ohly: *Hohelied-Studien: Grundzüge einer Geschichte der Hoheliedauslegung des Abendlandes bis um 1200*. Wiesbaden: Steiner Verlag 1958; Ann W. Astell: *The Song of Songs in the Middle Ages*. Ithaca & London: Cornell University Press 1990; Hannah W. Matis: Early-Medieval Exegesis of the Song of Songs and the Maternal Language of Clerical Authority. In: *Speculum*, 89, 2 (2014), p. 358–381; Ann E. Matter: *The Voice of My Beloved*. Philadelphia: University of Pennsylvania Press 1990; Marvin H. Pope: *Song of Songs: A New Translation and Commentary*. New York: Anchor Bible 1977; Gianfranco Ravasi: *Il Cantico dei cantici: Commento e attualizzazione*. Bologna: Edizioni Dehoniane 1992; Denys Turner: *Eros and Allegory: Medieval Interpretations of the Song of Songs*. Kalamazoo: Cistercian Publications 1995. On Dante and the Song of Songs, see Lino Pertile, *La puttana*, and Nasti, *Favole d'amore*; see also: cf. Erich Auerbach: *Studi su Dante*. Milan: Feltrinelli 1991, p. 248–256 and 261–268. Johan Chydenius: *The Typological Problem in Dante*. Helsinki: Societas Scientiarum Fennica 1960. Jean Leclercq O.S.B.:

monic poem, the bridegroom is repeatedly – even obsessively – referred to as "my beloved", a term which appears relatively infrequently throughout the Bible as a whole but is employed no fewer than thirteen times within the Song of Songs.[35] The bride describes the beauty, virtues and actions of her "beloved", but often employs the term simply to indicate or evoke the love that unites them. This is the case in expressions such as "Dilectus meus mihi et ego illi" (2:16), a passage the *Glossa Ordinaria* comments on in a topical manner:

> [interl.] Vox Ecclesie
> [marg.] DILECTUS MEUS MIHI. Sincero amore mihi copulatur et ego illi. Vel dilectus talem exhortationem mihi facit et ego illi faciem et vocem ostendo. Vel dilectus mihi non alteri cuilibet, scilicet gratiam prestabit et fructum rependet et ego ei, non alteri cuiquam non in alia turba hominum sed integra obedientia et devotione conglutinabor. Cunctis his sensibus apte convenit quod sequitur: qui pascitur inter lilia.

'Beloved' is thus a name of sincere love and a promise of fidelity and obedience. For the bride, however, calling the name of her beloved is also a request for help:

> [marg.] DILECTUS MEUS. Tali affatui dilecti mox amica columbini cordis simplicitate respondet et iniuncto officio se obedituram promittit, quasi dicat: non solum hortatur sed etiam adiuvat.

Exhortation of the beloved is necessary because, as the commentators note, on several occasions the bride calls on her bridegroom-Christ's help so that she may repent ("compuncta") and follow him without getting lost:

> [interl.] Vox Ecclesie de Christo
> [marg.] 49. DILECTUS MEUS. Ecclesia timente casum quia Dominus amorem erga se nostrum in proximorum maxime amore vult cognosci aperte subditur dilectus meus, quasi: pertimesco quidem seculi conversationem, sed intelligo quod caritas operit multitudinem peccatorum et confido in dilecti mei auxilio, a quo iam sunt compuncta corda eorum.

The Beloved must therefore remind the bride, who is fragile and bound to the earth, of the blessings of love. The Church / soul must be dragged from her spiritual inertia, questioned, spurred on by the beloved as in 2:10: "En dilectus meus loquitur mihi. [Sponsus.] Surge, propera, amica mea, columba mea,

---

Monks and Love in Twelfth-Century France. Oxford: Clarendon Press 1979, p. 137–144; Paul Priest: Dante and the Song of Songs. In: *Studi Danteschi*, 49 (1972), p. 79–113. For the *Convivio* in particular, see Peter Dronke: *Dante's Second Love: Originality and Contexts of Convivio* (Society For Italian Studies Occasional Papers). London: Maney Publishing 1997. On the *Vita nova*: Paola Nasti: La memoria del Canticum e la *Vita Nuova*: una nota preliminare. In: *The Italianist* 18 (1998), p. 14–27; Paola Nasti: Nozze e vedovanza: dinamiche dell'appropriazione biblica in Dante e Cavalcanti. In: *Tenzone. Revista de la Asociación Complutense de Dantología*, VII, (2006), p. 71–110.
35 Song of Songs 1:12; 1:13; 2:3; 2:9; 2:16; 5:1; 5:4; 5:9; 5:10; 5:16; 5:17; 6:1; 6:2.

formosa mea, et veni" (cf. the interlinear gloss: "venit et stat et sic de aliis convertendis mihi precipit"). For the commentators, this narrative and thematic nucleus of the Song of Songs had a clear theological meaning: the intervention of God (and his grace) is always necessary to ensure that the Christian soul remains on the path of love. But since God is good, his salvific intervention is never denied. In this sense, the Song and its gloss were used to reveal the mystery of saving grace and describe to the faithful Christian the salvific comings and goings of the beloved. We see this in the following episode, where the bridegroom 'comes' ("veni") to his beloved who calls him ("veniat"): "Veniat dilectus meus in hortum suum, et comedat fructum pomorum suorum. [Sponsus.] Veni in hortum meum, soror mea, sponsa (5:1)". Yet the bride too must react by 'hurrying', as we are told by the very incipit of the tale: "trahe me post te curremus introduxit me rex in cellaria sua" (1:3). It is no coincidence that in explaining this passage to his monks, Bernard noted the importance of divine intervention to revive the faltering love of weak men, but also the need to respond by following the path of revealed joy:

> Trahe me post te, in odore unguentorum tuorum curremus. Propterea opus habeo trahi, quoniam refriguit paulisper ignis in nobis amoris tui, nec valemus a facie frigoris huius currere modo, sicut heri et nudius tertius. Curremus autem postea, cum reddideris laetitiam salutis tuae, cum redierit melior temperies gratiae, cum sol iustitiae iterum incaluerit, et pertransierit tentationis nubes [...] atque ad lenem flatum aurae blandioris solito coeperint unguenta liquescere, et aroma fluere, et dare odoerem suum.[36]

If we now consider Dante's lexical choices in the terzine of *Paradiso* XI from which we began, reading them in light of the biblical intertext that the key word "diletto" (in combination with "sposa") reveals, it becomes clear that Dante's references to Solomon's text are very precise, indicating a specific narrative nucleus of the Song and its gloss. "The Providence ... / so that the Bride [...] might meet her love [*diletto*] / [...] commanded that there be two princes" (Par. XI 28–35): this is the Song of Song's story of the bride who, having faltered, must once again find her way ("might meet") in order to find her beloved, but also of the divine bridegroom who must intervene in her favour. The verb Dante employs to describe this intervention, however, is not the "venire" ("come") that appears so frequently in the Song, but "ordinare" ("command" or "set in order") – which, like "diletto" and "sposa" is a key word of Song of Songs and thus also of *Paradiso* XI. At line 2:4 of the biblical epithalamium, the bride declares that the groom "ordinavit in me cartitatem". The order of charity is one of the most important theological concepts

---

[36] Bernard of Clairvaux, Saint: *Sermones super Cantica Canticorum*. Edited by Jean Leclercq, C. H. Talbot, Henri M. Rochais. 2 vols. Rome: Editiones Cistercienses 1957, sermo XXI, 4.

for understanding the medieval reflection on love as the bond between heaven and earth, and was developed by the Church Fathers on the basis of precisely this Solomonic verse.[37] For the medieval Christian, to set in order charity implied an ability to select the object of one's love according to the correct hierarchy. The bridegroom of the Song therefore intervenes to remind the beloved-Church how and who to love: "Ordinat ergo Dominus in ecclesia caritatem qua eam vel ipse diligit vel ad suum amorem ac proximi rite tenendum inflammat".[38]

In Dante's *Paradiso*, the verb "ordinare" is thus repeated not at random but as part of the network of pericopes employed by the poet to modernise the story of the Song, or better still, to read the history of the Church in light of the mystery revealed by the Song of Songs. God thus sets in order charity, or rather re-establishes the foundation of the stray and disordered Church by sending two princes who become an example of the correct hierarchy of affection to follow.

Dante adopts many other key words from the Song in the Heaven of the Sun: we might consider the "gate of pleasure" (XI, 60) which is a clear reference to the gate described in the Song at 5:4, or even the hurrying of Francis's first follower, Bernard ("he hurried [. . .] and though he ran, he thought his pace too slow" (XI, 81)), which takes its inspiration from a verse we have already cited ("Trahe me post te curremus introduxit me rex in cellaria sua" [Song of Songs 1:3]). Like the bride of Par. XI 32, Bernard runs behind the prince who represents the bridegroom: Francis. This impassioned running figuratively translated the process of the *sequela Christi*, which every faithful Christian should follow to live in the name of the Incarnation.[39] The metaphor of sacred love which is developed throughout the Song of Songs thus allowed Dante to express the image of the

---

[37] Maria Cândida Monteiro Pacheco: Ordinatio caritatis. Réflexions sur l'ascèse et la mystique dans la pensée de Saint Bernard, In: *Ecriture et réécriture des textes philosophiques médiévaux: Volume d'hommage offert à Colette Sirat*. Edited by Jacqueline Hamesse and Olga Weijers . Turnhout: Brepols 2006, p. 367–380. For the theology of charity: Hélène Pétré: *Caritas. Etude sur le vocabulaire latin de la charité chrétienne*, Louvain, Administration du 'Spicilegium sacrum Lovaniense' 1948; Peter D. Fehlner: *The Role of Charity in the Ecclesiology of St. Bonaventure*. Rome: Editrice miscellanea francescana 1965.

[38] Bede: *In cantica canticorum allegorica exposition*. Edited by D. Hurst. CCSL 119B, I, ii, 4; pp. 166–375. Caritas, "as the supernatural love of fruition whereby the Christian loves God for his own sake and above all as his last end, thus entering the joy of the Lord", was for Bonaventure "the root of that ecclesial unity which makes the Church what she is" (Peter D. Fehlner, *The Role of Charity*, p. 143 and 145).

[39] "Sponsa sponsi lateri juncta ingreditur, post eam famulae ingrediuntur, quia perfecti exemplis praecedunt, alii imitando sequuntur. Quod ad tropologiam sic refertur: Cum viderint lapsi aliquem perfecte conversum, dicunt: Curremus in odore unguentorum tuorum hoc est, nos imitabimur tuum exemplum" (Honorius of Autun: Expositio Super Cantica canticorum. In: *Patrologia Latina* . Paris: Migne, 1844–1864 . Vol. 172, col. 366C).

friar's 'slow' running not only in the Christological sense triggered by the exaltation of Francis as an *alter-Christus*, but also and more crucially as a strong mystical and emotional message that placed *delectio* at the heart of the relationship between the just and God. The Franciscans run behind a dream of imitating the love that Christ and subsequently Francis – both bridegrooms and the Church's beloved – had ordered within the world.

4 Monads: "Worms"

Defining this category of biblical intertextuality is more complex. A monad could be any word present in the biblical concordances or *distinctiones*. As we know, concordances catalogued biblical vocabulary through the lens of intertextuality in order to allow exegetes and preachers to read various passages of the Bible in parallel. *Distinctiones*, meanwhile, facilitated the examination of the literal, mystical and allegorical meaning of passages that were connected by lexical equivalences. This is, in theory, a broad and fruitful field of investigation which might lead us to consider the 'technicality' of a vast number of lemmas employed by Dante. In practice, 'monads' are more probably a limited number of lemmas that introduce within the narrative questions of theology or sacred history, on which the poet comments, often with a certain measure of originality.

The monad that we shall examine by means of an example is "verme" ("worm"), a 'watchword' that Dante employs in the *Comedy* with a degree of frugality: he uses it only six times, four in the *Inferno* and no fewer than twice in *Purgatorio* X.[40] On each of these occasions, there are no long references to the biblical text. Nevertheless, recognition of the biblical 'prehistory' of this word is necessary in order to understand its semantic potential, as well as the problematic nature which Dante attributed to it and which his readers were (and are) called to recognise.

The most significant appearances of the worm on which we shall dwell are those in *Inferno*, where the worm is invariably a means of torture. "Sickening worms" feed on the blood and tears of the cowardly:

---

40 *Inferno* III, 67–68 ("fell at their feet, where it was gathered up by sickening worms"); *Inferno* VI, 22–23 ("When Cerberus, the great worm, noticed us, he opened wide his mouths, showed us his fangs"); *Inferno* XXIX, 61–62 ("all animals, down to the little worm, collapsed"), the only reference to worms as "earthly animals"; *Inferno* XXXIV, 108 ("the hair of the damned worm who pierces through the world"); *Purgatorio* X, 124 and 128–129 ("do you not know that we are worms"; "you are still like the imperfect grub, the worm before it has attained its final form"). I discuss the instances in *Purgatorio* in a forthcoming publication on *Le Tre Corone*.

> Con questa distinzion prendi 'l mio detto; The insects streaked their faces with their blood,
> e così puote star con quel che credi which, mingled with their tears, fell at their feet,
> del primo padre e del nostro Diletto. where it was gathered up by sickening worms.
>
> (*Inferno* III, 67–69)

The macabre image is unsurprising: medieval science, as Isidore of Seville neatly summarises, considered 'putrescence' and humidity to be the natural habitat of worms, and indeed the cause of their generation:[41]

> Sunt autem vermes aut terrae aut aquae aut aeris aut carnium aut frondium aut lignorum aut vestimentorum. [. . .] 18. Proprie autem vermis in carne putrefacta nascitur, tinea in vestimentis, eruca in olere, teredo in ligno, tarmus in lardo.[42]

The association between putrefaction, natural humours and worms remained unchanged even after the 'discovery' of Aristotle's *De animalibus*:

> Teredônus vocant Greci lignorum vermes, eo quod terendo edant, ut dicit Isidorus lib. 12. Ex humore autem corrupto in arboribus derelicto sub corticibus arborum et in medullis generantur. Maxime autem in arboribus generantur, quando in importuno tempore arbores resecantur vel plantatur, ut dicit idem. Et hoc est in plenilunio, potissime quando humiditas, que lunari virtute cum corporibus tunc abundat, non digeritur, et propter eius superfluitatem non regitur a natura, et ideo necesse est ut talis superfluitas corrumpatur, ac in vermes et in putredinem convertatur.[43]

The putrid scene the Pilgrim witnesses in the vestibule of Hell is thus scientifically precise. However, Dante's Hell also contains two other worms who do not wallow in *putredo* but they nonetheless torture the damned: Cerberus and Lucifer.[44]

---

41 On the worm in medieval science: Isabelle Draelants: Poux, puces et punaises chez les naturalistes du XIIIe siècle: de simples vermes ou des parasites nuisibles?. In: *Poux, puces, punaises: la vermine de l'homme. Découverte, descriptions et traitements. Antiquité, Moyen Âge, Époque moderne*. Edited by Franck Collard, Évelyne Samama. Paris: L'Harmattan 2015, p. 195–225; Maaike Van der Lugt: *Le ver, le démon et la Vierge: les théories médiévales de la génération extraordinaire ; une étude sur les rapports entre théologie, philosophie naturelle et médecin*. Paris: Les Belles Lettres 2004.

42 *Etymologies* XII, ch. 5, 1, in: Isidore of Seville (Isidorus Hispalensis): *Etymologiarum sive originum libri XX*. Edited by Wallace M. Lindsay. Oxonii: E typographeo Clarendoniano (1911), 2nd Ed. 1957.

43 Bartholomaeus Anglicus (1601), *De genuinis rerum coelestium, terrestrium et inferarum proprietatibus libr; XVIII [De rerum proprietatibus]*, Francofurti, Apud Wolfgangum Richterum, 1601 (Facsimile Minerva, G.M.B.H., Frankfurt a. M. 1964, p. 1120). On Aristotle's *De Animalibus* in the Middle Ages: *Aristotle's Animals in the Middle Ages and Renaissance*. Edited by Carlos Steel, Guy Guldentops and Pieter Beullens. Louvain: Leuven University Press 1999 (Medievalia Lovaniensia, Series I, Studia XXVII).

44 Leonardo Canova: Il "gran vermo" e il "vermo reo". Appunti onomasiologici sull'eteromorfia nell'"Inferno" dantesco. In: *TiconTre. Teoria Testo Traduzione*, IX (2018), p. 281–303; Christopher Kleinhenz: Infernal Guardians Revisited: "Cerbero, il gran vermo" ("Inf." VI, 22). In: *Dante Stud-*

Quando ci scorse Cerbero, il gran vermo,	When Cerberus, the great worm, noticed us,
le bocche aperse e mostrocci le sanne;	he opened wide his mouths, showed us his fangs;
non avea membro che tenesse fermo.	there was no part of him that did not twitch.
	(*Inferno* VI, 22–24)
Ed elli a me: "Tu imagini ancora	And he to me: "You still believe you are
d'esser di là dal centro, ov' io mi presi	north of the center, where I grasped the hair
al pel del vermo reo che 'l mondo fóra.	of the damned worm who pierces through the world.
	(*Inferno* XXXIV, 106–108)

By transforming (at least metaphorically) the two diabolical beings into worms, the poet was situating himself within an extensive popular tradition of visions of the afterlife, which often hosted tormenting worms, like the *Visio Pauli* and the work of Bonvesin da la Riva, but also 'foreign' texts such as the *Liber scalae*.

This symbolic tradition ultimately has its roots in biblical imagery. In the New Testament, and specifically the Gospel of Mark (9:43, 45, 47) and in the Acts of the Apostles (12:23), the worm is a symbol of the eternal corruption to which sinners will be condemned. As the 'intertextual cipher' of the worms described in Mark reveals, the wholly negative connotation of the image of worms has its origins in the Old Testament. The preferred *loci* for this infernal image of worms can be found for the most part in the book of Isaiah:

> detracta est ad inferos superbia tua concidit cadaver tuum subter te sternetur tinea et operimentum tuum erunt vermes (Isaiah 14:11)
>
> sicut enim vestimentum sic comedet eos vermis et sicut lanam sic devorabit eos tinea salus autem mea in sempiternum erit et iustitia mea in generationes generationum (Isaiah 51:8)
>
> et egredientur et videbunt cadavera virorum qui praevaricati sunt in me vermis eorum non morietur et ignis eorum non extinguetur et erunt usque ad satietatem visionis omni carni (Isaiah 66:24)[45]

---

ies, XCIII (1975), p. 185–199; Giuseppe Ledda: Animali di Malebolge. In: *Il bestiario dell'aldilà. Gli animali nella "Commedia" di Dante*. Ravenna: Longo 2019, p. 103–128. While I was revising the proofs of this chapter I received, with thanks Leonardo Canova's new monograph *Bestiario onomasiologico della "Commedia"*. Firenze: Franco Cesati Editore, 2022. He treats the 'vermes' in a very exhaustive way especially at p. 402–412. Of course some of our observations are similar, but our focus is different.

45 As Thomas Aquinas observes, there is a further correlation between these passages and several Old Testament verses: "Tum etiam quantum ad mortui afflictionem in Inferno, subter te sternetur. In quibus omnes poenae Inferni, Judith ult. dabit ignem et vermes et carnes eorum ut urantur, et sentiant usque in sempiternum" (Thomas Aquinas, *Expositio super Isaiam ad litteram*, ch. 14. Online: https://www.corpusthomisticum.org/cis01b.html, accessed 24.06.2022).

Beginning from these passages, the idea that the worm had been created to torture sinners became popular in the Middle Ages. Its association with putrefaction led Petrus Comestor to consider this "insect"[46] a postlapsarian punishment that served to discipline, correct and instruct sinful man:

> Dicitur quod ante peccatum hominis fuerunt mitia, sed post peccatum facta sunt nociva homini tribus de causis; propter hominis punitionem, correptionem, instructionem ; punitur [. . .]. Corrigitur [. . .] ; instruitur [. . .]: vel cum videt haec minima sibi posse nocere, recordatur fragilitatis sue, et humiliatur. Sed diceret quis quod quaedam animalia ledunt alia, quae nec inde puniuntur, vel corriguntur, vel instruuntur.[47]

Consistent with this notion, the *Glossa ordinaria* rationalised the presence of worms in Isaiah's infernal visions by equating them with the material and spiritual torments that await the damned:

> *sternetur tinea*
> [interl.] per tinea et vermes inferni tormenta designat
> *et operimentum tuum erunt vermes*
> [interl.] cum prius pallia auro gemmisque distincta
> [marg.] SUBTER. Putredo tinea et operimentum vermium pene eterne sunt quas propria gignit conscientia. Vel suppliciorum materia que ex propriis peccatis nascitur sicut enim quamdiu humor est in cadavere vermes nascentur ex putredine sic ex ipsa materia peccatorum gingnuntur supplicia.
> [marg.] Requies diaboli lectus temptationis qui dicebat hec omnia tibi dabo si cadens adoraveris me.
>
> *in me. Vermis eorum*
> [interl.] materialis vel conscientie
> [marg.] VERMIS EORUM. Materialis vel conscientie. Unde: Sicut tinea comedit vestimentum et vermis corrodit lignum et ignis devorat ligna sic meror et tristitia excrucia cor viri.

The idea that there were real worms in Hell was contested by those who, like Thomas Aquinas, followed Augustine in rejecting a literal interpretation of the 'infernal' worm of Isaiah (and Judith), considering the expression as a metaphor *spiritualis* for the *coscientiae remorsus* instead.[48] Nevertheless, as we have noted

---

46 The worm, an invertebrate, was included within Aristotelian taxonomy as an insect under the category of *entoma* or *entomata*.
47 Petrus Comestor: *Historia scolastica*, qu. 8, in PL 198, Paris, 1855, col. 1045. On this text see Isabelle Draelants: Poux, puces et punaises, p. 213.
48 "Nihil tamen prohibet quaedam etiam quae de damnatorum poenis in Scripturis dicta corporaliter leguntur, spiritualiter accipi, et velut per similitudinem dicta: sicut quod dicitur Isaiae ult.: vermis eorum non morietur: potest enim per vermem intelligi conscientiae remorsus, quo etiam impii torquebuntur; non enim est possibile quod corporeus vermis spiritualem cor-

and as was shown by Ledda's survey, medieval visions of Hell are teeming with real worms. In this sense, in *Inferno* III, Dante complies with this 'popular vision'. Yet he seems to apply the term "worm" to Cerberus and Lucifer in a more or less metaphorical manner. Even though the category of worms was relatively broad and generic in the Middle Ages, going so far as to include every kind of insect and various invertebrates, Cerberus and Lucifer do not have the appearance of the worm. They do possess, however, some worm-like qualities.

In medieval encyclopaedic and scientific literature, the identification of worms with putrefaction, and thus with sin to be corrected, was related to the observation of several biological and morphological aspects of the *minuta*. As Draelants has shown, these scientific observations were to a certain degree reflected in the exegesis and religious literature of the late thirteenth century. In my opinion, Dante's use of the term "worm" indicates that he should be numbered among the exegetes of religious sources who grasped the importance of scientific reflection for the interpretation of this biblical 'sign'. From this perspective, it is of no little importance for the reader of Dante that, at least from Bartholomeus Anglicus onwards, medieval science considered the mouth of the worm to be essential to both its movement and parasitic survival: "plus ore quam pedibus se trahit. Vilis est, flexibilis et exanguis" (*De proprietatibus rerum* XVIII, ch. 114, p. 1230). Moreover, the bite of some so-called worms, and of fleas in particular, was recognised in the wake of Avicenna's *Canon* (book IV, fen 6, tr. 5, ch. 14) as venomous by Albertus Magnus, who in his *De animalibus* (XXVI, ch. 1, no. 31) describes the relative medical process in copious and grotesque detail.[49] The worm's dependence on its mouth (and bite) also led moralists and preachers to consider *minuta* as a symbol or sign for gluttony and incontinence. In his *Ars praedicandi* (ch. 57),[50] for example, Alan of Lille

---

rodat substantiam, neque etiam corpora damnatorum quae incorruptibilia erunt. Fletus etiam et stridor dentium in spiritualibus substantiis non nisi metaphorice intelligi possunt: quamvis in corporibus damnatorum, post resurrectionem, nihil prohibeat corporaliter ea intelligi; ita tamen quod per fletum non intelligatur lacrimarum deductio, quia ab illis corporibus resolutio nulla fieri potest, sed solum dolor cordis et conturbatio oculorum et capitis, prout in fletibus esse solet." (Thomas Aquinas: *Summa contra Gentiles*, b. 4 ch. 90 ¶ 9. Online: https://www.corpusthomisticum.org, accessed 24.06.2022).

Although I reached this Aquinean locus independently, I note that Minnis has discussed it in similar terms in a work I have been unable to consult in its entirety: Alaistair Minnis: *Hellish Imaginations from Augustine to Dante: An Essay in Metaphor and Materiality*. Oxford: The Society for the Study of Literature and Language 2020, p. 87–88. This study deals with the question of the senses of metaphorical writing; I believe it to be consistent with the conclusions of the present essay.

49 Isabelle Draelants, Poux, puces et punaises, p. 210.
50 Alan of Lille: *Summa de arte praedicatoria*. PL 210, 109–198A.

cautioned: "O homo, memorare quod fuisti sperma fluidum, quomodo sis vas stercorum, quomodo eris esca vermium. Quod post mortem de lingua nascetur vermis, ut noletur peccatum linguae, de stomacho ascarites ut significetur pecatum gulae". Similarly, Anthony of Padua noted in one of his sermons: "In locis humentibus gula et luxuria designantur. Humiditas enim mater est corruptionis, ex qua vermes et similia generantur".[51]

It is therefore possible that, for Dante, Cerberus and Lucifer are "worms" on the basis of precisely this late but widespread moralising literature on the biology of the 'minute animal'. Indeed, they are symmetrical symbols of the sin of gluttony:[52] Cerberus is famously the guardian of the circle of the gluttons, while Lucifer, in turn, is the primary actor in Eve's sin of gluttony.[53] It is no coincidence that the throat and mouth (or indeed, three mouths!) are the most horrific and terrifying physiognomic traits of Dante's two monsters, instruments of torture and pain.

But to this aspect of moralised biology the other 'quality' that Dante undeniably attributed to certain insects and invertebrates must also be added: the 'genetic' imperfection hypothesised by Aristotle. The arrival of Aristotle's *De animalibus* on the thirteenth-century scientific scene had a significant impact in various areas, including the *scientia de verme*. It was above all Albertus Magnus, in his own *De animalibus*, who formalised the new acquisitions from Aristotle on the subject. Following the Stagirite, Albertus distinguishes between perfect and imperfect animals on the grounds of the circumstances of their generation.[54] Only

---

[51] Antonius Patavinus: *Sermo in dominica I post natiuitatem Domini*. Edited by B. Costa et al. (1979), t. 2, pars III, § 19, p. 546.

[52] It should be noted that Cerberus's inability to remain still ("there was no part of him that did not twitch" (*Inferno* VI, 24)) mimics one of the characteristics attributed to worms in the *Abies, arbor alta*, a compendium on natural properties of Cistercian origin (pre-1230): "Vermis. Sine semine [...] nascitur. Sine strepitu graditur. Vilis. Fragilis. Mollis. Terra pascitur. Proprie ex putrida carne gignitur. Porrigendo et contrahendo movetur. Rem consumit unde oritur. Nil eo dum tangitur melius est. Nil eo dum pungitur durius est. Incessantur moveri dicitur". (*Abies, arbor alta*. Mss Montpellier, École de médecine, H 470, s. v. and Bruxelles, Bibl. royale Albert Ier, II 1060, cited in Isabelle Draelants: *Ego sum vermis:* de l'insecte né de la pourriture à la conception du Christ sans accouplement. Un exemple de naturalisme exégétique médiéval. In: *Mélanges Catherine Jacquemard*. Edited by Brigitte Gauvin, M.-A. Lucas-Avenel. Caen: PUC 2019, p. 151–184, 155–56).

[53] As Kleinheinz has already observed, "considered against the backdrop of Genesis, the sin of gluttony, because of its connotations and implications in the Biblical context, becomes synecdochical for pride. So, too, in the *Comedy* these two notions are intertwined": Christopher Kleinhenz, Cerbero, il gran vermo, p. 191.

[54] For the Aristotelian understanding of the worm, see Reynolds: "A general reading of Generation of animals [4] and History of animals [5,6] in both of which this word is used many times,

animals born through the fertilisation of the male seed and the Pneuma, resulting in an embryo, could be described as in any way perfect. During embryonic morphogenesis, the animal is transformed according to sequences which Aristotle compares to the movements of automata in classical Greek temples. *Automata*[55] contain within themselves a potential that, when put in motion by an external agent, comes to be 'active'. In the absence of this external agent (the seed and the pneuma), animals that are born 'spontaneously', without coitus or fertilisation, are necessarily imperfect or incomplete. There thus exists a hierarchy in the animal world of Aristotle and teleological structure. *Entomata* (invertebrates, insects, arthropods etc.) are a vaguely defined category – not least because of the difficulties associated with observing such minute phenomena – and moreover are imperfect animals. While not all "worms" are equal in Aristotelian biology, most are attributed to spontaneous generation (*sine coito*) and imperfect embryonic evolution. Some *anulosa*, as Albertus Magnus calls the 'entoma', are imperfect because they are not generated from the male seed, and for this reason do not resemble their 'parents' at birth:

> Animalia autem quae sunt sine differentia perfecta sexus et sine coitu, generantia ex suis corporibus putrefactis, generant quidem etiam sicut alia, sed primo generant rem alterius generis: et in illis non est mas et femina secundum perfectam maris et feminae distinctionem: et hoc modo generant quaedam anulosorum. Quaedam etiam habent distinctum sexum et coeunt. Rationabiliter autem hoc accidit. Si enim haec secundum sua genera sibi similia generarent, necessario foret generatio eorum continua per successionem et propagationem unius ex alio: | hoc autem non convenit nisi perfectis animalibus sibi similia generantibus: || dieta autem animalia non sunt talia eo quod ex putrefactione sui aut ex aliis superfluitatibus putrefactis generentur. In talibus igitur non generatur simile generanti, sed potius gusanes qui dissimiles sunt generanti in figura et specie, sicut videtur: et in iilis stat generatio || quia illa dissimilia non alia ex se sibi et parentibus dissimilia generantur. Si enim semper per dissimilia procederet generatio. procederet in infinitum dissimilitudo: et hoc natura respuit eo quod infinitum imperfectum est: natura autem perfici et perfec-

---

however, reveals that Aristotle regards the perfect condition as that state of an animal which enables us to discern by its bodily form the species to which it belongs (i.e. to recognise it for what it is). Perfection is also an enabling condition, which allows the animal in question to generate another member of the same kind in the same perfect form: "Some animals bring their young to perfection and bring forth externally a creature similar to themselves . . . . [4] [GA 732a26-27]": Stuart Reynolds: "Cooking up the PerfectI: Aristotle's Transformational Idea about the Complete Metamorphosis of Insects". In: *Phil. Trans. R. Soc*, B 374: 20190074 (2019), p. 1–16, p. 6.

55 On *automata* in the context of Aristotle's understanding of generation, see Devin Henry: Embryological models in ancient philosophy. In: *Phronesis* 151 (2005), p. 1–42.

> tum semper desiderat. Generato tamen gusane in dissimili figura, gusanes est imperfectum animal sicut et ovum et pro tempore perficitur et tunc redit ad parentis sui similitudinem.[56]

As he demonstrates in *Purgatorio* X, 127–129 ("Why does your mind presume to flight when you / are still like the imperfect grub [*antomata*], the worm / before it has attained its final form?"), Dante has a reasonably precise familiarity with Aristotelian entomology. In an excellent essay, Minio-Paluello has shown that Dante derives 'antomata', the Aristotelian term for 'insect', from a textual tradition that, although corrupted, was widespread in the thirteenth and fourteenth centuries.[57] Dante's tercet clarifies, among other things, that the poet followed in the wake of Aristotle and his commentators by reflecting on the formation of the 'antomata' in terms of perfection and imperfection ("formazion falla"). If we reread the passage from Albertus Magnus above with closer attention, it is clear that the worm is imperfect and therefore 'dissimilar' from its parents:

> In talibus igitur non generatur simile generanti, sed potius gusanes qui dissimiles sunt generanti in figura et specie, sicut videtur: et in iilis stat generatio || quia illa dissimilia non alia ex se sibi et parentibus dissimilia generantur.

In this way, then, Cerberus and above all Lucifer are worms insofar as they are dissimilar from the creator God; and for this reason they are confined to the kingdom of "dissimilitudo", Hell. Having been created *in similitudine Dei*, Lucifer, in particular, is 'guilty' of having chosen the way of dissimilarity. However, as Albertus notes, dissimilarity cannot proceed to infinity because nature tends towards perfection:

> Si enim semper per dissimilia procederet generatio. procederet in infinitum dissimilitudo: et hoc natura respuit eo quod infinitum imperfectum est: natura autem perfici et perfectum semper desiderat.

In the perfect world experienced by Dante, the eternal exile of Cerberus and Lucifer is the weapon with which God contains the spiral of "dissimilitudo" triggered by the rebellion of his dearest angel. They are therefore not only torturing worms, but also *exempla* of the victory of perfection over the forces of chaos.

---

[56] Albertus Magnus: *De animalibus*. Edited by Hermann Stadler. Münster: Aschendorff 1916–1920, l. XV, tr. 1 ch. I, pp. 992–992.

[57] Lorenzo Minio Paluello: "Antomata", "Purg." X, 128, e i testi latini della biologia di Aristotele'. In: *Studi Danteschi*, 50 (1973), p. 111–153.

5 Towards a Sacred Vocabulary

Introducing his *Liber in distinctionibus* and citing an important series of *auctoritates* on theological language and the language of the Bible, Alan of Lille wrote:

> Quoniam juxta Aristotelicae auctoritates praeconium, qui virtutum nominum sunt ignari cito paralogizantur, in sacra pagina periculosum est theologicorum nominum ignorare virtutes, ubi periculosius aliquid quaeritur, ubi difficilius invenitur, ubi non habemus sermones de quibus loquimur, ubi rem ut est sermo non loquitur, ubi vocabula a propiis significationibus peregrinantur et novas admirari videntur; ubi divina descendit excellentia ut humana ascendat intelligentia; ubi nomina pronominatur, ubi adjectiva substantivantur, ubi verbum non est nota ejus de altero dicitur, ubi sine inhaerentia praedicatio, ubi sine materia subjecto, ubi affirmatio impropria, negatio vera, ubi constructio non subjacet legibus Donati, ubi translatio aliena a regulis Tulii, ubi enuntiatio peregrinia ad Aristotelis documento, ubi fidei remota a rationis argumento.[58]

As Luisa Valente summarises, in this passage "Alain présente de manière synthétique les déviations du discours théologique par rapport aux définitions des composants du discours données dans les arts du trivium".[59] The theologian believes that the Bible may be read with the support of logical science because the biblical text itself is not distant from rational argument: in understanding the sacred page, it is dangerous to forget the force of words – "virtus verborum". However, Alan insists, the 'Holy Scripture' and therefore the forms of its meaning distance themselves from rational argument because the 'sermo' is not sufficient to express the 'res'. But what is the *res* of the *verba Dei*?[60] According to Thomas Aquinas, the Bible's *res* is its spiritual meaning, the meaning that is expressed *per figuram* and which reveals the invisible:

> Sicut enim dictum est, sacra Scriptura veritatem quam tradit, dupliciter manifestat: per verba, et per rerum figuras. Manifestatio autem quae est per verba, facit sensum historicum sive litteralem; unde totum id ad sensum litteralem pertinet quod ex ipsa verborum significatione recte accipitur. Sed sensus spiritualis, ut dictum est, accipitur vel consistit in

---

[58] Alan of Lille: *In Distinctionibus Dictionum Theologicalium*. PL 210, 685–1011, 687–688.
[59] Luisa Valente: *Logique et théologie: les écoles parisiennes entre 1150 et 1220*. Paris: Vrin, 2008, p. 225.
[60] "La conclusion d'Alain est que la foi est éloignée de l'argumentation rationnelle, Mais cette conclusion ne doit pas faire oublier la phrase qui ouvre le prologue: dans la *sacra pagina*, il est dangereux d'oublier la force des mots – *virtus verborum*. La distance entre foi et argumentation rationnelle ne doit pas être entendu dans le sens d'une irrationalité radicale de la foi, mais plutôt dans celui d'une rationalité partielle. Ce texte peut être lu comme une sorte de manifeste de la scientificité relative de la théologie ante litteram. { . . . } il est dit en effet que, dans la *sacra pagina*, il est plus difficile de poser des questions et de trouver les réponses", *Ibidem*.

> hoc quod quaedam res per figuram aliarum rerum exprimuntur, quia visibilia solent esse figurae invisibilium, ut Dionysius dicit. Inde est quod sensus iste qui ex figuris accipitur, spiritualis vocatur. Veritas autem quam sacra Scriptura per figuras rerum tradit, ad duo ordinatur: scilicet ad recte credendum, et ad recte operandum. Si ad recte operandum; sic est sensus moralis, qui alio nomine tropologicus dicitur.[61]

To this end, the words of the Bible are to be studied both in light of the meanings that exegetes have 'found' within the text and by applying the laws of Donatus, Cicero and Aristotle. It is important to 'distinguish' words so as to avoid error, but also because this allows us to deeply enjoy the sacred text:

> Dignum duximus theologicorum verborum significationes distinguere, metaphorarum rationes assignare, occultas troporum positiones in lucem reducere, ut liberior ad sacram paginam pandatur introitus, ne ab aliena positione fallatur theologus, et sit facilior via intelligendi; minus intelligentes invivet, torpentes excitet, peritiores delectet.[62]

Like the medieval readers of the Bible described by Alan, Dante also knew the importance of distinguishing the sense of 'sermones / verba' in order to comprehend a text, as well as the need to understand the multiple meanings of the biblical word. But when Dante moves from being a reader of the Bible to an author, knowledge of "theologicorum verborum significationes" enables the poet to transform his own language into theological or sacred language, and to seek to anchor his own *sermo* to the *res*. If Dante's poem can be described as sacred, it is in no small part because his language is formed by the *verba theologica*, words that the poet uses while bearing in mind the *significationes* revealed by the great scholars of the Bible and by himself (as an interpreter of the word of God). In this sense, then, the word is the locus of the poem's sacred polysemy which the poet describes in his letter to Can Grande; and it is proof of the fact that the poet considers himself a *scriba Dei* because he does not compose lies, but recounts *res*.[63]

---

[61] Thomas Aquinas: *Quodlibet* VII, q. 6 art. 2 (Online: https://www.corpusthomisticum.org/q07.html, accessed 24.06.2022).
[62] Alan of Lille: *Liber in Distinctionibus Dictionum Theologicalium*, 688.
[63] A fundamental contribution on Dante's conception of *signa* is Zygmunt G. Baranski, *Dante e i segni. Saggi per una storia intellettuale di Dante Alighieri*. Naples: Liguori 2000.

Bibliographical References

Primary Literature and Early Authors

Abies, arbor alta. Mss Montpellier, École de médecine, H 470, s. v. and Bruxelles, Bibl. royale Albert Ier, II 1060.
Alan of Lille (Alanus de Insulis): *Liber in Distinctionibus Dictionum Theologicalium.* PL 210, 685–1011.
Alan of Lille (Alanus de Insulis): *Summa de arte praedicatoria.* PL 210, 109–198A.
Albertus Magnus (Albert the Great): *De animalibus.* Edited by Hermann Stadler. Münster: Aschendorff 1916–1920.
Antonius Patavinus: *Sermo in dominica I post natiuitatem Domini.* Edited by B. Costa et al. (1979). Online: http://www.documentacatholicaomnia.eu/04z/z_1195-1231__Antonius_Patavinus__Sermo_054_Dominica_I_Post_Nativitatem_Domini__LT.pdf.html.
Aquinas, Thomas: *Expositio super Isaiam ad litteram.* Online: https://www.corpusthomisticum.org.
Aquinas, Thomas: *Quodlibet.* Online: https://www.corpusthomisticum.org
Aquinas, Thomas: *Summa contra Gentiles.* Online: https://www.corpusthomisticum.org.
Aquinas, Thomas: *Super Evangelium S. Matthaei lectura.* Online: https://www.corpusthomisticum.org.
Augustine, Saint: *Enarrationes in Psalmos, I-L.* In: *Corpus Christianorum Series Latina,* vol. 38. Edited by D.Eligius Dekkers and Johannes Fraipont. Turnhout: Brepols 1956.
Bartholomaeus Anglicus (1601): *De genuinis rerum coelestium, terrestrium et inJerarum proprietatibus libr; XVIII [De rerum proprietatibus].* Francofurti, Apud Wolfgangum Richterum, 1601 [Facsimile Minerva, G.M.B.H., Frankfurt a. M. 1964.
Bede (Beda Venerabilis): *In cantica canticorum allegorica expositio.* Edited by David Hurst. CCSL 119B, I, ii, 4; pp. 166–375.
Bernard of Clairvaux, Saint: *Sermones super Cantica Canticorum.* Edited by Jean Leclercq, C. H. Talbot, Henri M. 2 vols. Rome: Editiones Cistercienses1957.
The Liturgy and Time. Vol IV. In: *The Church at Prayer.* Edited by Ir.n. H. Dalmais, Pierre Jounel and A. Georges Martimort. Collegeville: The Liturgical Press 1985, p. 75.
The Glossa Ordinaria: The Making of a Medieval Bible Commentary. Edited by Lesley Smith. Leiden: Brill 2009.
Glossa ordinaria: in accordance with *Biblia latina cum glossa ordinaria*, Adolf Rusch pro Antonio Koberger, [Strasbourg 23.IX.1481], 2415 p., amended, enriched with new prologues, sentences and unpublished collations. Online: https://gloss-e.irht.cnrs.fr/php/livres-liste.php?id=glo.
Honorius of Autun (Honorius Augustodunensis): *Expositio Super Cantica canticorum.* In: *Patrologia Latina.* Edited by Jacques Paul Migne. Vol. 172, col. 366C. Paris: 1844–1864.
Isidore of Seville (Isidorus Hispalensis): *Etymologiarum sive originum libri XX.* Edited by Wallace M. Lindsay. Oxonii: E typographeo Clarendoniano (1911), 2nd Ed. 1957 (Online: https://penelope.uchicago.edu/Thayer/E/Roman/Texts/Isidore/home.html).
Petrus Comestor (Pierre le Mangeur): *Historia scolastica,* PL 198. Paris: 1855, col. 1045.
Rabanus Maurus: *Opusculum de Passione Domini.* PL 112, coll. 1125–1430.

Waley, Thomas: *De modo componendi sermones*. In: *Artes Praedicandi: Contribution à l'Histoire de la Rhétorique au Moyen Age*. Edited by Thomas-Marie Charland. Ottawa: Institut D'Études Médiévales 1936.

Secondary Literature

Astell, Ann W.: *The Song of Songs in the Middle Ages*. Ithaca & London: Cornell University Press 1990.
Auerbach, Erich: *Studi su Dante*. Milan: Feltrinelli 1991.
Ayres, Larry: An Italian Romanesque Manuscript of Hrabanus Maurus' *De Laudibus Sanctae Crucis* and the Gregorian Reform. In: *Dumbarton Oaks Papers*, 41 (1987), p. 13–27.
Baranski, Zygmunt G.: *Dante e i segni. Saggi per una storia intellettuale di Dante Alighieri*. Naples: Liguori 2000.
Baranski, Zygmunt G.: 'Questio quedam exorta est': Dante's *Questio de aqua et terra* between *questio disputata* and *tractatus*, between rhetoric and *reportatio*, between fact and fiction, between Verona and Ravenna (forthcoming article).
Barblan, Giovanni: *Dante e la Bibbia. Atti del Convegno internazionale promosso da "Biblia" (Firenze, 26–28 settembre 1986)*. Florence: Olschki 1988.
Barney, Stephen A.: Peter the Chanter's Distinctiones Abel. In: *Allegory, Myth, and Symbol*. Edited by Morton W. Bloomfield. Cambridge, MA: Harvard University Press 1981, p. 87–107.
Bataillon Louis J.: Intermédiaires entre les traités de morale pratique et les sermons: les distinctiones bibliques alphabétiques. In: *Les genres littéraires dans les sources théologiques et philosophiques médiévales. Définition, critique et exploitation* (Actes du colloque de Louvain-la-Neuve, 25–27 mai 1981). Louvain-la-Neuve: Université catholique de Louvain 1982, p. 213–226.
Belting, Hans: *The Image and its Public in the Middle Ages: Form and Function of Early Paintings of the Passion*. New Rochelle, N.Y.: A.D. Caratzas 1990.
Benfell, V. Stanley: *The Biblical Dante*. Toronto: University of Toronto Press 2011.
Bériou, Nicole: Les Sermons latins après 1200. In: *The Sermon*. Edited by Beverly Kienzle. Turnhout: Brepols 2000, p. 363–447.
Bestul, Thomas H.: *Texts of the Passion: Latin Devotional Literature and Medieval Society*. Philadelphia: University of Pennsylvania Press 1996.
Boynton, Susan and Diane J. Reilly (eds): *The Practice of the Bible in the Middle Ages: Production, Reception, and Performance in Western Christianity*. New York: Columbia University Press 2011.
Canova, Leonardo: Il "gran vermo" e il "vermo reo". Appunti onomasiologici sull'eteromorfia nell'"Inferno" dantesco. In: *TiconTre. Teoria Testo Traduzione*, IX (2018), p. 281–303.
Canova, Leonardo: *Bestiario onomasiologico della "Commedia"*. Firenze: Franco Cesati Editore, 2022.
Capelle, Bernard: Aux origines du culte de la croix. In: *Questions liturgiques et paroissiales*, 27 (1946), p. 157–162.
Cerbo, Anna: Espiazione e recupero totale della libertà dal peccato (*Purgatorio* XXI, 58–78). In: *Dante oltre il medioevo. Atti dei Convegni in ricordo di Silvio Pasquazi* (Roma 16 e 30 novembre 2010). Edited by V. Placella. Rome: Pioda 2012, p. 39–57.

Chazelle, Celia: *The Crucified God in the Carolingian Era: Theology and Art of Christ's Passion*. Cambridge: Cambridge University Press 2001.

Chenu, Marie Dominique: *La théologie au XIIe siècle*. Paris: Vrin 1975.

Chydenius, Johan: *The Typological Problem in Dante*. Helsinki: Societas Scientiarum Fennica 1960.

Cousins, Ewert: The Humanity and the Passion of Christ. In: *Christian Spirituality: High Middle Ages and Reformation*, Edited by Jill Raitt, Bernard McGinn and John Meyendorff. New York: Crossroad 1987, p. 375–39.

Crépin, André: Bede and the Vernacular. In: *Famulus Christi: Essays in Commemoration of the Thirteenth Centenary of the Birth of the Venerable Bede*. Edited by Gerald Bonner. London: S.P.C.K. 1976, p. 170–192.

Cremascoli, Giuseppe and Francesco Santi (eds): *La Bibbia del XIII secolo. Storia del testo, storia dell'esegesi. Convegno della Società Internazionale per lo studio del Medioevo Latino (SISMEL) Firenze, 1–2 giugno 2001*. Florence: SISMEL, Edizioni del Galluzzo 2004.

Cristaldi, Sergio: Dalle beatitudini all'"Apocalisse". Il Nuovo Testamento nella "Commedia". In: *Letture classensi* 17, series Edited by Nicolò Mineo. Ravenna: Longo 1988, p. 23–67.

Dahan, Gilbert: *L'exégèse chrétienne de la Bible en occident médiéval XIIe–XIVe siècle. Patrimoines, christianisme*. Paris: Cerf 1999.

Davies, Oliver: Dante's *Commedia* and the Body of Christ. In: *Dante's Commedia: Theology as Poetry*. Edited by Vittorio Montemaggi and Matthew Treherne. Notre Dame IN: Notre Dame University Press 2010, p. 161–179.

de Lubac, Henri: *Exégèse médiévale: les quatre sens de l'écriture*, 4 vols. Paris: Aubier 1959–1964.

Delcorno, Carlo: Cadenze e figure della predicazione nel viaggio dantesco. In: *Lettere Italiane*, 37, 3 (1985), p. 299–320.

Delcorno, Carlo: Schede su Dante e la retorica della predicazione. In: *Miscellanea di studi danteschi in memoria di Silvio Pasquazi*. Edited by Alfonso Paolella, Vincenzo Placella, Giovanni Turco. Naples: Federico & Ardia, I, 1993, p. 301–312.

Delcorno, Carlo: 'Ma noi siam peregrin come voi siete'. Aspetti penitenziali del 'Purgatorio '. In: *Da Dante a Montale. Studi di filologia e critica letteraria in onore di Emilio Pasquini*. Edited by Gian Mario Anselmi, Bruno Bentivogli, Alfredo Cottignoli, Fabio Marri, Vittorio Roda, Gino Ruozzi, and Paola Vecchi Galli. Bologna: Gedit 2005, p. 11–30.

Derbes, Anne: *Picturing the Passion in Late Medieval Italy: Narrative Painting, Franciscan Ideologies, and the Levant*. Cambridge: Cambridge University Press 1996.

Draelants, Isabelle: Poux, puces et punaises chez les naturalistes du XIIIe siècle: de simples vermes ou des parasites nuisibles?. In: *Poux, puces, punaises: la vermine de l'homme. Découverte, descriptions et traitements. Antiquité, Moyen Âge, Époque moderne*. Edited by Franck Collard, Évelyne Samama. Paris: L'Harmattan 2015, p. 195–225.

Draelants, Isabelle: *Ego sum vermis*: de l'insecte né de la pourriture à la conception du Christ sans accouplement. Un exemple de naturalisme exégétique médiéval. In: *Mélanges Catherine Jacquemard*. Edited by Brigitte Gauvin, M.-A. Lucas-Avenel. Caen: PUC 2019, p. 151–184.

Draisma, Sipke (ed.): *Intertextuality in Biblical Writings*. Edited by by. Kampen: Kok 1989.

Dronke, Peter: *Dante's Second Love: Originality and Contexts of Convivio* (Society For Italian Studies Occasional Papers). London: Maney Publishing 1997.

Federici, Theresa: Dante's Davidic Journey: From Sinner to God's scribe. In: *Dante's "Commedia": Theology as Poetry*. Introduced and edited by Vittorio Montemaggi and Matthew Treherne: Notre Dame IN: Notre Dame University Press 2010, p. 180–209.

Fehlner, Peter D.: *The Role of Charity in the Ecclesiology of St. Bonaventure*. Rome: Editrice miscellanea francescana 1965.

Ferzoco, George: Dante and the Context of Medieval Preaching. In: *Reviewing Dante's theology*. Edited by Claire E. Honess and Matthew Treherne. Bern: Peter Lang, II, 2013, p. 187–210.

Fewell, Danna N. (ed.): *Reading between Texts: Intertextuality and the Hebrew Bible*. Edited by Louisville: Westminster / John Knox Press 1992.

Gaimari, Giulia: La letizia di Cristo nel *Purgatorio*: un'ipotesi di lettura. In: *Studi Danteschi*, 82 (2016), p. 165–18.

Gameson, Richard: *The Early Medieval Bible: Its Production, Decoration, and Use*. Cambridge| New York: Cambridge University Press 1994.

Genette, Gérard: *The Architext: An Introduction*. Berkeley: University of California Press 1992.

Genette, Gérard: *Palimpsests: Literature in the Second Degree*. Lincoln NE and London: University of Nebraska Press 1997.

Genette, Gérard: *Paratexts: Thresholds of Interpretation*. Lincoln NE and London: University of Nebraska Press 1997.

Ghisalberti, Alessandro: *Paradiso*, canto VII. Dante risponde alla domanda: perché un Dio uomo?. Edited by Ennio Sandal: *Lectura Dantis Scaligera 2009–2015*. Rome / Padua: Antenore 2016, p. 141–158.

Gigante, Claudio: 'Adam sive Christus'. Creazione, incarnazione, redenzione nel canto VII del *Paradiso*. In: *Rivista di Studi Danteschi*, 8, 2 (2008), p. 241–268.

Gragnolati, Manuele: *Experiencing the Afterlife: Soul and Body in Dante and Medieval Culture*. Notre Dame IN: University of Notre Dame Press 2005.

Hasenohr, Geneviève: Un recueil de 'Distinctiones' bilingue du début du XIVe siècle: Le Manuscrit 99 de la Bibliothèque Municipale De Charleville. In: *Romania*, 99, no. 393 (1) (1978), p. 47–96.

Hays, Richard B.: *Echoes of Scripture in the Letters of Paul*. New Haven: Yale University Press 1989.

Hays, Richard B.: *Echoes of Scripture in the Gospels*. Waco, TX: Baylor University Press 2016.

Henry, Devin: Embryological models in ancient philosophy. In: *Phronesis* 151 (2005), p. 1–42.

Hollander, Robert: Dante's Use of the Fifth Psalm. A Note on *Purg*. XXX, 84. In: *Dante Studies*, XCIX, 1973, p. 145–150.

Kleinhenz, Christopher: Infernal Guardians Revisited: "Cerbero, il gran vermo" ("Inf." VI, 22). In: *Dante Studies*, XCIII (1975), p. 185–199.

Kleinhenz, Christopher: The Poetics of Citation: Dante's "Divina Commedia" and the "Bible". In: Dante: *The Critical Complex. Vol. 4. Dante and Theology: The Biblical Tradition and Christian Allegory*. Edited by Richard Lansing. New York & London: Routledge 2003, p. 301–321.

Kuhry, Emmanuelle: Dictionnaires, distinctions, recueils de propriétés en milieu cistercien: outils pour la prédication, sources pour l'étude de la nature. In: *Les Cisterciens et la transmission des textes (XIIe–XVIIIe siècles)*. Edited by Thomas Falmagne, Dominique Stutzmann, Anne-Marie Turcan-Verkerk. Turnhout: Brepols 2018, p. 286–337.

Lanza, Adriano: Il 'sacrosanto segno' e il 'venerabil segno'. In: Idem: *Dante eterodosso. Una diversa lettura della Commedia*. Bergamo: Moretti Honegger 2004, p. 102–112.

Leclercq, Jean: Commentary on Biblical and Ecclesiastical Literature from Latin Antiquity to the Twelfth Century (trans. A. Kraebel). In: *The Mediaeval Journal*, 2.2 (2012), p. 27–53.

Leclercq, Jean: *Monks and Love in Twelfth-Century France*. Oxford: Clarendon Press 1979, p. 137–44.

Leclercq, Henri: Croix et crucifix. Edited by Fernand Cabrol and H. Leclercq: *Dictionnaire d'Archeologie Chretienne et de Liturgie*. Paries: Librairie Letouzey et Ané 1948, vol. 3, pt. 2, 3045–3131.
Ledda, Giuseppe (ed.): *La Bibbia di Dante. Esperienza mistica, profezia e teologia biblica in Dante. Atti del Convegno Internazionale di Studi (Ravenna: 7 novembre 2009)*. Ravenna: Centro Dantesco dei Frati Minori Conventuali 2011.
Ledda, Giuseppe: Sulla soglia del Purgatorio: peccato, penitenza, resurrezione. Per una 'lectura' di *Purgatorio* IX. In: *Lettere Italiane*, 66 (2014) 1, p. 3–36.
Ledda, Giuseppe: *La Bibbia di Dante*. Turin / Bologna: Claudiana – EMI 2015.
Ledda, Giuseppe: Animali di Malebolge. In: *Il bestiario dell'aldilà. Gli animali nella "Commedia" di Dante*. Ravenna: Longo 2019, p. 103–128.
Leftow, Brian: Anselm on the Cost of Salvation. In: *Medieval Philosophy and Theology*, 6 (1997), p. 73–92.
Leonard, Jeffery M.: Inner-Biblical Interpretation and Intertextuality. In: *Literary Approaches to the Bible*. Edited by Douglas Mangum and Douglas Estes. Bellingham, WA: Lexham Press 2017, p. 97–141.
Levering, Matthew: Christ's Fulfillment of Torah and Temple: Salvation According to Thomas Aquinas. Notre Dame IN: University of Notre Dame Press 2002.
Levy, Ian Christopher: The Literal Sense of Scripture and the Search for Truth in the Late Middle Ages. In: *Revue d'Histoire Ecclesiastique*, 104, 3–4 (2009), p. 783–827.
Liere, Frans Van: *An Introduction to the Medieval Bible*. Cambridge: CUP 2014, p. 230–233.
Light, Laura: Non-Biblical Texts in Thirteenth-Century Bibles. In: *Medieval Manuscripts, Their Makers and Users*. A Special Issue of Viator in Honor of Richard and Mary Rouse. Los Angeles University of California: Center for Medieval and Renaissance Studies. Brepols, Turnhout 2011, p. 169–83.
Loewe, William P.: *Lex Crucis: Soteriology and the Stages of Meaning*. Philadelphia: Fortress Press 2016.
Lugt, Maaike Van der: *Le ver, le démon et la Vierge: les théories médiévales de la génération extraordinaire ; une étude sur les rapports entre théologie, philosophie naturelle et médecin*. Paris: Les Belles Lettres 2004.
Lund-Mead, Carolynn: The "Vulgata" in the "Commedia": Self-Interpreting Texts. In: *Dantean Dialogues: Engaging with the Legacy of Amilcare Iannucci*. Edited by Maggie Kilgour and Elena Lombardi. Toronto: University of Toronto Press 2013, p. 155–173.
MacDonald, Alasdair A.; Bernhard Ridderbos, Rita M. Schlusemann (eds): *The Broken Body: Passion Devotion in Late Medieval Culture*. Groningen: Egbert Forsten 1998.
Maldina, Nicolò: *In Pro del Mondo: Dante, la Predicazione e i Generi della Letteratura Religiosa Medievale*. Rome: Salerno 2018.
Maldina, Nicolò: "Per poenitentiam factum prophetam". Filigrane davidiche nel prologo della "Commedia". In: *Poesia e profezia nell'opera di Dante*. Edited by Giuseppe Ledda. Ravenna: Centro Dantesco dei Frati Minori Conventuali 2019, p. 163–17.
Manescalchi, Romano: Il Cristo lieto (*Purg.* XXIII 74) a confronto con analoghe rappresentazioni. In: *Parola del testo: semestrale di filologia e letteratura italiana comparata*, 20, 1 / 2 (2016), p. 23–40.
Marsden, Richard and E. Ann Matter (eds): *The New Cambridge History of the Bible, ii: From 600 to 1450*. Cambridge: Cambridge University Press 2012.
Martinez, Ronald L.: Dante's Forese, the Book of Job, and the Office of the Dead: A Note on Purgatorio 23. In: *Dante Studies*, 120 (2002), p. 1–16.

Matis. Hannah W.: Early-Medieval Exegesis of the Song of Songs and the Maternal Language of Clerical Authority. In: *Speculum*, 89, 2 (2014), p. 358–381.
Matter, Ann E.: *The Voice of My Beloved*. Philadelphia: University of Pennsylvania Press 1990.
Mellone, Attilio: Il primato di Cristo secondo Dante. In: Idem: *Saggi e letture dantesche*. Salerno: Editrice Gaia 2005, p. 373–391.
Minio Paluello, Lorenzo: "Antomata", "Purg." X, 128, e i testi latini della biologia di Aristotele'. In: *Studi Danteschi*, 50 (1973), p. 111–153.
Minnis, Alastair J.: Quadruplex Sensus, Multiplex Modus: Scriptural Sense and Mode in Medieval Scholastic Exegesis. In: *Interpretation and Allegory*. Leiden, The Netherlands: Brill 2000.
Minnis, Alaistair J.: *Hellish Imaginations from Augustine to Dante: An Essay in Metaphor and Materiality*. Oxford: The Society for the Study of Literature and Language 2020, p. 87–88.
Monteiro Pacheco, Maria Cândida: *Ordinatio caritatis. Réflexions sur l'ascèse et la mystique dans la pensée de Saint Bernard, Ecriture et réécriture des textes philosophiques médiévaux: Volume d'hommage offert à Colette Sirat*. Edited by Jacqueline Hamesse and Olga Weijers. Turnhout: Brepols 2006, p. 367–380.
Moyise, Steve: Intertextuality and the Study of the Old Testament in the New Testament. In: *The Old Testament in the New Testament*. Edited by S. Moyise. Sheffield: Sheffield Academic Press 2000, p. 14–41.
Moyise, Steve: Intertextuality and Biblical Studies: A Review. In: *Verbum et Ecclesia*, 23, 2 (2002), p. 418–431.
Moyise, Steve: Dialogical Intertextuality. In: *Exploring Intertextuality: Diverse Strategies for New Testament Interpretation of Texts*. Edited by B. J. Oropeza and Steve Moyise. Eugene, OR: Cascade Books 2016, p. 3–15.
Mulchahey, Marian Michele: *First the Bow is Bent in Study: Dominican Education Before 1350*. Toronto: Pontifical Institute of Mediaeval Studies 1998, p. 509–513.
Nasti, Paola: La memoria del Canticum e la *Vita Nuova*: una nota preliminare. In: *The Italianist* 18 (1998), p. 14–27.
Nasti, Paola: Nozze e vedovanza: dinamiche dell'appropriazione biblica in Dante e Cavalcanti. In: *Tenzone. Revista de la Asociación Complutense de Dantología*, VII, (2006), p. 71–110.
Nasti, Paola: *Favole d'amore e 'saver profondo': La tradizione salomonica in Dante*. Ravenna: Longo 2007.
Nasti, Paola: 'Caritas' and Ecclesiology in Dante's Heaven of Sun. In: *Dante's "Commedia": Theology as Poetry*. Introduced and edited by Vittorio Montemaggi, and Matthew Treherne, Notre Dame IN: Notre Dame University Press 2010, p. 210–244.
Nasti, Paola: Dante and Ecclesiology. In: *Reviewing Dante's Theology*. Edited by Claire E. Honess and Matthew Treherne. Oxford / Bern / Berlin: Peter Lang, II, 2013, p. 43–88.
Nasti, Paola: Soteriologia e Passione nella 'Commedia'. In: *Theologus Dantes*. Edited by Luca Lombardo, Diego Parisi, Anna Pegoretti. Venice: Edizioni Ca' Foscari 2018, p. 103–138.
Nasti, Paola: Dante e la tradizione scritturale. In: *Dante*. Edited by Robert Rea and Justin Steinberg. Rome: Carocci 2020, p. 267–285.
Ohly, Friedrich: *Hohelied-Studien: Grundzüge einer Geschichte der Hoheliedauslegung des Abendlandes bis um 1200*. Wiesbaden: Steiner Verlag 1958.
Patout Burns, J.: 'The Concept of Satisfaction in Medieval Redemption Theory', *Theological Studies*, 36, 2 (1975), p. 285–304.

Pertile, Lino: *La puttana e il gigante. Dal Cantico dei Cantici al Paradiso Terrestre di Dante*. Ravenna: Longo 1998.
Pertile, Lino: Sul dolore nella Commedia. *Letteratura e filologia tra Svizzera e Italia. Studi in onore di Guglielmo Gorni*. Edited by Maria Antonietta Terzoli, Alberto Asor Rosa, Giorgio Inglese. 3 vols. Rome: Edizioni di Storia e Letteratura 2010, I, p. 105–120.
Pope, Marvin H.: *Song of Songs: A New Translation and Commentary*. New York: Anchor Bible 1977.
Pétré, Hélène: *Caritas. Etude sur le vocabulaire latin de la charité chrétienne*, Louvain, Administration du 'Spicilegium sacrum Lovaniense' 1948.
Prentice, Robert: O. F. M.: The Voluntarism of Duns Scotus, as Seen in His Comparison of the Intellect and the Will. In: *Franciscan Studies*, 28 (1968), p. 63–103.
Priest, Paul: Dante and the Song of Songs. In: *Studi Danteschi*, 49 (1972), p. 79–113.
Ravasi, Gianfranco: *Il Cantico dei cantici: Commento e attualizzazione*. Bologna: Edizioni Dehoniane 1992.
Ravasi, Gianfranco: *I salmi nella "Divina Commedia"*. Foreword by Enrico Malato. Rome: Salerno 2013.
Riché, Pierre and Guy Lobrichon (eds): *Le Moyen Âge et la Bible*. Paris: Beauchesne 1984.
Rigo, Paola: *Memoria classica e memoria biblica in Dante*. Florence: Olschki 1994.
Roberts, Phyllis B.: The *Ars Praedicandi* and the Medieval Sermon. In: *Preacher, Sermon and Audience in the Middle Ages*, Edited by by Carolyn Muessig. Leiden: Brill 2002, p. 39–62.
Roest, Bert: Mendicant School Exegesis. In: *The Practice of the Bible in the Middle Ages: Production, Reception, and Performance in Western Christianity*. Edited by S. Boynton and D. J. Reilly. New York: Columbia University Press 2011, p. 179–204.
Rokseth, Yvonne: La liturgie de la passion vers la fin du Xe siècle. In: *Revue de musicologie*, 31 (1949), p. 9–26 and *Ibidem*, 32 (1950), p. 1–58.
Rouse, Richard H. and Mary A. Rouse: The Verbal Concordance to the Scriptures. In: *Archivum Fratrum Praedicatorum*, 44 (1974), p. 5–30.
Rouse, Richard H. and Mary A. Rouse: Biblical Distinctiones in the Thirteenth Century. In: *Archives d'histoire doctrinale et littéraire du moyen âge*, 41 (1975), p. 27–37.
Rouse, Richard H. and Mary A. Rouse: The Development of Research Tools in the Thirteenth Century. In: *Authentic Witness. Approaches to Medieval Texts and Manuscripts*. Notre Dame IN: University of Notre Dame Press 1991, p. 221–255, p. 203.
Ryan, Christopher: Paradiso VII: Marking the Difference between Dante and Anselm. In: *Dante and the Middle Ages: Literary and Historical Essays*. Edited by John Barnes and Cormac Ó Cuilleanaìn. Dublin: Irish Academic Press 1995, p. 117–137.
Sabbatino, Pasquale: La Croce nella *Divina Commedia*. In: *Critica letteraria*, 115–116 (2002), p. 275–298.
Sasso, Gennaro: . . . a far vendetta corse / della vendetta del peccato antico (Pd VI 92–3). In: *Bollettino di Italianistica. Rivista di critica, storia letteraria, filologia e linguistica*, 3, 1 (2006), p. 15–40.
Schnapp, Jeffrey T.: Unica spes hominum, crux, o venerabile signum. In: *The Transfiguration of History at the Center of Dante's* Paradise. Princeton: Princeton University Press 1986.
Smalley, Beryl: Use of the Spiritual Senses of Scripture in Persuasion and Argument by Scholars in the Middle Ages. In: *Recherches de Théologie et Philosophie Médiévales*, 52 (1985), p. 44–63.

Smith, Lesley: *The Glossa Ordinaria: The Making of a Medieval Bible Commentary*. Leiden: Brill 2009, p. 145–153.
Steel, Carlos; Guy Guldentops and Pieter Beullens (eds): *Aristotle's Animals in the Middle Ages and Renaissance*. Louvain: Leuven University Press 1999 (Medievalia Lovaniensia, Series I, Studia XXVII).
Thomson, S. Harrison: Grosseteste's Topical Concordance of the Bible and the Fathers. In: *Speculum*, 9, 2 (1934), p. 139–144.
Trone, George A.: The Cry of Dereliction in *Purgatorio* XXIII. In: *Dante Studies*, 113 (1995), p. 111–129.
Turner, Denys: *Eros and Allegory: Medieval Interpretations of the Song of Songs*. Kalamazoo: Cistercian Publications 1995.
Valente, Luisa: *Logique et théologie: les écoles parisiennes entre 1150 et 1220*. Paris: Vrin 2008.
Vettori, Alessandro: *Dante's Prayerful Pilgrimage: Typologies of Prayer in the Comedy*. Leiden-Boston: Brill 2019, p. 67–80.
Viladesau, Gerard R.: *The Beauty of the Cross: The Passion of Christ in Theology and the Arts from the Catacombs to the Eve of the Renaissance*. Oxford: Oxford University Press 2006.
Viladesau, Gerard R.: *The Crucifixion of Jesus: History, Myth, Faith*. Minneapolis: Fortress Press 1995.
Walsh, Katherine and Diana Wood (eds): *The Bible in the Medieval World: Essays in Honour of Beryl Smalley*. Studies in Church History Subsidia 4. Oxford: Blackwell 1985.
Ward, Thomas M.: Voluntarism, Atonement, and Duns Scotus. In: *Heythrop Journal*, 58 (2017), p. 37–43.
Watt, Mary Alexandra: *The Cross that Dante Bears: Pilgrimage, Crusade, and the Cruciform Church in the Divine Comedy*. Gainesville: University Press of Florida 2005.

Albert Russell Ascoli
Dante and the Faith of the Reader

Before turning to the way in which Dante himself invokes and represents "the faith of the reader," which is the primary subject of this lecture (*lectio*?) turned essay, I think it proper to say a few words about myself as a reader, faithful and unfaithful by turns, of Dante and his works, and the place of "faith" within the tradition that has shaped my reading practices over the decades. I came to the conference where I first presented these materials, as well, with my own specific family history very much in mind. It was, in fact, from Lisbon in October of 1941, that my Italian-Jewish father (Giulio Ascoli), then 17 years, old travelled from Lausanne, Switzerland, to Lisbon, where he took passage to join *his* father (Abram Alberto Ascoli), mother (Paola Ascoli-Segre) and sister (Ida Ascoli Freiberger) who had preceded him to the United States. It was there, after the end of the war, and after obtaining citizenship in his adoptive country, that he married my mother (Marian Loomis Ascoli), who came from the branching trees old New England families (in the first instance, the Loomis's and the Russell's). My own interest in Dante then, in some sense, can be located geographically and historically between a desire to recover my exiled father's culture of origin through a filter provided by its most famous and accomplished poet, himself, notoriously, an exile, but perhaps as well from affinities for some of the cultural traditions of my mother's natal region, where, for instance, Dante had found his first, eminent, translator and critic, Henry Wadsworth Longfellow.[1] In other words, one of the many different readers of Dante whose "faith" is in some, partially sublimated, way, at issue in this essay is myself, the mixed product of a marriage between a non-practicing Jew and an Emersonian deist. My values, professional and personal, were shaped by both traditions (and by a midwestern boyhood!), and I placed and place considerable "fede" in the enduring moral, social, political, intellectual, imaginative, and, yes, spiritual, significance of the *Divina Commedia*, for a wide spectrum of readers from many times and places, religious credos and national and ethnic identities.

---

[1] On Longfellow, and his cultural context, in relation to Dante, see the special issue of *Dante Studies Dante Studies*, 128 (2010). Edited by Arielle Saiber and Giuseppe Mazzotta (introduced by Mazzotta). On the larger tradition of American Dante Studies, see Giuseppe Mazzotta: The American Criticism of Charles Singleton. In: *Dante Studies* 104 (1986), p. 27–44, and Giuseppe Mazzotta: Reflections on Dante Studies in America. In: *Dante Studies* 118 (2000), p. 323–330, as well as the anthology of essays previously published in this journal and its precursors in that same issue. See also the issue of *Annali d'Italianistica*, 8 (1990), devoted to "Dante and Modern American Criticism," especially the essays in the first section.

Nonetheless, as diverse as the scholarly tradition, the North American, into which I entered as a young scholar, may be, it would be hard to deny the central importance of the bright red thread that passes from Charles Singleton to the late Robert Hollander (the first raised as a Protestant in the western U.S., the other born to an immigrant Jewish family in New York), and thence to many of their successors, namely the claim that Dante is a "theologus-poeta", whose greatest poem takes as its subject "the state of the souls after death" in the Christian afterlife and for its author a status comparable if not equivalent to that of the human authors of the Bible, and for itself a fourfold mode of allegorical signification comparable if not equivalent to Holy Writ.[2] Whether this interpretation is correct or not (and many critics myself very much included have modified, challenged, and / or denied it), it does represent the context out of which my own thinking about the *Commedia* emerged, additionally filtered through the work of John Freccero, Giuseppe Mazzotta, Teodolinda Barolini, and Ronald Martinez, among many others, and it puts the question that concerns me today front and centre.[3] That, is do the poem and its author demand a faith, a belief, from its readers that complements the faith that is due to the Christian God, to his Scriptures, and to his one and only Church?[4]

My own work has had at its centre the way in which, over his career, at least from the *Vita Nuova* forward, Dante conceived and constructed the idea of author-

---

[2] Charles S. Singleton, *Dante Studies 1: Elements of Structure*. Cambridge MA: Harvard University Press 1954; Robert Hollander: Dante as Theologus-Poeta. Ravenna: Longo, 1980 (this essay first published 1976), pp. 39–89. For my understanding of the question of the "poeta-theologus" and the related issue of allegory in Dante, see Albert Russell Ascoli: Access to Authority: Dante in the Letter to Cangrande. In: *Proceedings of the First International Dante Symposium*. Edited by Zygmunt Baranski. Florence: Le Lettere Editore 1997, p. 309–352; Blinding the Cyclops: Petrarch after Dante. In: *Petrarch and Dante*. Edited by T. Cachey and Z. Baranski. Notre Dame: Notre Dame University Press 2009, p. 114–173; Poetry and Theology. In: *Reviewing Dante's Theology Volume 2*. Edited by Matthew Treherne and Claire Honess. Bern: Peter Lang 2014, p. 3–42.

[3] John Freccero: *Dante: The Poetics of Conversion*. Edited by Rachel Jacoff. Cambridge MA: Harvard University Press 1986; Giuseppe Mazzotta: *Dante, Poet of the Desert*. Princeton: Princeton University Press 1979 and *Dante's Vision and the Circle of Knowledge*. Princeton: Princeton University Press 1992; Teodolinda Barolini: *Dante's Poets: Textuality and Truth in the "Comedy"*. Princeton: Princeton University Press 1984 and *The Undivine Comedy: Detheologizing Dante*. Princeton: Princeton University Press 1992. As for last name on the list, there are too many debts to enumerate here, so I will offer as an example one particularly salient essay: Ronald L. Martinez: The Pilgrim's Answer to Bonagiunta and the Poetics of the Spirit. In: *Stanford Italian Review* 4 (1983), p. 37–63.

[4] Though my emphases are very different, I gladly acknowledge that my first steps down the path to understanding the problematic intertwining of these two types of "fede" in the *Commedia* were guided by Giuseppe Mazzotta: *Poet of the Desert*, ch. 7: "The Language of Faith: Messengers and Idols."

ship and *autorialità* that he proposed to claim for himself.[5] It is, however, an essential part of Dante's "auto-costruzione" that as author he is in constant dialogue with readers, real and imaginary, past-present-future, and that whatever innovations he may have brought to a Western concept of authorship, his contributions to what it means to be a reader also are extraordinary.[6] In what follows, I will show how this dialogue is articulated over the course of his major Italian works, both drawing on and synthesizing partial treatments offered in earlier work, and introducing some new materials, especially as regards the *Commedia* itself.

Let us begin with the *Vita Nuova*. There, in the chapter traditionally numbered XXV, Dante poses and answers the question that he imagines a skeptical reader might ask: Why has he referred to "Amore" as a person, a substantive being, when in fact it is "an accident in a substance," i.e., the emotional experience of a person who is "in love." His extensive answer falls back on the authority of the classical Greek and Latin "poets" to justify the potentially deceptive use of the trope of personification, with the specification that modern "dicitori in rima" such as himself must be ready to "explain themselves," i.e., to make plain why and how they are using it, as, in fact, he is doing here:

> ... prima è da intendere che anticamente non erano dicitori d'amore in lingua volgare, anzi erano dicitori d'amore certi poete in lingua latina .... *E non è molto numero d'anni passati, che appariro prima questi poete volgari; ché dire per rima in volgare tanto è quanto dire per versi in latino*, secondo alcuna proporzione. E segno che sia picciolo tempo, è che se volemo cercare in lingua d' "oco" e in quella di "sì," noi non troviamo cose dette anzi lo presente tempo per cento e cinquanta anni. E la cagione per che alquanti grossi ebbero fama di sapere dire, è che quasi fuori li primi che dissero in lingua di "sì." *E lo primo che cominciò a dire sì come poeta volgare, si mosse però che volle fare intendere le sue parole a donna, a la quale era malagevole d'intendere li versi latini. E questo è contra coloro che rimano sopra altra matera che amorosa*, con ciò sia cosa che cotale modo di parlare fosse dal principio trovato per dire d'amore. *Onde, con ciò sia cosa che a li poete sia conceduta maggiore licenza di parlare che a li prosaici dittatori, e questi dicitori per rima non siano altro che poete volgari,*

---

[5] Albert Russell Ascoli: *Dante and the Making of a Modern Author*. Cambridge: Cambridge University Press 2008.

[6] I am, obviously, not the first to address, in one way or another, the questions of Dante and reading, Dante and his readers. Among many possible, I will mention here: Susan Noakes: *Timely Reading: Between Exegesis and Interpretation*. Ithaca NY: Cornell University Press 1988; John Ahern: The New Life of the Book: The Implied Reader of the *Vita nuova*. In: *Dante Studies*, 110 (1992), p. 1–16; William Franke: *Dante's Interpretive Journey*. Chicago: University of Chicago Press 1996; Justin Steinberg: *Accounting for Dante: Urban Readers and Writers in Late Medieval Italy*. Notre Dame IN: University of Notre Dame Press 2007; Elena Lombardi: *Imagining the Woman Reader in the Age of Dante*. Oxford: Oxford University Press 2018. Others will appear as we proceed. I also acknowledge a longstanding debt to the late Armando Petrucci, particularly his *Writers and Readers in Medieval Italy*. Trans. Charles Radding. New Haven CT: Yale University Press 1995.

degno e ragionevole è che a loro sia maggiore licenzia largita di parlare che a li altri parlatori volgari: *onde, se alcuna figura o colore rettorico è conceduto a li poete, conceduto è a li rimatori.* Dunque, *se noi vedemo che li poete hanno parlato a le cose inanimate, sì come se avessero senso e ragione,* e fattele parlare insieme; e non solamente cose vere, ma cose non vere, cioè che detto hanno, di cose le quali non sono, che parlano, e detto che molti accidenti parlano, sì come se fossero sustanzie e uomini; *degno è lo dicitore per rima di fare lo somigliante, ma non sanza ragione alcuna, ma con ragione la quale poi sia possibile d'aprire per prosa.* Che li poete abbiano così parlato come detto è, appare per Virgilio; lo quale dice che Iuno, cioè una dea nemica de li Troiani, parloe ad Eolo, segnore de li venti, quivi nel primo de lo Eneida: "Eole, nanque tibi," e che questo segnore le rispuose, quivi: "Tuus, o regina, quid optes explorare labor; michi iussa capessere fas es." Per questo medesimo poeta parla la cosa che non è animata a le cose animate, nel terzo de lo Eneida, quivi: "Dardanide duri." Per Lucano parla la cosa animata a la cosa inanimata, quivi: "Multum, Roma, tamen debes civilibus armis." Per Orazio parla l'uomo a la scienzia medesima sì come ad altra persona; e non solamente sono parole d'Orazio, ma dicele quasi recitando lo modo del buono Omero, quivi ne la sua Poetria: "Dic michi, Musa, virum." Per Ovidio parla Amore, sì come se fosse persona umana, ne lo principio de lo libro c'ha nome Libro di Remedio d'Amore, quivi: "Bella michi, video, bella parantur, ait." E per questo puote essere manifesto a chi dubita in alcuna parte di questo mio libello. *E acciò che non ne pigli alcuna baldanza persona grossa, dico che né li poete parlavano così sanza ragione, né quelli che rimano deono parlare così non avendo alcuno ragionamento in loro di quello che dicono; però che grande vergogna sarebbe a colui che rimasse cose sotto vesta di figura o di colore rettorico, e poscia, domandato, non sapesse denudare le sue parole da cotale vesta, in guisa che avessero verace intendimento. E questo mio primo amico e io ne sapemo bene di quelli che così rimano stoltamente.*[7]

---

[7] (3) To clarify this matter suitably for my purpose, I shall begin by saying that, formerly, there were no love poets writing in the vernacular, the only love poets were those writing in Latin: among us (and this probably happened in other nations as it still happens in the case of Greece) it was not vernacular poets but learned poets who wrote about love. (4) It is only recently that the first poets appeared who wrote in the vernacular; I call them "poets" for to compose rhymed verse in the vernacular is more or less the same as to compose poetry in Latin using classical meters. And proof that it is but a short time since these poets first appeared is the fact that if we look into the Provençal and the Italian literatures, we shall not find any poems written more than a hundred and fifty years ago. (5) The reason why a few ungifted poets acquired the fame of knowing how to compose is that they were the first who wrote poetry in the Italian Language. (6) The first poet to begin writing in the vernacular was moved to do so by a desire to make his words understandable to ladies who found Latin verses difficult to comprehend. And this is an argument against those who compose in the vernacular on a subject other than love, since composition in the vernacular was from the beginning intended for treating of love. (7) Since, in Latin, greater license is conceded to the poet than to the prose writer, and since these Italian writers are simply poets writing in the vernacular, we can conclude that it is fitting and reasonable that greater license be granted them than to other writers in the vernacular; therefore, if any image or coloring of words is conceded to the Latin poet, it should be conceded to the Italian poet. (8) So, if we find that the Latin poets addressed inanimate objects in their writings, as if these objects had sense and reason, or made them address each other, and that they did this not only with real things but also with unreal things (that is: they have said, concerning things that do not exist,

(*Vita Nuova*, XXV, 3–10)⁸

In this one dense chapter we find many of the key issues that Dante will elaborate over the course of his career. For our purposes, however, the main points are two: first, that he concedes to his readers the right, perhaps even the obligation, to question his intentions; second, that he claims for *himself* the symmetrical right to require that readers respect his clarified authorial intentions. Note that the *Vita Nuova* as a whole posits implicitly and explicitly many different readers: notably the "fedeli d'amore" (the faithful of Love) (ch.III); Guido Cavalcanti (chs. III, XXIV, XXV); Beatrice; "donne che [hanno] intelletto d'amore" (chs. XVIII–XIX); pilgrims passing through Florence on their way to Rome or to Jerusalem (ch. XL); two "donne gentili" who ask him for some of his poems (ch. XLI); and various others. Note also that Dante himself is perhaps the most obvious reader of his own poetry, in the "ragioni" that explain the circumstances and motivation of composition, and in the "divisioni" where he breaks down the structure of each poem in turn.⁹ Note finally that there is an underlying tension throughout the *libello*,

---

that they speak, and they have said that many an accident in substance speaks as if it were a substance and human), then it is fitting that the vernacular poet do the same – not, of course, without some reason, but with a motive that later can be explained in prose. (9) That the Latin poets have written in the way I have just described can be seen in the case of Virgil, who says that Juno, a goddess hostile to the Trojans, spoke to Aeolus, god of the winds, in the first book of the Aeneid: Eole, nanque tibi, and that this god answered her: Tuus, o regina, quid optes explorare labor; michi iussa capessere fas est. This same poet has an inanimate thing speak to animate beings in the third book of the Aeneid: Dardanide duri. In Lucan the animate being speaks to the inanimate object: Multum, Roma, tamen debes civilibus armis. In Horace a man speaks to his own inspiration as if to another person, and not only are the words of Horace but he gives them as if quoting from the good Homer, in this passage of his Poetics: Dic michi, Musa, virum. In Ovid, Love speaks as if it were a human being, in the beginning of the book called The Remedy of Love: Bella michi, video, bella parantur, ait. From what has been said above, anyone who experiences difficulties in certain parts of this, my little book, can find a solution for them. (10) So that some ungifted person may not be encouraged by my words to go too far, let me add that just as the Latin poets did not write in the way they did without a reason, so vernacular poets should not write in the same way without having some reason for writing as they do. For, if any one should dress his poem in images and rhetorical coloring and then, being asked to strip his poem of such dress in order to reveal its true meaning, would not be able to do so – this would be a veritable cause for shame. And my best friend and I are well acquainted with some who compose so clumsily.

8 While I accept the critique initiated by Guglielmo Gorni and Dino Cervigni as regards the arbitrary nature of Michele Barbi's critical edition of the *Vita Nuova*, I adopt this system of numbering for lack of a better, or more widely recognised, alternative. For an earlier reading of this passage, see Ascoli: *Dante and the Making*, esp. chapter 4, section ii.

9 On Dante's self-commentary, most notably in *Vita Nuova*, *Convivio*, and the so-called *Epistle to Cangrande*, begin with the following, and the extensive bibliography they provide: Alistair J. Minnis and A. B. Scott, with David Wallace (eds): *Medieval Literary Theory and Criticism, c. 1100–c. 1375*:

present also in chapter XXV (and the preceding chapter XXIV), between the poetic faith of those belonging to the cult of love and the Christian Fith of the pilgrims.[10] And, of course, in various ways, as is well known, Dante gestures toward bridging the gap between these two "faiths" through his love of Beatrice, she who blesses.

In the *Convivio*, composed more than 10 years later, after his traumatic expulsion from Florence, we again find a complex understanding of the act of reading, of Dante's relationship to his readers, and of his own role as self-reader.[11] Let me begin again with a specific passage, this one from book IV, chapter 6, in which Dante offers a definition, the first and only time he does so in his canon, of the "autore," the author, as one who is "degno di fede e di obbedienza," to be "creduta e obbedita":

> L'altro principio, onde "autore" discende, sì come testimonia Uguiccione nel principio de le sue *Derivazioni*, è uno vocabulo greco che dice "autentin," che tanto vale in latino quanto "degno di fede e d'obedienza." E così "autore," quinci derivato, si prende per ogni persona degna di essere creduta e obedita. E da questo viene questo vocabulo del quale al presente si tratta, cioè "autoritade"; per che si può vedere che "autoritade" vale tanto quanto "atto degno di fede e obedienza." [Onde, avvegna che Aristotle sia dignissimo di fede e d'obedienza,] manifesto è che le sue parole sono somma e altissima autoritade.[12] (*Convivio* IV, iv, 5)[13]

The Commentary Tradition. Oxford: Clarendon 1988. Zygmunt Baranski: Dante Alighieri: Experimentation and (Self-) Exegesis. In: *The Cambridge History of Literary Criticism; Vol. 2: The Middle Ages*. Edited by Alastair Minnis and Ian Johnson. Cambridge: Cambridge University Press 2005, p. 561–82; and see again Ascoli: *Dante and the Making*, ch. 4, and "Access to Authority."

10 For an interpretation of chapter 25 by Robert Durling, differing in emphasis from mine, that focuses specifically on the apparent contradiction with the preceding chapter, see the discussion in *Dante and the Making*, pp. 195–196 and n. 44.

11 Richard Lansing: Dante's Intended Audience in the *Convivio*. In: *Dante Studies* 110 (1992), p. 17–24; Franziska Meier: Educating the Reader: Dante's *Convivio*. In: *L'Alighieri* 45 (2015), p. 21–33; Stanley Levers: From Revelation to Dilation in Dante's *Convivio*. In: *Dante Studies* 134 (2016), p. 2–25. For an additional bibliography, see Albert Russell Ascoli: Ponete mente almen come sono bella: Poetry and Prose, Goodness and Beauty. In: *Dante's 'Convivio': Or, How to Restart a Career in Exile*. Edited by Franziska Meier in the University of Leeds Dante Studies series. Bern: Peter Lang 2018, p. 115–144.

12 "The other source from which "author" derives, as Uguccione attests in the beginning of his book Derivations, is a Greek word pronounced "autentin" which in Latin means "worthy of faith and obedience." Thus "author," in this derivation, is used for any person deserving of being believed and obeyed. From this comes the word which we are presently treating, namely "authority"; hence we can see that authority means "pronouncement worthy of faith and obedience." Consequently, when I prove that Aristotle is most worthy of faith and obedience, it will be evident that his words are the supreme and highest authority."

13 Cited from Dante Alighieri, *Convivio*. In: Dante Alighieri: *Opere minori, tomo I, parte II*. Edited by Cesare Vasoli and Domenico de Robertis. Milan and Naples: Ricciardi 1988. For further discussion of this passage, with additional bibliography, see Ascoli: *Dante and the Making*, esp. ch. 2.

This of course is a strong definition of the relatively impersonal authority of an "auctor," and it is traditional in the Middle Ages. But it is also, prima facie, a definition of authorship and authority *in relation to* a reader or hearer, the one who, their "faith" on the author and is therefore brought to obey him in ways specific to the field in which he is authoritative.[14] It is also, again, but now explicitly, not "fede" in the religious sense, but rather belief in the truths to be find in the writings of certain human beings, specifically Aristotle, the Greek philosopher as translated into medieval Latin, whose influence on 13th century scholastic philosophy and theology, especially that of Thomas Aquinas, is very well-known.

I will come back shortly to the relationship between this kind of "fede" and that of the religious believer, but for now let me point out some of the various ways in which Dante's recourse to this definition tells something about his own status as reader and aspiring "author / authority." As I have argued at length in other work, the explicit reason behind this discourse on authority is to show respect for traditional authorities, even as he apparently contradicts them, while at the same time insinuating the possibility that he too, as self-commentator on his "philosophical" canzoni, may deserve a reader's "fede e obedienza." In other words, and in several different ways, Dante here both compromises traditional models of human *auctoritas* even as he appropriates some of their qualities for himself, both as poet and as philosopher. One route to understanding how this process unfolds is to look carefully, as, again, I have done elsewhere, at the definition of the *poetic* "autore" that immediately precedes that concerning The Philosopher, but, here again, I must briefly delay that discussion, while we look at how Dante, in *Convivio*, as in the *Vita Nuova*, offers an extensive justification of his authorial role in relation to prospective readers in the opening book of the treatise.

Books 2 through 4 of the unfinished treatise are all presented as commentaries by Dante on three of his own philosophical *canzoni* written at an earlier time and, to his mind, misinterpreted by their first readers. In other words, here Dante again appears in the doubled roles of author and of reader – though a reader who is explaining the author's intentions to other readers, this time for explicitly didactic purposes. The first book, however, serves both to define this twofold process, this doubled Dante, to prospective readers to be educated and to those, among whom contemporary intellectuals, who might criticise him for a variety of transgressions (first person reference, the use of an elevated style to acquire

---

14 Albert Russell Ascoli: Worthy of Faith? Authors and Readers in Early Modernity. In: *The Renaissance World*. Edited by John Martin. New York and London: Routledge 2007, p. 435–451, and: 'Favola Fui': Petrarch Writes his Readers. In: *The Bernardo Lecture series*. Binghamton NY: Center for Medieval & Renaissance Studies (Spring 2011), p. 1–35.

"maggiore autoritade," and, above all writing in the vernacular of his parents rather than in the more authoritative *grammatica*, that is, Latin).

Dante frames the twin problems of his readership and his authorship first in terms of the dramatic shift in his personal circumstances – namely his politically-motivated exile from Florence (I, ii, 3–6) – but also his greater maturity (I, i, 16) and his immersion in the philosophical works of Cicero and Boethius (XX, xii, 2–3), as well as the Latin Aristotle. He now presents himself as one who will humbly mediate between the "pan degli angeli" that he has found in that metaphorical Banquet of classical philosophy (I.vii.1), and a collection of readers primarily literate in the vernacular who do not have the time or skill to read the originals:

> [L]o volgare [as against Latin *grammatica*] servirà veramente a molti. Ché la bontà de l'animo, la quale questo servigio attende, è in coloro che per malvagia disusanza del mondo hanno lasciata la litteratura a coloro che l'hanno fatta di donna meretrice; veramente a molti . . . *e questi nobili [by virtue of "bontà de l'animo] sono principi, baroni, cavalieri e molt'altra nobile gente non solamente maschi ma femmine*, che sono molti e molte in questa lingua, volgari, e non literati (*Convivio* I, ix,.4–5)[15]

Both in the shift away from the autobiographical mode of the *Vita Nuova* and the explicit dedication to the transfer of knowledge, Dante claims a greater, more authoritative role for himself, his poetry, and the vernacular language than in the "youthful work," and to a pan-Italian audience rather the Florence and Tuscan-centred readership he addresses there (excepting the pilgrims, of course, who he presumes don't hear him).

As to the question of a reader's possible faith in his poetic-philosophical writings, he primarily claims the humble role of mediator of the *autori* who he will later say are the ones truly "worth of faith and obedience." And he apparently remains within the domain of the rational wisdom to be had from the love of a neo-Boethian Lady Philosophy. From this latter specification, many scholars – Nardi, Freccero, Hollander – have made a sharp distinction between *Convivio* as philosophical (and, for Nardi, potentially heretical) work and the *Commedia* as theologically motivated.[16] There are, however, some indirect signs, as there were

---

[15] "[The] vernacular will be of service to many. For goodness of mind, which this service attends to, is found in those who because of the world's wicked neglect of good have left literature to those who have changed it from a lady into a whore; and these noble persons comprise princes, barons, knights, and many other noble people, not only men but women, of which there are many in this language who know only the vernacular and are not learned."

[16] Bruno Nardi: Dal "Convivio" alla "Commedia". In: *Studi Storici* (fasc. 35-9). Rome: Istituto Storico Italiano 1960; John Freccero: Casella's Song (*Purg*. II.112) (1973). In: *Poetics of Conversion*, p. 186–94; Robert Hollander: *Purgatorio* II: Cato's Rebuke and Dante's 'Scoglio' (1975). In Idem:

in *Vita Nuova*, that the faith Dante desires from his readers is implicitly rooted in and / or analogous to the Christian Faith in divinity. Let me review these summarily:

1. The metaphorics of bread, which stand both for the content and the linguistic form of the treatise throughout the first book, generally support Dante's assertion of modesty. However, the first and last references suggest something different. The phrase "pan de li angeli" clearly refers to the angelic nature as being that of pure intellect, but just as clearly it cannot be entirely separated from the fact that *what* the angels contemplate primarily is their Creator. And while this article of Christian belief does not directly affect the reader's perception of Dante himself, it does prepare the way for the closing image of Book 1 in which Dante gives a very different account of the "bread" he has prepared for his readers and its relationship to "grammatica":

> Così rivolgendo li occhi a dietro, e raccogliendo le ragioni prenotate, puotesi vedere questo pane, col quale si deono mangiare le infrascritte canzoni, essere sufficientemente purgato da le macule, e da l'essere di biado; per che tempo è d'intendere a ministrare le vivande. Questo sarà quello pane orzato del quale si satolleranno migliaia, e a me ne soperchieranno le sporte piene. Questo sarà luce nuova, sole nuovo, lo quale surgerà là dove l'usato tramonterà, e darà lume a coloro che sono in tenebre e in oscuritade, per lo usato sole che a loro non luce.[17] (*Convivio* I, xiii, 11–12)

As has often been observed, this passage clearly describes Dante's "volgare" in Christological terms and projects a language that supplants the "usato sole," i.e., Latin, shortly after he describes his desire to confer "stabilitade" on his natal tongue through the meter and rhymes of his poetry:

Studies in Dante. Ravenna: Longo 1980, p. 91–105. For a critique of the way that the notion of the "palinode" had been used by Dante criticism in the wake of these readings, with additional bibliography, see Ascoli: *Dante and the Making*, esp. ch. 6, and for a specific review of the readings of *Purgatorio* II on which Freccero and Hollander first articulated their understanding of it, see my Performing Salvation in Dante's *Commedia*. In: *Dante Studies* 135 (2017), p. 74–104.

[17] "(11) So turning our gaze backwards and gathering together the reasons already noted, we can see that this bread, with which the canzoni placed below must be eaten, is sufficiently cleansed of its impurities and of being oaten. Therefore it is time to think of serving the meat. (12) This commentary shall be that bread made with barley by which thousands shall be satiated, and my baskets shall be full to overflowing with it. This shall be a new light, a new sun which shall rise where the old sun shall set and which shall give light to those who lie in shadows and in darkness because the old sun no longer sheds its light upon them."

> Ciascuna cosa studia naturalmente a la sua conservazione: onde se lo volgare studiare per sé potesse, studierebbe a quella; e quella sarebbe acconciare sé a piu stabilitate, e più stabilitade non potrebbe avere che in legare sé con numero e con rime. E questo studio è stato mio.[18] (*Convivio* I, xiii. 6–7)[19]

2. At the beginning of book II, in a very famous passage, he offers guidance to his readers in how to interpret this "pane" both literally and allegorically.

> Ma però che più profittabile sia questo mio cibo, prima che vegna la prima vivanda voglio mostrare come mangiare si dee. Dico che, sì come nel primo capitolo è narrato, questa sposizione conviene essere litterale e allegorica. E a ciò dare a intendere, si vuol sapere che le scritture si possono intendere e deonsi esponere massimamente per quattro sensi. L'uno si chiama litterale, [e questo è quello che non si stende più oltre che la lettera de le parole fittizie, sì come sono le favole de li poeti. L'altro si chiama allegorico,] e questo è quello che si nasconde sotto 'l manto di queste favole, ed è una veritade ascosa sotto bella menzogna: sì come quando dice Ovidio che Orfeo facea con la cetera mansuete le fiere, e li arbori e le pietre a sé muovere; che vuol dire che lo savio uomo con lo strumento de la sua voce fa[r]ia mansuescere e umiliare li crudeli cuori, e fa[r]ia muovere a la sua volontade coloro che non hanno vita di scienza e d'arte: e coloro che non hanno vita ragionevole alcuna sono quasi come pietre. E perché questo nascondimento fosse trovato per li savi, nel penultimo trattato si mosterrà. Veramenti li teologi questo senso prendono altrimenti che li poeti; ma però che mia intenzione è qui lo modo de li poeti seguitare, prendo lo senso allegorico secondo che per li poeti è usato. Lo terzo senso si chiama morale, e questo è quello che li lettori deono intentamente andare appostando per le scritture, ad utilitade di loro e di loro discenti: sì come appostare si può ne lo Evangelio, quando Cristo salio lo monte per transfigurarsi, che de li dodici Apostoli menò seco li tre; in che moralmente si può intendere che a le secrete cose noi dovemo avere poca compagnia. Lo quarto senso si chiama anagogico, cioè sovrasenso; e questo è quando spiritualmente si spone una scrittura, la quale ancora [sia vera] eziandio nel senso litterale, per le cose significate significa de le superne cose de l'etternal gloria: sì come vedere si può in quello canto del Profeta che dice che, ne l'uscita del popolo d'Israel d'Egitto, Giudea è fatta santa e libera. Che avvegna essere vero secondo la lettera sia manifesto, non meno è vero quello che spiritualmente s'intende, cioè che ne l'uscita de l'anima dal peccato, essa sia fatta santa e libera in sua potestate. E in dimostrar questo, sempre lo litterale dee andare innanzi, sì come quello ne

---

18 "Everything by nature pursues its own preservation; thus if the vernacular could by itself pursue anything, it would pursue that; and that would be to secure itself greater stability, and greater stability it could gain only by binding itself with meter and with rhyme. (7) This has been precisely my purpose"

19 For my reading of these passages, with additional bibliography, see Ascoli: 'Ponete mente'. And for Dante's use of the metaphorics of bread (and other comestibles), see Danielle Callegari, *Dante's Gluttons: Food and Society from* Convivio *to the* Comedy. Amsterdam: Amsterdam University Press 2022.

la cui sentenza li altri sono inchiusi, sanza lo quale sarebbe impossibile ed inrazionale intendere a li altri, e massimamente a lo allegorico.[20] (*Convivio* II, i, 1–9.)

As I have argued elsewhere,[21] the passage, at least initially, focuses not, as has so often been argued, on Dante's method of writing, but rather on how his work should be "eaten," that is interpreted, *by its readers*, while it also deliberately conflates and confuses two models of reading appropriate to two different kinds of texts: those of poets, notably classical poets such as Ovid, and those of "theologians," that is of the human authors of the Bible. On the one hand he claims (or seems to, since the passage in question is a reconstruction of a lacuna in the textual traditions) to be steering his readers toward the moralizing interpretation

---

20 "But so that this food of mine may be more profitable, I wish to show, before it appears, how the first course must be eaten. (2) As I stated in the first chapter, this exposition must be both literal and allegorical. To convey what this means, it is necessary to know that writings can be understood and ought to be expounded principally in four senses. (3) The first is called the literal, and this is the sense that [does not go beyond the surface of the letter, as in the fables of the poets]. The next is called the allegorical, and this is the one that is hidden beneath the cloak of these fables, and is a truth hidden beneath a beautiful fiction. Thus Ovid says that with his lyre Orpheus tamed wild beasts and made trees and rocks move toward him, which is to say that the wise man with the instrument of his voice makes cruel hearts grow tender and humble and moves to his will those who do not devote their lives to knowledge and art; and those who have no rational life whatsoever are almost like stones. (4) Why this kind of concealment was devised by the wise will be shown in the penultimate book. Indeed the theologians take this sense otherwise than do the poets; but since it is my intention here to follow the method of the poets, I shall take the allegorical sense according to the usage of the poets. (5) The third sense is called moral, and this is the sense that teachers should intently seek to discover throughout the scriptures, for their own profit and that of their pupils; as, for example, in the Gospel we may discover that when Christ ascended the mountain to be transfigured, of the twelve Apostles he took with him but three, the moral meaning of which is that in matters of great secrecy we should have few companions. (6) The fourth sense is called anagogical, that is to say, beyond the senses; and this occurs when a scripture is expounded in a spiritual sense which, although it is true also in the literal sense, signifies by means of the things signified a part of the supernal things of eternal glory, as may be seen in the song of the Prophet which says that when the people of Israel went out of Egypt, Judea was made whole and free. (7) For although it is manifestly true according to the letter, that which is spiritually intended is no less true, namely, that when the soul departs from sin it is made whole and free in its power. (8) In this kind of explication, the literal should always come first, as being the sense in whose meaning the others are enclosed, and without which it would be impossible and illogical to attend to the other senses, and especially the allegorical. (9) It would be impossible because in everything that has an inside and an outside it is impossible to arrive at the inside without first arriving at the outside; consequently, since in what is written down the literal meaning is always the outside, it is impossible to arrive at the other senses, especially the allegorical, without first arriving at the literal."
21 Albert Russell Ascoli: Tradurre l'allegoria: *Convivio* 2.1. In: *Critica del Testo* (triple issue *Dante Oggi*. Edited by Piero Boitani and Roberto Antonelli), vol. 1 (2011), p. 153–175.

of poetic fictions, but at the same time he offers examples of four different senses, as was traditionally prescribed for Biblical exegesis. One of these examples is the scene of the Transfiguration, though interpreted in a way more suitable to a non-Biblical text. The last example, of anagogy, examines the prophetic text "In exitu Israel de Aegypto" (Psalm 113 |114), and refers to the Christian escatological interpretation thereof as revealing "le superne cose dell'eterna gloria." In other words, Dante both "humbly" aligns himself with the limited allegorical project of poetry and at the same time invites his readers to contemplate the possibility that they should read his words as the exegetical tradition reads the Bible. Furthermore, Dante's use of the first allegorical sense, what would be the "quo credas" – what should you believe – of the exegetes, actually aligns himself with Orpheus and Orpheus with Christ that, again, subtly pushes his readers toward an exceptional "faith" in his words.[22]

3. My final example takes us back to book 4 and that second (though it comes first) definition of "autore":

> Questo vocabulo, cioè "autore" . . . può discendere da due principii: l'uno si è d'uno verbo molto lasciato da l'uso in gramatica, che significa tanto quanto "legare parole," cioè "auieo." E chi ben guarda lui, ne la sua prima voce apertamente vedrà che elli stesso lo dimostra, che solo di legame di parole è fatto, cioè di solo cinque vocali, che sono anima e legame di ogni parola, e composto da esse per modo volubile, a figurare imagine di legame. Ché, cominciando da l'A, ne l'U quindi si rivolve, e viene diritto per I ne l'E, quindi si rivolve e torna ne l'O; sì che veramente imagina questa figura: A, E, I, O, U, la quale è figura di legame. E in quanto "autore" discende da questo verbo, si prende solo per li poeti, che con l'arte musaica le loro parole hanno legate: e di questa significazione al presente non s'intende . . .[23] (*Convivio* IV, vi, 3–4)

---

[22] On Dante's treatment of Orpheus here, see again, Ascoli: "Tradurre l'allegoria," as well as Zygmunt Barański: Notes on Dante and the Myth of Orpheus. In: *Dante, mito e poesia, Atti del secondo seminario dantesco internazionale, Monte Verità, Ascona, 23–27 giugno 1997*. Edited by Michelangelo Picone and Tatiana Crivelli. Florence: Cesati 1999, p. 133–154; and, especially, Enrico Fenzi: L'esperienza di sé come esperienza dell'allegoria (a proposito di Dante, *Convivio* II i 2). In: *Studi danteschi*, 67 (2002), p. 161–200.

[23] "This word, namely "auctor" without the third letter c, has two possible sources of derivation. One is a verb that has very much fallen out of use in Latin and which signifies more or less "to tie words together," that is, "auieo." Anyone who studies it carefully in its first form will observe that it displays its own meaning, for it is made up only of the ties of words, that is, of the five vowels alone, which are the soul and tie of every word, and is composed of them in a different order, so as to portray the image of a tie. (4) For beginning with A it turns back to U, goes straight through to I and E, then turns back and comes to O, so that it truly portrays this image: A, E, I, O, U, which is the figure of a tie. Insofar as "author" is derived and comes from this verb, it is used

Admittedly, I have spoken a great deal about this paragraph elsewhere, indeed, my reading of it was the initial impetus behind what would become *Dante and the Making of a Modern Author*, but since it represents a critical step in today's argument, I find I must go there again. As hinted above it represents one of the indirect attempts that Dante is making in this part of the treatise to claim for himself the qualities of the second "autore," the one who is "worthy of faith and obedience," and, at the same time, it implies, admittedly in a covert manner, a relationship between belief in Dante's text as a source of truth and belief in God as the source of all truth. Despite the assertion that this definition is irrelevant, Dante has made it virtually impossible for us to believe this claim of his. After all, the whole of *Convivio* is constructed as commentary on Dante's own philosophically charged *poetry*, while the fact that the verb "avieo" is specifically cast as a first-person singular suggests an identity with the first person author of the treatise. Notably, as can be seen in comparing the motif of poetic ligature in the two passages, it also takes us back to Dante's claims at the end of book I concerning the relationship between his versifying and the purified and stabilised "volgare" as a quasi-sacramental "pane orzato": as the vowels bind together language in general, so the poet binds together the words of that language. And, as we have seen, Dante has expressly stated that his love for his natal tongue leads him to confer stability on it through "number and rhyme," what he here calls "l'arte musaica." Finally, as will only really become apparent toward the end of the *Commedia* itself, in the end it is God who is the Author of all authors (*auctores, autori*), as well as of the two books, the Bible and Nature, through which we build our faith. In other words, Dante either consciously or unconsciously creates an oblique analogy, whose consequences he will only later fully unfold, between human and divine "poetry" understood as creative, truthful, "making."[24]

In the final part of this essay, then, let me turn to the culminating work in this sequence, the one in which Dante clearly makes the most extravagant demands on the faith of his readers in his text, and most tightly binds that "poetic faith" to the project of building the faith of Christians in God's justice and mercy. I refer, obviously, to the *Commedia*.

---

only to refer to poets who have tied their words together with the art of poetry; but at present we are not concerned with this meaning."

24 On this culminating episode, see Ascoli: *Dante and the Making*, ch. 7, sec. v–vi. My work was particular inspired by Robert Hollander's seminal analysis of Dante's use and transformation of the language of authorship and authority in *Inferno* Cantos I and IV, and then in *Paradiso* XXVI, in: Dante's Use of *Aeneid* I in *Inferno* I and II. In: *Comparative Literature*, 20 (1968), p. 142–56, as well as Mazzotta: *Poet of the Desert*, pp. 258–259.

As anyone who knows the *Commedia* will remember, when Dante encounters Virgil in the first Canto of *Inferno*, he addresses him as follows:

O de li altri poeti onore e lume,	O light and honor of all other poets,
vagliami 'l lungo studio e 'l grande amore	may my long study and the intense love
che m'ha fatto cercar lo tuo volume.	that made me search your volume serve me now.
Tu se' lo mio maestro e 'l mio autore	You are my master and my author, you are
tu se' solo colui da cui io tolsi	the only one from whom my writing drew
lo bello stilo che m'ha fatto onore.	the noble style for which I have been honored.

(*Inferno* I, 82–87)

Having just looked at Dante's explicit two definitions of the word "autore," it should be clear that he here has conflated those two definitions – Virgil will be a guide "worthy of faith and obedience," but he has also served as Dante's master in the art of poetry. Here the character Dante, sometimes, misleadingly, called Dante *agens*,[25] and at others, reductively, Dante-pilgrim,[26] presents himself, once again, as both reader (of Virgil's poetry) and as himself a poet honored for his "beautiful style." In the *Commedia*, then, while the structural doubling of Dante as poet and Dante as commentator is gone, he clearly remains a model for his readers: as one who traces a moral-spiritual itinerary that they might imitate, and as one who lays claim to their faith in him and promotes their faith in the divine Grace that sponsors his journey and is the ultimate guarantor of whatever faith they put in him as poet. In fact, to skip blithely over the 60 intervening cantos, when Virgil "crowns and mitres" Dante over himself in *Purgatorio* XXVII, I would argue that in some sense he passes on both types of *auctoritas* to his grateful pupil.[27]

That said, at various points during the course of *Inferno*, Dante puts in doubt both his faith in Virgil's writings and the claim he makes on his own readers beliefs. Let me offer two quick examples. In Canto XIII, the canto of the suicides, Virgil justifies inflicting pain on the plant that contains the soul of Pier delle Vigne:

---

[25] Ascoli: "Access to Authority," p. 336–338, and nn. 88, 89, 92, 95.
[26] Corey Flack: Is Dante a Pilgrim? Pilgrimage, Material Culture, and Modern Dante Criticism. In: *Forum Italicum*, 55 (2021), p. 372–398.
[27] Ascoli: *Dante and the Making*, ch. 7, sec. iii.

"S'elli avesse potuto creder prima," rispuose 'l savio mio, "anima lesa, ciò c'ha veduto pur con la mia rima,	My sage said: "Wounded soul, if, earlier, he had been able to believe what he had only glimpsed within my poetry,
non averebbe in te la man distesa; ma la cosa incredibile mi fece indurlo ad ovra ch'a me stesso pesa".	then he would not have set his hand against you; but its incredibility made me urge him to do a deed that grieves me deeply".
	(*Inferno* XIII, 46–51)

As is well known, Virgil refers to the analogous Polydorus episode in Canto III of the *Aeneid*, and insists upon the fact that the pilgrim could not possibly have believed the truth of that part of his text. As various critics have noted, and most recently and completely Alison Cornish,[28] this canto focuses intently on the thematics of faith and faithfulness, highlighting Piero's misplaced faith in Emperor Frederic II, which has effectively blinded him to the possibility of God's grace and mercy in the world to come.

A few cantos later, Dante restages his disbelief in Virgil's incredible text as his own readers' disbelief in the scene he is about to describe, that is in:

Sempre a quel ver c'ha faccia di menzogna de' l'uom chiuder le labbra fin ch'el puote, però che sanza colpa fa vergogna;	Faced with that truth which seems a lie, a man should always close his lips as long as he can – to tell it shames him, even though he's blameless;
ma qui tacer nol posso; e per le note di questa comedìa, lettor, ti giuro, s'elle non sien di lunga grazia vòte . . .	but here I can't be still; and by the lines of this my Comedy, reader, I swear – and may my verse find favor for long years –
	(*Inferno* XVI, 124–129)

In swearing by the notes of his own poem, Dante highlights the fact that whatever claims he has made to being "worthy of faith and obedience" are at their roots tautological and unsustainable, unless, of course that "grazia" of the last quoted line is not understood, as it has so often, and on the whole convincingly, been the case, to favor among its future readers, but rather to an underpinning of divine grace. While this passage refers specifically to the upcoming depiction of Geryon, "quella sozza imagine di froda" (XVII, 7), it might well be taken to stand for the problems Dante-*author* faces in relation to his readers throughout the *Inferno* and, potentially, throughout the poem as a whole. That Geryon is not only a poetic creation of Dante but also a figure of poetry and rhetoric, seems

---

[28] I refer to a Keynote Address given by her at the Dante Society of America Conference "Dante Somma Luce," on "fede" in *Inferno* XIII, now revised in her new book, *Believing in Dante*. Cambridge: Cambridge University Press, 2022.

clear. Not only does he have obvious affinities with Horace's composite monster in the *Ars Poetica*, but his arrival, "vien notando" (131), echoes Dante's reference to the "note" of the poem which encloses him. In other words, the monster represents, apotropaically a risk that Dante runs in his quest to capture a reader's "fede e obbedienza."

Clearly Dante does not leave his readers in this state of suspended doubt (that is, in a condition opposed to belief) for long, once he has arrived in *Purgatorio*. Let me offer three more examples to illustrate how he, progressively, moves to overcome it.

1. In *Purgatorio* II, as is well known, he juxtaposes two songs. The singing of the psalm "In Exitu" by souls arriving in the afterlife from our world, on the one hand, and on the other, the singing of Dante's own canzone "Amor che nella mente mi ragiona" by his old friend Casella, which enraptures those same souls and Dante himself, distracting them from continuing their journey of purgation. The canto then offers two textual models, the same two we saw operative in *Convivio* II.1, biblical and poetic, and with them two forms of readerly response: active, faith-driven "performance" of the text leading toward salvation, passive spectatorship that puts the divine imperative of upward movement on hold. One way of understanding this is to see a radical divide between poetic and divine authorship that suggests that "faith" in the human author is contrary to the divinely sponsored authority of the Bible. Another way, one frequently adopted in North American scholarship, is to argue that Dante is leaving behind a past model of writing for a new one, which leads him to assimilate the *Commedia* to the Bible itself.[29] At the same time, and from the perspective of the present essay, we can say both that even as dramatises two forms of reading, at the same time, he puts his readers in the position of having to actively decide between them interpretatively and, more importantly, existentially (i.e., to choose which kind of reader they wish to be themselves).

2. Two later episodes suggest precisely that some version of the latter model is where Dante convinces his readers that the *Commedia* constitutes a place where faith in the human author and faith in Christian revelation may be seen to coincide. The first comes in the meeting of Dante and Virgil with Statius, where the latter declares not only that he was a crypto-Christian, but that his conversion was carried out through a reading of Virgil's fourth *Eclogue*. The double paradox,

---

[29] For an extend reading of this episode, see again Ascoli: "Performing Salvation."

signaled first by Barolini,[30] is that Virgil himself did not know that his poem could or would inculcate a faith from which he remained excluded, while Statius, now a Christian, did not dare reveal his faith, or attempt to lead others to it, through his poem. The resolution of this duality is to be found in, implicitly of course, Dante, who as an active reader of both poets, enacts a synthesis between them, simultaneously possessing Christian faith and inscribing it in the poem he will write (and which we are reading), on divine instruction, at journey's end. The second, of course, is his encounter with Bonagiunta da Lucca, a poet, but also his uncomprehending reader, in Canto XXIV: those extraordinary lines echo in an exceptionally compact way his meta-poetic treatment of "Amore" personified in *Vita Nuova* XXV, his opposition of the two types of song in *Purgatorio* II, and the Virgil, Statius, Dante triad in *Purgatorio* XXII:

"Ma dì s'i' veggio qui colui che fore trasse le nove rime, cominciando *'Donne ch'avete intelletto d'amore.'"*	"But tell me if the man whom I see here is he who brought the new rhymes forth, beginning: 'Ladies who have intelligence of love.'"
E io a lui: "I' mi son un che, quando Amor mi spira, noto, e a quel modo ch'e' ditta dentro vo significando."	I answered: "I am one who, when Love inspires in me, takes note; and in the manner that He dictates, within I go forth signifying."
"O frate, issa vegg' io," diss' elli, "il nodo che 'l Notaro e Guittone e me ritenne di qua dal dolce stil novo ch'i' odo!	"O brother, now I see," he said, "the knot that kept the Notary, Guittone, and me short of the sweet new manner that I hear.
Io veggio ben come le vostre penne di retro al dittator sen vanno strette, che de le nostre certo non avvenne;	I clearly see how your pens follow closely behind him who dictates, and certainly that did not happen with our pens; and he
e qual più a riguardar oltre si mette, non vede più da l'uno a l'altro stilo."	who sets himself to look further can find no other difference between the two styles."
	(*Purgatorio* XXIV, 49–62)[31]

Though this instantiation of Love is clearly referred back to the *Vita Nuova*, chapter XIX, it is just as clearly not a personified trope, but rather the Triune God which, though the person of the Holy Spirit, offers inspiration to the writer, who

---

[30] Barolini: *Dante's Poets*, pp. 258–270, esp. 270; see also my discussion of this episode in *Dante and the Making*, pp. 317–322.
[31] The translation adopted here partially diverges from Mandelbaum's.

notes what he has been told by the "dittatore."[32] The figures of "notation" clearly recall and resignify the implications of *Inferno* XVI.[33] The explicit citation of yet another Dantean canzone recalls and resolves the stand-off between *In Exitu* and "Amor che nella mente" of *Purgatorio* II, by implicitly aligning Dante's poetry with the human authors of the Bible while at the same time he is "performing" the language of divine Love as the souls who sing the Psalm had done before him. Removing the obligation to "believe" Dante as an 'autore,' the passage invites faith in the texts he notes and writes down under the dictation of God's Love.

3. As many critics have observed, once in the Earthly Paradise, Dante more explicitly puts himself on the same plane as the Biblical authors. Notably, in depicting the Triumphal pageant of salvation history, he compares his representations of the four allegorical animals that stand for the four Gospels to both Ezechiel and to the Revelation of John, affirming that in one detail where the two biblical authors differ "Giovanni è meco," John agrees with him (and not vice-versa!), in a passage explicitly directed to his readers:[34]

A descriver lor forme piú non spargo
rime, lettor; ch'altra spesa mi strigne
tanto ch'a questa non posso esser largo;

ma leggi Ezechïel, che li dipigne
come li vide da la fredda parte
venir con vento e con nube e con igne;

e quali i troverai ne le sue carte,
tali eran quivi, salvo ch'a le penne
Giovanni è meco e da lui si diparte.

Reader, I am not squandering more rhymes
in order to describe their forms; since I
must spend elsewhere, I can't be lavish here;

but read Ezekiel, for he depicts those animals
approaching from the north; with wings and
cloud and fire, he depicts them.

And just as you will find them in his pages,
such were they here, except that as to the
feathers; John is with me, and departs from him.
(*Purgatorio* XXIX, 97–105)[35]

---

32 Here I follow Martinez: "The Pilgrim's Answer," and Mazzotta: *Poet of the Desert*, pp. 202–210. See also, my "Performing Salvation," for additional discussion and bibliography.
33 On the connection between *Inferno* XVI and *Purgatorio* XXIV, see Albert Russell Ascoli: *Ariosto's Bitter Harmony: Crisis and Evasion in the Italian Renaissance*. Princeton: Princeton University Press 1987, p. 277–278. See also Ascoli: *Dante and the Making*, p. 323, n. 27, for additional discussion with bibliography.
34 See Peter Hawkins: John is with Me (1988). In Idem: *Dante's Testaments: Essays in Scriptural Imagination*. Stanford: Stanford University Press 1999, p. 54–71.
35 The translation adopted here partially diverges from Mandelbaum's.

And shortly thereafter Dante compares himself to the three favored disciples who witness the Transfiguration,[36] once again with specific reference to John:

S'io potessi ritrar come assonnaro li occhi spietati udendo di Siringa, li occhi a cui pur vegghiar costò sì caro;	Could I describe just how the ruthless eyes (eyes whose long wakefulness cost them so dear), hearing the tale of Syrinx, fell asleep,
come pintor che con essempro pinga, disegnerei com' io m'addormentai; ma qual vuol sia che l'assonnar ben finga.	then like a painter painting from a model, I'd draw the way in which I fell asleep; but I refrain – let one more skillful paint.
Però trascorro a quando mi svegliai, e dico ch'un splendor mi squarciò 'l velo del sonno, e un chiamar: "Surgi: che fai?"	I move, therefore, straight to my waking time; I say that radiance rent the veil of sleep, as did a voice: "Rise up: what are you doing?"
Quali a veder de' fioretti del melo che del suo pome li angeli fa ghiotti e perpetüe nozze fa nel cielo,	Even as Peter, John, and James, when brought to see the blossoms of the apple tree – whose fruit abets the angels' hungering,
Pietro e Giovanni e Iacopo condotti e vinti, ritornaro a la parola da la qual furon maggior sonni rotti,	providing endless wedding-feasts in Heaven – were overwhelmed by what they saw, but then, hearing the word that shattered deeper sleeps,
e videro scemata loro scuola così di Moïsè come d'Elia, e al maestro suo cangiata stola;	arose and saw their fellowship was smaller – since Moses and Elijah now had left – and saw a difference in their Teacher's dress;
tal torna' io …	so I awoke

(*Purgatorio* XXXII, 64–82)

We have already seen the use that Dante makes of the Transfiguration in his definition of allegorical reading and writing in *Convivio* II.1, and it is clearly no accident that immediately after the comparison to Peter, James and John that he receives his first prophetic commission from Beatrice as Christ, a commission that may certainly be interpreted as divinely authorizing the writing of the *Commedia* itself (XXXII, 100–105).

There is, of course, much to be said about the ways in which Dante continues his negotiation between the reader's faith in his text and the reader's faith

---

[36] On Dante's use of the Transfiguration in the *Commedia*, see Peter Hawkins: Transfiguring the Text: Ovid, Scripture, and the Dynamics of Allusion. In: Idem: *Dante's Testaments* Stanford: Stanford University Press 2000, p. 180–93 (this chapter published in 1985). See also, more generally, Jeffrey Schnapp: *The Transfiguration of History at the Center of Dante's "Paradise"*. Princeton: Princeton University Press 1986; as well as Ascoli: *Dante and the Making*, pp. 377–384 passim.

in God over the course of *Paradiso*. But before turning, if only symptomatically, to the final canticle, I need to speak briefly about one of the many ways, though perhaps the most obvious, that Dante imagines his relationship with his readers throughout the *Commedia*: namely, in the "addresses to the reader" (whether directed specifically at the "lettor" or to an apostrophised "Voi") that recur at relatively regular intervals throughout the poem, for a total of twenty-one.[37] We have already seen examples in the passages from *Inferno* XVI and *Purgatorio* XXIX.

These apostrophes, as is very well known, inspired a seminal critical debate some sixty years ago, one which seems especially apposite to the topic I have been developing here. In two very famous essays from the 1950's, both written by German Jewish emigrés to the U.S., which to this very day are often taken to represent the state of the question, Erich Auerbach (developing a problem defined by Herman Gmelin) and then Leo Spitzer (responding polemically to Auerbach and to unnamed others, primarily his Johns Hopkins colleague, Charles Singleton) assessed the significance of these addresses to the readers in the *Commedia*.[38] Leaving aside important details in their arguments, and that of Gmelin, such as what actually counts, numerically and semantically, as an address to the reader, let me simply focus on the primary divergence between the two. For Auerbach, the addresses to the reader highlight Dante's assumption of a unique status for himself as poet-prophet, one which creates an abyssal difference between authorial knowledge and readerly ignorance:

> Dante addresses the reader as if everything that he has to report were not only factual truth, but truth containing Divine Revelation. The reader, as envisioned by Dante (and in point of fact, Dante creates his reader), is a disciple. He is not expected to discuss or to judge, but to follow; using his own forces, but the way Dante orders him to do (p. 276)

For Spitzer, instead, Dante's relationship to the reader is that of an exemplary model, readily available and imitable, that presumes essential equality of status between writer and reader, based on the Christian principal (observed largely in the breach, then as now) of the parity of all human souls in the eyes of the Lord:

> Dante's discovery of a new auctorial relationship with the reader was the consequence of the nature of his vision in which the presence of the reader for whom it is told is required.

---

[37] Of these two kinds there are 6 in *Inferno* (Cantos VIII, IX, XVI, XX, XXV, XXXIII), 8 in *Purgatorio* (VIII, IX, X, [2], XVII, XXIX, XXXI, XXXIII), and 5 in *Paradiso* (II, V, X [2], XXII).

[38] Erich Auerbach: Dante's Addresses to the Reader. In: *Romance Philology* 7 (1954), p. 268–278; Leo Spitzer: The Addresses to the Reader in the *Commedia* (1955). In Idem: *Romanische Literaturstudien, 1936–56*. Tübingen: Niemeyer 1959, p. 574–95 (this essay first published 1955). See Hermann Gmelin: Die Anrede an den Leser in Dantes *Göttliche Komödie*. In: *Deutsches Dante Jahrbuch* 29–30 (1951), p. 130–140, for the origins of the discussion, and cf. Franke, *Dante's Interpretive Journey*, ch. 1, esp. sec. 4, for a different yet important perspective on it.

> Although Dante presents himself as actually having been in the beyond . . . he surely thought no more of himself as belonging to a superhuman category of prophets than did any truly religious poet in other ages . . . his "I" is indeed . . . a poetic-didactic "I" that stands for any other Christian (p. 160)

Auerbach, in the terms I have been stressing, emphasises the reader's faith in Dante as poet-prophet. Spitzer emphasises the role of Dante-character in mediating the reader's faith in the Christian God. Both of them are, in some sense, right, both are also wrong, at least according to this reader.[39] The one point they apparently agree on is on the "constructedness" and novelty of Dante's reader, a phenomenon whose evolution through Dante's works I have been outlining in this essay.

There is one especially important difference that needs to be noticed between Dante's staging of his own role as reader and his relationship to his imagined readership in both *Vita Nuova* and *Convivio*, on one hand, and the *Commedia*, on the other. In both of those earlier works, by occupying the roles both of author (of poems) and reader-commentator (of those poems), as we have seen, he puts himself in the position akin to that of his readers, but also declares the superiority of his interpretive grasp of the poems he asks them to understand. And within this structure we can once more see, looming in the distance, the complex relationship between Dante and his readers in the *Commedia* (where he is at once above them [Auerbach] and equal to them [Spitzer]). At the same time, an obvious distinction between the *Commedia* and those earlier works is that there is no obvious formal equivalent to the division between Dante the poet and Dante the privileged interpreter or reader of his own poetry.[40] This difference can be read, however, in either a Spitzerian or an Auerbachian key, or perhaps it must be read in both. On one hand, in frequently entrusting his readers with the task of deciphering the text (as he does conspicuously in *Inf.* IX, XX, and XX; and in *Purg.* VIII) he, in some sense, potentially promotes them to the position of interpretive freedom and potential mastery that he arrogated to himself in the earlier works. On the other, of course, he apparently promotes himself to the status of an "au[c]

---

39 While Spitzer's patent contempt for Singleton no doubt had and has its justifications, it is also true that the American critic's seminal distinction between Dante (character) as everyman, stand in for his reader, and Dante (poet) as uniquely blessed and talented individual, could be said convincingly to take some account of both aspects of the quarrel (Singleton, *Dante Studies I*, esp. ch. 1. There have since been a number of important reformulations of this opposition that have tended blur the difference between these two poles. I think especially of Gianfranco Contini: Dante come personaggio-poeta della *Commedia*. In: Idem: *Un'idea di Dante*. Turin: Einaudi 1976 (this essay published 1957), p. 33–62; as well as a number of the essays collected in Freccero: *The Poetics of Conversion*.
40 For a more nuanced account of this issue, see Ascoli: *Dante and the Making*, pp. 218–226.

tor" whose words merit the kind of faithful attention previously reserved for the classical philosophical and poetic *auctores* and, perhaps, to that of the human authors of the Bible. On this latter view, it would seem that in the *Commedia* he elevates himself to the status that he moved toward implicitly in both *Convivio* and *De Vulgari Eloquentia*, without, in those works, ever himself abandoning the explicit rhetorical position of "lettore."

In conclusion, then, let me turn to three of the explicit addresses to the reader in *Paradiso*, where the problem of the readers' faith once again comes to the fore. The first of these comes very near the beginning of the canticle, in a passage that contains a clear recollection of *Convivio*, along with its complex formulation of Dante both as poet and as commentator on his poetry to his readers:

O voi che siete in piccioletta barca,	O you who are within your little bark,
desiderosi d'ascoltar, seguiti	eager to listen, following behind
dietro al mio legno che cantando varca,	my ship that, singing, crosses to deep seas,
tornate a riveder li vostri liti:	turn back to see your shores again: do not
non vi mettete in pelago, ché forse,	attempt to sail the seas I sail; you may,
perdendo me, rimarreste smarriti.	by losing sight of me, be left astray.
L'acqua ch'io prendo già mai non si corse;	The waves I take were never sailed before;
Minerva spira, e conducemi Appollo,	Minerva breathes, Apollo pilots me,
e nove Muse mi dimostran l'Orse.	and the nine Muses show to me the Bears.
Voialtri pochi che drizzaste il collo	You other few who turned your minds in time
per tempo al pan de li angeli, del quale	unto the bread of angels, which provides
vivesi qui ma non sen vien satollo,	men here with life – but hungering for more –
metter potete ben per l'alto sale	you may indeed commit your vessel to
vostro navigio, servando mio solco	the deep salt – sea, keeping your course within
dinanzi a l'acqua che ritorna equale.	my wake, ahead of where waves smooth out again.

(*Paradiso* II, 1–15)

Here, conspicuously, Dante, while affirming the novelty and exalted status of his poem, distinguishes between two types of readers: the unprepared in their "little boats" who could fall into intellectual and spiritual error attempting to follow the flight of the poet's imagination up through the heavens, as against the very few who have already eaten of the "bread of angels" and are thus up to the challenge. There is, of course, much more to say about this passage, much of which has already been discussed in the great sea of Dante criticism. Let me focus then on a few key points that bear on the question of the readers' faith in both senses. First, of all, there is the notion that there are two types of readers, whose abilities are, apparently, not determined by Dante's authoritative communication of the experiences he will now represent. In other words, the lines suggest a degree of autonomy in the reader that Dante was far less willing to concede in his earlier works (and even, to some degree, in the earlier canticles). At the same time, there is the equally obvious assertion that Dante insists upon the special value ("acqua ... già mai si corse") of what he is about to write for readers who come to it with special intellectual and / or spiritual knowledge. There is also, perhaps a bit less obviously, a hint that the latter group may already have *been* Dante's readers, and that they may have achieved their status in part by what they gained from reading the *Convivio*, whose avowed purpose, as we have seen, is to divulge "the bread of angels."[41] There is an even more problematic insinuation, that while a reader's faith in Dante's text might not be useful or even necessary for salvation (as, on the other hand, the matters treated in the earlier canticles might be – after all, this warning is delivered only after readers have come this far), excessive trust in it might actually be responsible for confusing one's faith in the one true "Author," the triune God. The use of the words "smarriti" and "pelago" in particular suggests a condition of spiritual error akin to the one Dante-character was experiencing at the beginning of the poem (*Inferno* I, 3, 13–14; II, 64), risking a damnation

---

[41] This reading faces two obstacles, which I will not attempt to refute in detail here. The first is that the *Convivio* remained unfinished and did not circulate widely, i.e., could and would have been read only by a few people. Here the only possible answers are (1) that a few could have read the treatise, a few of those could have understood it or even have read and understood Dante's philosophical *canzoni* without a prose commentary (both those included in the treatise and those, like "Tre Donne" that didn't make it in but have an obvious allegorical content), and (2) that Dante imagined that others had followed a path parallel to his own in reading and understanding the philosophical and theological *auctoritates* he refers to there. The second is that this "bread of angels" is strictly theological – i.e., rooted in faithful reading of Scripture and commentaries thereon – while in the *Convivio* it is rational-philosophical. In other words, that Dante has here undertaken a palinodic re-reading and refutation of his earlier authorial stance. This position was strongly argued by Daniel J. Ransom quite some time ago in: *Panis Angelorum*: A Palinode in the *Paradiso*. In: *Dante Studies* 95 (1977), p. 81–94. To this I would simply say that while Dante clearly does make frequent use of such palinodic allusions, it may well be that here, as on occasion elsewhere, he is attempting to have his angelic "cake" and eat it too (on the Dantean palinode more generally, see note 16 above) To this latter point, I would note, following Jason Aleksander (The *Divine Comedy*'s Construction of its Audience in *Paradiso* II, 18. In: *Essays in Medieval Studies*, Volume 30 (2014), pp. 1–10, esp. p. 7) the interesting ambiguity of the word "qui" which could indicate either that "Dante-poet" is referring to our world, where he is *here and now* writing and the elect few are reading him, or to the Other World, where Dante-character is *here and now* traveling, where he has good hope of returning after death, where those same readers' faith might eventually lead them as well.

for which, Beatrice will later say to him, only his subsequent journey through the Other World would prevent (*Purgatorio* XXX, 133–138).

All that said, I will close my discourse with a slightly longer look at the opening address to a twice-invoked reader, which is also a kind of farewell to and authorization of that reader, in Canto X, as Dante enters the Heaven of the Sun, the home of those who have best understood and explicated the Word of God:

Guardando nel suo Figlio con l'Amore	Gazing upon His Son with that Love which
che l'uno e l'altro etternalmente spira,	One and the Other breathe eternally,
lo primo e ineffabile Valore	the Power – first and inexpressible –
quanto per mente e per loco si gira	made everything that wheels through mind and
con tant' ordine fé, ch'esser non puote	space so orderly that one who contemplates
sanza gustar di lui chi ciò rimira.	that harmony cannot but taste of Him.
Leva dunque, lettore, a l'alte rote	Then, reader, lift your eyes with me to see
meco la vista, dritto a quella parte	the high wheels; gaze directly at that part
dove l'un moto e l'altro si percuote;	where the one motion strikes against the other;
e lì comincia a vagheggiar ne l'arte	and there begin to look with longing at
di quel maestro che dentro a sé l'ama,	that Master's art, which in Himself he loves
tanto che mai da lei l'occhio non parte.	so much that his eye never parts from it.
[. . .]	[. . .]
Or ti riman, lettor, sovra 'l tuo banco,	Now, reader, do not leave your bench, but stay
dietro pensando a ciò che si preliba,	to think on that of which you have foretaste;
s'esser vuoi lieto assai prima che stanco.	you will have much delight before you tire.
Messo t'ho innanzi: omai per te ti ciba;	I have prepared your fare; now feed yourself,
ché a sé torce tutta la mia cura	because that matter of which I am made
quella materia ond' io son fatto scriba.	the scribe calls all my care unto itself.

(*Paradiso* X, 1–12, 22–27)

We begin with an invocation of the Trinity, starting with the Son, whose creative Word informed the Heavens, and all of nature, then passing to the Holy Spirit, the Love which inspires Dante to understand the meaning of that Word and write what he has been given down, and the finally to God the Father. Dante then invites his reader to follow his example in lifting his eyes up to the visible heavens, which give testimony to the *invisibilia*, illustrating, as it were, the Pauline definition of faith, as "the evidence of that which does not appear, the argument of things hoped for" (Hebrews 11:1). The second address to the reader may be the most cogent in the poem for my topic, since it not only refers to the reader's ingestive experience (recalling the primary metaphor of *Convivio*) of the content that Dante (or, rather, in this case, obviously, God) has provided, but at the same time to the specific situation and activity of reading and to the ongoing process of writing. The image of the reader hunched over the texts he is studying strangely reverses the upward glance to which Dante has just invited him, and suggests a doubled experience of reading the metaphorical book of Nature and literally written books, like the Bible, and perhaps like the *Commedia* itself. I would argue, in addition, that the image evokes not only the reading of a vernacular work such as the *Commedia*, but also the *lectio* of a student of theology, absorbing the text furnished by the *auctor* or *magister* as may be, an assertion in keeping with the prevalence of Latin sages among in the fourth heaven.[42] In this way Dante is cast bi-valently in the two roles he had at the outset assigned to Virgil, while at the same time he defines himself not as the originator of that text, but rather as faithful transcriber of a "materia" that is now clearly not his own journey but God's celestial "regno" (cf. *Paradiso* I, 10–12, 26–27). The passage suggests a potential parallel between Dante writing on his "bench" and the reader reading at his, but then, perhaps, becoming a writer himself (I take this from a suggestion of the late Robert Durling), even as, at the same time, there is a clear separation between the reader ingesting what has been set before him and Dante the solitary, privileged scribe continuing his textual journey.

I would like to believe that *my* readers, having come to the end of this essay, will not arrive at the conclusion that I have in any sense resolved the intertwined questions incessantly posed by Dante concerning either of the two kinds of faith he juxtaposes – that of the reader in a human author and that of the Christian in the Holy Trinity. What I hope to have suggested instead is that Dante's complex and intense reflections on the relationship of author to reader through the medium of the texts, whether governed by rational understanding or a suprarational faith (of whichever kind) or some combination of the two. are worthy of serious consideration – all the more so because they *cannot* be easily resolved. Whether this consideration should be that of a medieval poet's "thinking with the stars" invoked in *Paradiso* X; of an academic's ostensibly dispassionate sifting through the objects of her or his or their study; of the existential grappling of any-per-

---

[42] This notion culminates in the examination sequence of *Paradiso* XXIV–XXVI, notably in Dante's comparison of himself responding to St. Peter's examination on the theological virtue of Faith to a "baccialiere" responding to a *quaestio* posed by a "maestro." On this passage specifically see Ascoli. "Starring Dante," in a special issue of the online journal *Religions* entitled "Teaching Dante," eds. Christopher Metress and Brian Johnson (*Religions* 10, 319 , Spring 2019). On my understanding of the significance of the examination sequence – conducted by, who else, the three favored apostles of the Transfiguration – and especially Canto XXVI, where the Dantean discourse on author and authority reaches its climax, see the references in note 24 above.

son with the constantly impinging issues of what might be might prove worthy of their trust, or belief, or faith, not to say "obedience" in our own conflicted times; or some other configuration stimulated, or not, by an engaged reading of Dante's text, or mine for that matter, I frankly cannot say.

Bibliographical References

AA.VV.: Dante and Modern American Criticism. *Annali d'Italianistica*, 8 (1990).
Ahern, John: The New Life of the Book: The Implied Reader of the *Vita nuova*. In: *Dante Studies*, 110 (1992), p. 1–16.
Aleksander, Jason: The *Divine Comedy*'s Construction of its Audience in *Paradiso* II, 18. In: *Essays in Medieval Studies*, Volume 30 (2014), pp. 1–10.
Alighieri, Dante: *Opere minori, tomo I, parte II*. Edited by Cesare Vasoli and Domenico de Robertis. Milan and Naples: Ricciardi 1988.
Ascoli, Albert Russell: *Ariosto's Bitter Harmony: Crisis and Evasion in the Italian Renaissance*. Princeton: Princeton University Press 1987.
Ascoli, Albert Russell: Access to Authority: Dante in the Letter to Cangrande. In: *Proceedings of the First International Dante Symposium*. Edited by Zygmunt Baranski. Florence: Le Lettere Editore 1997, p. 309–352.
Ascoli, Albert Russell: Palinode and History in the Oeuvre of Dante. In Amilcare A. Ianucci (ed.): *Dante: Contemporary Perspectives*. Toronto-Buffalo-London: University of Toronto Press 1997, pp. 23–50.
Ascoli, Albert Russell: Worthy of Faith? Authors and Readers in Early Modernity. In: *The Renaissance World*. Edited by John Martin. New York and London: Routledge 2007, p. 435–451.
Ascoli, Albert Russell: *Dante and the Making of a Modern Author*. Cambridge: Cambridge University Press 2008 (Ital. Transl. by Anna Montanari available online: *Dante e l'invenzione di un autore moderno* through Academia.edu: https://www.academia.edu/15586290/Dante_e_linvenzione_di_un_autore_moderno_trans_of_Dante_and_the_Making_of_a_Modern_Author_trans_Anna_Montanari).
Ascoli, Albert Russell: Blinding the Cyclops: Petrarch after Dante. In: *Petrarch and Dante*. Edited by T. Cachey and Z. Baranski. Notre Dame: Notre Dame University Press 2009, p. 114–173.
Ascoli, Albert Russell: 'Favola Fui': Petrarch Writes his Readers. In: *The Bernardo Lecture series*. Binghamton NY: Center for Medieval & Renaissance Studies (Spring 2011), p. 1–35.
Ascoli, Albert Russell: Tradurre l'allegoria: *Convivio* 2.1. In: *Critica del Testo* (triple issue *Dante Oggi*). Edited by Piero Boitani and Roberto Antonelli), vol. 1 (2011), p. 153–175.
Ascoli, Albert Russell: Poetry and Theology. In: *Reviewing Dante's Theology Volume 2*. Edited by Matthew Treherne and Claire Honess. Bern: Peter Lang 2014, p. 3–42.
Ascoli, Albert Russell: Performing Salvation in Dante's *Commedia*. In: *Dante Studies* 135 (2017), p. 74–104.
Ascoli, Albert Russell: "Ponete mente almen come sono bella": Poetry and Prose, Goodness and Beauty. In: *Dante's 'Convivio': Or, How to Restart a Career in Exile*. Edited by Franziska Meier in the University of Leeds Dante Studies series. Bern: Peter Lang 2018, p. 115–144.

Ascoli, Albert Russell: "Starring Dante," in *Teaching Dante*. Special Issue ed. by Christopher Metress and Brian Johnson, *Religions* 10, 319 (Spring 2019) doi:10.3390/rel10050319.
Auerbach, Erich: Dante's Addresses to the Reader. In: *Romance Philology* 7 (1954), p. 268–78.
Barański, Zygmunt: Notes on Dante and the Myth of Orpheus. In: *Dante, mito e poesia, Atti del secondo seminario dantesco internazionale, Monte Verità, Ascona, 23–27 giugno 1997*. Edited by Michelangelo Picone and Tatiana Crivelli. Florence: Cesati 1999, p. 133–154.
Baranski, Zygmunt: Dante Alighieri: Experimentation and (Self-) Exegesis. In: *The Cambridge History of Literary Criticism; Vol. 2: The Middle Ages*. Edited by Alastair Minnis and Ian Johnson. Cambridge: Cambridge University Press 2005, p. 561–82.
Barolini, Teodolinda: *Dante's Poets: Textuality and Truth in the Comedy*. Princeton: Princeton Univ. Press. 1984.
Barolini, Teodolinda: *The Undivine Comedy: Detheologizing Dante*. Princeton: Princeton University Press 1992.
Callegari, Danielle: *Dante's Gluttons: Food and Society from* Convivio *to the* Comedy. Amsterdam: Amsterdam University Press 2022.
Contini, Gianfranco: Dante come personaggio-poeta della *Commedia* (1957). In: Idem *Un'idea di Dante. Saggi danteschi*. Turin: Einaudi (1970 / 1976) 2001, p. 33–62.
Cornish, Alison: *Believing in Dante*. Cambridge: Cambridge University Press 2022.
Fenzi, Enrico: L'esperienza di sé come esperienza dell'allegoria (a proposito di Dante, *Convivio* II i 2). In: *Studi danteschi*, 67 (2002), p. 161–200.
Flack, Corey: Is Dante a Pilgrim? Pilgrimage, Material Culture, and Modern Dante Criticism. In: *Forum Italicum*, 55 (2021), p. 372–398.
Franke, William: *Dante's Interpretive Journey*. Chicago: University of Chicago Press 1996.
Freccero, John: *Dante. The Poetics of Conversion*. Edited by Rachel Jacoff. Cambridge MA: Harvard University Press 1986.
Freccero, John: Casella's Song (*Purg*. II.112) (1973). In: Idem: *Dante: The Poetics of Conversion*. Edited by Rachel Jacoff. Cambridge MA: Harvard University Press 1986.
Gmelin, Hermann: Die Anrede an den Leser in Dantes *Göttliche Komödie*. In: *Deutsches Dante Jahrbuch* 29–30 (1951), p. 130–140.
Hawkins, Peter: John is with Me (1988). In Idem: *Dante's Testaments: Essays in Scriptural Imagination*. Stanford: Stanford University Press 1999, p. 54–71.
Hawkins, Peter: Transfiguring the Text: Ovid, Scripture, and the Dynamics of Allusion (1985). In: Idem: *Dante's Testaments* Stanford: Stanford University Press 2000, p. 180–93.
Hawkins, Peter S.: *Dante's Testaments: Essays in Scriptural Imagination*. Stanford: Stanford University Press 1999.
Hollander, Robert: Dante's Use of *Aeneid* I in *Inferno* I and II. In: *Comparative Literature*, 20 (1968), p. 142–156.
Hollander, Robert: *Purgatorio* II: Cato's Rebuke and Dante's 'Scoglio' (1975). In: Idem: *Studies in Dante*. Ravenna: Longo 1980, p. 91–105.
Hollander, Robert: Dante as Theologus-Poeta (1976). Ravenna: Longo 1980, p. 39–89.
Lansing, Richard: Dante's Intended Audience in the *Convivio*. In: *Dante Studies* 110 (1992), p. 17–24.
Levers, Stanley: From Revelation to Dilation in Dante's *Convivio*. In: *Dante Studies* 134 (2016), p. 2–25.
Lombardi, Elena: *Imagining the Woman Reader in the Age of Dante*. Oxford: Oxford University Press 2018.

Martinez, Ronald L.: The Pilgrim's Answer to Bonagiunta and the Poetics of the Spirit. In: *Stanford Italian Review* 4 (1983), p. 37–63.

Mazzotta, Giuseppe: *Dante, Poet of the Desert*. Princeton: Princeton University Press 1979.

Mazzotta, Giuseppe: *Dante's Vision and the Circle of Knowledge*. Princeton: Princeton University Press 1992.

Mazzotta, Giuseppe: The American Criticism of Charles Singleton. In: *Dante Studies* 104 (1986), p. 27–44.

Mazzotta, Giuseppe: Reflections on Dante Studies in America. In: *Dante Studies* 118 (2000), p. 323–330.

Meier, Franziska: Educating the Reader: Dante's *Convivio*. In: *L'Alighieri* 45 (2015), p. 21–33.

Minnis Alistair J. and A. B. Scott, with David Wallace (eds): *Medieval Literary Theory and Criticism, c. 1100–c. 1375: The Commentary Tradition*. Oxford: Clarendon 1988.

Nardi, Bruno: *Dal "Convivio" alla "Commedia"*. In: *Studi Storici* (fasc. 35-9). Rome: Istituto Storico Italiano 1960.

Noakes, Susan: *Timely Reading: Between Exegesis and Interpretation*. Ithaca NY: Cornell University Press 1988.

Petrucci, Armando: *Writers and Readers in Medieval Italy*. Trans. Charles Radding. New Haven CT: Yale University Press 1995.

Ransom, Daniel J.: *Panis Angelorum*: A Palinode in the *Paradiso*. In: *Dante Studies* 95 (1977), p. 81–94.

Saiber, Arielle and Giuseppe Mazzotta (eds): *Dante Studies*, 128 (2010).

Schnapp, Jeffrey: *The Transfiguration of History at the Center of Dante's "Paradise"*. Princeton: Princeton University Press 1986.

Singleton, Charles S.: *Dante's* Commedia: *Elements of Structure*. Baltimore and London: John Hopkins University Press 1977 (orig. *Dante Studies 1: Elements of Structure*. Cambridge MA: Harvard University Press 1954).

Spitzer, Leo: The Addresses to the Reader in the *Commedia* (1955). In Idem: *Romanische Literaturstudien, 1936–56*. Tübingen: Niemeyer 1959, p. 574–95.

Steinberg, Justin: *Accounting for Dante: Urban Readers and Writers in Late Medieval Italy*. Notre Dame IN: University of Notre Dame Press 2007.

Teresa Bartolomei
Dante: Talking to the Dead – Giving a Voice to Silence

Introduction. Autobiographical Discourse in the *Comedy* as the Integration of Prosopopoiea and Typological-Figural Metalepsis

Determining whether it is generally possible to establish a boundary between autobiography and autofiction – and precisely what this might be – is the primary subject of the theoretical conflict currently being waged in studies of 'life writing'[1], just as for many years a similar debate over the difference between historical fact and narrative reconstruction took place in historiographical scholarship.[2] The questionable temptation to unite all confessional, lyrical and autobiographical discourse under the title of autofiction is founded in the unquestionable observation that its fundamental figural tool, prosopopoeia (as highlighted by Paul de Man, in a groundbreaking contribution on the matter),[3] is incapable of guaranteeing the truth of narrative report, not only in the eyes of the recipient but even those of the author of autobiographical writing, since it articulates a contradictory polarisation.

On the one hand, biographical discourse is produced as 'self-testimony', embodying a suspicious coincidence of the roles of 'spectator' and 'agent' inherent in every narrative report that claims factual relevance. The temporal dissociation of the roles (the agent becomes their own spectator through retrospective distortion of the vision inherent in the time sequence) is not sufficient to structurally guarantee the mutual independence of their respective performative interests (the spectator desires narrative truth; the actor desires the successful outcome of their own strategy of self-representation). The suspicion that the narrative is

---

[1] The monumental three-volume manual recently issued by de Gruyter altogether declines to choose between the terms: beginning with the title, the difference is inconclusively evaded by a punctuation mark. See MartinWagner-Egelhaaf: *Handbook of Autobiography / Autofiction*. Berlin: De Gruyter, 2019.
[2] See Carlo Ginzburg: *Il filo e le tracce* (2006). Milan: Feltrinelli 2015.
[3] Paul de Man: Autobiography as De-Facement. In: Id.: *The Rhetoric of Romanticism*. New York: Columbia University Press 1984, p. 67–81.

Note: Translated from the Italian by Matthew Coneys Wainwright.

manipulated by the actor to favour their self-rehabilitation constantly looms over the autobiographical report, casting the shadow of an irresolvable *self-testimonial fallacy*.

On the other hand, autobiographical narration is threatened by an opposing movement that inscribes an incurable textual discontinuity in the continual flux of memory through the reflective doubling of the 'I' as subject and object, thus doubling their diegetic roles and rhetorical and epistemological functions, which are interchangeable but not equivalent. The narrative reconfiguration of the 'I' is certainly necessary in order to reunite the plurality of a self splintered by the discontinuity of the passage of time (as asserted by twentieth-century theorists of narrative identity, from A. MacIntyre to P. Ricoeur). Yet it can also simultaneously deepen this plurality as a consequence of the problematic structural nature of narrative truth, of the impending fallacy of reconfiguration itself. The non-coincidence of story and plot, of the factuality of events and their narrative elaboration (facts do not change, but their representation, as cognitive appropriation, represents a seriously fallible interpretation, highly unstable and permanently open to review), exacerbates the distance between the narrated 'I' and the narrating 'I'. It is burdened with the epistemological distance between life and writing, in which it is evident that phenomenological truth depends on its hermeneutically mediated expression but doesn't coincide with the truth of the latter.[4]

Prosopopoeia, the superimposition upon the past 'I' (rendered mute and inanimate by the passage of time) of the present 'I' as a mask that speaks in its stead (placing words in its mouth)[5] is the central figure of autobiographical discourse – and indeed of writing in general, which gives a voice to silence, revealing the irremediable difference between experience and its expression to be the law of sense. The text is a mask: it is interposed between the denoted, what it envisages to signify, and the recipient; but it is also interposed between the denoted and the author (who is co-created by their own text, made an interpretant of their

---

[4] See Alasdair MacIntyre: *After Virtue: A Study in Moral Theory* (1981). 2nd ed. London: Duckworth 1985; Paul Ricoeur: *Temps et Récit*. 3 Vols. Paris: Seuil 1983|1984|1985 and *Soi-même comme un autre*. Paris: Seuil 1990. For a discussion of the limits of the reconfigurative power of narrative from the perspective of personal (and collective) identity, see Teresa Bartolomei: *Figura hujus mundi: Figuras líricas da temporalidade na poesia de Emily Dickinson*. Doctoral Thesis (UL), p. 396 et seq.

[5] Prosopopoeia, de Man claims, is "the fiction of an apostrophe to an absent, deceased, or voiceless entity, which posits the possibility of the latter's reply and confers upon it the power of speech. Voice assumes mouth, eye, and finally face, a chain that is manifest in the etymology of the trope's name, *prosopon poien*, to confer a mask or a face (*prosopon*). Prosopopeia is the trope of autobiography, by which one's name [. . .] is made as intelligible and memorable as a face" (Paul de Man: Autobiography, p. 75–76).

own signification relationship with the signified experience). Autobiography (as the genetic figure of all textuality) "veils", de Man states, a "defacement of the mind of which it is itself the cause" (Paul de Man: Autobiography, p. 81).

The problematic paradox of this hermeneutic circle – by which the condition of meaning given to the subject (only the experience that is represented, narrated, is understood, made known) becomes the very factor that structurally problematises the truth of the meaning in question – is particularly significant in the case of autobiographical discourse. Here, the risk of writing cannibalising life rather than preserving it as memory, and on the other hand of life cannibalising writing (by prioritising self-rehabilitation over narrative truth), may take on grotesquely dramatic proportions. Autobiographies are generally read to discover what the author thinks of themselves, rather than to discover what his life was like. At the end of the day, a good autobiography therefore does not draw a line under biographical research but instead facilitates it by becoming a catalyst for heterobiography.[6]

This problem has been articulated and confronted not only in contemporary times. Indeed, beginning from Plato's *Phaedrus*,[7] it has repeatedly emerged within Western thought; and the reflection that follows, without entering into a historical reconstruction of its *status quaestionis*, seeks quite simply to reveal the centrality of this theme in the construction of the autobiographical monument that is the *Divine Comedy*. The proposal advanced herein is that Dante's work can be read (in one of so many possible ways) as a solution to the epistemological impasse associated with the contradiction inherent in the autobiographical mode of writing, a means to interpret the masked separation and duplication of the 'I' into signifier and signified by a narrator who coincides with the spectator, who is a 'self-witness'. This mechanism of connection and disconnection, which is rhetorically identifiable as prosopopoeia,[8] invigorates the entire *Divine Comedy* in its nature as a confessional discourse, combined with poetic allegory in the classical topos of the journey to the kingdom of the dead. Nevertheless, it is precisely Dante's recourse to this classical and eminently poetic trope[9] of the descent into

---

[6] "The interest of autobiography, then, is not that it reveals reliable self-knowledge – it does not – but that it demonstrates in a striking way the impossibility of coming into being) of all textual systems made up of tropological substitutions" (Paul de Man: Autobiography, p. 71).

[7] As shown by Jacques Derrida: *La dissémination*. Paris: Seuil 1972, p. 69 et seq.

[8] "Therefore I turn to the canzone and under the pretense of teaching her how she must excuse herself, I excuse her; to address inanimate things in this way is a figure of speech, one which the rhetoricians call prosopopoeia and which the poets use quite frequently. This third part begins: My song, it seems you speak contrary" (*Convivio* III, ix, 2).

[9] The topos of the journey to the afterlife was assimilated into medieval hagiographic, parenetic and devotional literature much earlier than Dante, becoming a cornerstone of the edifying hom-

Hell (*nekyia*) and its exploration (*katabasis*)[10] that allows him to position his autobiographical discourse as an apologetic and theological discourse in a paraenetic and prophetic mould. He endows poetic allegory with a new Christian meaning as theological allegory, making his apologetic and confessional report of a profoundly personal event a universal *exemplum salutis*, supported by its investiture as transcendent prophecy.

In formulating the autobiographical account of his conversion and reunion with the beloved woman as a pilgrimage to the afterlife, Dante draws on a deeply pagan symbolic code to redeem his report of any doubt concerning its possible narrative inconsistency and rescue his own reconstruction of the facts from any interpretative problematisation. In doing so, he ensures the illegitimacy of alternative versions of the narrative by articulating his own viewpoint as the Christian vector for the redemptive universalisation of the human condition. The pagan and literary topos of the journey to the afterlife (which, theologically speaking, is spurious and highly suspect)[11] is reconfigured in the *Comedy* as a Christian code through which to reread the individual and contingent experience of existence in universal terms and *sub specie aeternitatis*. The use of prosopopoeia to animate the inanimate object of autobiographical discourse (making the extinct past 'I' speak through the present 'I') functions through the dead, who interact and converse with the present (living) 'I',[12] becoming the voice and agent of the autobiographical narrative that is woven into the account of the otherworldly journey.

The polarity of the 'I' as subject and object, as present and past, underpins the autobiographical discourse and is enhanced by the triangulation of author (Dante the writer), character-*agens*[13] (Dante the pilgrim in the afterlife), and

---

iletic inventory of *exempla salutis* that undoubtedly provided Dante with a great deal of emblematic and doctrinal material. Nevertheless, this contribution seeks to establish that the corpus of medieval 'precursors' was not a poetic model for the *Comedy*, but solely an intertextual library that permitted Dante to relate his autobiographical writing to classical antecedents, as unequivocally indicated by the fact that his guide for the first part of the journey is Virgil, a pagan poet.

10 The journey of Ulysses, who travels only to the shores of Hades, is strictly a *nekyia*, while that of Aeneas (and of Orpheus, Hercules and Theseus) is a fully-fledged *katabasis*.

11 See section III herein.

12 The fact that the pilgrim is living is attested throughout the *Comedy* with an emphasis that is not merely of diegetic importance as proof of the supernatural nature of his journey, but also functions as a metadiegetic guarantee of the truth of the autobiographical report that it carries through the witness of the dead.

13 The Epistle to Can Grande explicitly identifies Dante's duality as agent and author: "(37)(13) The title of the book also is clear. For the title of the whole book is 'Here begins the Comedy', &c., as above; but the title of the part is 'Here begins the third cantica of the Comedy of Dante, which is called Paradise'. (38) (14) These three points, in which the part differs from the whole, having been examined, we may now turn our attention to the other three, in respect of which there is no

empirical *persona* (the terrestrial, historical Dante).[14] The duplication of the 'I' as narrative object, in the form of both the historical *persona* and literary character, does not seek to diminish the truth of the autobiographical account through autofiction, but rather precisely the opposite: to reinforce it through the authority of an external voice, one that cannot be historically contested because it is metatemporal. The poetic *autofiction* Dante exercises in developing an autobiographical narrative presented in the work as a biographical account expressed by the dead (damned, penitent and blessed) in dialogue with the depicted 'I' (in the guise of a character) is what enables the conversion of the empirical 'I' – the object of the confessional representation mediated by its transformation as a literary character (the traveller through the afterlife) – into a metaliterary 'I'-agent, who embodies a universal figure of salvation (the Everyman, *homo viator*) and confers the author-poet with the prophetic status of *scriba dei*. Any possible doubt concerning the autobiographical truth of the empirical 'I' – of the historical Dante whose political, moral and amorous experiences are described to us by the eloquent and loquacious dead, who are remarkably well-informed concerning the terrestrial world – is excluded as a matter of principle.

In this process, the disjunctive reciprocity between universes of discourse that is entailed by prosopopoeia, which oscillates 'indecisively' between truth and fiction, between life and writing,[15] and exposes their proximity as mutual irreducibility,[16] is integrated and stabilised by a metaleptic[17] mechanism of typo-

---

difference between the part and the whole. The author, then, of the whole and of the part is the person mentioned above, who is seen to be such throughout." ("Agens igitur totius et partis est ille qui dictus est, et totaliter videtur esse").

14 On this distinction, see the pioneering essay of Gianfranco Contini: Dante come personaggio-poeta della *Commedia* (1957). In: Id.: *Un'idea di Dante. Saggi danteschi*. Turin: Einaudi (1970 / 1976) 2001, p. 33–62.

15 Is the speaking mask into which the (autobiographical) text converts the transmitted and represented subject a vector of dissimulation, simulation or revelation? Cf. Paul de Man: Autobiography, p. 70.

16 The supernatural prosopopoeic presence of the Commendatore in *Don Giovanni* 'unmasks' the naturalistic illusion of the represented story by exposing, through an eruption of the fantastique, the fiction inherent in the operatic apparatus which is masked by mimetic realism. In its explicit duality, the prosopopoeic mask 'unmasks' the mask of identity activated by the mechanism of mimetic naturalism.

17 "In modern criticism, the term metalepsis is used primarily to indicate shifts between narrative levels: that is, between the world of the narrator and the world that she or he describes. The term as the phenomenon itself is identified already in Servius' commentary on Vergil's *Aeneid* 1. The concept of metalepsis (μετάληψις / *transumptio*) derives originally from the classical rhetorical doctrine of figures of speech. In antiquity, metalepsis refers to a semantic shift by means of tropes like metonymy or synecdoche, or on the basis of synonymy and homonymy.

logical-figural interpretation of Christian origin. It is this that connects ontologically separate worlds (the here and now and the afterlife), temporally distinct planes (the past, present and future), different diegetic agents (narrator, character, extra-textual reference) and different degrees of knowledge.[18] These come together in the poetic fiction of an intradiegetic, homodiegetic character who externalises the textual omniscience of the author with respect to the character, establishing divine historical and existential omniscience with respect to the empirical 'I' that is represented. Dante the author knows the whole truth, not only

---

Thus, in Vergil's "post aliquot mea regna videns mirabor aristas" (after several corn-ears, I shall marvel at seeing my reign: Verg. *Ecl.* 1.69), *aristas* (corn-ears) stands for harvests, harvests for summers, *summers* for years, so *aristas* can be understood as *years*. This shift can be extended to the replacement of what precedes with what follows, and then to the exchange of acting / creating and speaking / representing if poetic discourse is understood performatively. [...] The process of describing the fictional world is therefore replaced by the reality created within that world; and so the boundary between the world of narration and the narrated world is transgressed" (Peter v. Möllendorff: Metalepsis. In: *Oxford Classic Dictionary*). The most complete formulation of metalepsis as a figure linking the field of rhetoric with those of narratology and artistic fiction is offered by Gérard Genette, who summarises it in his 2004 essay of the same name (following an initial formulation in Gérard Genette: *Figures III*. Paris: Seuil 1972, p. 243 et seq.). In demonstrating how the metaleptic encounter of different universes of discourse in the text (and more generally in artistic production) is the semantic key to all mimetic representation, Genette brings to light a far-reaching symbolic mechanism, converting the traditional pair of metaphor and metonymy into a triad where metalepsis is liberated from its traditional classification as a particular instance of metonymy. Genette's position nevertheless suffers from a limitation to theory of fiction that undermines the initial intuition of identifying the referential grammar, the mimetic code applied by a text or work in the metaleptic architecture adopted. This limitation is resolved in more recent elaborations of the concept: "This transgressiveness is the defining characteristic of narrative metalepsis, first identified by Gérard Genette, and which designates a transgression of internally diegetic boundaries by figures and narrator(s). Further elaborations – not least by Genette himself – have resulted in an extension of the concept, so that today any kind of transgressing of narrative boundaries is often understood as a metalepsis" (*Ibidem*). Typological-figural metalepsis (the so-called theory of the four senses, which Dante made his own) can be recognised as the specific metaleptic architecture inherent in the conjunction of Christian biblical hermeneutics as an anthropological-ontological and eschatological paradigm. The transgression of diegetic boundaries in the *Comedy* is articulated as an eschatological transgression of 'natural' ontological boundaries (between the here-and-now and the beyond, past and future, time and eternity).

18 Gérard Genette: *Métalepse: De la figure à la fiction*. Paris: Seuil 2004, p. 104 et seq. isolates the metaleptic dimension of autobiographical discourse with concise brilliance in an implicit critique of the unilateralism of de Man, who reconstructs it exclusively in prosopopoeic terms. For a comprehensive analysis of the integration of prosopopoeic and metaleptic figurality in autobiographical narrative, see Sidonie Smith & Julia Watson: Metalepsis in Autobiographical Narrative. In: *European Journal of Life Writing*, Vol VIII, 1–27 (2019).

of the Dante-character but also the historical Dante, with whom, by the grace of God, he finally coincides at the end of his journey, at the end of the story, acquiring the crystal-clear vision of the dead.

The classical and pagan figure of *katabasis* is, in other words, the symbolic means by which Dante can integrate poetic and theological allegory, prosopopoeia with typological-figural metalepsis: a joining of time and eternity, real life and writing, past and future, in which the rhetorical device acquires ontological depth. In typological-figural metalepsis, the hermeneutic mechanism becomes the metaphysical key to an ontological architecture of history, implying an asymmetrical but structural reciprocity between past and future, historical and eschatological reality, the particular and the universal. The textual artifice of the metaleptic connection between different universes of discourse is expanded to encompass historical and ontological genealogy, exposing the fact that, alongside causality, meaning is a true and full law of the historical being. Typological-figural metalepsis, the allegorical machine on which the entire *Comedy* is based – because it is the foundation of history and the universe itself[19] – rescues prosopopoeia, lyrical-confessional writing, from its impotence as a purely subjective discourse, integrating it with the metaphysical power of a textual tool, allegory, that is recognised not merely as a hermeneutic but also an ontological key.

Dante triumphs in the confessional account of his own life, his autobiographical narration, apologetically oriented towards personal rehabilitation from the ignominy of condemnation and exile and performatively oriented towards reunification with his beloved (a purely virtual and imaginary reunification, but one that is poetically effective). The *Comedy* imposes itself as the irrefutable word of the *scriba dei*, of the prophet who does not offer his own subjective, individual and fallible version of the facts, but transmits the interpretation of his own life as the *littera* of a universal message of salvation received directly from the afterlife.[20]

---

19 See Erich Auerbach: *Dante: Poet of the Secular World*, New York: NYRB Classics (1929|1961) 2007; Figura (1938). Rpt. in: Id. *Time, History, and Literature: Selected Essays of Erich Auerbach*. Edited by James I. Porter. Princeton: Princeton University Press 2014; *Mimesis: The Representation of Reality in Western Literature* (1946). Princeton: Princeton University Press (1955) 2014 (with a New Introduction by E. Said), p. 189 et seq.
20 The principal difference between poetic and theological allegory (as illustrated in *Convivio* I, ii, 3) is not formal but one of content: in theological allegory 1) *littera* always claims historical truth (occasionally, this may also be the case in poetry: Dante treats many mythological stories as factual information); 2) *res gestae* also possess their own allegorical power, are endowed with authentic figural meaning. Theological allegory is *in factis*, poetic allegory is *in verbis*. On the longstanding question of the tension between the two forms of allegory in Dante's work, especially the *Comedy*, see the overview provided Teodolinda Barolini: *The Undivine Comedy: Detheologizing Dante*. Princeton: Princeton University Press 1992, p. 3 et seq. For specific and

The prosopopoeic process of giving a voice to the dead is diegetically literalised as narrative content, without slipping into a fictional evasion of the autobiographical account, through the facilitation of typological-figural metalepsis. This device guarantees that the narrative duplication of the empirical 'I' as the 'I'-protagonist (of the otherworldly journey) remains within the bounds of mimetic description and does not err towards fantastical invention.

While the genesis, mechanism and implications of the *Comedy*'s Christian-rooted, metaleptic-figural allegorical tool are well known and have been widely studied, little analysis has been dedicated to its interaction with the lyrical-confessional prosopopoeic tool (of classical lineage) within the articulation of the *Comedy*'s autobiographical discourse. It is precisely this aspect that will be briefly examined in this essay, where we shall seek in particular to highlight their respective functions – complementary but also contradictory, and not without tension – in constructing the role of the dead as mouthpieces for the author-protagonist's autobiographical account.

1 Presence as the Falsification of the 'I': The Mask of the Text as its Revelation

In an essay on the classical lineage of the *Divine Comedy*, the scholar Stefano Carrai notes that Dante's dead speak like epitaphs, employing expressions that draw directly on classical and medieval Latin funerary epigraphy: "the genre which above all others influenced the poetic language of the *Comedy* is undoubtedly that of the sepulchral epigram" (Carrai 2020, 336).[21]

---

particularly illuminating insights, cf. Robert Hollander: *Allegory in Dante's 'Comedy'*, Princeton: Princeton University Press 1969; Charles S. Singleton: *Dante's* Commedia: *Elements of Structure*. Baltimore and London: John Hopkins University Press (1954) 1977, p. 84 et seq.; Roberto Mazzotta: *Dante, Poet of the Desert*. Princeton: Princeton University Press 1979, p. 227 et seq.; John Freccero: Introduction to Inferno. In: *The Cambridge Companion to Dante*. Edited by Rachel Jacoff. Cambridge UK: Cambridge University Press 1993, p.172–191 (p. 179 et seq.).

21 Stefano Carrai (Dante e la tradizione classica. In: *Dante*. Edited by Robert Rea and Justin Steinberg. Rome: Carocci 2020, p. 329–344) offers a timely review of the epitaphic utterances directed towards Dante by his otherworldy interlocutors: from the entrance of Virgil to Farinata (a "soul who delivers a canonical address to the *viator*", p. 337); from Charles Martel to Bocca degli Abati; from Manfredi to Pier della Vigna, Brunetto Latini, Pia de' Tolomei, Ciacco and Adrian V (p. 338). Among all these characters, recourse to the stereotypical formulae of ancient epigraphy is repeated and multifaceted. "Dante above all knew how to draw on the influence of this obituary tradition by making it the cornerstone of his dialogues, which punctuate the narration of the

Dante travels through the afterlife as if it were a boundless cemetery, pausing to read the inscriptions on the headstones (and making them speak). He is following an itinerary traced by a guide who lives within the graveyard and can never leave it, but who has the authority and expertise to navigate its immense labyrinth. He progresses through a combination of coincidence and causality, with interruptions and encounters decided by his guide – who with didactic precision selects the most prestigious mausoleums, monuments to memorable individuals – as well as spontaneous pauses, prompted by happenstance or the attractive force of singularly conspicuous tombs and particularly eloquent epitaphs. In the course of his cemeterial exploration, the pilgrim evokes the memory of "souls that unto fame are known" (*Paradiso* XVII, 138), along with others who are less well known; he discovers that in one part of the cemetery are gathered those twice dead, who will never be able to leave their destined tombs, while in another are found souls who travel through the graveyard and are desperate to leave it. He finally reaches the tombstone of his agonisingly desired beloved, only to discover that the tomb is empty and that she, along with an elect host of her fellows, is even more alive than him, in a radical inversion of earthly coordinates (the body obeys the soul, space is but an appearance, linear time is condensed in the absolute present) encapsulated in the verb "passing beyond the human" ("trasumanar") (*Paradiso* I, 70).

Through speaking with the dead, listening to their autobiographical confessions and their historical, political, philosophical and doctrinal lessons, Dante also gathers biographical revelations concerning himself. These range from descriptions of his past errors (by Virgil and Beatrice) and exceptional merits (by Brunetto, but also Virgil, Beatrice and Cacciaguida) to *ex post* prophecies concerning his turbulent political and existential experiences.[22] His exile, which he

---

prophetic journey and the otherworld pilgrim's encounters with the souls of the deceased. [. . .] As a consequence, it becomes clear that the construction of the poem's protagonist and authorial alter ego is at least in part influenced by the figure of the *viator*, typical of the epigraphic-sepulchral canon, who follows a road scattered with tombs and pauses from time to time to read the words inscribed on the tombstones in a kind of ideal dialogue with the dead" (p. 339).

22 Ciacco's indirect prophecy refers to the outcome of the struggle between Florentine political factions, which would have dire consequences for Dante's personal circumstances (*Inferno* VI, 58–75). Direct prophecies concerning the poet's individual vicissitudes include those of Farinata degli Uberti (*Inferno* X, 77–81); Brunetto Latini (*Inferno* XV, 61–64); Vanni Fucci (*Inferno* XXIV, 140–142); Corrado Malaspina (*Purgatorio* VIII 133–139); and Oderisi da Gubbio (*Purgatorio* XI, 137–139). The entirety of *Paradiso* XVII constitutes a broad prophetic depiction in which Dante's ancestor Cacciaguida 'foretells' the poet's destiny of political exile, interpreting it as providential design and thus sealing the elevation of his self-understanding from "exul immeritus" to prophet.

had already endured for some time when the work was written, is announced through the backdating of the journey to 1300, less than a year before his condemnation in January 1301: a diachronic manipulation of memory through divinatory anticipation, reinforcing the truth of his autobiographical narration of facts and the providential interpretation that the poem provides.

Reading the *Comedy*, we essentially find ourselves within a poetic universe that, beyond its substantial differences, is directly connected to that evoked by Wordsworth in his three essays dedicated to burial inscriptions: the celebrated *Essays upon Epitaphs* (1810). The manifesto of a poetics that juxtaposes the classicist register of satire, whose key trope is antithesis (polemically embodied by Pope), with the romantic register of the inclusive and not totalising compatibility of contradictions, whose key trope is prosopopoeia, Wordsworth's three essays are themselves, as Paul de Man observes in his analysis, an "exemplar autobiographical text" (Paul de Man: Autobiography, p. 72). The work "turns compulsively from an essay upon epitaphs to being itself an epitaph and, more specifically, the author's own monumental inscription or autobiography" (*Ibidem*). This twisting of Wordsworth's text from critical-descriptive analysis of a literary form, the epitaph as an exemplary condensation of (auto)biographical writing into the confessional implementation of this discourse, is reconstructed by de Man beginning from Wordsworth's autobiographical-literary identification with figures of deprivation throughout his work (vagabonds, cripples, blind beggars, dying children). In the essays, such figures are brought together in the character of a deaf man who seeks to compensate for his inability to hear the sounds of nature by reading books. The entire autobiographical discourse, de Man argues, moves in reality from an experience of (existential and temporal) deprivation by establishing itself as an operation of "self-restoration", of reintegrating an 'I' wounded and wearied by adverse personal circumstances or simply the passage of time, the entropic attrition of that finite resource that is the individual's life. This "restorative need", de Man observes, is at the root of the peculiar performative connotation that characterises autobiographical writing in general, which is never a simple descriptive account in a confessional mould but rather a vector of precise practical demands: "Writers *of* autobiographies as well as writers *on* autobiography are obsessed by the need to move from cognition to resolution and to action, from speculative to political and legal authority" (*Ibidem*, p. 71). This, moreover, is the insight that underpins the work of Philippe Lejeune, one of the fathers of studies on this subject:[23] autobiography "is not only representational and cognitive but contractual" (*Ibidem*).

---

23 See Philippe Lejeune: *Le Pacte autobiographique* (1975). Paris: Seuil 1996.

The restorative and not purely descriptive strategy of autobiographical discourse justifies the paradoxical thesis of Wordsworth's three studies, according to which such discourse finds its most effective realisation not in narrative account but in the epitaph: a permanent inscription of the 'I' in the terrain of the present; a textual incorporation of each human being's memory as a declaration of immortality, *beyond* the threadbare condition of mortality attested by the tomb. In the epitaph (and in portraiture), in verbal (or figurative) inscription, upon the stone that guards their body: here, the deceased is once more given a voice, a tool of self-representation. It is for this reason that "the dominant figure of the epitaphic or autobiographical discourse is, as we saw, the prosopopoeia, the fiction of the voice-from-beyond-the-grave" (*Ibidem*, p. 74).[24]

Come, perché di lor memoria sia,	As, on the lids of pavement tombs, there are
sovra i sepolti le tombe terragne	stone effigies of what the buried were
portan segnato quel ch'elli eran pria,	before, so that the dead may be remembered;
onde lì molte volte si ripiagne	and there, when memory – inciting only
per la puntura de la rimembranza,	the pious – has renewed their mourning, men
che solo a' pïi dà de le calcagne;	are often led to shed their tears again

(*Purgatorio* XII, 16–21)

The epitaph or portrait (photograph, bas-relief) is an 'effigy' of what the deceased once was; it is the signifier through which their life is transmitted as the signified, endowing their memory with an emotionally engaging force that underlines and at the same time lessens their absence (remembrance shortens the distance, but also

---

24 In a sophisticated reading of de Man's essay on autobiography, which is simultaneously textual analysis, biography and autobiography, Jacques Derrida: *Mémoires pour Paul de Man*. Paris: Seuil 1988, p. 27 et seq.) develops a reflection on the intrinsically "mournful", "funerary" dimension of all biographical and autobiographical discourse, in so far as it is the textual inscription of the intrinsic finitude of the subject and their relations with the other, of the "non-totalisability of every act of memory". In this sense, Derrida observes, "tout ce que nous inscrivons dans le présent vivant de notre rapport aux autres porte déjà, toujours, une signature de *mémoires d'outre-tombe*. Mais cette finitude, qui est aussi la finitude de la mémoire, n'a pas d'abord la forme d'une *limite*, d'une capacité, d'une aptitude ou d'une faculté limitée, d'un pouvoir borné, limite qui nous pousserait à multiplier les signes testamentaires, les traces, les hypogrammes, les *hypomnemata*, les signatures et les épitaphes, les *mémoires* autobiographiques. Non, elle ne peut prendre cette forme que par la trace de l'autre en nous, sa préséance irréductible, autrement dit la trace tout court, qui est toujours trace de l'autre, finitude de la mémoire, et donc venir ou souvenir du futur. S'il y a une finitude de la mémoire, c'est parce qu'il y a de l'autre, et de la mémoire comme mémoire de l'autre, qui vient de l'autre et revient à l'autre. Elle défie toute totalisation et nous voue à une scène de l'allégorie, à une fiction de prosopopée, autrement dit à des tropologies du deuil: mémoire du deuil et deuil de la mémoire " (*Ibidem*, p. 49–50).

intensifies its weight). When we speak of epitaphs, we do not simply speak of dead women and men. Rather, we allow the dead to speak; and at the same time, we speak of ourselves as beings relentlessly posthumous to ourselves, needing to regain the voice and face, at least virtually, of "what we were before", becoming masks animated by the same inanimate version of ourselves buried in the tomb of the past. Whoever speaks of epitaphs (or of writing in general) becomes their own epitaph, inscribing their end in writing in order to re-establish themselves in the memories of those who have access to the text, to the inscription, as an inextinguishable voice capable of giving "tears when memory has renewed their mourning".

But what "memory"? That determined by the deceased, or by those who remain? Epitaphs, Wordsworth observes, fluctuate between two forms: those that speak in the first person and those that give voice to survivors; and for him the second are the happier, since they avoid the "tender fiction"[25] of the voice from beyond the grave that risks condemning the living to death by petrification, since it restores not only the memory of the deceased but establishes the inexorable superiority of those from whom death has not taken the final and greatest word (like the Shakespeare of Milton's poetry). Having the last word with respect to oneself, control over one's own memory and the "effigy of what one was before", is the fundamental objective of autobiographical discourse, of the epitaph. It is by definition written on stone to ensure that the word of the deceased will not mortally fade away, but will await the immortality of the 'I' that is only ostensibly imprisoned in the tomb (from which it can lead the living "to shed their tears again").

---

[25] "These sensations and judgments, acted upon perhaps unconsciously, have been one of the main causes why epitaphs so often personate the deceased, and represent him as speaking from his own tomb-stone. The departed Mortal is introduced telling you himself that his pains are gone; that a state of rest is come; and he conjures you to weep for him no longer. He admonishes with the voice of one experienced in the vanity of those affections which are confined to earthly objects, and gives a verdict like a superior Being, performing the office of a judge, who has no temptations to mislead him, and whose decision cannot but be dispassionate. Thus is death disarmed of its sting, and affliction unsubstantialised. By this tender fiction, the survivors bind themselves to a sedater sorrow, and employ the intervention of the imagination in order that the reason may speak her own language earlier than she would otherwise have been enabled to do. This shadowy interposition also harmoniously unites the two worlds of the living and the dead by their appropriate affections. And it may be observed, that here we have an additional proof of the propriety with which sepulchral inscriptions were referred to the consciousness of immortality as their primal source.

[.] This latter mode, namely, that in which the survivors speak in their own persons, seems to me upon the whole greatly preferable: as it admits a wider range of notices; and, above all, because, excluding the fiction which is the ground-work of the other, it rests upon a more solid basis", William Wordsworth: Upon Epitaphs (from *The Friend*, Feb. 22.1810). In: *The Prose Work of William Wordsworth*. Vol. II (London 1876). New York: AMS Press, Inc 1967, p. 24–75 (p. 39).

The pact with the recipient that underpins every autobiographical discourse[26] points precisely towards this posthumous (prosopopoeic) control of memory of the self by establishing the author themselves as the guarantee of the credibility of their own self-representation. This guarantee is nevertheless founded on a hermeneutic circle that is not lacking in vicious redundancy (the autobiographical testimony's content is the material proof of the testimony's credibility, adopted in order to achieve the requested trust; but this credibility is a prerequisite for belief in the content of the testimony) and its efficacy is relative: the coincidence between the judicial figures of witness and defendant (the "person judged")[27] produced in 'self-testimony' leads, as a matter of principle, to suspicion concerning the interested party's version of the facts. The prosopopoeic operation implied by self-narration is called into question by the recipient as a "fiction" (perhaps a "tender" one), and in order to reach the truth of the facts and their interpretation it is preferable to resort to alternative sources: the testimony of survivors is generally considered more trustworthy than that of the deceased. Such is the *self-testimonial fallacy* that afflicts every confessionally or historiographically autobiographical statement.

This condition of the structural problematisation of epitaphic truth transmitted in the first person can develop into a painful existential crisis when the self-witness is not only virtually but actually 'indicted': that is, when a specific personal event of destabilising dissonance directly enables the restorative application of autobiographical testimony in order to right a presumably suffered wrong, reinstate a presumably denied truth, or help the interested party to redeem themselves from what is felt to be a grave injustice, a slanderous falsehood. The impotence of the self-witness, the resistance of the recipients of the self-representation, may become a tragic personal threat for those who find themselves in a particularly acute situation of deprivation, of existential isolation and 'mutilation' deriving from misunderstanding or genuine personal calamities:

> 12. Veramente, al principale intendimento tornando, dico, come è toccato di sopra, per necessarie cagioni lo parlare di sè è conceduto: e intra l'altre necessarie cagioni due sono più manifeste. 13. L'una è quando sanza ragionare di sè grande infamia o pericolo non si può

---

[26] See Philippe Lejeune: *Pacte*, p. 13–46.

[27] Every autobiographical discourse, Dante piercingly remarks in his reflection on the question in the opening of the *Convivio*, establishes a dynamic of judgment that places the subject of the confessional discourse in the position of "person judged" with respect to the recipient, who automatically becomes "the one who judges": "(2) I say then that there are three reasons why a man's presence makes him less worthy than he really is. The first of these is immaturity, and I do not mean of age but of mind; the second is envy--and these two reside in the one who judges; the third is human imperfection--and this resides in the person judged" (*Convivio* I, iv, 2).

cessare; e allora si concede, per la ragione che de li due sentieri prendere lo men reo è quasi prendere un buono. E questa necessitate mosse Boezio di se medesimo a parlare, acciò che sotto pretesto di consolazione escusasse la perpetuale infamia del suo essilio, mostrando quello essere ingiusto, poi che altro escusatore non si levava. 14. L'altra è quando, per ragionare di sè, grandissima utilitade ne segue altrui per via di dottrina; e questa ragione mosse Agustino ne le sue Confessioni a parlare di sè, chè per lo processo de la sua vita, lo quale fu di [non] buono in buono, e di buono in migliore, e di migliore in ottimo, ne diede essemplo e dottrina, la quale per sì vero testimonio ricevere non si potea. 15. Per che se l'una e l'altra di queste ragioni mi scusa, sufficientemente lo pane del mio formento è purgato de la prima sua macula. Movemi timore d'infamia, e movemi desiderio di dottrina dare la quale altri veramente dare non può.16. Temo la infamia di tanta passione avere seguita, quanta concepe chi legge le sopra nominate canzoni in me avere segnoreggiata; la quale infamia si cessa, per lo presente di me parlare, interamente, lo quale mostra che non passione ma vertù sia stata la movente cagione. (*Convivio* I , ii, 12–16)[28]

Teaching others, transmitting useful and important doctrine through the example of one's own life, and seeking to bring an end to a great infamy or looming danger: these are the two reasons that justify autobiographical discourse, observes the proemial Dante of the *Convivio*. Here, he combines didactic, parenetic ambition (the "desire" to present his own life as "example and instruction") with a burning "fear of infamy" linked to an urgent need for self-restoration: to save his skin (averting a grave "danger") and his own name, to defend his honour as a man and as a writer in the face of a devastating injustice, an undeserved exile, and a ruinous hermeneutic error (the interpretation of his poetic work as the fruit of passion rather than virtue, as blind love poetry rather than the

---

28 (12) To return to the main topic, however, I say that (as touched on above) speaking about oneself is allowed in cases of necessity, and among the several cases of necessity two are very evident. (13) One is when great infamy or danger cannot be avoided except by talking about oneself; then it is permissible, for the reason that to take the less evil of two paths is almost the same as taking a good one. This necessity moved Boethius to speak of himself, so that under the pretext of consolation he might defend himself against the perpetual infamy of his exile, by showing it to be unjust, since no other apologist came forward. (14) The other arises when by speaking of oneself very great benefit comes to another by way of instruction; and this reason moved Augustine to speak of himself in his *Confessions*, because by the progress of his life, which proceeded from bad to good, good to better, and better to best, he gave us an example and instruction which could not be provided by any other testimony so true as this. (15) Consequently, if each of these reasons may serve as my excuse, the bread made from my wheat is sufficiently cleansed of its first impurity. A fear of infamy moves me, and a desire to give instruction moves me, which in truth others are unable to give. (16) I fear the infamy of having yielded myself to the great passion that anyone who reads the canzoni mentioned above must realise once ruled me. This infamy will altogether cease as I speak now about myself and show that my motivation was not passion but virtue.

poetry of "salvation").[29] Like Boethius before him, "since no other apologist came forward", Dante must take the stand to defend his own poetry and his own 'good name', which has been stained by the unjust punishment of exile and poverty (*Convivio* I, iii, 3) and the "cheapening" ("invilimento") of his person and work resulting from such disgrace (*Ibidem*, 5). He must do so with "difficulty"[30] and in a new way, because all previous efforts in this regard have not only failed, but have in fact been counterproductive: "Therefore since, as has been said above, I have presented myself to virtually everyone in Italy, by which I have perhaps made myself more base than truth warrants, not only to those to whom my fame had already spread but also to others, whereby my works as well as my person are without doubt made light of" (*Convivio* I, iv, 13).[31]

The problem with this task of self-rehabilitation, Dante observes, is that a presence is damaging to fame. According to this remark he develops a brief yet extraordinary treatise on the falsification of personality produced by "presence", the immediacy of an interhuman relationship not filtered through the distancing

---

29 In the *De vulgari eloquentia*, Dante claims to be a poet of "integrity" ("rettitudine"), juxtaposing love poetry (whose object is the "most important thing" to achieve pleasure: physical love) and the poetry of virtue, which in the *Divine Comedy* will be exalted in an identification that recasts salvation as a merging together of what is "useful", "pleasurable" and "good": "But we must discuss what these things of greatest importance may be. To begin with what is useful: here, if we carefully ponder the goal of all those who seek what is useful, we will find that it is nothing other than their own well-being. Secondly, what is pleasurable: here I say that what is most pleasurable is what is the most highly valued object of our desires; and this is love. Thirdly, what is good: and here no-one will doubt that the most important thing is virtue. So these three things, well-being, love, and virtue, appear to be those most important subjects that are to be treated in the loftiest style; or at least this is true of the themes most closely associated with them, prowess in arms, ardour in love, and control of one's own will. (9) On these themes alone, if I remember rightly, we find that illustrious individuals have written poetry in the vernacular: Bertran de Born on arms, Arnaut Daniel on love, Giraut de Borneil on integrity; Cino da Pistoia on love, his friend on integrity." (*De vulgari eloquentia* II,II, 8–9).

30 "Now that my bread has been cleansed on the one side, it is necessary for me to cleanse it on the other to escape a censure of this kind, for my writing, which can almost be called a commentary, is intended to remove the defect of the canzoni mentioned above, and this may itself prove to be perhaps a little difficult in part. This *difficulty* is deliberate here so as to escape a greater defect, and is not due to a lack of knowledge" ("E però che lo mio pane è purgato da una parte, convienlomi purgare da l'altra, per fuggire questa riprensione, che lo mio scritto, che quasi comento dir si può, è ordinato a levar lo difetto de le canzoni sopra dette, ed esso per sè fia forse in parte alcuna un poco duro. La qual *durezza*, per fuggir maggiore difetto, non per ignoranza, è qui pensata") (*Convivio* I, iii, 2).

31 "Onde con ciò sia cosa che, come detto è di sopra, io mi sia quasi a tutti li Italici apprensentato, per che fatto mi sono più vile forse che 'l vero non vuole non solamente a quelli a li quali mia fama era già corsa, ma eziandio a li altri, onde le mie cose sanza dubbio meco sono alleviate".

protection of the word ("I say then that there are three reasons why a man's presence makes him less worthy than he really is", *Ibidem*, 2).[32] The audience of an 'in-person' autobiographical discourse do not give it credit because the absence of any distance between self and self-representation is damaging to that discourse, to fame, and to the reception of the authentic interpretation of meaning signified by personality and existential history. In this perspective, the textual caesura between the narrating and narrated 'I', the prosopopoeic mask with which the 'I' reanimates the past 'I', represents a tool of performative success: apologetic discourse *pro domo sua* rarely registers a hit when it lacks the distancing protection of textual mediation. The "presence" of the 'I' before oneself and others must be overcome through the textual distance that writing guarantees. Such disjunctive inscription is necessary to re-establish personal truth, since "presence diminishes the good and the evil in everyone more than truth warrants" (*Ibidem*, 12).[33] Without the prosopopoeic mask of confessional-autobiographical discourse, without an epitaph inscribed in the stone of writing, the subject's authenticity is not recognised by others or even by the subject themselves, because of the congenital impurity that "blemishes every person" ("macula ogni uomo") (*Ibidem*, 9–11).

The confessional text is a restorative buffer for both Dante the poet (it is necessary to "remove the defect of the canzoni mentioned above", III, 2) and Dante the man, the victim of a historical and political disgrace that has stripped him of his dignity twice over, inducing those who witnessed his fall to lay the blame for it at his door ("displaying against my will the wound of fortune for which the wounded one is often unjustly accustomed to be held accountable", *Ibidem* 4).

The Dante of the *Convivio* is a "wounded" man who is tired of displaying his own wound, his mutilation, and is therefore predisposed to donning a "difficult" textual mask behind which his "presence" can hide in order to reveal the truth of his own life and work ("the true meaning [. . .] hidden beneath the figure of allegory", *Convivio* I, ii, 17).

This confessional exercise, which combines Augustinian doctrinal parenesis with Boethian self-rehabilitation, will prove altogether inadequate as a means of restoration. The *Convivio* brings no resolution on either a literary or a biographical level. The path of philosophical lyric does not lead its author to the longed-for destination of a "poetry of virtue" transformed into an authentic "poetry of salvation" (following the distinction drawn in the *De vulgari eloquentia*);[34] neither

---

[32] "Dico adunque che per tre cagioni la presenza fa la persona di meno valore ch'ella non è".
[33] La "presenza ristringe lo bene e lo male in ciascuno più che 'l vero non vuole".
[34] The *Divine Comedy* 'returns' to love poetry, following the philosophical departure enacted in the *Convivio*, by reembracing the central theological thesis of the *Vita nuova* concerning the salvific potential of human love (see Lino Leonardi: Dante e la tradizione lirica. In: Robert Rea

does it allow him to gain the "greater authority" (*Convivio* I, iv, 13) needed to bring the painful infamy of exile to a close and return him to the "sweet bosom" of "the most beautiful and famous daughter of Rome, Florence", there to rest "my weary mind and to complete the span of time that is given to me" (*Convivio* I, iii, 4).

Dante is poetically delegitimised by the "defect" attributed to his literary production and his inability to re-establish his own biographical truth in the eyes of his contemporaries (and even in his own eyes, due to the "shadow", the "blemish" – "macula"–, marring the clarity of his self-perception, his own "presence" and lack of distance from himself);[35] he is literally "lost" ("Truly I have been a ship without sail or rudder, brought to different ports, inlets, and shores by the dry wind that painful poverty blows", *Convivio* I, iii, 5). He must seek an alternative textual key, another prosopopoeic mask to negate the biographically falsifying effect of his own presence, the historical immanence of the empirical 'I'.

This new way will be opened up by classical poetry. Emerging from the shadows of lengthy obscurity ("one who seemed faint because of the long silence", *Inferno* I, 63), Virgil "appears before the eyes" (62) of Dante to offer him "another path" by which he might "leave this savage wilderness" (93) of the desperation associated with his tragic condition of exile poverty, infamy and moral disorientation. The authenticating distance of autobiographical truth established by textual mediation must be radicalised. The prosopopoeic mask of the past

---

and Justin Steinberg (eds): *Dante*, p. 354 –361). In this sense, as Teodolinda Barolini observes, "The *Commedia* is a poem of epic dimension, epic scale, and yet it is also the most lyric of epics: it is the epic of the "I". The autobiographical and amorous essence of the poem is the mark "of a lyric past that [Dante] chose never to leave behind" (p. 32, in: Dante and the Lyric Past. In: Rachel Jacoff [ed.]: *Cambridge Companion to Dante*, p. 14–33).

35 "9. La terza ["cagione" per cui la presenza fa la persona di meno valore ch'ella non è] si è l'umana impuritade, la quale si prende da la parte di colui ch'è giudicato, e non è sanza familiaritade e conversazione alcuna. Ad evidenza di questa, è da sapere che l'uomo è da più parti maculato, e come dice Agustino, nullo è sanza macula. [. . .] 11. E queste macule alcuna ombra gittano sopra la chiarezza de la bontade, sì che la fanno parere men chiara e men valente. [. . .] 12. E questa terza cagione può essere così nel male come nel bene, se le cose de la sua ragione si volgano ciascuna in suo contrario. Per che manifestamente si vede che per impuritate, sanza la quale non è alcuno, la presenza ristringe lo bene e lo male in ciascuno più che 'l vero non vuole" (Convivio I, iv, 9, 11–12). "(9) The third ["cause" for which the presence of a person reduces their worth] is human imperfection, which attaches to him who is judged and does not obtain without some familiarity and intimacy with him. To make this clear, we must observe that man is blemished in many ways, for as Augustine says, 'no one is without blemish'. [. . .] (11) These blemishes cast a shadow on the brightness of his goodness, so that they make it seem less bright and less worthy. [. . .] (12) This third cause may obtain for evil as well as for good, if each term in the argument is turned to its opposite. Thus it is clearly seen that because of imperfection, from which no man is free, presence diminishes the good and the evil in everyone more than truth warrants".

'I' reanimated by the present 'I', of the dead man who speaks from the tomb of the past: this must be exteriorised, resituating the autobiographical narrative in the mouths of other dead souls, third parties, metatemporal witnesses who are therefore beyond questioning on the grounds of the truth of that narrative. The textual distance from the *presence* of the empirical 'I' produced by writing, which was adopted systematically in the *Convivio*, is reimagined in the *Comedy* as metaphysical distance. It is a literary ruse that extracts the posthumous relationship between the narrating / present 'I' and the narrated / past 'I' from the plane of immanence and transfers it to external witnesses, who guarantee that the author's self-testimony will receive the absolute credibility reserved for an annunciation *sub specie aeternitatis*.

This is the solution proposed by classical *katabasis*. In order to know who he is and where he must go, what to do with his own life, which path to take (as in the case of Ulysses) and its meaning (as for Aeneas) – in short, to discover his own autobiographical truth – the hero must descend into the underworld to question the souls that inhabit it, whose metahistorical knowledge of history transmits a prophetically infallible vision of existential events.

By converting the autobiographical strategy of the *Convivio* with its twofold parenetic-doctrinal (Augustine) and rehabilitative (Boethius) appeal into *katabasis*, a journey into the afterlife, Dante surmounts the deficit of credibility resulting from the *self-testimonial fallacy*, from the coincidence of "judged" and "judge". He divides the object-narrated 'I' into the historical-empirical 'I' and the literary-character 'I', the latter of which becomes a witness to the testimony concerning the empirical 'I' that is provided by the dead when they are encountered and questioned (up to the autobiographical apotheosis of the encounter with his ancestor Cacciaguida in *Paradiso* XV–XVII). The dead speak with the "greater authority" of the prophetic power conferred upon the inhabitants of eternity by virtue of their eschatological position (regardless of whether they are damned, penitent or blessed: their historical clear-sightedness is independent from their moral status).[36]

---

[36] In their magisterial reconstruction of Dante's life beginning from the autobiographical thread interwoven with his writings, Elisa Brilli, and Giuliano Milani (*Vite nuove. Biografia e autobiografia di Dante*. Rome: Carocci 2021) suggest a characterisation of the *Comedy* under the category of 'testament', in contrast to the polarity of monumental and documentary approaches into which 'biographical' readings of the work have traditionally been divided. To this end, they underline how the *Comedy* moves beyond the model of self-textualisation and self-commentary characteristic of the poet's mature works, returning instead to "narration of self" along the lines of *Vita Nuova*. The interpretation of the *Comedy* as an epitaph that we propose here emphasises the poet's narrative doubling, by which the "narration of self" intersects with a "narration of him" constructed through a metahistorical lens, in a solution of radical continuity that claims to be

2 Two Models of Katabasis, Concerning the Hero and the Author, and their Christianisation in the *Comedy*

Dante's adoption of the literary device of *katabasis* as a radical reformulation of his own autobiographical discourse presents him with two problems: one theological and one poetic. The first is that this model of classical lineage is fundamentally antichristian; the second that its epic formulation (relating to a hero searching for the truth of his own life) implies a departure from the love poetry that the experiment of the *Convivio* purported to reclaim, not with entirely satisfactory results, by rescuing a philosophically instituted "poetry of virtue" from the limited "poetry of passion". To resolve these issues, Dante implements a revolutionary twofold strategy, both theological and literary, in order to Christianise the classical model.

First of all, he integrates the epic model of the *katabic* hero, who descends into underworld to discover his own biographical truth, with the lyrical, Orphic model of the *katabic* author,[37] one who here, however, descends into the underworld not to save but to be saved, not to reclaim who or what he loves from death but rather, through death, to find a form of eternal life. The author writes not to produce a memory of his life that will be devoured by the all-consuming hunger of Chronos, but rather to transfigure human memory into a transcendent vision. In this way, the lyrical model of *katabasis* is Christianised by Dante through an inversion of the logic of the action of salvation: Beatrice, the Christian Eurydice, does not have to be brought back to life on earth. It is the 'dead' Beatrice who must return the lost poet to the life of Grace, for he is at risk of losing eternal life. In this reversal of roles, the *katabasis* of the author is Christianised while avoiding poetic dryness, the erotic aridity of the allegorisation of Eurydice as the very

---

more than mere textual artifice. This difference does not pertain to philological reconstruction of the poet's biographical history, but it is essential from a textual perspective: the separation of the two narrative perspectives is the poetic device through which the *Comedy* is born.

37 In the *De vulgari eloquentia*, Dante explicitly assimilates the figure of katabasis to the office of the poet by adopting and allegorically adapting the advice of the Cumaean Sybil to Aeneas (*Aeneid* VI, 126–131) concerning the difficulty of returning from the underworld. Poets are the chosen loved by God, or exalted by their own ardent virtue, who succeed in returning from their otherworldly journey: "And those who succeed are those whom the author of the Aeneid, in the sixth book, calls God's beloved, raised to the heavens by their ardent virtue and made the children of God – though he is speaking figuratively." "Et hii sunt quos Poeta Eneidorum sexto Dei dilectos et ab ardente virtute sublimatos ad ethera deorumque filios vocat, quanquam figurate loquatur" (*De vulgari eloquentia* II, IV 10).

soul of the poet, led astray by sin, that besets traditional Christian re-readings of the Orphic paradigm – which Dante certainly borrows from Boethius and his interpreters,[38] while nevertheless reinvigorating them with his incomparable literary intelligence. The Dante of the *Comedy* goes in search of Beatrice, knowing that reuniting with her will be the salvation of a soul placed at risk by his moral, spiritual and literary crisis. At the same time, he is firm in his conviction that this search will itself be the source of a new artistic register. The pilgrim of the afterlife is a poet convinced that love will save both his soul and his writing; who sees the conversion of "poetry of passion" to "poetry of virtue" not as erotic and literary abdication, but an opportunity to transform his own "passion" into a supreme condition of spiritual and artistic achievement, a condition of "salvation" and poetic greatness.

Having guaranteed the assimilation of epic, heroic *katabasis* with love poetry through its integration with a Christianised version of the lyrical *katabasis* of the author, the Dante of the *Comedy* next proceeds to neutralise the transgressive potential of classical *katabasis* in relation to Christianity. He does so through a metaleptic device of a typological-figural nature of New Testament origin, which ensures the biographical rehabilitation of the epic hero in the key of Christian prophecy. Renewing an exegetic tradition of late antiquity in which pagan providentialism is recast as prophetic anticipation of Christianity – beginning in particular from Virgil's *Aeneid* and *Eclogue* IV[39] – Dante cleanses the model of epic *katabasis* of its theologally transgressive burden (a contravention of the Christian prohibition of divination, summoning the dead and communicating with the afterlife). This is achieved through a typological interpretation that converts the separation of past, present and future, of terrestrial and eschatological condition, history and eternity, into the semantic interdependence of its anticipatory meaning.

The adoption of the classical and pagan model of *katabasis* radically differentiates the *Comedy* from the medieval canon of visions and narrations of the afterlife (the most emblematic being the *Voyage of Saint Brendan the Abbot*), all

---

[38] The allegorical rereading of the figure of Orpheus as a sinner who falls back into sin when he looks behind himself, developed in the final carmen of the third book of the *De consolatione philosophiae* (XII. 49–58), would be resumed by numerous later commentators. On this tradition see Stefano Carrai, Tradizione classica, p. 340 et seq.

[39] On the risks and structural limitations of the Christianisation of the classical and especially Virgilian model, with the fluctuations and ambiguity that characterise Dante's relationships with the Virgil character (or "source") throughout the *Comedy*, see Kevin Brownlee (Dante and the Classical Poets. In: Rachel Jacoff [ed.]: *Cambridge Companion to Dante*, p. 100–119) and Teodolinda Barolini: *Dante's Poets: Textuality and Truth in the Comedy*. Princeton: Princeton University Press 1984, p. 201.

of which are essentially conceived in an allegorical manner, a laborious means of respecting the taboo of necromancy and divination central to the Judeo-Christian tradition. In this religious context, speaking with the dead has been stigmatised as an extremely serious sin since the episode of the damned king Saul (the great intertext of Shakespeare's *Macbeth*), who on the eve of the battle in which he will lose his kingdom and life, despairing at the lack of any prophetic guide following the death of Samuel, asks the Witch of Endor to summon the spirit of the prophet himself (1 Samuel 28:3–25). Similarly, in the gospel parable of the Rich Man (Luke 16:19–31) the parenetic utility of any form of contact between living and dead is repudiated: the living will not believe the word of a dead man if they have not believed that of the prophets ("the great chasm" that separates Paradise from Hell and the kingdom of the dead from that of the living cannot be crossed, *Ibidem*, p. 26). Medieval literature of the journey to the afterlife is thus configured as a parenetic anthology of *exempla salutis* (the eschatological vision of reward and punishment for earthly conduct is an incentive for virtue and the search for salvation) in which the transgressive dimension of a direct and personal relationship with deceased souls is generally avoided, set aside in favour of a neutral and abstract description of otherworldly suffering and glory in a rigidly allegorical mould. The register of the narrative is descriptive, rather than dramatic: with few exceptions (most notably St Brendan's conversation with Judas Iscariot),[40] there is no interaction between the traveller and the souls who are witnessed, no cognitive exchange between the two worlds. The kingdom of the dead remains a simple object of experience for the living traveller, who in turn is not experienced by the dead. The visionary aspect of the account generally remains disassociated from any divinatory dimension (fortune telling) or prophetic proclamation (with the partial exception of the apocryphal text of the *Visio Sancti Pauli*),[41] and above all from any autobiographical or confessional relevance. In contrast, classical episodes of *nekyia* and *katabasis* are endowed with genuine dramatic action, as well as cognitive and practical exchange between this world and the next: the living traveller speaks with the dead, is known and recognised by them, seeks to obtain personal information of a divinatory nature (Ulysses and Aeneas) which may reveal predestination (Aeneas), and in certain cases (Hercules, Theseus, Orpheus) even actively intervenes to remove a human or divine being from the underworld (Cerberus, Persephone, Eurydice).

---

40 See in *La leggenda di S. Brandano* (in Pasquale Villari [ed.]: *Antiche leggende e tradizioni che illustrano la Divina commedia* [1848]. Bologna: Forni 1979 [fascimile reproduction of the 1865 edition], p. 118 et seq.) the chapter dedicated to this singular encounter: "How they met Judas Iscariot, who was sitting on a rock in the middle of the sea" (*Ibidem*, p. 129 et seq.).

41 See Pasquale Villari (ed.), *Antiche leggende*, p. 114 et seq.

It is this dramatic dynamic that Dante reintroduces, borrowing it directly from the classical model as an alternative to its medieval counterpart. Dante 'speaks with the dead', listens to them and makes them listen to him, questions them about his own future. Such a relationship would constitute sinful practice of necromancy and divination were it not justified by the prophetic predestination that makes him a new Paul and is articulated in the typological-figural character of the narrative, constructed as a metaleptic bridge between earthly and celestial life, between history and eternity, between present, past and future. It reveals the true meaning of earthly life, manifested in the eschatological fulfilment conferred upon it by divine judgment on the plane of eternity.

The prophetic redemption of the truth of the autobiographical account that is guaranteed by its provenance – by the fact that the Dante character hears it spoken by the dead and relates it not in the first person but second-hand (through a deceased intermediary) – is possible within the *Comedy* because this poetic repositioning corresponds to theological truth revealed by typological-figural metalepsis.[42] The poet's prosopopoeic allegory[43] develops into the metaleptic

---

[42] Simone Marchesi (The Poet in the Mirror: Epic and Autobiography in Dante's Inferno. In: *Sacred Heart University Review*, Vol. 24: Iss. 1, Article 5 [2010]) observes that the autobiographical "project of writing" (in a 'romance' mould) and that of epic writing (in a classical mould) are clearly characterised as two distinct canons, to be kept separate, in Dante's production prior to the *Divine Comedy*, yet converge in his paradoxical project of an autobiographical epic. The epic 'we-story' does not remain impersonally allegorical (as in the *Roman de la rose*) but is founded in an 'I-story' whose protagonist is a concrete individual, historically identified through personal narrative. This contribution suggests that it is precisely the combination of figural prosopopoeia with its metaleptic-typological counterpart that enables the combination of these two "projects of writing", while simultaneously rescuing autobiographical writing from its structural self-testimonial fallacy.

[43] de Man's thesis according to which "the lyric" is "the instance of represented voice" because it is the "transformation of trope into anthropomorphism" (p. 261, in Paul de Man: Anthropomorphism and Trope in the Lyric. In: Id.: *The Rhetoric of Romanticism*, p. 239–266) peculiarly echoes the central thesis of *Vita Nuova* XXV, where Dante a) illustrates the centrality of the prosopopoeic trope of personification, the animation of the inanimate that is given a voice and face through writing, to the lyric poetry of love; and b) identifies this figure as key to the continuity between vernacular lyric and the classical tradition, establishing an authorial genealogy that harks back directly to the greatest Latin poets. For the Dante of the *Vita Nuova*, the use of prosopopoeia is, in other words, fundamental to defining the self-awareness of the lyrical love poet (for a splendid commentary on this conceptual passage, see Albert Russell Ascoli: *Dante and the Making of a Modern Author*. Cambridge | New York: Cambridge University Press 2008): "XXV. (1) At this point it may be that someone worthy of having every doubt cleared up could be puzzled at my speaking of Love as if it were a thing in itself, as if it were not only an intellectual substance, but also a bodily substance. This is patently false, for Love does not exist in itself as a substance, but is an accident in a substance. (2) And that I speak of Love as if it possessed a body, further still, as if it

allegory of the theologian, who through figural interpretation is capable of reconstructing facts as authentic *littera*: historical veracity depends on the validity of their interpretation (and not vice versa). The agent 'does not understand' what is happening to him, nor is he capable of recording it as historical truth, if he is incapable of reading it as signified through the mediation of the eternal interpretant constituted by divine judgement. For this reason, the rhetorical mechanism of *ex post* prophecy – by which the autobiographical narrative of the historical 'I' woven within the poetic narrative of the otherworldly journey is formulated as a supernatural foretelling of events yet to come, rather than a historical account of events that have happened – is not in this context of metaphysical hermeneutics a mere literary ploy, intended to create an illusory effect of diachronic connection between event and knowledge, through which the anticipation of knowledge concerning what has happened legitimises the claim of interpretative validity with regards to the event (by announcing what will occur, the oracle also establishes what the future event *is*). The *ex post* prophecies by which Dante discovers the course of his earthly life during his unearthly journey serve as a poetic tool, underlining the fact that it is only by learning his own biographical story *sub specie aeternitatis* that it comes to be recognised as the *littera* of a text whose supreme decoder – historical, moral and eschatological – is God, judge and interpreter in one.

If the dead of the *Comedy* speak as epitaphs, the metaleptic-figural inscription of their discourse, which is presented as an account and eschatological commentary on both the historical situation of the time and the autobiographical story of the poet, ensures that such a discourse is not ("tender" or "difficult") prosopo-

---

were a human being, is shown by three things I say about it. I say that I saw it coming; and since "to come" implies locomotion, and since, according to the Philosopher, only a body may move from place to place by its own power, it is obvious that I assume Love to be a body. I also say that it laughed and even that it spoke – acts that would seem characteristic of a human being, especially that of laughing; and so it is clear that I assume love to be human. (3) To clarify this matter suitably for my purpose, I shall begin by saying that, formerly, there were no love poets writing in the vernacular, the only love poets were those writing in Latin: among us (and this probably happened in other nations as it still happens in the case of Greece) it was not vernacular poets but learned poets who wrote about love. (4) It is only recently that the first poets appeared who wrote in the vernacular; [. . .]. (8) So, if we find that the Latin poets addressed inanimate objects in their writings, as if these objects had sense and reason, or made them address each other, and that they did this not only with real things but also with unreal things (that is: they have said, concerning things that do not exist, that they speak, and they have said that many an accident in substance speaks as if it were a substance and human), then it is fitting that the vernacular poet do the same – not, of course, without some reason, but with a motive that later can be explained in prose. (9) That the Latin poets have written in the way I have just described can be seen in the case of Virgil," and of Lucan, Horace and Ovid."

poeic "fiction", but rather a revelation of the interdependence between time and eternity, between life and death, immanence and transcendence, which remains hidden from the eyes of the flesh but is visible to the eyes of authentic faith.

For this reason, the *Comedy* claims, the supreme epitaph for each one of us, entrusted with having the final word on what we are, is ultimately written neither by the dead or by those who survive, but by God alone. The ambition to be a "judge" – even merely as a 'depicter', a mimetic portraitist of human experience, a narrator of the biographical story of oneself or others – is acceptable only if it is contained by the floodgates of an awareness of our own radical inadequacy, our infallibility, our mimetic impotence, which derives from the fundamental hermeneutic limit represented by the fact that the *littera* of every human life may only be reconstructed on the basis of its eschatological interpretation. The validity of the prosopopoeic expression of lived experience depends on its correct metaleptic-figural interpretation. Without such mediation, the epitaph is empty; it becomes a pure rhetorical gimmick, a shapeshifter fluctuating between fiction and reality.[44]

3 Humanly Attainable 'Visible Speech'

It is in the three cantos of the entry into Purgatory (X–XII) that we encounter an explicit poetic manifesto for this Christianisation of the lyrical device of prosopopoeia, in its classical form and through its integration with the metaleptic-typological device, implemented in the reconnection of the *katabasis* of the author with that of the hero.

As Dante and Virgil ascend the first terrace where souls atone for the sin of pride – of which Dante recognises he is sorely guilty[45] – the poet consummates his definitive departure from a "poetry of love" that is lyrical and purely individual, which cannot be transformed into a Christian "poetry of salvation" on account of its metaleptic-figural, prophetic-doctrinal and historical-communal nature. The sin that Dante casts aside forever is not only moral, but also poetic.

---

[44] Indeed, the epitaph that Boccaccio places (or may have placed – the attribution is uncertain) in Dante's mouth in the spectral "Prosopopea di Dante" is a mere rhetorical expedient. The literalisation of the tropological mechanism results in an "obscure Minerva", an opaque allegorical mask in which the historicity of biographical information is frozen by artifice (Wordsworth rightly emphasises that a good epitaph rejects all narrative and ideally contains only the name of the deceased) (see *Rime* 32, in the edition of Boccaccio's *Rime* edited by Vittore Branca, Milan: Mondadori 1992).

[45] *Purgatorio* XI, 118–119; XII, 136–138.

He is a new Orpheus, but unlike his predecessor he does not fall into the corrupting temptation of the 'petrifying'[46] lament of immanence:

Poi fummo dentro al soglio de la porta	When I had crossed the threshold of the gate
che 'l mal amor de l'anime disusa,	that – since the soul's aberrant love would make
perché fa parer dritta la via torta,	the crooked way seem straight – is seldom used,
sonando la senti' esser richiusa;	I heard the gate resound and, hearing, knew
e s'io avesse li occhi vòlti ad essa,	that it had shut; and if I'd turned toward it,
qual fora stata al fallo degna scusa?	how could my fault have found a fit excuse?

(*Purgatorio* X, 1–6)

The ethical renunciation of the clutches of sin celebrated in this entry into the penitential itinerary of the purifying ascent will also be 'sculpted', here and in the following two cantos, as an artistic renunciation. Dante distances himself from an autobiographical discourse that remains anchored in the falsifying self-certification of earthly "presence" without ever measuring its eschatological distance from eternity. He offers an exquisite expression of this detachment in his subtle critique of the unwavering pride of human mimetic pretention, through which figurative art becomes a synecdoche for the epistemological ambition to re-create (through image, narration or cognition) the real through its depiction.[47]

The scenes of exemplary humility and punished pride that are depicted on the white marble walls and stone path of the first terrace constitute a supernatural work of art in which every difference between the object and its representation, between reality and image, 'appears' to be surmounted the moment it is established:[48]

---

[46] "As soon as they had brought them out, one of them [the angels] said, 'Flee for your lives! Don't look back, and don't stop anywhere in the plain! Flee to the mountains or you will be swept away!' [. . .] But Lot's wife looked back, and she became a pillar of salt" (Genesis 19:17, 26).

[47] As we have already underlined, it is important to remember that this rejection of lyric poetry founded in an entirely immanent, figuratively prosopopoeic autobiography is embodied as a return to the love poetry repudiated in the *Convivio*. In order to return to Beatrice, Dante must not look back but must follow new paths upon which he "shall need some ingenuity" (*Purgatorio* X, 10). As John Freccero observes, the "insistence on the recuperability of his erotic past distinguishes Dante's confession from virtually all others in the Christian tradition" (Introduction, p. 178).

[48] Teodolinda Barolini (*The Undivine Comedy*, p. 173 et seq.) develops a formidable critical analysis of the three cantos of the terrace of the prideful as a poetic manifesto of sublime ambition, in which Dante inscribes his identity as an artist capable of competing with the mimesis of the Omnipotent, a virtuous antitype to Arachne's emulation of divine artistic power. However, this illuminating reflection does not take into account the character of aesthetic palinode of the three cantos as the sanctioning of a unilateral model of immanent self-sufficiency for artistic creation

[L'angelo dell'annunciazione,]   [The angel of the Annunciation]

dinanzi a noi pareva sì verace   after long interdict, appeared before us,
quivi intagliato in un atto soave,   his gracious action carved with such precision –
che non sembiava imagine che tace.   he did not seem to be a silent image.

(*Purgatorio* X, 37–39)

The vision presented by this work of art is made disturbing by its conspicuous contradiction. On the one hand, it unequivocally exposes the very nature of the image through its manifest inscription in its material support, the white marble (31) where the scenes are "storïate" ("presented") (73), "imposte" ("engraved") (52); the angel is "carved" ("quivi intagliato"). On the other, the sculpture contradicts its own iconographic status ("he did not seem to be a silent image") by virtue of the 'truthfulness' of its appearance, of its emergence not as presence or representation, but genuine apparition: "dinanzi a noi *pareva* sì verace" ("*appeared* before us").

This material inscription, repeatedly hammered home through explicit references to the support and indexical references of a locative nature ("here", "there", "in that same marble"),[49] exposes the apparition's nature as an image. Dante is only contemplating 'scenes', not real events but "stories engraved upon the rock" (52). The 'graven images' on the wall do not 'dissimulate', conceal, themselves in an illusory manipulation of their own mimetic substance, creating the fictitious effect (*trompe l'oeil*) of an image that 'simulates' reality or unreality (which is pure *simulacrum*). The difference between image and reality is neither denied nor avoided: it is 'material' and, as such, insurmountable. The images contemplated by the pilgrim are pure images ("these effigies of true humility", 98), or more precisely pure narration through image, "stories" (71), as is unequivocally exposed by the fact that they are made from stone and marble, rather than flesh. Reality is not a simple question of ideas and depictions: without material embodiment, it has no substance, no existence (other than angelic and divine). The Virgin of the Annunciation is merely an "effigy" (is "ivi imaginata") (41); the scornful Michal is merely "effigïata" ("shown as at the window") (67); it is merely "figurato, quanto

---

which is incapable of metaleptically uniting earthly and eschatological perspectives, thus allowing human writing to be "shared by heaven and by earth" (*Paradiso* XXV, 1–2).

49 "*[W]as of white marble* and adorned with carvings / so accurate" (31–32); "his gracious action carved *[here]* with such precision" (38); "for *in that scene* there was the effigy of one" (41); "another story engraved *upon the rock*" (52); "*There*, carved *in that same marble*" (55); "shown *there*" (62); "*Facing that scene*, and shown as at the window" (67); "To look more closely at another carving, / *which I saw gleaming white beyond Michal*" (71–72); "And *there* the noble action [. . .] was presented" (73) (*Purgatorio* X, m.e.).

per via di fuor del monte avanza" (all are "effigies on all the path protruding from the mountain") (*Purgatorio* XII,23–24).

Nevertheless, these images differ from those that are made by human hands or result from natural phenomena, because they present themselves as apparitions, which both materially confirm their own nature as images, as "likeness"[50] – and belie it in the perception of the viewer ("pareva" e "non sembiava" – "seemed" and "did not seem"). Actually, the receiver perceives them as presence, overwhelmed by the mimetic (poetic) power which surpasses his hermeneutic ability as a sensory and rational codifier of natural phenomena and human artwork:

Giurato si saria ch'el dicesse 'Ave!' (40)	One would have sworn that he was saying, 'Ave!' (40)
e avea in atto impressa esta favella 'Ecce ancilla Deï', propriamente come figura in cera si suggella. (43–45)	and in her stance there were impressed these words, "Ecce ancilla Dei," precisely like a figure stamped in wax. (43–45)
a' due mie' sensi faceva dir l'un 'No', l'altro 'Sì, canta'. (59–60)	made two of my senses speak – one sense said, "No," the other said, "Yes, they do sing"; (59–60)
Similemente al fummo de li 'ncensi che v'era imaginato, li occhi e 'l naso e al sì e al no discordi fensi. (61–63)	just so, about the incense smoke shown there, my nose and eyes contended, too, with yes and no. (61–63)

(*Purgatorio* X)

The synaesthetic collapse of the visual image into auditory and olfactory perception is a sensorial phenomenon that takes place not in the depiction itself but in its reception. The mimetic potency of the depiction is so great (superior even to that of nature)[51] that it undermines the distinction between the senses inherent in the very act of the visual observer. That the graven images do not appear as a "silent image" is not because they materially transform mimesis (by *simulating* the bodily life they represent), but because they transform it symbolically, revealing the bodily life as the signifier of the meaning disclosed by its exemplificative, figural portrayal. What Dante encounters is a remarkable case of metaleptic figural interpretation. Divine mimesis, which makes human history narrative art, is not imitation but interpretation, which reveals the hidden truth

---

[50] *Purgatorio* XII, 23. The occurrence is particularly significant since it is a *hapax legomenon* in the *Comedy*.
[51] "[D]'intagli sì, che non pur Policleto, / ma la natura lì avrebbe scorno" ("[S]o accurate – not only Polycletus / but even Nature, there, would feel defeated") (32–33).

of immanence by reading and exposing it through the establishment of a typological bridge between the earthly event and its eschatological fulfilment, between past and present, between history and eternity. What Dante sees carved in stone is the meaning, the truth of the event of the Annunciation, of the figure of the psalmist king, of Trajan's gesture of charity, of the terrible fate of the prideful (from Lucifer to Arachne). Figural divine mimesis overwhelms the sensory order when it reveals that figurally interpretative vision, which recognises a symbolic order in the real, is superior to its natural counterpart, limited to purely fleshly experience and blind to the full meaning of empirical appearance.

The panels of Purgatory depict reality as God sees it, in full light of its moral, typological and anagogical meaning. The image is not a copy of the real but rather its interpreter, in a triangulation where the referent, the historical event, is signified as eternal life. In other words, the referent is read as significant of an eschatological sense and through this comes to life in the prosopopoeia of the image, which finally gives it a voice, making it speak what is, truly and eternally,

Colui che mai non vide cosa nova	[...] the speech made visible by One
produsse esto visibile parlare,	within whose sight no thing is new – but we,
novello a noi perché qui non si trova.	who lack its likeness here, find novelty.

(*Purgatorio* X, 94–96)

History contains nothing "new" for God,[52] because he observes it in the eternal light of unchanging truth. In the exposition of the celestial vision ("the peace that opened heaven after long interdict", 36–37) presented by the marble panels of Purgatory, history is received as "immagine che non tace" (an image that is "not [...] silent") (39), unlike on earth where events do not declare their own meaning. Here, in Purgatory, on earth rising out of itself,[53] history is received not as presence but as apparition. In the art of divine sculpture, the event *speaks* (acquires meaning) and sight becomes text, producing "*visibile parlare*" ("visible speech").[54] The miraculous prosopopoeia produced by mimetic divine "likeness"

---

[52] Unlike human beings, who have an insatiable desire for novelty: "Li occhi miei, ch'a mirare eran contenti / per veder novitadi ond' e' son vaghi" ("My eyes, which had been satisfied in seeking / new sights – a thing for which they long") (*Purgatorio* X, 103–104).

[53] Within the poetic and theological geography of the *Comedy*, Purgatory, like Hell, is a terrestrial region governed by supernatural laws and inaccessible to the living, except by special divine grace.

[54] The Augustinian precedent ("visible words") for this expression (see Giuseppe Mazzotta, *Poet of the Desert*, p. 242 and Barolini *The Undivine Comedy*, p. 175–176) reenforces its hermeneutic, rather than supernatural, connotation. It is not a prodigious technical feat (a perfectly believable simulation), but rather a refined semantic code following a divine model (destined for the purifying instruction of the souls of Purgatory) that unnerves the flesh-and-blood observer, who is

does not originate from technical virtuosity but from a metaleptic intersection of levels: it is not mimesis of the referent (the object of vision, in its historical *littera* shared by God and man) but mimesis of divine vision, as indicated by the metaleptic warning of the author Dante, who bursts into the text to distance his own human experience from that of the Dante character: here, on earth, "we lack its likeness". In history, it is impossible for man to see through the eye of God; yet in this mimetic depiction it pedagogically becomes an optical tool to supplement human vision, the vision of the penitents who, in Purgatory, are still on earth but are simultaneously making their way towards heaven. They are in a condition of transition, moving towards the unearthly fullness of communion with God, in which there will be less need for any didactic "artifice"[55] or mimetic mediation:

Qual di pennel fu maestro o di stile	What master of the brush or of the stylus
che ritraesse l'ombre e ' tratti ch'ivi	had there portrayed such masses, such outlines
mirar farieno uno ingegno sottile?	as would astonish all discerning minds?
Morti li morti e i vivi parean vivi:	The dead seemed dead and the alive, alive:
non vide mei di me chi vide il vero,	I saw, head bent, treading those effigies,
quant' io calcai, fin che chinato givi.	as well as those who'd seen those scenes directly.

(*Purgatorio* XII, 64–69)

"Non vide mei di me chi vide il vero" ("I saw [. . .] as well as those who'd seen those scenes directly.") The direct witness of the historical event does not see the truth any better than the observer of this iconographic reproduction crafted by God. The revealed image is not a mimetic filter, a figurative–narrative 'copy' of

---

not prepared to receive it. The divine artist here realises what de Man recognises to be "the claim of all poetry" (of all art), which is "to make the invisible visible" ("a figure to the precise extent that it undoes the distinction between sign and trope") (p. 50 in Paul de Man: Hypogram and Inscription. In: Id.: *The Resistance to Theory*. Minneapolis: University of Minnesota Press 1986, p. 27–57). That this semiotic collapse does not abolish the distinction between hallucination and perception, as sustained by de Man against Riffaterre (in their debate concerning a poem of Victor Hugo which metapoetically thematises the conversion of the invisible to visibility), shows that in this instance Riffaterre is firmly on the side of Dante. The effect of visibility produced by the sculptures of Purgatory "is not a hallucination but a hallucinatory effect" (*Ibidem*, p. 49). That Dante's figuration of "visible speech" follows not only a patristic and textual model but also the figurative, pictorial and epigraphic examples of artistic production contemporary to the author – in particular, Giotto's Paduan frescoes – has been widely studied by critics, including recently Marcello Ciccuto: Dante, Giotto e il "visibile parlare". In: *La Commedia: filologia e interpretazione*. Edited by Maria G.Riccobono. Milan, LED, 2020. For an exhaustive review of the critical literature on "visible speech", see Faibisoff, Leah: ISCAD Annotated Bibliography: *Visibile Parlare,*" *International Seminar on Critical Approaches to Dante*. Website, May 2019.

55 [S]o did I see, but carved more skilfully, / with greater sense of likeness, effigies / on all the path protruding from the mountain" (*Purgatorio* XII, 22–24).

the event (in Platonic terms, a further screen that increases the distance between the metaphysical truth of the idea and its material substantiation),[56] but a figural unveiling of its eschatological truth: a hermeneutic decoding not of the eternal and immutable idea underlying the empirical appearance,[57] but of the transcendent significance of earthly contingency. By producing a figural rather than a figurative vision of the event, divine mimesis reveals its inscription in eternity, recognised as irrevocable truth, of salvation or condemnation, by divine justice.[58]

The disorientation of the pilgrim – the living man who, confronted with this unearthly vision intended for the dead, lacks the perceptive strength to withstand the dizzying semantic concentration of the historical event produced by God's mimesis of His own vision[59] – is counterbalanced by the lucidity of the author, who develops this striking ekphrastic sequence (which continues for a full three cantos) as a narrative device that facilitates a robust corrective anamnesis of his own poetics and artistic self-understanding. The superiority of divine mimesis over its natural and human counterparts lies in the fact that it draws forth the prosopopoeic mechanism of animation by which the object is represented (giving a voice and face to the event, depicting it) from the metaleptic mechanism of its

---

[56] This is the central argument of the famous polemic against artistic mimesis (and in particular against painting, labelled as "illusion" and charlatanism), which is no more than the production of semblance of semblance (see in particular Book X of the *Republic*: ""To which is painting directed in every case, to the imitation of reality as it is or of appearance as it appear (μιμήσασθαι, ἢ πρὸς τὸ φαινόμενον, ὡς φαίνεται,?) Is it an imitation of a phantasm (φαντάσματος) or of the truth?" "Of a phantasm" he said. "Then the mimetic art is far removed from truth, and this, it seems, is the reason why it can produce everything, because it touches or lays hold of only a small part of the object and that a phantom (εἴδωλον)" (*Republic* 598b; see also 365c, 523b, 583b, 586b; 602d) (*The Republic of Plato*. In: *Platonis Opera*. Ed. By John Burnet. Oxford: Oxford University Press 1903. Engl. Transl.: *Plato in Twelve Volumes*. Vols. 5 & 6 translated by Paul Shorey. Cambridge, MA: Harvard University Press; London: William Heinemann Ltd. 1969) (Online: http://www.perseus.tufts.edu/hopper/text?doc=Perseus%3Atext%3A1999.01.0168%3Asection%3D598b).

[57] In a radical departure from ("eikastike") 'truthful' Platonic mimesis (which reproduces the truth in its appearance), as opposed to ("phantastike") 'illusionist' mimesis (which imitates appearance) (see *Sophist* 234b et seq.).

[58] The sculpted panels represent a sublime example of hypotyposis, a symbolic mechanism closely interconnected with metalepsis. On this association see Gérard Genette, *Métalepse*, p. 10 et seq., who also analyses the classical precedent for Dante's ekphrasis: Homer's description of the shield of Achilles in the *Iliad* (81 et seq.), which is constructed precisely as a "tableau vivant", an "animated image". The transformation of the metaleptic blueprint of hypotyposis is at the heart of the 'transgressive' production of an image that is produced as an 'apparition', phenomenologically surpassing the event as simple presence.

[59] For this reason, as we have seen, his senses enter into a lively squabble, contradicting one another: "one sense said, 'No,' the other said, 'Yes, they do sing'".

eschatological interpretation, rejecting the figurative mechanism as a figural device. As Dante establishes in the formidable *ars poetica* of *Purgatorio* X–XII, it is only by integrating mimetic and figurative representation of the event and persona (the mask) with its figural understanding that its historical truth can be articulated; only this way, therefore, is it possible to guarantee the truth of the account, of the narrative report of the event.[60] Factuality is not separable from its meaning. Story can only be reconstructed as plot, and to be authentic it must weave together the earthly and eschatological dimensions, must metaleptically unite the here-and-now with the afterlife, the world of the living with that of the dead, separating representation from the falsification of presence.

Within this perspective, it is evident that the only credible autobiographical (and biographical) report is one received *sub specie aeternitatis*, as "*a thing not new*". The only credible epitaph is the one inscribed by God (who in the *Comedy* speaks through the mouths of the dead), because the "judged" cannot instantiate himself as "judge". Ultimately, no human being can be either their own judge or narrator. To claim a valid incarnation of such identification through the prosopopoeic mechanism of animating the past beginning from the present, the 'I'-object beginning from the 'I'-subject – to claim to give voice to an inherently "silent image", to the dead soul that is the past 'I', the 'I' of another reduced to an object – is an act of mimetic pride in which the subject is consumed by the madness of comparing themselves, even if only virtually, with God. It is the error of Orpheus, the sin of Lot's wife. Only by uniting the autobiographical, confessional and apologetic ambition, in a mimetic-narrative, prosopopoeic mould, to restore the present 'I' with the metaleptic device of figural interpretation (of an eschatological reading of history, reconnecting oneself to the "opening of the heaven" achieved by Christ's incarnation) that elevates the earthly man into the heavenly man (1 Corinthians 15: 47–49), can the man, the artist, aspire not to reach but at least start out upon the way to truth, to his own life, to representation (leaving the "evil path" of perdition, *Purgatorio* XII, 72).

The ekphrastic pedagogy concerning the need to integrate the propsopopeic-confessional and metaleptic-figural device in the mimetic representation, which is developed across these three cantos of the *Purgatorio*, is thus eloquently counterpointed by the contrapasso of the penitence required of the prideful man who claims to be his own autonomous judge; of the artist who trusts solely in immanently imitative (figurative) rather than transcendentally interpretative

---

[60] See Giuseppe Mazzotta, *Poet of the Desert*, p. 227 et seq., for a sophisticated discussion of the theoretical significance of Canto X for Dante's poetics and conception of allegory. Mazzotta's starting point and the critical outcome of his analysis differ from the reading presented here, though the two are by no means incompatible.

(figural) mimesis, in purely horizontal historical narration, in the exclusively prosopopoeic connection of the past 'I' with its present counterpart. If the miniaturist Oderisi da Gubbio is the outstanding character of the first terrace's gallery of penitents, it is because his diatribe against worldly fame expresses, with extraordinary poetic power, the censure of the deepest illusion inherent in pride. Such is the pride of a man who believes he can 'immortalise' himself through his own earthly work by prosopopoeically projecting the memory of what he has achieved, rather than "passing beyond the human" (*Paradiso* I, 70) through metaleptic attainment of transcendence.[61]

Contemplating the ephemeral nature of worldly fame, the penitent artist considers and condemns the madness of seeking to conquer the transitory nature of human life through earthly memory founded on figurative work, on the poetic word. Moral sin is qualified as artistic sin. Dante is now the anti-Orpheus, because the scope of his poetry is no longer to save the dead Beatrice-Eurydice (she whom he loves, she who loves him) through poetic memory. Orpheus will always fall, because human memory is looking backwards, tirelessly searching for the past. The true Christian poet, the poet of *salvation*, does not look back: he directs his word and gaze forwards towards eternity, knowing that he cannot deliver salvation from death, but instead receives salvation from death.

The ekphrastic lesson concerning the correct mimetic register for artistic representation thus finds a didactic-parenetic application in the contrapasso of the penitential sentence of the prideful, which is produced as a form of dishumanisation, disanimation, petrification, and deprivation of a face, in a clear inversion of the prosopopoeic mechanism of animation of the object by the subject:

Io cominciai: "Maestro, quel ch'io veggio muovere a noi, non mi sembian persone, e non so che, sì nel veder vaneggio".	"Master," I said, "what I see moving toward us does not appear to me like people, but I can't tell what is there – my sight's bewildered."
Ed elli a me: "La grave condizione di lor tormento a terra li rannicchia, sì che ' miei occhi pria n'ebber tencione.	And he to me: "Whatever makes them suffer their heavy torment bends them to the ground; at first I was unsure of what they were.

(*Purgatorio* X, 112–117)

---

61 *Purgatorio* is the canticle in which "the poem rise[s] again from Hell's dead realm" (*Purgatorio* I, 7), in which Dante learns he cannot rely on his political, intellectual, artistic and civil works to achieve 'immortality', as Ser Brunetto taught (an illusion in which the pilgrim still indulges in *Inferno* XXVI, 85). Rather, it is necessary for him to *pass beyond the human*: to transfigure himself through receiving a transcendence that cures human beings of their hereditary "blemish" and "imperfection" (*Convivio* I, iv).

The visual disorientation caused by the humanly unobtainable perceptual density of the images engraved in the marble, which present themselves as an apparition superior to presence, is here overturned in a visual "bewilderment" provoked on the contrary by a perceptual deficit that dispels the referential content of what is viewed ("people") in the image that is transmitted ("what I see [. . .] does not appear to me like people"). The excess of the "visible speech" of divine mimesis here gives rise to the deficiency of the *invisible speech* of the penitents' condition:

Le lor parole, che rendero a queste	These words, which had been spoken by my guide,
che dette avea colui cu' io seguiva,	were answered by still other words we heard;
non fur da cui venisser manifeste;	for though it was not clear who had replied,
ma fu detto:	an answer came:
	(*Purgatorio* XI, 46–49)

The prideful are reduced to an invisible voice because their faces are lost, hidden beneath a stone that visually substitutes their persona:

Ma guarda fiso là, e disviticchia	But look intently there, and let your eyes
col viso quel che vien sotto a quei sassi:	unravel what's beneath those stones: you can
già scorger puoi come ciascun si picchia.	already see what penalty strikes each.
	(*Purgatorio* X, 118–120)

The effect is one of petrification: like the wife of Lot, the prideful are (at least visually) converted into sculpture:

Come per sostentar solaio o tetto,	Just as one sees at times – as corbel for
per mensola talvolta una figura	support of ceiling or of roof – a figure
si vede giugner le ginocchia al petto,	with knees drawn up into its chest (and this
la qual fa del non ver vera rancura	oppressiveness, unreal, gives rise to real
nascere 'n chi la vede; così fatti	distress in him who watches it): such was
vid' io color, quando puosi ben cura.	the state of those I saw when I looked hard.
Vero è che più e meno eran contratti	They were indeed bent down – some less, some more –
secondo ch'avien più e meno a dosso;	according to the weights their backs now bore;
	(*Purgatorio* X, 130–137)

This 'contraction' of the penitents' humanity, this subtractive regression, is not real but a purely visual effect. Even the punishment received by the prideful is a work of art, further proof of the skill which the supreme master of "artifice" adds to the sculptures of the terrace. Indeed, while the image transmitted by the penitents may appear to be pure appearance and not apparition (unlike the "engravings", the "images" "carved" in the marble), like true art it produces authentic emotional and spiritual effects: "this oppressiveness, unreal, gives rise to real distress in him who watches it".

The lessening of the penitents' humanity through petrification and the loss of their faces is produced as a copy of a copy: the penitents do not appear "like people" but "seem" to be caryatids ("such was / the state of those I saw") which, in turn, have been copied from living beings. The mimetic process of the prosopopoeic animation of the inanimate, who are given a speaking face by the artist,[62] is here 'imitated' and inverted in an exemplary contrapasso that punishes the pride of a man who, like Eve, makes his likeness with God, his own creative capacity, a means of independence, judgment, and distance from Him:

Or superbite, e via col viso altero,	Now, sons of Eve, persist in arrogance,
figliuoli d'Eva, e non chinate il volto	in haughty stance, do not let your eyes bend,
sì che veggiate il vostro mal sentero!	lest you be forced to see your evil path!
	(*Purgatorio* XII, 70–72)

The prideful man does not hide, but openly defies God, losing sight of the path he should follow and instead turning towards the "crooked way", the "evil path" of sin, which "seems straight" on account of the soul's "aberrant love" (*Purgatorio* X, 2–3). He 'arrogantly' raises his gaze and face towards Heaven, not to learn and to be transformed but rather to ape the Almighty, to be '*like* Him', denying the limits of his own finite nature. For this reason, the artist who has dared to give a face and voice to matter, to the event, to the past, rather than reading them figurally in light of their eternal significance, loses his "mouth", "eyes" and "face", "contracting" to become an inanimate statue. Penitential antiprosopopoeia – the deanimation and deprivation of a face enacted by the supreme judge, the supreme celestial artist – reveals the error of an art that trusts solely in itself, which seeks to carry Eurydice out from the jaws of death, claims to redeem historical truth solely with the efforts of the subject, measuring it against the brief time of human understanding rather than the eternity of its eschatological fulfilment.[63]

---

62 Like Love, which in the *Vita nuova* (XXV) is, as we have already seen, represented by the lyric poet, the "vernacular poet", "as if it were a thing in itself, as if it were not only an intellectual substance, but also a bodily substance, "as if it possessed a body, further still, as if it were a human being", saying "that it laughed and even that it spoke". Like those "inanimate objects" of which the classical poets spoke "as if [they] had sense and reason, or made them address each other"; "they did this not only with real things but also with unreal things (that is: they have said, concerning things that do not exist, that they speak, and they have said that many an accident in substance speaks as if it were a substance and human)".

63 In other words, what is punished is the artistic pretence of inverting the relationship of mortal dependence between subject and time through a figurative mimesis that by inscribing the subject in the text deprives it of its entropic and transitory condition. If the autobiographical

Noi salavam per una pietra fessa,	Our upward pathway ran between cracked rocks;
che si moveva e d'una e d'altra parte,	they seemed to sway in one, then the other part,
sì come l'onda che fugge e s'appressa.	just like a wave that flees, then doubles back.
"Qui si conviene usare un poco d'arte",	"Here we shall need some ingenuity,"
cominciò 'l duca mio, "in accostarsi	my guide warned me, "as both of us draw near
or quinci, or quindi al lato che si parte".	this side or that side where the rock wall veers."

(Purgatorio X, 7–12)

Virgil's pronouncement at the entrance to Purgatory invites not only the pilgrim but also the author to broadly reconsider his spiritual and artistic path: "we shall need some ingenuity [*arte*]" not only to tackle the singular geological structure of the first of Purgatory's paths, a wall of rock that sways dangerously, but also the purifying ascent that it heralds and its poetic expression. This is different from the purely earthly ingenuity employed by Oderisi in his clumsy navigation of the fickle wind of human history, the uncontrollable blowing of worldly vanity:

Non è il mondan romore altro ch'un fiato	Worldly renown is nothing other than
di vento, ch'or vien quinci e or vien quindi,	a breath of wind that blows now here, now there,
e muta nome perché muta lato.	and changes name when it has changed its course.

(Purgatorio XI, 100–102)[64]

In their fear-inducing fluctuation, the "cracked rocks" of the first path through Purgatory are an exemplary petrification of the sin punished on the terrace of the prideful. They constitute a figurally interpretative 'image' of inconsistent 'vanity', of the vacuous instability of earthly contingency, upon which the prideful rely as a humanistic sign of dignity, arrogantly placing worldly value above its eschatological counterpart, prioritising the ethics of honour and fame over that of charity. The rock wall advances and retracts ominously: it is as treacherous

---

"inscription of the self in the text [is] the very definition of the lyric" (p. 111 in Michael Riffaterre: Prosopoeia. In: *Yale French Studies*, Nr. 69 (1985), *The Lesson of Paul De Man*, p. 107–123), in the contrapasso of the prideful Dante expresses his own disassociation from the poetic reconfiguration of temporality achieved solely through the lyrical device of prosopopoeia and not also through metaleptic and figural means. The hypogrammatical inscription of the subject in the text (of the artist in his work) as the prosopopoeic anthropomorphisation of symbolic figuration is at the heart of the debate between Michael Riffaterre, Prosopoeia, and Paul de Man, Hypogram.
64 "The wind blows to the south and turns to the north; round and round it goes, ever returning on its course" (Ecclesiastes 1:6). "Better what the eye sees than the roving of the appetite. This too is meaningless, a chasing after the wind" (Ecclesiastes 6:9). The term Kohelet, or vanity (Latin *vanitas*) is a translation of the Greek ματαιότης, itself a translation of a Hebrew term (hă-ḇêl) literally meaning 'breath' or 'vapour' but used metaphorically to indicate anything evanescent or in vain (see https://biblehub.com/hebrew/1892.htm) (cf. Psalm 39 [40], 5–6).

as human glory, as the earthly memory in which man deludedly believes he can 'immortalise' himself, ultimately proving to be scattered and without voice, pure "rumour [*romore*]". It is as lifeless as swirling dust, helpless before the inconstant elements:

> La vostra nominanza è color d'erba, Your glory wears the color of the grass
> che viene e va, e quei la discolora that comes and goes; the sun that makes it wither
> per cui ella esce de la terra acerba. first drew it from the ground, still green and tender.
> (*Purgatorio* XI, 113–115)

The created condition of man is that of a puppet whose strings are pulled by the forces of nature,[65] the inexorable alternation of life and death, a combination of the fatality of the cyclical return of the ever unchanged and the lability of individual existence and events, generated by the same law that will cause their decay, in the inseparable temporal interdependence between beginning and end, birth and death.

For the Christian reader of Paul, liberty means breaking this cycle "to be brought into the freedom and glory of the children of God", escaping the inertia of the created being's enslavement to sin and transience through the revitalising breath of the Spirit, accessing the glory of filiation. Having passed the trial of the path threatened by the menace of the moving rock, Virgil and Dante once again find themselves "released from it, in open space":

> che noi fossimo fuor di quella cruna; [we had] made our way through that needle's eye;
>   but when
> ma quando fummo liberi e aperti we were released from it, in open space
> sù dove il monte in dietro si rauna, above, a place at which the slope retreats,
> (*Purgatorio* X, 16–18)

'Liberated' from the disorienting confusion of contingency and now within the redemptive condition of Purgatory – though still uncertain and confused ("I was exhausted; with the two of us uncertain of our way", 19) – the two poets begin to take in the purifying experience of the first terrace, with its combination of artistic exemplification and expiatory contrapasso. Still searching for themselves and their own art ("uncertain of our way"), they receive a lesson that is at once moral and aesthetic. It majestically alternates images endowed with the force of presence of apparition by the power of divine mimesis, and presences deprived of their own appearance by the knowing hand of the artist and judge, "contracted"

---

[65] These verses clearly evoke Paul's great portrayal of creation's servitude, its slavery to its own transient nature, in Romans 8:20–21: "For the creation was subjected to frustration, not by its own choice, but by the will of the one who subjected it, in hope that the creation itself will be liberated from its bondage to decay and brought into the freedom and glory of the children of God".

antiprosopopoeically in a petrification that exhibits and purifies the pride of a human mimesis that has neither sought nor known how to find eschatological communion with eternity.

> Più non dirò, e scuro so che parlo
> I say no more; I know I speak obscurely
> (*Purgatorio* XI, 137)

Oderisi closes his tirade against the vanity of human glory with an obscure prophecy *post eventum*, adding another piece to the epitaph which Dante has the dead dictate over the course of the *Comedy*. The past is articulated as a future that cannot be deciphered from the present, for such is the 'perspective' of eternity (*Paradiso* XVII, 17–18): what we have done is a condition of that which is yet to come, which awaits in the beyond where "all times are present" (18). In the sight of eternity nothing is new, and for this very reason nothing is lost. The past, lost like dust in the fickle wind of temporal contingency, is retained whole, like a "painted" image, in the eyes of God:[66]

> E 'n la sua volontade è nostra pace:
> ell' è quel mare al qual tutto si move
> ciò ch'ella crïa o che natura face».
>
> And in His will there is our peace: that sea
> to which all beings move – the beings He
> creates or nature makes – such is His will."
> (*Paradiso* III, 85–87)

There is no one better placed to describe time than one who has left it behind; none more fitting to tell us who we are than one who has freed himself from the falsifying weight of "presence". Consequently, Dante's *Comedy* still today asks that we read it as an *inscription* of the narration and interpretation of the poet's life, which he acquired by speaking with the dead:

> Ciò che narrate di mio corso scrivo,
> e serbolo a chiosar con altro testo
> a donna che saprà, s'a lei arrivo.
>
> What you have told me of my course, I write;
> I keep it with another text, for comment
> by one who'll understand, if I may reach her.
> (*Inferno* XV, 88–90)

---

66 La contingenza, che fuor del quaderno
de la vostra matera non si stende,
tutta è dipinta nel cospetto etterno;

necessità però quindi non prende
se non come dal viso in che si specchia
nave che per torrente giù discende.

Contingency, while not extending past the book in which
your world of matter has been writ, is yet
in the Eternal Vision all depicted

(but this does not imply necessity,
just as a ship that sails downstream is not
determined by the eye that watches it).
(*Paradiso* XVII, 37–42)

Bibliographical References

Ascoli, Albert Russell: *Dante and the Making of a Modern Author*. Cambridge: Cambridge University Press 2008.
Auerbach, Erich: *Dante: Poet of the Secular World*, New York: NYRB Classics (1929|1961) 2007.
Auerbach, Erich: Figura (1938). Rpt. in: Id. *Time, History, and Literature: Selected Essays of Erich Auerbach*. Edited by James I. Porter. Princeton: Princeton University Press 2014.
Auerbach, Erich: *Mimesis: The Representation of Reality in Western Literature* (1946). Princeton: Princeton University Press (1955) 2014 (with a New Introduction by E.Said).
Barolini, Teodolinda: *Dante's Poets: Textuality and Truth in the Comedy*. Princeton: Princeton Univ. Press. 1984.
Barolini, Teodolinda: *The Undivine Comedy: Detheologizing Dante*. Princeton: Princeton University Press 1992.
Barolini, Teodolinda: Dante and the Lyric Past. In: *The Cambridge Companion to Dante*. Edited by Rachel Jacoff. Cambridge UK: Cambridge University Press 1993, p. 14–33.
Bartolomei, Teresa: *Figura hujus mundi: Figuras líricas da temporalidade na poesia de Emily Dickinson*. Doctoral thesis available through the Repository of the Literary Theory Programme (UL), 2016. Online: http://www.letras.ulisboa.pt/images/areas-unidades/literaturas-artes-culturas/programa-teoria-literatura/documentos/bartolomei2_def.compressed.pdf.
Boccaccio, Giovanni: *Rime*. Edited by Vittore Branca. Milan: Mondadori 1992.
Brilli, Elisa & Giuliano Milani: *Vite nuove. Biografia e autobiografia di Dante*. Rome: Carocci 2021.
Brownlee, Kevin: Dante and the Classical Poets. In: *The Cambridge Companion to Dante*. Edited by Rachel Jacoff. Cambridge UK: Cambridge University Press 1993, p. 100–119.
Carrai, Stefano: Dante e la tradizione classica. In: *Dante*. Edited by Robert Rea and Justin Steinberg. Rome: Carocci 2020, p. 329–344.
Ciccuto, Marcello: Dante, Giotto e il "visibile parlare". In: *La Commedia: filologia e interpretazione*. Edited by Maria G. Riccobono. Milan, LED 2020. Online: http://dx.doi.org/10.7359/930-2020-cicc (accessed 24.10.21).
Gianfranco Contini: Un'interpretazione di Dante (1965) In: Idem: *Un'idea di Dante. Saggi danteschi*. Turin: Einaudi (1970 / 1976) 2001.
de Man, Paul: Autobiography as De-Facement. In: Id.: *The Rhetoric of Romanticism*. New York: Columbia University Press 1984, p. 67–81.
de Man, Paul: Anthropomorphism and Trope in the Lyric. In: Id.: *The Rhetoric of Romanticism*. New York: Columbia University Press 1984, p. 239–266.
de Man, Paul: Hypogram and Inscription. In: Id.: *The Resistance to Theory*. Minneapolis: University of Minnesota Press 1986, p. 27–57.
Derrida, Jacques: *La dissémination*. Paris: Seuil 1972.
Derrida, Jacques: *Mémoires pour Paul de Man*. Paris: Seuil 1988.
Faibisoff, Leah: ISCAD Annotated Bibliography: *Visibile Parlare," International Seminar on Critical Approaches to Dante*. Website, May 2019. Online: https://dante.medieval.utoronto.ca/visibile-parlare/ (accessed 24.10.2021).
Freccero, John: Introduction to Inferno. In: *The Cambridge Companion to Dante*. Edited by Rachel Jacoff. Cambridge UK: Cambridge University Press 1993, p. 172–191.
Genette, Gérard: *Figures III*. Paris: Seuil 1972.

Genette, Gérard: *Métalepse: De la figure à la fiction*. Paris: Seuil 2004.
Ginzburg, Carlo: *Il filo e le tracce* (2006). Milan: Feltrinelli 2015.
Hollander, Robert: *Allegory in Dante's 'Comedy'*, Princeton: Princeton University Press 1969.
Lejeune, Philippe: *Le Pacte autobiographique*. (1975) Paris: Seuil 1996.
Leonardi, Lino: Dante e la tradizione lirica. In: *Dante*. Edited by Robert Rea and Justin Steinberg. Rome: Carocci 2020, p. 354–361.
MacIntyre, Alasdair: *After Virtue: A Study in Moral Theory* (1981). 2nd Ed. London: Duckworth 1985.
Marchesi, Simone: The Poet in the Mirror: Epic and Autobiography in Dante's Inferno. In: *Sacred Heart University Review*, Vol. 24: Iss. 1, Article 5. (2010). Online: http://digitalcommons.sacredheart.edu/shureview/vol24/iss1/5 (accessed 24.10.21).
Mazzotta, Giuseppe: *Dante, Poet of the Desert*. Princeton: Princeton University Press 1979.
Möllendorff v., Peter: Metalepsis. In: *Oxford Classic Dictionary*. Online: https://doi.org/10.1093/acrefore/9780199381135.013.8231 (accessed 24.11.2021).
Plato: *The Republic*. In: *Platonis Opera*. Ed. By John Burnet. Oxford: Oxford University Press 1903. Engl. Transl.: *Plato in Twelve Volumes*. Vols 5 & 6 translated by Paul Shorey. Cambridge, MA: Harvard University Press; London: William Heinemann Ltd. 1969. Online: perseus.tufts.edu (accessed 27.07.2022).
Rea, Robert and Justin Steinberg (eds): *Dante*. Rome: Carocci 2020.
Ricoeur, Paul: *Temps et Récit*. 3 Vols. Paris: Seuil 1983|1984|1985.
Ricoeur, Paul: *Soi-même comme un autre*. Paris: Seuil 1990.
Riffaterre, Michael: Prosopoeia. In: *Yale French Studies*, Nr. 69 (1985), *The Lesson of Paul De Man*, p. 107–123.
Singleton, Charles S.: *Dante's* Commedia: *Elements of Structure*. Baltimore and London: John Hopkins University Press 1977 (orig. *Dante Studies 1: Elements of Structure*. Cambridge MA: Harvard University Press 1954).
Smith, Sidonie & Julia Watson: Metalepsis in Autobiographical Narrative. In: *European Journal of Life Writing*, Vol VIII, 1–27 (2019), doi: 10.21827/ejlw.8.35479.
Steinberg, Justin: *Accounting for Dante: Urban Readers and Writers in Late Medieval Italy*. Notre Dame IN: University of Notre Dame Press 2007.
Villari, Pasquale (ed.): *Antiche leggende e tradizioni che illustrano la Divina Commedia* (1848). Bologna: Forni 1979 (fascimile reproduction of the 1865 edition).
Wagner-Egelhaaf, Martina: *Handbook of Autobiography / Autofiction*. Berlin: De Gruyter 2019.
Wordsworth, William: Upon Epitaphs (from *The Friend*, Feb. 22.1810). In: *The Prose Work of William Wordsworth*. Vol. II (London 1876). New York: AMS Press, Inc 1967, p. 24–75.

Lina Bolzoni
Dante: Memory Matters in the *Comedy*

Let us begin our journey with Giovanni di Paolo's fascinating miniature (Figure 1) depicting the white rose and some of its inhabitants, which Dante and Saint Bernard encounter in Canto XXXII of the *Paradiso*; it appears in a codex now housed in the British Library (MS Yates Thompson 36) that was produced between 1444 and 1450 at the commission of the King Alfonso V of Naples.[1] The miniaturist places before us an important aspect of the text: the fact that even in Paradise, the indescribable place *par excellence*, Dante does stop making us 'see', communicating his visions to us in words – which also means emphatically and efficiently constructing our memory of his journey. As Cardinal José Tolentino de Mendonça noted in his paper, the *Comedy* is in fact a "pedagogy of sight", because "we are all called to have visions". Indeed, at the very beginning of the text Dante's guide, Virgil, teaches him to see, to look with the eyes of the body so that he might see with the eyes of the mind. Expressions such as "to look intently" (*guardare fisso*) and variations thereon appear regularly.[2] For instance, on the terrace of the prideful, who are contorted into unrecognisable forms under the weights they carry (sin strips away the image of man, who God created according to his own image and likeness), Virgil says:

Ma guarda fiso là, e disviticchia	But look intently there, and let your eyes
col viso quel che vien sotto a quei sassi:	unravel what's beneath those stones
	(*Purgatorio* X, 118–119)

In these verses, "unravel" (*disviticchia*), a "crude and scrannel" rhyme, communicates with expressionistic force the effort of extricating the image from what has enveloped it, almost suffocated it, like a parasitic plant.

Knowing how to see, how to accompany the pilgrim on his journey and reconstruct his itinerary in our minds, and by thus to create our own memory of his experience: all this is essential. It is part of our duty as readers, or as those

---

[1] See Luca Azzetta: *Il duplice volto di un manoscritto quattrocentesco: il codice Yates Thompson*. In: *La* Commedia *di Dante nello specchio delle immagini*. Edited by Lina Bolzoni, Rome: Istituto della Enciclopedia italiana 2021, p. 117–149.

[2] Lina Bolzoni: "Quinci su vo per non esser più cieco" (Purg. XXVI,57): l'educazione dello sguardo, in Il "visibile parlare" di Dante: dalla *Commedia* alle arti dei nostri giorni. In: Idem: *La* Commedia *di Dante nello specchio delle immagini*, p. XIII–XXXVI.

Note: Translated from the Italian by Matthew Coneys Wainwright.

https://doi.org/10.1515/9783110796049-007

who listen to his verses. Indeed, the important role that memory plays in Dante's world is one we have forgotten; one which, immersed in our highly technological world that apparently frees us from the need to remember, we will struggle to recover.

By the Middle Ages, memory was already laden with a long and complex history. In Archaic Greece, an oral society with no knowledge of writing, memory played a fundamental role in guaranteeing the survival and identity of the human community.[3] For this reason, memory appears in Greek myth as a goddess, Mnemosyne, the mother of the Muses; memory and poetry are thus closely intertwined. This situation changed with the diffusion of handwriting and the birth of the *polis*, the city. The spread of handwriting diminished the importance of memory and thus its sacred nature; nevertheless, the need to remember survived, and indeed assumed a new importance in the life of the city, where it was the task of the orator and poet to recite their discourses and poems publicly and effectively. Memory became an art, precisely something that could be taught and practised.[4]

According to tradition, the art of memory was invented by Simonides of Ceos (554–468 BC), a lyric poet of the Pre-Socratic era, who is also credited with being the first to receive payment for his verses and to compare poetry with painting. Plutarch (*De gloria Atheniensium*, 3) claims that he defined painting as silent poetry and poetry as a speaking painting, thus delineating the boundaries which, according to Dante, divine art is capable of transgressing, as in the example of the "visible speech" that characterises the sculptures of the *Purgatorio* (X, 95). We can observe that, from its very origins in ancient Greece, to discover and practise the art of memory has meant becoming an expert in mental images, their qualities and their extraordinary effectiveness. Connected with this is the recognition – facilitated by the new urban reality – of an environment in which different

---

[3] See Eric A. Havelock: *Cultura orale e civiltà della scrittura*. Rome / Bari: Laterza 1963; Marcel Detienne: *I maestri di verità nella Grecia arcaica*, Rome / Bari: Laterza 1977; Jesper Svenbro: *La parola e il marmo. Alle origini della poetica greca*, Turin: Boringhieri 1984.

[4] On the art of memory, see Paolo Rossi: *Clavis universalis. Arti della memoria e logica combinatoria da Lullo a Leibniz*. Milan / Naples: Ricciardi 1960; Frances A. Yates: *L'arte della memoria*. Turin: Einaudi 1972; M. Carruthers: *The Book of Memory: A Study of Memory in Medieval Culture*. Cambridge: Cambridge University Press, 1990; Lina Bolzoni: *La stanza della memoria. Modelli letterari e iconografici nell'età della stampa*. Turin: Einaudi 1995; Mary Carruthers: *The Craft of Thought: Meditation, Rethoric, and the Making of Images, 400–1200*. Cambridge: Cambridge University Press 1998; Lina Bolzoni: *La rete delle immagini. Predicazione in volgare dalle origini a Bernardino da Siena*. Turin: Einaudi, 2002; Aleida Assmann: *Ricordare. Forme e mutamenti della memoria culturale*. Bologna: il Mulino 2002.

arts, such as painting, poetry and sculpture, can encounter one another beyond the various tools they employ.

Writing, meanwhile, recreates memory in its own image and likeness. Ancient witnesses – such as the *Rhetorica ad Herennium*, (III,30), traditionally attributed to Cicero – tell us that those who practice the art of memory behave in exactly the same way as scribes. The scribe engraves the wax tablet, methodically following the lines and marks that form letters and words; even with the passing of time, the tablet will relay the message with which it has been entrusted. So too mnemonics teaches its practitioner to fix an ordered progression of *loci* within the space of the mind: here, *imagines agentes* can be located, connected by association with the things and words to be remembered. Like written words, these too will convey the memories they guard even after much time.

In the Latin world, the art of memory was employed above all by orators: as we have already seen, a text of fundamental importance, the *Rhetorica ad Herennium*, was attributed to Cicero. In the Middle Ages, the recovery of this ancient tradition – whose highest reinterpretations appear in the works of Albertus Magnus and Thomas Aquinas – meshed with the long experience that had matured above all in monastic contexts, an experience in which memory, its qualities and functions, were of strong moral and spiritual value. The techniques of memory were closely linked with those of meditation. A "force of thought" – to reappropriate the title of Mary Carruthers' book – was developed and cultivated, allowing the mental construction of temples, tabernacles, palaces, gardens, or staircases, trees, and similar. In every case this consisted of fixing an itinerary to be followed step by step, *locus* by *locus*. Each stage of the itinerary entails both progression in knowledge and moral transformation, culminating in a mystical experience, an encounter with God.

This idea and experience of memory is particularly stimulating when we consider the *Comedy*. Indeed, various studies have adopted this perspective since Frances Yates first posed the question many years ago, fully aware that it might provoke outcry or appear crude or impracticable.[5] Yates noted that the *Comedy* – or rather what Contini somewhat snobbishly termed the "libretto" of the *Comedy*[6] – is also a system for memorising the vices and virtues: the structure of the three canticles corresponds with a system of *loci* whose *order* – we might add – is gradually explained so that it can be understood and remembered (*Inferno* XI, 19 et seq., *Pur-*

---

[5] Frances Yates, *L'arte della memoria*, p. 87 et seq. For subsequent studies (including bibliography), see Lina Bolzoni, *Dante o della memoria appassionata*. In: *Lettere italiane*, LX (2008), p. 169–193.
[6] Gianfranco Contini: Un'interpretazione di Dante. In: Idem: *Un'idea di Dante. Saggi danteschi*. Turin: Einaudi 1976, p. 69.

gatorio XVII, 85 et seq., etc.), albeit with the occasional discrepancy.[7] The circles of Hell, the terraces of Purgatory and the heavens of Paradise place before us the classification of the vices and virtues. The encounters with various characters function as *imagines agentes*, in the sense that they help us to understand and remember the specific nature of the vice that is condemned and virtue that is rewarded.

It is important to underline that when we speak of a system of vices and virtues, we refer to something that was familiar to the average audience that read and / or listened to the poem. Meticulously constructed through the writings of philosophers and scholars, the order of vices and virtues was proclaimed by preachers and entrusted to images – or rather diagrams that combined words and images – which had a remarkable dissemination in Europe between the twelfth and fourteenth centuries; having emerged in a monastic setting, from the Trecento they also circulated among the laity.[8] We might take as an example the tree of virtues and tree of vices (Figure 2), which are rooted respectively in humility and pride. They form part of a cycle conserved in the Biblioteca Laurenziana of Florence (cod. Pluteo, 20.24, ff. 3v-4r) dating probably from the late Trecento or early Quattrocento, which also includes images such as the *lignum vitae*, inspired by the famous work of Saint Bonaventure; the cherub, who guides the sinner to repentance and confession; and the *turris sapientiae* (Figure 3). Such diagrams allow the individual to remember, undertake and say everything required for them to repent, contemplate, purify themselves, and in short accomplish a work of inner edification (according to a metaphor that the *turris sapientiae*, for example, takes literally).[9] It was a kind of condensed, visual moral library, ready to be used by preachers and the educated laity alike. As a cycle, its individual components might vary; what remained consistent was its structure, which brought together memory and invention, biblical exegesis and its moral application, visual diagram and numerical correspondences.

---

[7] Theodore J. Cachey outlines this structure, highlighting Dante's "cartographic impulse", in: *Cartografie dantesche: mappando Malebolge*. In: *Critica del testo*, XIV / 2 (2011), *Dante oggi / 2*. Edited by Roberto Antonelli, Annalisa Landolfi, Arianna Punzi, p. 229–260.

[8] See Lina Bolzoni: Allegorie e immagini della memoria: il 'Colloquio spirituale' e il ciclo della 'Torre della Sapienza. In: Id. *La rete delle immagini*, p. 47–99; *The Medieval Craft of Memory: An Anthology of Texts and Pictures*. Edited by M. Carruthers and J. Ziolkowski. Philadelphia: University of Pennsylvania Press 2002; Lucy Freeman Sandler: *Religious Instruction and Devotional Study: The Pictorial and the Textual in Gothic Diagrams*. In: *The Visualization of Knowledge in Medieval and Early Modern Europe*. Edited by Marcia Kupfer, Adam S. Cohen, J.H. Chajes. Turnhout: Brepols 2020, p. 429–448.

[9] On architectural images, their use and their connections with biblical exegesis, see the rich documentation provided by Henri De Lubac: *Exégèse médiévale. Les quatre sens de l'Écriture*. Paris: Aubier 1959–1964 (in particular II, 2. p. 42 et seq.).

To be aware of the system of vices and virtues is to acknowledge something that was familiar to much of the public of Dante's time, who were therefore well placed to recognise it in his poem. Seeing and recognising the classification of vices and virtues was essentially part of what Baxandall has termed "the period eye".[10] It is perhaps also useful to recall that the master of rhetoric Boncompagno da Signa (ca. 1165–1250) had defended the use of artificial *memory* in his *Rhetorica novissima*, including in relation to the need of the faithful to remember the punishments of Hell and joys of Paradise.[11]

We shall now seek to retrace the *Comedy* using the building blocks of the art of memory, which is to say order, *loci* and *imagines agentes*. It has not been forgotten that the *Comedy* presents an order, a precise diagram that can easily be visualised: it is sufficient to consider school textbooks, or even recent editions of the poem, where diagrams of the Hell, Purgatory and Paradise can easily be found. Such representations help us to remember, to orient ourselves within the vast sea of the text, to recognise in every passage and verse the *locus* in which we find ourselves (with '*locus* indicating both the place in the text and the place in the corresponding classification and journey: an experience familiar to anyone of a certain age who has been questioned on the *Divine Comedy* in an exam). Alberto Manguel has clearly underlined this aspect in his contribution to our conference. Dante, he writes, has mapped out "a meticulous travel guide . . . with a geological, architectural and theological precision". To follow Dante's journey, to fix it in our minds, is indeed to internalise an order that is at once cosmic and moral.

It is fascinating to observe how this dimension comes to the fore in visual representations of the poem. Even very early illustrated manuscripts contain diagrams that set out the structure of Dante's journey for the reader to see and comprehend.[12] Particularly in Florence, such diagrams enjoyed a remarkable dissemination: evidence for this includes Domenico di Michelino's famous painting of 1465, currently in the Duomo, where behind the poet we see a depiction of the mountain of Purgatory, with its various terraces (Figure 4). Graphic reconstruction is also interwoven with studies of Dante's cosmography, beginning the work of the mathematician and architect Antonio Manetti (1423–1498) on the *Sito, forma e misura dello Inferno*, a text cited by Cristoforo Landino in his commentary and published in 1506 by Gerolamo Benivieni. Even the young Galileo was

---

[10] Michael Baxandall: The Period Eye. In: *Painting and Experience in Fifteenth Century Italy: A Primer in the Social History of Pictorial Style*. Oxford: Oxford University Press 1985, p. 29–108.
[11] *Rhetorica novissima*. Edited by by Augusto Gaudenzi. Bologna: Bibliotheca iuridica Medii Aevi, II 1892, p. 249–297 (see pp. 275–279).
[12] See Lucia Battaglia Ricci: *Dante per immagini. Dalle miniature trecentesche ai giorni nostri*. Turin: Einaudi 2018; Lina Bolzoni: *La* Commedia *di Dante nello specchio delle immagini*.

associated with geographical reconstruction of the afterlife when, between 1587 and 1588, he intervened to defend Manetti against the criticism of Alessandro Vellutello. This scholar from Lucca (and thus not a Florentine, as Michelangelo would observe with a note of disdain) had an edition of the *Comedy* published at Venice in 1544 by Marcolini, accompanied not only by a *Nova espositione* but also tables that precisely depict the structure of Dante's journey, with "mathematical precision" – as Volkmann, one of its first scholars, critically observes – and "continuous maps and cross-sections".[13] This is a telling example of an approach to reading the poem that sought to bring emphasise its order, in a realistic way that at each stage of the journey seeks to remind us of our position on the map (Figure 5). In 1568, the only illustrations included with Bernardino Daniello's commentary on the *Comedy* would be depictions of the three kingdoms of the afterlife. We would also like to recall a peculiar diagram of the *Inferno* (Figure 6) found in the splendid exemplar of the 1491 edition of the *Comedy* held in the Casa di Dante in Rome, whose pages are accompanied by a dense handwritten commentary and over 400 colour miniatures, probably executed between 1497 and 1499 by Antonio Grifo. The diagram, Andrea Torre writes, "does indeed reproduce a pattern utilised in other visualisations of the poem, but interprets it through graphical details belonging to Grifo's *modus figurandi* (the scrolls, which here mark the various circles of Hell and elsewhere denote the identity of characters, or give iconic substance to memorable verses), as well as the original solution of having the beast-like legs of Lucifer emerge from the infernal topography, covered in the ice of Cocytus, to form a singular, monstruous *corpus* from the many hands which is made a receptacle for all the sins of humanity."[14]

We may observe the characteristics of the *loci* within the various kingdoms of the afterlife. Within the *Inferno*, the order is fixed forever: each of the damned souls that Dante meets will remain there, tied to their punishment and their appointed locus even after the Last Judgment, within the shadow without time. In the other two canticles the situation is different. Not only is Purgatory destined to disappear, but the very order which Dante follows is itself in a certain sense precarious. Indeed, the penitents Dante meets are positioned on specific terraces

---

13 See Paolo Procaccioli: *La proposta di Marcolini (1544): la* Commedia *commentata da Vellutello*. In: Lina Bolzoni: *La* Commedia *di Dante nello specchio delle immagini*, p. 237–265, who cites (p. 239) Michelangelo (letter of 9 May 1545), in Michelangelo Buonarroti: *Carteggio di Michelangelo. Edizione postuma di G. Poggi*. Edited by Paola Barocchi and Renzo Ristori. Florence: SPES 1979, p. 212, n. MXLII, and Ludwig Volkmann: *Iconografia dantesca. Le rappresentazioni figurative della Divina Commedia*. Florence / Venice: Olschki 1898, p. 73.
14 Andrea Torre: "Il vero chiodo". L'incunabolo della Casa di Dante col commento figurato di Grifo. In: Lina Bolzoni: *La* Commedia *di Dante nello specchio delle immagini*, p. 217–236 (p. 219).

only so that the main fault with which they have blemished themselves is made clear and memorable. Before or after their encounter with Dante, they are destined to purify themselves of other errors on the other terraces of the *Purgatorio*.[15] Dante observes this in relation to himself while travelling through the terrace of the envious:

"Li occhi", diss' io, "mi fieno ancor qui tolti, ma picciol tempo, ché poca è l'offesa fatta per esser con invidia vòlti.	"My eyes," I said, "will be denied me here, but only briefly; the offense of envy was not committed often by their gaze.
Troppa è più la paura ond' è sospesa l'anima mia del tormento di sotto, che già lo 'ncarco di là giù mi pesa".	I fear much more the punishment below; my soul is anxious, in suspense; already I feel the heavy weights of the first terrace."

(*Purgatorio* XIII, 133–138)

If we wish to indulge Dante's pact with the reader, we might at this point say that Dante has engineered it so that the pilgrim's journey coincides with the moment at which the structure of Purgatory is most legible, best suited to becoming a system of memory and spiritual purification. On the other hand, we might say that Dante's poetry remodels the divine order according to his own needs, including those which relate to memory.

This aspect of the question is clarified in the *Paradiso*. In the sphere of the Moon, Beatrice explains to Dante that the souls of the blessed are not really located in the *loci* that he observes: rather, God uses this means of representation (that is, positioning) to render the variety of degrees of blessing that the souls enjoy comprehensible to the frail human intellect. Moses, Samuel, John, and the Madonna do not have

non hanno in altro cielo i loro scanni che questi spirti che mo t'appariro,	[...] their place in any other heaven than that which houses those souls you just saw,
né hanno a l'esser lor più o meno anni;	nor will their blessedness last any longer.
ma tutti fanno bello il primo giro, e differentemente han dolce vita	But all those souls grace the Empyrean; and each of them has gentle life – though some
per sentir più e men l'etterno spiro.	sense the Eternal Spirit more, some less.

---

15 I owe this observation to Luigi Blasucci, who has studied the particular role that time plays in the second canticle. See Luigi Blasucci: Tempo e penitenza nel *Purgatorio*. In: *Soglie*, II (2000), p. 33–45.

> Qui si mostraro, non perché sortita
> sia questa spera lor, ma per far segno
> de la celestïal c'ha men salita.
>
> Così parlar conviensi al vostro ingegno,
> però che solo da sensato apprende
> ciò che fa poscia d'intelletto degno.

> They showed themselves to you here not because
> this is their sphere, but as a sign for you
> that in the Empyrean their place is lowest.
>
> Such signs are suited to your mind, since from
> the senses only can it apprehend
> what then becomes fit for the intellect.
>
> (*Paradiso* IV, 31–42)

The relationship between place and image in Paradise is thus purely illusory. It is part of the rhetorical strategy, the system of memory employed by the souls and God for Dante's benefit. In other words, Dante's poetry presents itself on this level, too, as a reproduction of divine language.[16]

We now come to another essential component of a system of memory: *imagines agentes*. In accordance to the tradition described above, these are to be associated with the thing to be remembered and must be singularly striking, capable of eliciting horror or pleasure. They therefore absolutely must not be banal, or even merely commonplace and predictable. Weinrich has underlined that the basic technique Dante uses is that of contrapasso, the principle of justice whereby the punishment corresponds with the crime. It is significant, he notes, that the explicit declaration of this principle is voiced by Bertran de Born ("and thus, in me one sees the law of counter-penalty [*contrapasso*]", *Inferno* XXVIII, 142), and therefore serves as a comment on one of the most terrible and fantastical apparitions of the *Inferno*.[17] Bertran is in fact a decapitated corpse who carries his own head by its hair. He is punished in this way, placed among the sowers of discord, because he spurred the young prince Henry III to rebel against his father, the king of England. His image as a damned soul makes visible the nature and

---

[16] Recent studies have interpreted this passage in various ways. Freccero comments on Beatrice's words by highlighting the illusory character of the structure of the *Paradiso*: "The structure of the *cantica* depends, not upon a principle of *mimesis*, but rather upon metaphor" (John Freccero: *Dante. The Poetics of Conversion*. Edited by Rachel Jacoff. Cambridge MA: Harvard University Press 1986, p. 222). Teodolinda Barolini notes that Dante projects "onto the souls a concern for representing themselves to the pilgrim which is in fact a displaced articulation of his own concerns as writer of this texts" and maintains that such a strategy is necessary in order to allow him to write the *Paradiso*, providing him with a similar structure to the other two canticles (Teodolinda Barolini: *The Undivine Comedy: Detheologizing Dante*. Princeton: Princeton University Press 1992).

[17] Harald Weinrich: *La memoria di Dante*. Florence: Accademia della Crusca 1994, an essay partially reprised in: Memoria e oblio davanti a Dio e agli uomini (Dante). In: Idem: *Lete. Arte e critica dell'oblio*. Bologna: Il Mulino 1999, p. 39–60.

very essence of his actions: he mutilated the body of the State, severing its head from its torso. Put differently, Dante's contrapasso makes analogy visible; it take the metaphor literally. In this way the damned become *imagines agentes*, signalling both the sin that has been committed and divine justice.

Encounters with various damned souls and description of the punishments they suffer serve to construct *imagines agentes*, impressing in our mind both knowledge of the sin and horror at the consequent punishment. That Dante's memory is charged with emotions and passions – that it is an impassioned memory – is extremely important. This is demonstrated to us in some of the most famous passages of the *Inferno*. "There is no greater sorrow than thinking back upon a happy time in misery," says Francesca da Rimini (*Inferno* V, 121), quoting Virgil (*Aeneid* II, 3–4; "and this your teacher knows") and thus causing the story of Aeneas and Dido to resurface. For Master Adam, the counterfeiter of coins condemned to never-ending thirst, memory itself becomes part of the punishment:

Li ruscelletti che d'i verdi colli	The rivulets that fall into the Arno
del Casentin discendon giuso in Arno,	down from the green hills of the Casentino
faccendo i lor canali freddi e molli,	with channels cool and moist, are constantly
sempre mi stanno innanzi, e non indarno,	before me; I am racked by memory –
ché l'imagine lor vie più m'asciuga	the image of their flow parches me more
che 'l male ond' io nel volto mi discarno.	than the disease that robs my face of flesh.

(*Inferno* XXX, 64–69)

Ugolino (*Inferno* XXXIII, 4–6) begins his story by saying: ""You want me to renew / despairing pain that presses at my heart / even as I think back, before I speak." Numerous other examples could be given, but it is more interesting to see how this impassioned memory assails Dante and plays a role of considerable relevance to our discussion. At the very beginning of the poem, and thus an extremely memorable locus, we read:

Nel mezzo del cammin di nostra vita	When I had journeyed half of our life's way,
mi ritrovai per una selva oscura	I found myself within a shadowed forest,
ché la diritta via era smarrita.	for I had lost the path that does not stray.
Ahi quanto a dir qual era è cosa dura	Ah, it is hard to speak of what it was,
esta selva selvaggia e aspra e forte	that savage forest, dense and difficult,
che nel pensier rinova la paura!	which even in recall renews my fear

(*Inferno* I, 1–6)

Here we encounter a strong contrast in verb tenses, as happens in many similar passages, above all in the *Inferno*: "the darkened plain / *quaked* so tremendously – the memory / of terror then, *bathes* me in sweat again" (*Inferno* III,

131–132); "and there within I *saw* a dreadful swarm / of serpents so extravagant in form – / remembering them still *drains* my blood from me (*Inferno* XXIV, 84); "It *grieved* me then and now *grieves* me again / when I *direct* my mind to what I *saw*" (*Inferno* XXVI, 19–20); "And when I heard him speak so angrily, / I *turned around* to him with shame so great / that it still *stirs* within my memory" (*Inferno* XXX, 133); "And now – with fear I *set it down* in meter – / I *was* where all the shades were fully covered" (*Inferno* XXXIV, 10); "'Love that discourses to me in my mind' / he then *began* to sing – and *sang* so sweetly / that I still hear that sweetness *sound* in me" (*Purgatorio* II, 112–114); and so on. In calling to mind the opposition between the world that is narrated and the world that is commented, the contrast of verb tenses neatly highlights the complexity of the question of who the "I" is in the *Comedy*: there is the past tense of the pilgrim, of the *agens*, and the present tense of the *auctor*, he who remembers, writes and comments.[18] However, it is precisely the emotive force of memory that tends to destroy the distinction between times and functions. The fear that the memory of the forest carries certainly serves to construct the *auctoritas* of the writer Dante, in the sense that it is proof of the truth of his lived experience, and at the same time underlines its quality, its particular force; yet these are not its only functions. The pilgrim Dante also represents the ideal reader of his poem, in the sense that he proposes a model 'ethics of reading', showing us how we should respond to the poem, the transformations the various cantos should progressively enact within us. In other words, he offers us a model to imitate: we readers, too, must ensure the images act upon us with full efficacy. In this perspective, it is essential to observe how impassioned memory is intimately interwoven with contrapasso, and thus with the fundamental technique which, as we have stated, serves to construct *imagines agentes*. We might consider Caina, the deepest part of Hell, where those who betrayed their relatives are trapped within the lake of ice:

Poscia *vid'* io mille visi cagnazzi	And after that *I saw* a thousand faces
fatti per freddo; onde *mi vien riprezzo*,	made doglike by the cold; for which *I shudder* –
e *verrà sempre*, de' gelati guazzi.	and *always will* – when I face frozen fords.

(*Inferno* XXXII, 70–72)

This is the same contrast of verb tenses that we observed in the *incipit*, reinforced and expanded by the future ("and always will"), except here the interplay of associations is even more refined. A tangible experience, one belonging to the earthly world – the sight of "frozen fords", of icy lakes – calls the infernal setting to mind

---

[18] See Harald Weinrich: *Tempus. Le funzioni dei tempi nel testo*. Bologna: Il Mulino 2004. See also Franca Ageno Brambilla: Osservazioni sull'aspetto e il tempo del verbo nella *Commedia*. In: *Studi danteschi*. Padua: Antenore 1990, p. 138–183.

by means of analogy. Those who have undermined the law of love, who were indifferent to its warmth, are embedded in ice: contrapasso creates an image that reveals the nature of the sin. The memory and horror that this generates in Dante not only remain intact in the present but are reinforced by the sight of icy lakes. In other words, moral horror is prolonged in physical horror, in the unbearable icy feeling that the earthly experience regenerates each time through analogy. The boundary between body and psyche is transcended: the force of imagination, so crucial for memory, knows precisely how to accomplish this. We readers are invited to share with Dante the entire process of memory, with its components of knowledge and of moral and physical rejection.

But how far does the process of memory go? Images, imprinted in our inner faculties, in our imagination, intellect and memory, constitute a guide, an aid in following the path that leads to God. At the culminating moment of the journey, however, they cease to exist and to operate, linked as they are to the specific human condition, and thus also to its weakness. The rhetorical component of the question is negatively expressed: that which cannot be recalled through images cannot be expressed in words:

> Da quinci innanzi il mio veder fu maggio
> che 'l parlar mostra, ch'a tal vista cede,
> e cede la memoria a tanto oltraggio.
>
> From that point on, what I could see was greater than speech can show: at such a sight, it fails – and memory fails when faced with such excess.
> (*Paradiso* XXXIII, 55–57)

In reality, the verses that we have cited do not bring the use of images to an end, but rather underline the increasing difficulty of using them to effectively represent and ensure the remembrance of vision as it progresses. Here too, at this final stage of the journey, the emotional quality of memory is not lessened:

> cotal son io, ché quasi tutta cessa
> mia visïone, e ancor mi distilla
> nel core il dolce che nacque da essa.
>
> [. . .] my vision almost fades completely, yet it still distills within my heart the sweetness that was born of it.
> (*Paradiso* XXXIII, 61–63)

And shortly after:

> La forma universal di questo nodo
> credo ch'i' vidi, perché più di largo,
> dicendo questo, mi sento ch'i' godo.
>
> I think I saw the universal shape which that knot takes; for, speaking this, I feel a joy that is more ample.
> (*Paradiso* XXXIII, 91–93)

We have truly reached the end of the journey; and once again memory leaves in the soul – of the poet, and of those who read or listen – a trace of the emotions it carries with it.

Bibliographical References

Ageno Brambilla, Franca: Osservazioni sull'aspetto e il tempo del verbo nella *Commedia*. In: *Studi danteschi*. Padua: Antenore 1990, p. 138–183.

Assmann, Aleida: *Ricordare. Forme e mutamenti della memoria culturale*. Bologna, il Mulino 2002.

Azzetta, Luca: *Il duplice volto di un manoscritto quattrocentesco: il codice Yates Thompson*. In: *La* Commedia *di Dante nello specchio delle immagini*. Edited by Lina Bolzoni, Rome: Istituto della Enciclopedia italiana 2021, p. 117–149.

Barolini, Teodolinda: *The Undivine Comedy: Detheologizing Dante*. Princeton: Princeton University Press 1992.

Battaglia Ricci, Lucia: *Dante per immagini. Dalle miniature trecentesche ai giorni nostri*. Einaudi: Turin 2018.

Baxandall, Michael: The Period Eye. In: *Painting and Experience in Fifteenth Century Italy: A Primer in the Social History of Pictorial Style*. Oxford: Oxford University Press 1985, p. 29–108.

Blasucci, Luigi: Tempo e penitenza nel *Purgatorio*. In: *Soglie*, II (2000), p. 33–45.

Bolzoni, Lina: *La stanza della memoria. Modelli letterari e iconografici nell'età della stampa*. Turin: Einaudi 1995.

Bolzoni, Lina: *La rete delle immagini. Predicazione in volgare dalle origini a Bernardino da Siena*. Turin, Einaudi 2002.

Bolzoni, Lina: Allegorie e immagini della memoria: il 'Colloquio spirituale' e il ciclo della 'Torre della Sapienza'. In: Id. *La rete delle immagini*, p. 47–99.

Bolzoni, Lina: *Dante o della memoria appassionata*. In: *Lettere italiane*, LX (2008), p. 169–193.

Bolzoni, Lina (ed.): *La* Commedia *di Dante nello specchio delle immagini*. Roma: Istituto della Enciclopedia Italiana, Treccani 2021.

Bolzoni, Lina: "Quinci su vo per non esser più cieco" (Purg. XXVI,57): l'educazione dello sguardo, in Il "visibile parlare" di Dante: dalla *Commedia* alle arti dei nostri giorni. In: Idem: *La* Commedia *di Dante nello specchio delle immagini*, p. XIII–XXXVI.

Boncompagno da Signa: *Rhetorica novissima*. Edited by Augusto Gaudenzi. Bologna: Bibliotheca iuridica Medii Aevi, II 1892, p. 249–297.

Buonarroti, Michelangelo: *Carteggio di Michelangelo. Edizione postuma di G. Poggi*. Edited by Paola Barocchi and Renzo Ristori. Florence: SPES 1979, p. 212, n. MXLII.

Cachey, Theodore J.: *Cartografie dantesche: mappando Malebolge*. In: *Critica del testo*, XIV / 2 (2011), *Dante oggi / 2*. Edited by Roberto Antonelli, Annalisa Landolfi, Arianna Punzi, p. 229–260.

Carruthers, Mary J.: *The Book of Memory: A Study of Memory in Medieval Culture*. Cambridge: Cambridge University Press 1990.

Carruthers, Mary J.: *The Craft of Thought: Meditation, Rethoric, and the Making of Images, 400–1200*. Cambridge: Cambridge University Press 1998.

Carruthers J. Mary and Jan M. Ziolkowski (eds.): *The Medieval Craft of Memory: An Anthology of Texts and Pictures*. Philadelphia: University of Pennsylvania Press 2002.

Contini, Gianfranco: Un'interpretazione di Dante (1965) In: Idem: *Un'idea di Dante. Saggi danteschi*. Turin: Einaudi (1970 / 1976) 2001.

Detienne, Marcel: *I maestri di verità nella Grecia arcaica*. Rome / Bari: Laterza 1977.

Freccero, John: *Dante. The Poetics of Conversion*. Edited by Rachel Jacoff. Cambridge MA: Harvard University Press 1986.

Freeman Sandler, Lucy: *Religious Instruction and Devotional Study: The Pictorial and the Textual in Gothic Diagrams.* In: *The Visualization of Knowledge in Medieval and Early Modern Europe.* Edited by Marcia Kupfer, Adam S. Cohen, J.H. Chajes. Turnhout: Brepols 2020, p. 429–448.

Havelock, Eric A.: *Cultura orale e civiltà della scrittura.* Rome / Bari: Laterza 1963.

Lubac, Henri de: *Exégèse médiévale: les quatre sens de l'écriture*, 4 vols. Paris: Aubier 1959–1964.

Procaccioli, Paolo: *La proposta di Marcolini (1544): la* Commedia *commentata da Vellutello.* In: Lina Bolzoni: *La* Commedia *di Dante nello specchio delle immagini*, p. 237–265.

Rossi, Paolo: *Clavis universalis. Arti della memoria e logica combinatoria da Lullo a Leibniz.* Milan / Naples: Ricciardi 1960.

Svenbro, Jesper: *La parola e il marmo. Alle origini della poetica greca.* Turin: Boringhieri 1984.

Torre, Andrea: "Il vero chiodo". L'incunabolo della Casa di Dante col commento figurato di Grifo. In: Lina Bolzoni: *La* Commedia *di Dante nello specchio delle immagini*, p. 217–236.

Volkmann, Ludwig: *Iconografia dantesca. Le rappresentazioni figurative della Divina Commedia.* Florence / Venice: Olschki 1898.

Weinrich, Harald: La memoria di Dante. Florence: Accademia della Crusca 1994, an essay partially reprised in: Memoria e oblio davanti a Dio e agli uomini (Dante). In: Idem: *Lete. Arte e critica dell'oblio.* Bologna: Il Mulino 1999, p. 39–60.

Weinrich, Harald: *Tempus. Le funzioni dei tempi nel testo.* Bologna: Il Mulino 2004.

Yates, Frances A.: *L'arte della memoria.* Turin: Einaudi 1972.

Figures

Figure 1: *The Celestial Rose, where Dante and Saint Bernard see Mary and the Archangel Gabriel, Saint Anna and Moses*; miniature by Giovanni da Paolo. In: *Paradiso*, Canto XXXII. London: British Library, MS Yates Thompson 36 (1440–1450), fol. 188r.

Figure 2: *The Tree of Vices and Virtues*, miniature, late 14th century / early 15th century. Florence: Biblioteca Medicea Laurenziana, cod. Pluteo 30.24, fols. 3v-4r.

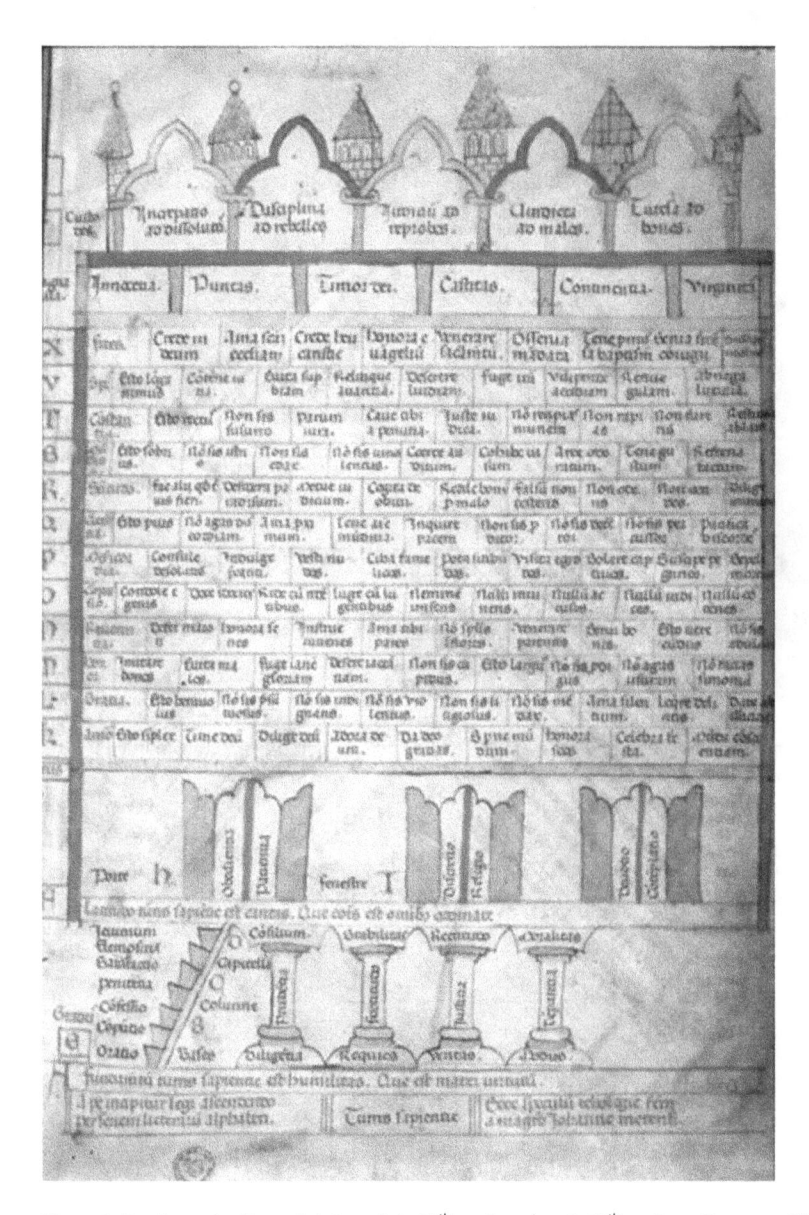

Figure 3: *Turris sapientiae*, miniature, late 14th century / early 15th century. Florence: Biblioteca Medicea Laurenziana, cod. Pluteo 30.24, fol. 1r.

Figure 4: Domenico di Michelino, *Dante, Florence, the Comedy*. Painting in Santa Maria del Fiore, Florence, 1465.

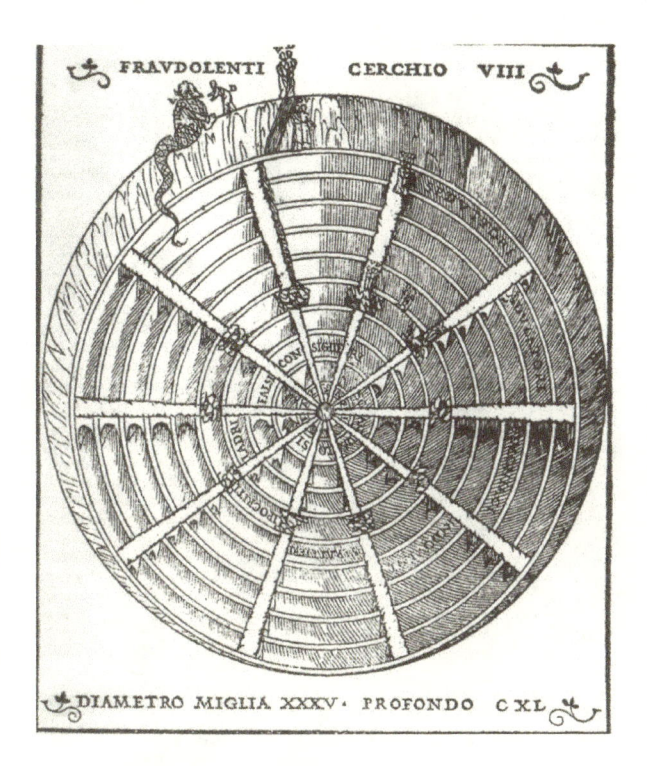

Figure 5: *Description of the Inferno*, woodcut. In: *La comedia di Dante Alighieri con la nova esposizione di Alessandro Vellutello*. Venice: Marcolini, 1544.

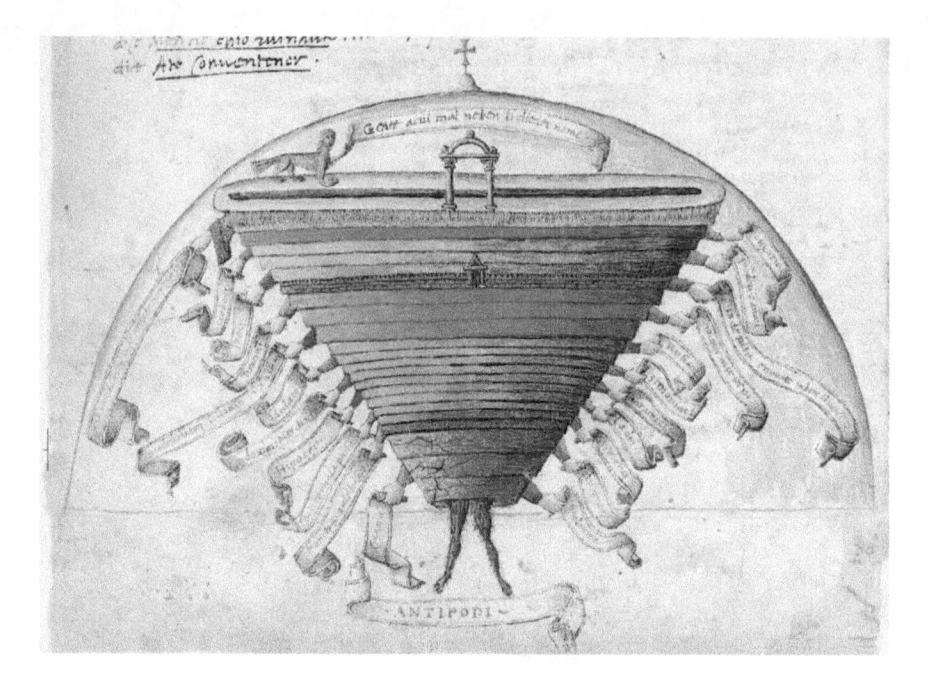

Figure 6: *Diagram of the Inferno*, Antonio Grifo, miniature, 1497–1499. In: *Commedia with the Commentary of Cristoforo Landino*. Venice 1491, fol. XIVr. Rome: Casa di Dante.

Giulio Ferroni
Dante, Poet of a Europe to Come

In Ernst Robert Curtius's monumental book, *Europäische Literatur und lateinisches Mittelalter*, Dante is afforded the utmost prominence, almost as the culmination and resolution of the literature of the Latin Middle Ages and its projection towards that of modern Europe. The Dante of Curtius is one whose prophetic anticipation is like

> a leaven which Dante casts into the tradition of the medieval West. The leaven penetrates the coagulated mass to its most remote regions and organizes it into a realm of new forms. It is the projection of Dante's personality on 'the book and school of the ages' (George) – on the total literary tradition [...] A single man, a solitary man, sets himself face to face with an entire millennium and transforms that historical world.[1]

The great philologist, such a keen observer of and participant in early twentieth-century poetry (and so close to T. S. Eliot, an exceptional connoisseur of Dante), placed Dante at the centre of European literature, on account both of his of having gathered the legacy of the medieval West and his stretching towards European literary modernity. And I believe that even today, after so many years and albeit with some partial repositioning, we may still fundamentally subscribe to Curtius's position. It is possible to follow the meandering and sometimes deep-running waters of the 'modern' presence (including its relative eclipse in the sixteenth and seventeenth centuries), above all on two essential fronts: the prominence of the author and that of the character.

We can indeed attribute to Dante the foundation of the image of the author in relation to the literary work, in terms of a coincidence between universality and individuality: the link between the work and the life and deeds of the subject, the *poet-character* (the *personaggio-poeta*, following Contini's famous formula), and the projection of the same subject as an image of the human, of every possible human being, as an everyman. Within this nexus lies the birth and construction of the modern author (and it is impossible not to recall Albert R. Ascoli's work and its significant title, *Dante and the Making of the Modern Author*). Nor, moreover, should we forget that in the prominence of his being an author (not only in the *Comedy*, but in all of Dante's texts, beginning from the *Vita nuova*), the image of

---

[1] Ernst Robert Curtius: *European Literature and the Latin Middle Ages* (1948). Princeton: Princeton University Press 1953. Reprint Ed. 2013, p. 359.

Note: Translated from the Italian by Matthew Coneys Wainwright.

https://doi.org/10.1515/9783110796049-008

Dante is imposed and characterised within the tradition and very iconography of his persona; and that the modern tradition of portraits of writers stems precisely from the way in which he represents himself and other writers (above all Virgil, his *master and author*). It is no coincidence that the many images that have been dedicated to Dante's poem and human figure establish the *author* Dante as their character, often in a gruff and disdainful depiction; and that in the many biographies dedicated to him, it is his very role as author, of a human figure consubstantial with his work, that has provided a fixed sense of his personality.

Yet if the author presents himself as a character, the prominence of other characters, of all the figures encountered in the otherworldly journey, is no less significant. This prominence and conspicuousness draws its strength from the fact that the majority of these individuals are drawn from the real world of Dante's time, from his present day; and that even historical and mythical characters are perceived as truly present, as part of the author's world. Again, it is Curtius who observes that the multiplicity and variety of persons "in the *Comedy* is explained by the most impressive and most fertile innovation which Dante's genius incorporated into the antique and medieval heritage: his drawing upon contemporary history". He adds that within the *Comedy* "the entire cosmos of history is unfolded, to be apportioned anew in the astrophysical cosmos of the structure of the world and in the metaphysical cosmos of the transcendent. Physical cosmology and the metaphysical realm of values are interconnected in the strictest correlation".[2]

This representation of a world understood as contemporary, in the terms in which it has been portrayed by Gaetano De Sanctis and Erich Auerbach, is oriented towards establishing the concreteness of human beings – the individuals the pilgrim encounters during his journey through the afterlife – in the completeness of their otherworldly destiny, the determinateness they receive through death, and, beyond death, in the distillation of their lives' meanings in the 'end products' which are the souls of the departed. The hereafter of Dante's poem is populated by formidable figures whose presence collects the meaning of completed lives: it is the kingdom of a humanity that has reached fulfilment (and this, in reference to the past life, is also true of the souls of the *Purgatorio*, who are nevertheless still focused on the further fulfilment of celestial blessing). This situation reaches the most absolute level of "valuable determinateness" that stems from perception of the death of another, to quote the existential reflection of Michail Bachtin (in *Author and Hero in Aesthetic Activity*, an essay written between 1920 and 1924). The Russian scholar traced the individuation of the literary hero, his original

---

[2] Ernst R. Curtius: *European Literature*, p. 366.

"birth", to the recognition of the death of another, the perception of another's life as complete:

> A *determined* life, a life freed from the claws of what-is-yet-to-be, of the future, of purpose and meaning – such a life becomes emotionally measurable, musically expressive, and self-sufficient (sufficient to itself as totally present-on-hand); its being-already-determined becomes a *valuable* determinateness. [. . .] Inner determinateness – the embodiment of meaning in mortal flesh – is born and dies *in* the world and *for* the world; it is given totally in the world and can be totally consummated in the world; the whole of it is gathered and consolidated into a finite object. As such, inner determinateness *can* have the significance of a plot or story, it *can* be a hero. [. . .] It is only in the world of others that an aesthetic, plot-bearing, intrinsically valuable movement is possible – a movement in *the past* which has value regardless of the future and in which all obligations and debts are forgiven and all hopes are abandoned.[3]

Dante inhabits this perspective with much greater acuity. His characters are all real individuals (or understood as such by the poet), his contemporaries and, in many cases, people he personally knew. Death has bestowed on them their status as 'ultimate' presences, marking the conclusion and fulfilment of the entire journey of their existence. The meaning of their being is condensed in this otherworldly and poetic presence, in their depiction by poet and the words they speak; sometimes even in their fleeting appearances between the lines. It is this that makes them personalities, entities who impose themselves upon the imagination, reaching beyond their poetic substance, the written space in which they are made manifest (and of course many of Dante's characters have given rise to narrative developments, fabrications and continuations, including on a popular level, "treating the shades as one treats solid things"). Through his progress, the author-character is reflected in the characters he meets, "protagonist and spectator, witness and patient, for whom the 'trials' of others become the 'documents' of himself".[4]

If the intensity of this poetic world and its leaning towards the absolute, towards a radical essentiality of experience and the word, have nurtured European literary modernity, this can in part be attributed to the fundamentally European character of Dante's culture. His anthropological and political background is already Italian insofar as it is already European; and not merely on account

---

[3] M. M. Bakhtin, M. Holquist, V. Liapunov: *Art and Answerability. Early Philosophical Essays*. Austin: University of Texas Press 1990, p. 108, 111, 112.
[4] Here I repeat an observation made by Salvatore Battaglia in his still essential work (first published in 1967): *Mitografia del personaggio*. See the edition edited by V. Russo, with a prefatory 'Memoria' by M. Pomilio. Naples: Liguori 1991, p. 43.

of his relationship with the Latin Middle Ages, but also because of his constant dialogue with the new vernacular culture of *oc* and *oïl*.

In the expressive tension of his great poem, geographical space is unfurled with the formidable realism afforded by his metrical and linguistic arrangement, the cohesion of that which the author himself termed "the rules of poetry". This has been observed by an extremely perceptive connoisseur of Dante, Andrea Zanzotto, who claims it is precisely the interweaving / chain of the *terza rima*, the "framing" it offers, that allows his language to reach a truly "ultra-realistic condensation".[5]

All this enables the force of Dante's representation, its emphasising of physical and geographical reality, its capacity to make objects, volumes, places and spaces perceptible, as if they were present before the reader, almost protruding into their mental horizon. All this lies within a crucial geographical culture, one in which the recognition of Europe is also inscribed, in terms which commentators often recall (also traced back to Brunetto Latini's *Trésor*). These are already at play in the canzone "Io son venuto al punto de la rota" (Europe and Ursa Major) and in *De vulgari eloquentia* I, 8, in the preliminary distinction between the three great languages of Europe, northern, southern and eastern, followed by the more specific division of their various forms (the languages of *oc*, *oïl* and *sì* of the threefold southern tongue).

In the *Comedy*, the term 'Europe' is encountered on only four occasions, each in a markedly different context (*Purgatorio* VIII, 123; *Paradiso* VI, 5; *Paradiso* XII, 48; *Paradiso* XXVII, 84). While in the first instance it is used generically by the pilgrim Dante to indicate the great fame of the Malaspina family, in the others it appears among broad geographical dimensions, panoramic views of distant horizons. This is the case in the splendid image of western Europe that indicates the homeland of Saint Dominic ("In that part of the West where gentle zephyr / rises to open those new leaves in which / Europe appears reclothed, not far from where, / behind the waves that beat upon the coast, / the sun, grown weary from its lengthy course, at times conceals itself from all men's eyes . . .", *Paradiso* XII, 46–51).[6] Later, when for a second time the pilgrim looks down towards the earth from the sphere of the fixed stars, having cast his eye across ninety degrees of celestial space (from the meridian of Jerusalem to that of Cadiz), he perceives at the western limit of his visual range the endpoint of the journey of Ulysses and, at the eastern limit, the coast of Phoenicia (where, according to myth, the abduction of Europa took place):

---

[5] Lorenzini, Niva: Il "miglior fabbro", il realismo, il corpo-parola (interview with Andrea Zanzotto, Pieve di Soligo, 5 January 2009). In: *il verri*, n. 39 (2009), p. 19–25 (on p. 19).

[6] "In quella parte ove surge ad aprire / Zefiro dolce le novelle fronde / di che si vede Europa rivestire, / non molto lungi al percuoter de l'onde / dietro a le quali, per la lunga foga, / lo sol talvolta ad ogne uom si nasconde".

Da l'ora ch'ïo avea guardato prima i' vidi mosso me per tutto l'arco che fa dal mezzo al fine il primo clima;	I saw that, from the time when I looked down before, I had traversed all of the arc of the first clime, from its midpoint to end,
sì ch'io vedea di là da Gade il varco folle d'Ulisse, e di qua presso il lito nel qual si fece Europa dolce carco.	so that, beyond Cadiz, I saw Ulysses' mad course and, to the east, could almost see that shoreline where Europa was sweet burden. (*Paradiso* XXVII, 79–84)

Beyond the name of Europe, however, various places within the continent are identified more specifically within the *Comedy*, both to draw comparisons with the landscape of the afterlife and as places of origin of characters or settings of historical and political events. They are great geographical spaces, truly comprehensive views, panoramic vistas that seem to carry the physical consistency of the space within the expressiveness of their language, almost as if Dante knows how to employ a kind of ideal cartographic measure to convey the real substance of the setting. He should be termed a poet of setting, the setting of Italy and of Europe, of Italy because it *is* Europe.

As an example, I will offer only the remarkable similarities of the stone embankments of the third ring of the seventh circle of Hell. Here, the mention of geographical places is grounded in the human work that built them and which simultaneously connects them, despite their distance from each other (an equivalence between the waters and embankments of two different and distant settings, the North Sea and the Brenta, and an interrelation between the plains of Padua and the climate of Carinthia, *Carentana*):

Quali Fiamminghi tra Guizzante e Bruggia, temendo 'l fiotto che 'nver lor s'avventa, fanno lo schermo perché 'l mar si fuggia;	Just as between Wissant and Bruges, the Flemings, in terror of the tide that floods toward them, have built a wall of dykes to daunt the sea;
e quali Padoan lungo la Brenta, per difender lor ville e lor castelli, anzi che Carentana il caldo senta:	and as the Paduans, along the Brenta, build bulwarks to defend their towns and castles before the dog days fall on Carentana;
a tale imagine eran fatti quelli, tutto che né sì alti né sì grossi, qual che si fosse, lo maestro félli.	just so were these embankments, even though they were not built so high and not so broad, whoever was the artisan who made them. (*Inferno* XV, 4–12)

Dante's perspective on historical and political matters, that which we would term geopolitics, is evidently European. Although the historical and political junctures of each of the sixth cantos broaden the outlook from Florentine space to that of Italy and the universal space of the Empire, all three canticles pay constant attention to European space, and to the intertwining of Florentine and Italian politics with that of Europe as a whole. The famous invective of *Purgatorio* VI – "abject Italy, you inn of sorrows" ("serva Italia, di dolore ostello") – is situated within the denouncement of the emperor ("German Albert") and definition of Italy as "the garden of the Empire" (105). In Canto XX of the same canticle, the encounter with Hugh Capet focuses on the kingdom of France, with a summary of the affairs and misdeeds of its various rulers. And in the *Paradiso*'s discourse of the eagle in the heaven of Jupiter, we will encounter harsh condemnation of the rulers of Europe, arranged in three groups of three *terzine* whose first letters form the acrostic LUE, the plague that casts its shadow over Europe. This denunciation appears within a singular sequence of geographical details (in which a single verse mentions the rulers of its remotest kingdoms, "he of Portugal and he of Norway", *Paradiso* XIX, 139).[7]

In the condemnation of Christian princes, here and elsewhere, decisive emphasis is placed on what Dante sees as their particularism, their stubborn clinging to a space of limited powers, which is opposed to the need for a universal political organism that will guide humanity towards a peaceful terrestrial existence. We know that the brief years of Henry VII of Luxembourg's descent into Italy led Dante to hope for the restoration of imperial order on a wholly European level; yet it is unclear whether the *Monarchia* was composed at the time of the emperor's descent, shortly beforehand, or – as appears most likely – in the years immediately after. It is however clear that the universalistic tension of the political treatise concludes by situating Dante's entire political ideology within the aspiration for a Christian Europe unified under the banner of imperial power. This is an altogether medieval ideology in which a historically 'reactionary' character may also be identified, a misunderstanding of the social and economic developments that were beginning to emerge within the European space. Yet despite such limitations, the need for transnational openness shines through the *Monarchia* and may still shine through it today, even when it encounters the prospects and demands of our globalised world; the need for a unified human race, which within our space must assume as its fundamental starting point the unity of Europe. We can therefore identify the *Monarchia* as a book about Europe, one of the earliest manifestations of an ideal that would be undermined and riven by the ever-increasing violence of the centuries, but ever more deeply explored and enriched through the practice of culture, science and the arts in

---

[7] Also present among the 'mystical' souls of the first crown is the Portuguese Petrus Hispanus, author of the *Summulae logicales*, "who, with his twelve books, glows on earth below" (134–135). Taking the name of John XXI, he was the first and only Portuguese pope for just a few months in 1277, prior to his death and burial in the cathedral of Viterbo.

that unity of the European ethos, which persists despite the continuing threat of particularism, populism and sovereignism.

For Dante, the territory over which the Empire should rule is rooted in Christian Europe but expands beyond the boundaries of Europe itself, following the model of ancient Rome. He affirms this explicitly in *Epistola* VII, 11, addressed in 1311 to the same Henry VII to caution him against the too limited nature of his current campaigns in northern Italy, "non prorsus, ut suspicamur, advertens, quoniam Romanorum gloriosa potestas nec metis Ytalie nec tricornis Europe margine coarctatur".[8] Here Dante not only cites a passage of *Aeneid* I, 286–287, which identifies the ocean as the limit of Roman power, but also records the edict of Augustus demanding a universal census, which emanated from an entirely just power, as shown by the divine incarnation and the birth under the edict of he who fulfils all justice. In parallel, *Monarchia* I, XI, 12 affirms that the jurisdiction of the empire is limited only by the ocean, while within the demonstration of Rome's superior nobility of II, III, 10–13 it is shown on the basis of various authorities that Rome's most distant Trojan ancestors came from each of the three parts of the world: Assaracus from Asia (Phrygia), Dardanus from Europe (Italy) and Electra from Africa (Atlas).

In a reference to the contemporary situation and in response to the Church's affirmation of its own primacy over imperial power, *Monarchia* III, XIV, 7 affirms that such a claim is not recognised by universal consensus, since it is rejected not only by Asia and Africa, but also much of Europe:

> And who can doubt that it did not receive it from the consent of all men or of the most exceptional among them, given that not only all Asians and Africans, but also the greater part of those who live in Europe find the idea abhorrent?

On several occasions, including in the *Comedy*, Dante insists on the providentiality of the empire and the peace of Augustus: through the historical moment ordained by God for the incarnation of the Word, *Monarchia* I, XIV, 2 evokes the Pauline notion of *plenitudo temporis* (from Galatians 4:4).

The claim of the Empire's universality nevertheless constitutes the basis of the entire theoretical and doctrinal development of the *Monarchia*. The European dimension of the treatise, like the entire unitary image of Europe and its culture that emerges from Dante's work, is framed within a broader awareness of the unity of the human race: a certainty that, beyond the distant and perhaps 'reactionary' imperial ideology, seems essential even so many centuries later, in our globalised world and amid the ever-increasing urgency of environmental threats to the future of the human race.

---

8 "[F]orgetting in sooth, as we apprehend, that the glorious dominion of the Romans is confined neither by the frontiers of Italy, nor by the coast-line of three-cornered Europe".

From Dante's viewpoint, the unity of humanity is determined in the first instance by the essential aspiration to realise the power of the potential intellect, to reach the highest level of knowledge, from which point alone its human members and the civil body may achieve authentic happiness. This perspective, moreover, is not lacking in Averroeistic roots:

> It is thus clear that the highest potentiality of mankind is his intellectual potentiality or faculty. And since that potentiality cannot be fully actualised all at once in any one individual or in any one of the particular social groupings enumerated above, there must needs be a vast number of individual people in the human race, through whom the whole of this potentiality can be actualised; just as there must be a great variety of things which can be generated so that the whole potentiality of prime matter can continuously be actualised; otherwise one would be postulating a potentiality existing separately from actualisation, which is impossible. And Averroes is in agreement with this opinion in his commentary on the *De anima*. (*Monarchia*, I, III, 7–9).

It is this aspiration to attain the power of the potential intellect that makes universal peace necessary:

> Now it has been sufficiently explained that the activity proper to mankind considered as a whole is constantly to actualise the full intellectual potential of humanity, primarily through thought and secondarily through action (as a function and extension of thought). And since what holds true for the part is true for the whole, and an individual human being "grows perfect in judgment and wisdom when he sits at rest", it is apparent that mankind most freely and readily attends to this activity – an activity which is almost divine, as we read in the psalm: "Thou hast made him a little lower than the angels" – in the calm or tranquillity of peace. Hence it is clear that universal peace is the best of those things which are ordained for our human happiness. (*Monarchia*, I, IV, 1–2).

From this follows the need for a single coordinator, a monarch tasked with guiding the complex collection of kingdoms and communities in which the human race is arranged towards the supreme goal:

> If this holds true in these cases and in individuals who are ordered to one particular goal, then the proposition advanced above is true; now it is agreed that the whole of mankind is ordered to one goal, as has already been demonstrated: there must therefore be one person who directs and rules mankind, and he is properly called "Monarch" or "Emperor". And thus it is apparent that the well-being of the world requires that there be a monarchy or empire. (*Monarchia*, I, v, 9–10).[9]

---

9 The unity of the human race and the necessity of the monarch who rules over it and guides it to the power of knowledge does not preclude the autonomy of individual communities and political institutions, within the broader arrangement of the universe: "Amplius, humana universitas est quoddam totum ad quasdam partes, et est quedam pars ad quoddam totum. Est enim quoddam

The entire reasoning of the *Monarchia* follows from this unitary principle, which is addressed to all humanity and which, in the development of the discourse, avoids invoking limits, divisions, or religious and ethnic conflicts, in an ideal vision of the totality of the human community. Only in later periods would this notion begin to make inroads, and only in our times is it becoming acknowledged as the only possible chance to safeguard the environment and ensure the very survival of humanity and our planet. This unitary vision entails a call for unity of judgment and justice, with the need for a supreme and final judge who can be none other than the emperor himself (I, X and XIII), the guarantor of the freedom of free will and, as such, *minister omnium* (I, XII).

It is moreover evident that in Dante's political context, this unitary call ultimately concluded by identifying itself with Christian Europe. The *Monarchia* – within Dante's cultural situation and his personal and political history, and above all in the polemical development of the third book, directed against the Church's temporal ambitions and its rejection of the supremacy of imperial power – came to stand as an implicit identification of the space of the Empire with the space of Europe, and the hope for unity and peace in a continent riven by multiple conflicts. A Europe whose identity was centred on and justified by ancient Rome, in the broadening of a civil outlook nurtured in the bosom of Italy, that "low-lying Italy for which / the maid Camilla died of wounds, / and Nisus, Turnus, and Euryalus".[10] The same Italy which had yearned in vain for salvation from Europe, for the descent of the German emperor, and which instead of fulfilment had encountered stubborn opposition, divisions and conflicts of every kind. Dante could only translate this lost hope to the plane of the imagination, entrusting to it a seat in the Empyrium, in the heaven beyond the heavens; a still empty seat that Beatrice shows him within the rose of the blessed, before leaving him to be guided by Saint Bernard:

E 'n quel gran seggio a che tu li occhi tieni	And in that seat on which your eyes are fixed
per la corona che già v'è sù posta,	because a crown already waits above it,
prima che tu a queste nozze ceni,	before you join this wedding feast, shall sit
sederà l'alma, che fia giù agosta,	the soul of noble Henry, he who is,
de l'alto Arrigo, ch'a drizzare Italia	on earth, to be imperial; he shall
verrà in prima ch'ella sia disposta.	show Italy the righteous way – but when

she is unready.
(*Paradiso* XXX, 132–138)

---

totum ad regna particularia et ad gentes, ut superiora ostendunt; et est quedam pars ad totum universum" (*Monarchia* I, VII, 1).
10 "Di quella umile Italia fia salute / per cui morì la vergine Cammilla, / Eurialo e Turno e Niso di ferute." (Inferno I, 106–108).

Bibliographical References

Ascoli, Albert Russell: *Dante and the Making of a Modern Author*. Cambridge: Cambridge University Press 2008.
Curtius, Ernst Robert: *European Literature and the Latin Middle Ages* (1948). Princeton: Princeton University Press 1953. Reprint Ed. 2013.
Bakhtin, Michail M., Holquist, Michael, Liapunov, Vadim: *Art and Answerability. Early Philosophical Essays*. Austin: University of Texas Press 1990.
Battaglia, Salvatore: *Mitografia del personaggio* (1967). Edited by Vittorio Russo. Naples: Liguori 1991.
Lorenzini, Niva: Il "miglior fabbro", il realismo, il corpo-parola (interview with Andrea Zanzotto, Pieve di Soligo, 5 January 2009). In: *il verri*, n. 39 (2009), p. 19–25 (on p. 19).

Section II: **Dante in Portugal**

Isabel Almeida
Dante in the Century of Camões

Those who seek to understand 16th-century Portuguese literature and its relationship to other literatures occasionally detect false absences or apparent gaps that do not hold up to subsequent scrutiny. A refinement of perspective or a redirection of inquiry towards a particular area are often sufficient to discard this supposed absence, which leads to intriguing questions, such as: how in reality has this void been filled? By what means and processes? Under which conditions? Due to what intentions or circumstances?

One might also mention false presences. Or perhaps it might be best to distinguish between what constitutes, in actual fact, a presence, and what is little more than a vague recollection or an indirect reference to a piece of work and its author. Invocation or allusion is not the same as knowledge. On the contrary – as Jean Bayard cautions[1] – it is eminently possible to speak of what has not been read. What is the meaning, then, of such a gesture? What risks does it carry and what expectations does it entail?

An example of this is the reception of Dante during the century of Camões. In Portugal, although no texts by the Florentine poet were printed or copied in manuscript form, as far as we know, he was nonetheless remembered, and part of what he wrote – disseminated in the original language or in Castilian versions – did leave a trail. We can trace this in direct references and in intertextual phenomena, or infer it from bibliographical exchanges and occurrences. But would these be another instance of a false absence? The answer varies. We shall see how and at what pace, by exploring, in a diachronic axis, a multiplicity of signs.[2]

---

[1] See Jean Bayard: *Comment parler des livres que l'on n'a pas lus?* Paris: Les Éditions de Minuit 2007.
[2] The present article takes up information disseminated in works by authors such as Achile Pellizzari, Bernardo Sansiventi, Arturo Farinelli, Vincenzo Cioffari, Giacinto Manuppella, Vasco Graça Moura, Daniela di Pasquale, and Rita Marnoto.

Note: Translated from the Portuguese by Cassilda Alcobia-Murphy.

https://doi.org/10.1515/9783110796049-009

The Age of the *Cancioneiro Geral*

In the mid-15th century, Gomes Eanes de Zurara, "Chief Keeper of the Library and Archives of Torre do Tombo,"[3] invoked in the *Crónica do Conde Dom Pedro de Menezes* (c. 1458–1464) "the renowned Poet Dante," according to whom, "spirits, through an inmost mystery, glimpse many things, which are yet to come."[4] Full of erudite zeal, and yet without evincing any measure of close contact with the *Commedia*, Gomes Eanes equates matter included in the "first Cantica" of this *opus magnum*, with the *Facta et Dicta Memorabilia* by Valerius Maximus and with Livy's *Decades*. Dante and the classics: this association suggests both appreciation and trust and, in effect, in the *Chronica do Conde D. Duarte de Menezes* (c. 1464–1469), Zurara often emphasises it in order to, according to the commentator "Johaõ Flamano,"[5] acclaim a bellicose *ethos* that would have been particularly appreciated by King Dom Afonso V of Portugal and the nobility around him. The Count D. Duarte, he explains, was the embodiment of this code:

> how magnanimous, and a man of such lineage that he pledged all his good fortune in this world to gain that which the Philosopher averred to be the main prize and accolade of the most noble and excellent gentlemen in this life – and the next – for according to Johaõ Flamano, in his gloss of the first Cantica [of] Dante, 'May yet in Hell be spared some pain to those who were, in this world, excellent knights.'[6]

Might there have been copies of the *Commedia* in the libraries of Portuguese sovereigns and their subjects?[7] C. 1521, there are no Dantean vestiges in the roll

---

3 Gomes Eanes de Zurara: *Crónica do Conde Dom Pedro de Menezes*. Reprodução facsimilada com nota de apresentação por José Adriano de Freitas Carvalho. Porto: Comissão Organizadora do Congresso Internacional "Bartolomeu Dias" 1988, p. [5].

4 *Ibidem*, p. [262] (Ch. LXXIX): "As the human will may oftentimes present to mortals, through a silent secret, the world to come, as that renowned Poet Dante sings of in his first Cantica, or if you will, Valerius Maximus in that Book, whereby he abridged Livy's fourteen Decades, where you shall find spirits, that through an inmost mystery, glimpse many things, which are yet to come...".

5 Perhaps Giovanni Flaminio? See Daniela Di Pasquale: Le prime ricezioni della *Divina Commedia* in Portogallo. Indizi e ipotesi. In *Studi Danteschi*, vol. LXXIII (2008), pp. 167–169.

6 Gomes Eanes de Zurara: *Chronica do Conde D. Duarte de Menezes*. In *Collecçaõ de Livros Ineditos de Historia Portugueza, dos Reinados de D. Joaõ I., D. Duarte, D. Affonso V., e D. Joaõ II*. Publicados de Ordem da Academia Real das Sciencias de Lisboa. Por José Corrêa da Serra, vol. III. Lisboa: [Academia Real das Sciencias de Lisboa] 1793, pp. 248–249 (Ch. CIX).

7 Teófilo Braga, guided by Zurara's quotations, conceded that King Dom Afonso V's library might offer validation as to the existence of the "Canticas of Dante" (*Historia da Universidade de Coimbra nas suas relações com a Instrucção Publica Portugueza*, vol. I. Lisboa: Por Ordem e na Typographia da Academia Real das Sciencias 1892, p. 236).

of King Dom Manuel I's possessions ("a man who derived much pleasure from books"[8]), but this list demands prudence in the conclusions to be drawn from its analysis.[9] As for any reverberations in terms of the literary forms and genres cultivated in the court of Dom Manuel I (known as "the Fortunate") or under the patronage of his sister, Dona Leonor,[10] these also require cautious research, albeit for different reasons. If the silences in an inventory leave much unsaid, the same applies to what is voiced in texts.

Gil Vicente, in the *Auto da Barca do Inferno* (written in 1517; in print *c.* 1520), most likely appropriated the idea of the "two barges"[11] that await souls for the final crossing,[12] not from the *Commedia* but from the glosses produced by Pedro Fernández de Villegas (1515). And what of the redemption of the "Knights of the Order of Christ"?[13] Would this equally be inspired by the commentary highlighted by Zurara? A survey of the *Cancioneiro Geral* (1516) leads one to ask, moreover, whether in Álvaro de Brito's outrage at the corruption of scribes, notaries, and judges, skilled at "turning, through Latin / a no into a yes, & a yes into a no,"[14] there might be an echo of the indictment of the city of Lucca, where "ogn'uom [. . .] è barattier" and "del no, per li denar vi si fa *ita*" (*Inferno* XXI, 41–42). Although there can be no absolute certainty, the connection is, nonetheless, plausible: Álvaro de Brito most likely travelled to Italy as part of the following of Infanta Dona Leonor, bride of Emperor Frederick III;[15] and he would have been aware of the passage, through Lisbon, of "foreign," "Flemish, Genovese, / Florentine, &

---

8 Gaspar Correia: *Crónicas de D. Manuel e de D. João III (até 1533)*. Leitura, Introdução, Notas e Índice por José Pereira da Costa. Lisboa: Academia das Ciências 1992, p. 174.
9 Braamcamp Freire: Inventario da Guarda-Roupa de D. Manuel. In *Archivo Historico Portuguez*, vol. II (1904), pp. 381–417. The inventory, produced in 1521, does not offer a complete account of all the volumes that Dom Manuel I possessed throughout his life.
10 See Isabel Vilares Cepeda: Os Livros da Rainha D. Leonor, segundo o códice 11 352 da Biblioteca Nacional, Lisboa. In *Revista da Biblioteca Nacional*, série 2, vol. 2, n.° 2 (1987), pp. 51–81; Isabel dos Guimarães Sá: *Leonor de Lencastre. De princesa a rainha-velha*, pp. 257–258. Lisboa: Temas e Debates 2016. Dante's works are not contained in the set of books bequeathed to the Convent of Madre de Deus that were itemised in 1537.
11 *Obras Completas de Gil Vicente*. Reimpressão Facsimilada da Edição de 1562. Lisboa: Biblioteca Nacional 1928, f. XLIIIv.
12 See Eugenio Asensio: Las Fuentes de las Barcas de Gil Vicente, pp. 68–69.
13 *Obras Completas de Gil Vicente*, f. XLIX.
14 "Senhor, Jam Pero Loys", in *Cancioneiro Geral de Garcia de Resende*. Nova edição. Introdução e Notas de Andrée Crabbé Rocha. Lisboa: Centro do livro Brasileiro 1973, vol. I, p. 248.
15 See "Carta de Pedro de Sousa Senhor de Prado que escreveo ao Duque de Bargança D. Jayme [. . .]", in D. A. Caetano de Sousa, *Provas da História Genealógica da Casa Real Portuguesa*. Coimbra: Atlântida Editora 1947, vol. I, l. III, p. 386. It is important to bear in mind that homonymy was prevalent at the time. See: Introdução. In *Obras de Álvaro de Brito*. Edição, introdução e notas

Castilian" merchants;[16] he took an interest in the poetry produced in the Spain of the Catholic Kings, where Alighieri had acquired an audience.[17]

One might also wonder: could an episode in the katabasis of the *Commedia* (*Inferno* V) underlie Diogo Brandão's "fingimento d'amores"[18] or the motto in a song by Bernardim Ribeiro? It is more likely that this affinity echoes the influence of intermediate sources, such as the "Infierno de enamorados" by the Marquis of Santillana, for whom Enrique de Villena had translated, c. 1428, Dante's[19] "sacred poem" (*Paradiso* XXV, 1). A comparison of excerpts sheds light on this indebtedness, most acutely in two memorable passages: the interpellation of the condemned and the acknowledgement (philosophical, aphoristic, Virgilian) of the sorrows of remembrance.

| ... O anime affannate,
venite a noi parlar, s'altri nol niega!
(*Inferno* V, 80–81) | '¡O, ánimas afanadas,'
...
'dezidme, ¿de qué materia
tractades, después del lloro,
en este limbo e miseria
do Amor fizo su thesoro?'[20] | O jentes atribuladas,
por que rrazam de vos de,
dizey a causa por que
soës assy atormentadas.[21] |

---

de Isabel Almeida. Lisboa: Comissão Nacional para a Comemoração dos Descobrimentos Portugueses 1997, pp. 17–18.

16 "Daluaro de brito pestana a Luys fogaça sendo vereador na çidade de Lyxboa, ẽ q lhe daa maneyra para os ares maos serem fora dela", in Garcia de Resende, *Cancioneiro Geral*, vol. I, p. 221.

17 Note, for example, as conspicuous evidence of this connection to Castile, in addition to the praise of the Catholic Kings ("These eight trovas were composed by Álvaro de Brito Pestana for King Dom Fernando, to which he appended his name, & can be read in as many ways as to add up to four and sixty"; "These further eight did he compose for Queen Dona Isabel his wife in the same manner and are written in Castilian"); the "Glosses by Álvaro de Brito entitled *terribles coytas deseo*"; or the texts after a song deemed to be heretical, by Antón de Móntoro. See Garcia de Resende, *Cancioneiro Geral*, vol. I, pp. 250–255, 279–283, 284–293.

18 Of all the 'infernos of the enamoured' included in the *Cancioneiro Geral*, it is the one by Diogo Brandão that supports (by revealing the indirect character of the relationship) a degree of familiarity with Dante's work. See Valeria Tocco: Gli Inferni d'Amore Portoghesi e la Tradizione Allegorica Europea. In *Filologia Medievale e Umanistica*, 127 (1993), pp. 297–359.

19 See Biblioteca Nacional de Espanha, Mss 10186 (available online).

20 Marqués de Santillana: Infierno de los enamorados. In *Comedieta de Ponza, Sonetos, Serranillas y Otras Obras*, pp. 95–96.

21 "Fyngymento damores feyto per Dyoguo brandam". In Garcia de Resende, *Cancioneiro Geral*, vol. III, p. 47.

... Nessun maggior dolore che ricordarsi del tempo felice ne la miseria; e ciò sa 'l tuo dottore. (*Inferno* V, 121–123)	La mayor cuita que haver puede ningún amador es membrarse del plazer en el tiempo del dolor, e ya sea que el ardor del fuego nos atormenta, mayor pena nos augmenta esta tristeza e langor.[22]	Que neste fogo penados sejamos sem esperança, matanos mays a lembrança dos prazeres ja passados.[23]
		Nũca foy mal nẽhũ moor nemno a hy nos amores caa lembrança do fauor no tempo dos desfauores.[24]

At this time, all signs indicate that Dante's presence in Portugal was minimal and piecemeal. In fact, any quest for a direct permeability towards Italian standards in the poetic discourse proves fruitless.[25] What is noticeable, instead, is a strong connection to Castile, which extended the cultural interchange that, despite political tensions and beyond vicious conflicts, had taken root in the previous century. Occasional citations and assertions in the *Cancioneiro Geral* are evidence of this bond: the models and *auctoritates* that take undeniable precedence are Iberian in origin, such as Mancías, Juan de Mena, Estúñiga, and Juan Roiz del Padrón.

Varied practices and options, however, coexisted in the world of the Iberian Peninsula. One might compare the *Cancioneiro Geral* (1516) with the *Cancionero General* coordinated by Hernando del Castillo and printed for the first time in Valencia, in 1511. That the *Commedia* was disseminated in Castile via Catalonia is demonstrable not only through the "Infierno de enamorados" but also through the above-mentioned work by Villena. In the *Cancionero General*, particularly in the work of the Marquis of Santillana (Íñigo López de Mendoza), Dante enjoys a status of which poets and troubadours in the collection by Resende (assuming this to be, in effect, representative) remained heedless.

The Tuscan bard is added, in the compilation by Hernando del Castillo, to an honourable lineage – a beloved common heritage – that the Marquis out-

---

[22] Marqués de Santillana: Infierno de los enamorados. In *Comedieta de Ponza, Sonetos, Serranillas y Otras Obras*, p. 96.
[23] "Fyngymento damores feyto per Dyoguo brandam". In Garcia de Resende, *Cancioneiro Geral*, vol. III, p. 48.
[24] Garcia de Resende, *Cancioneiro Geral*, vol. V, p. 99. Sousa Viterbo drew attention to this text in: Dante, o marquez de Santilhana e Bernardim Ribeiro. In *A Revista: Sciencias e Letras*, n.º 11 (1904), pp. 177–178. See Giacinto Manuppella: *Dantesca Luso-Brasileira. Subsídios para uma Bibliografia da Obra e do Pensamento de Dante Alighieri*. Coimbra: Por Ordem da Universidade 1966, p. 144.
[25] See R. Marnoto: *O Petrarquismo Português do* Cancioneiro Geral *a Camões*. Lisboa: Imprensa Nacional-Casa da Moeda 2015.

lines while mourning the death of Enrique de Villena (c. 1434): "We have lost Livy and the Mantuan [Virgil], / Macrobius, Valerius, Sallust and Magnentius [Lucan] / but let's not forget the moral Anneus [Seneca], / much lauded by the Roman People: / we have lost Tullius [Cicero] and Casaliano, / Alano [Alain de Lille], Boethius, Petrarca, Fulgentius; / we have lost Dante, Gaufredo [Galfredo de Vinsauf], Terence, / Juvenal, Statius and Quintilian."[26] If, conversely, the author of the *Commedia* is demeaned in the lament for Don Íñigo (d. 1458), composed by his nephew, Gómez Manrique, this serves merely to underscore the magnitude of his tribute: "for in rhyme, Dante proves / a simpleton side by side."[27] In the same funereal occasion, the "secretary" Diego de Burgos employed a similar strategy, by constructing a "Dante" willing to bow in grateful tribute to the Marquis: ". . . if I am renowned, if I am familiar, / it is by virtue of his wish to gaze upon my work."[28]

To these examples of the appreciation bestowed on "Aliger" – a true measure of worth[29] – one must add those included in the *Cancionero de Baena* or the *Cancionero de Stúñiga*. Undoubtedly, some of the praise heaped on the "lofty poet and rhetorician, Dante,"[30] "a man of letters / and a great poet,"[31] is somewhat superficial, and this superficial references, for the most part, simply betray a desire for good opinion. Villasandino distinguishes between "los torpes" [the inept], unworthy of the "gaya çiençia" ["joyful wisdom"], and the pleiad that

---

[26] "Comiençan las obras del Marqués de Santillana, Yñigo Lopez de Mendoça: y esta primera es vna que hizo à la muerte de Don Enrique de Villena" ("Robadas auian el Austro y Borea"), in *Cancionero General de Hernando del Castillo segundo la edición de 1511. . .* 2 vols. Madrid: La Sociedad de Bibliófilos Españoles 1882, vol. I, p. 87.

[27] "Comiençan las obras de Gomez Manrique; y esta primeira es vna que hizo à la muerte del Marqués de Santillana, Iñigo Lopez de Mendoça" ("mis sospiros, despertad"), in *Ibidem*, vol. I, p. 165. In the "Carta Rimada entre Manrique y el Marqués de Santillana" ["Rhymed letter between Manrique and the Marquis of Santillana"], the recipient's praise equally stands out for the modesty with which Gómez Manrique states: "Estrema cobdicia de algo saber / en ésta discreta e tan gentil arte / en que yo tengo tan poca de parte / como en parayso tiene Lucifer, / me haze vergüença, Señor, proponer, / e hablar en ella, seyendo ignorante, / con vos que emendays las obras del Dante / y otras más altas sabeys componer." (*Ibidem*, vol. I, pp. 190–191).

[28] "Comienza el tractado intitulado Triunfo del Marqués, á loor y reuerencia del yllustre y marauilloso señor don Yñigo Lopez de Mendoça, primero Marqués de Santillana, Conde del Real; compuesto por Diego de Búrgos, su secretario" ("Tornado era Febo á ver el tesoro", *Ibidem*, vol. I, p. 245).

[29] One should bear in mind the lines by Gomez Manrique: "maestro muy elegante, / digno de veneracion, / más que Virgilio ni Dante" ("No teniendo del saber", *Ibidem*, vol, I, p. 631).

[30] "Replicaçion de Juan Alfonso contra Ferran Manuel" ("Lyndo fydalgo en la luna menguante"), in *El Cancionero de Juan Alfonso de Baena*. Ed. Francisque Michel. Con las notas y los indices de la edición de Madrid del año 1851. Leipzig: F. A. Brockhaus 1860, vol. III, p. 823.

[31] "Este dezir fyzo el dicho Alfonso Aluarez de Villasandino a Don Pedro Tenoryo [. . .]" ("Muy noble sseñor onrrado"), *Ibidem*, vol. I, p. 285.

adds "Virgil and Dante, Horace and Plato" to "other legendary poets."[32] Juan de Mena imagines: "Solomon have I seen, the wise, / Euclid, Seneca, and Dante, / Aristotle, Plato, / Virgil, and Horace, the passionate."[33] Where does the weight of these names lie? Their exemplary dimension is unequivocal, and is reinforced by the prestigious kinship that binds them.

Determined to extol "a handsome lady of Seville,"[34] Francisco Imperial updated the Latin trope "taceat superata venustas."[35] Dante had already deployed it, in Canto XXV of the *Inferno*, and Micer Imperial turns the formula against those who had appropriated it: "Silence the poets and silence the authors, / Homer, Horace, Virgil and Dante, / and with them silence Ovid *the Lover* / and all who wrote in praise of the masters."[36] Such inflammatory euphoria was intended to cause a stir, and it succeeded. Diego Martines de Medina entered the fray with the protest: ". . . if her love has so enthralled you / well might you praise her, but not so / as to silence Dante, the Florentine / whom you have read, if you are wise."[37] To censure "the good Florentine"[38] thus amounts to an act of folly, the expression of a disorder:

> Dante, the poet, and great wordsmith,
> I am told, my friend, you have reproached,
> if this be true, little did you heed
> what the world deems worthy;
> but so do we go from bad to worse,
> yet I cannot credit it; and how perverse,

---

[32] "These words were written by Alfonso Aluares de Villasandino, and very well composed and well-founded, with the greatest of mastery and art, in reply and in query of the troubadours" ("A mi bien me plaze porque se estienda"), *Ibidem*, vol. I, p. 170.

[33] *Cancionero de Lope de Stúñiga. Códice del Siglo XV. Ahora por vez primera publicado*. Madrid: Imprenta y Estereotipia de M. Rivadeneyra 1872, p. 233.

[34] "These words were written by the said Miçer Françisco Imperial for love and praise of a beauteous lady of Seville, whom he named his star Diana, on a day when he sighted her aspect as she walked by the bridge of Seville towards the Church of Sant'Ana outside the city" ("Non fue por çierto mi carrera vana", *El Cancionero de Juan Alfonso de Baena*, vol. II, p. 455).

[35] See E. Robert Curtius: *Literatura Europea y Edad Media Latina*, 2 vols. Mexico-Madrid-Buenos Aires: Fondo de Cultura Económica 1984, vol. I, pp. 235–239.

[36] *El Cancionero de Juan Alfonso de Baena*, vol. II, p. 456.

[37] "These words were written by Diego Martines de Medina, a Judge of Seville, in response to previous words written by the said Miçer Françisco to the Star Diana . . ." ("Muy enperial e de grant vffana", *Ibidem*, vol. II, p. 460).

[38] *Ibidem*, vol. II, p. 458.

that ofttimes in Spain the rebuked
should reign over their rebukers.[39]

Francisco Imperial – a Genoese national – went as far as to proclaim: "Many poets have I read, / Homer, Virgil, Dante, / Boethius, Lucan / and Ovid's *Loves*; / but let misfortune befall me, / if in all their poesy / ever I read such genteel words / as those of the Infante."[40] Proud of his familiarity with the 'jurist, theologian poet Dante,"[41] Imperial did not conceal his admiration for the *Commedia*. It is for this reason that he retains the astonishing neologism coined in Canto I of the *Paradiso* ("nor, after Dante, *trasumanar* / might any language, however ingenious"[42]) and discusses the definition of Fortune as God's creature, as well as his "general ministra e duce" (*Inferno* VII, 78) ("And while I praise you / and condone the style / of Dante who knows much, / from what I've read and seen");[43] and for this reason, in a dreamlike register, he bestows on a book "penned entirely in the finest gold," and whose *incipit* was *En medio del camino*,[44] the aura that Saint Augustine, in

---

[39] A Dante el poeta, grant conponedor,
me disen, amigo, que rreprehendistes;
sy esto es verdat, en poco touistes
lo que el mundo tiene por de grant valor;
mas pues van las cosas de mal en peor,
non se que me diga, nin puedo entender,
por que en España suele contesçer
vençer el rrectado a su rrectador.
        ("Ferrant Manuel, amigo e señor", *Ibidem*, vol. II, p. 524.)

[40] "Muchos poetas ley, / Homero, Vergilio, Dante, / Boeçio, Lucani, de sy / en Ouidio De amante; / mas yo ssea mal andante, / sy en toda su escriptura / ley tan gentil fygura / como es la del infante" "These words were written by the said Miçer Françisco Ynperial in praise and devotion to the Infante Don Ferrando, King of Aragon, which were later published, for their virtues and great beauty bestowed on them by the grace of God" ("Muchos poetas ley", *Ibidem*, vol. II, p. 495).

[41] "These words were written by the said Miçer Françisco Ynperial, of Genoa, extant and inhabitant of the noblest city of Seville. . ." ("En dos seteçientos e mas doss e tres", *Ibidem*, vol. II, p. 423).

[42] "nin, segunt Dante, trasvmanar / podria lengua por bien que fable" in "Vuestra llaga, amigo, es incurable", *Ibidem*, vol. III, p. 1036.

[43] "E maguer que te alabe / e escuse en su estilo / Dante que tanto bien sabe, / segunt ya ley e vylo": "These words were written by the said Miçer Françisco Imperial by way of question and demand against master Fray Alfonso de la Monja, of the Order of Saint Pablo of Seville, requesting him to declare the definition of Fortune ("O Ffortuna! Çedo priue", *Ibidem*, vol. II, p. 485).

[44] "Address by Miçer Françisco to the Seven Virtues" ("El tienpo poder pesa a quien mas sabe", *Ibidem*, vol. II, p. 501).

his *Confessions*,[45] associated with the Gospel or the "codex of the Apostle" ("and I awoke, as if roused by force,/ to find in my hands an opened-up Dante,/ in the chapter where he is met by the Virgin").[46]

One might assume that some of these texts would have circulated in Portugal and served to arouse curiosity about Dante, but the data available, revisited above, are far from confirming this. Which is not to say that, between the end of the 15th and the beginning of the 16th centuries, the pull towards Italy was anything less than formidable. However, what was particularly esteemed about Italy were its classical origins and their corresponding rebirth. For example, in the *Cancioneiro Geral*, some invoke, with patent devotion and reverence, the names of Cicero, Ovid, and Plato;[47] while those of Petrarca, Boccaccio and Dante are ignored or neglected.

The intense Italianisation that began in Portugal in the 1530s would subsequently change this outlook, but only partially: Dante was, for the most part, sidelined, without ever generating consensus.

Just Before Sundown

Contrary to what is normally the case regarding the periodisation and the characterisation of the poetics and dynamics of Portuguese literature, a single date, that of 1527, has been used to identify a turning point in its history. It was from this

---

[45] Saint Augustine recalls how he "had heard of Antony, that, accidentally coming in while the gospel was being read, he received the admonition as if what was read were addressed to him ...". "By such oracle," he points out, had Antony immediately converted. His would be a similar experience with "the codex of the Apostle": "I grasped, opened, and in silence read that paragraph on which my eyes first fell .... No further would I read, nor did I need to. For instantly, as the sentence ended – by a light, as it were, of security infused into my heart – all the gloom of doubt vanished away." (Augustine of Hippo: *Confessions*. Translated by J.G. Pilkington. In *Nicene and Post-nicene Fathers*, First Series, vol. 1. Edited by Philip Schaff. Buffalo, NY: Christian Literature Publishing co. 1887, book VIII, xii, p. 29.)
[46] "e acorde, como a fuerça despierto,/ e falle en mis manos a Dante abierto,/ en el capitulo que la Virgen salua" in "Desir de Miçer Françisco a las syete virtudes", *El Cancionero de Juan Alfonso de Baena*, vol. II, p. 514.
[47] See, for example, in the *Cancioneiro Geral de Garcia de Resende*, the "Pregunta de dom Joham manuel a Aluaro de bryto" and the "Reposta Daluaro de brito polos consoantes" (vol. II, pp. 8–9). See also Ana Maria Sánchez Tarrío: O obscuro fidalgo João Rodrigues de Lucena, tradutor das *Heroides*. In *Euphrosyne*, 30 (2002), pp. 371–384; A tradição dos clássicos e a poética do *Cancioneiro Geral*. In Cristina Almeida Ribeiro e Sara Rodrigues de Sousa (eds.): Cancioneiro Geral de Garcia de Resende: um livro à luz da história. Lisboa: Húmus 2012, pp. 61–72.

year onwards that Francisco de Sá de Miranda, having completed his journey to Rome, popularised new experiences in form and genre, as well as new (although some were very old) standards. However, while this poet did not conceal his pride at having completed this pilgrimage; while he vaunted his predilection for Petrarca, Bembo, Sannazzaro, Boiardo and Ariosto; if, while never disavowing the Spanish tradition of the *old measure*, he raised in value those who had discovered "furthermore";[48] while all of the above is inescapable, it is nonetheless true that Miranda only included Dante sparingly in the collection, without qualifying this author as a master or a model.

In his reply to an epistle by Jorge de Montemor, and for the purpose of proving himself equal to those who had reached "the heights of the Parnassus,"[49] Sá de Miranda deployed erudite information, although, according to Rita Marnoto, this was "enumerative, rather than analytical, in nature":[50]

> A second life to Beatrice gave Dante
> And Laura, by Petrarca, gained such fame
> As hums from these shores to the Levant,
> Boccaccio raised Fiammetta in verse and prose,
> And from Pistoya, the good Cino, his Selvaggia,
> O, for such days, o for such a happy age.[51]

This acclaim of the power of poetry and of one of the *ætas aurea* is woven based on Petrarca's "Triumphus Cupidinis" (IV, 31–32): "ecco Dante e Beatrice, ecco Selvaggia,/ ecco Cin da Pistoia...." Is it thus conceivable that Sá de Miranda would pejoratively apply Dante's name in the epistle "in the Italian fashion, to Dom Fernando de Meneses"? Let us compare the *Obras*, printed in 1595, with the contents of the manuscript to which Carolina Michaëlis de Vasconcelos gave primacy during its edition:

---

[48] Francisco de Sá de Miranda: *Obras. Edição Fac-Simile da Edição de 1595*. Estudo introdutório de Vítor Aguiar e Silva. Braga: Universidade do Minho 1994, f. 59v.
[49] *Ibidem*, f. 64v.
[50] R. Marnoto: *O Petrarquismo Português do Renascimento e do Maneirismo*. Coimbra: Por Ordem da Universidade 1997, p. 169.
[51] Otra vida a Beatriz ha dado el Dante,
A Laura hizo el Patracha tan famosa,
Que suena deste mar al de Leuante.
Bocacio alço Fiumeta en verso y prosa,
De Pistoya el buen Cino a su Seluaja,
Ah que buenos años, buena edad dichosa. (Francisco de Sá de Miranda, *Obras*, f. 67v).

Despois coa melhor lei, entrou mais lume	Correndo mais o tempo, correu mais lume
Suspirouse milhor, veo outra gente	Sospirou se melhor, veu outra gente
De que Petrarcha fez tão rico ordume.	De que o Petrarca fez tam rico ordume.
Eu digo os Proençaes, de que ao presente	Eu digo os provençais, que inda se sente
Inda rithmas ouuimos que entoarão	O som das brandas rimas que entoárão
As Musas delicadas altamente.	De novo assi d'amor tam altamente
Aquelles *Dantes*, que *versos danarão*,	Despois (ah que vergonha!) em fim tornárão
Perdoem, ah que o digo vergonhoso,	A cair muitos neste amor vicioso;
Com doo de *bõs engenhos* que *enganarão*.[52]	O fino os finos peitos o salvárão.[53]

Several questions arise when one looks at the 1595 text: what is encompassed in the plural "Dantes"? What are "damaging verses" ("versos danarão")? What "good talents" ("bõs engenhos") are being deceived ("enganarão")? If one accepts that both texts are mutually illuminative, then "damaging verses" would correspond to the propagation of "wicked love" (as opposed to the salvific qualities of "refined" love). In which case, perhaps "Dantes," rather than vague antonomasia, is instead a derogatory designation of the poet himself or, better yet, of one aspect of his work; namely where, in Canto XXX of the *Purgatorio* of the *Commedia*, Dante is confronted by a stern Beatrice, "quasi ammiraglio" (*Purgatorio* XXX, 58) or "madre al figlio [. . .] superba" (*Purgatorio* XXX, 79), ferocious in her rebuke of her lover. Dante, an expert in the art of palinody,[54] is thus staging repentance, or "vergogna" (*Purgatorio* XXX, 78) for deviations such as those represented by the significance of the "rime petrose" in his "cammin." These "rime" (in particular, the song "Così ne 'l mio parlar voglio esser aspro")[55] contrast with the ideal of *dolcezza* professed in the *Vita Nuova* and with the sublimation of Eros which becomes progressively accentuated in the *Convivio* and in the *Commedia*.

---

52 *Ibidem*, p. 51.
53 Francisco de Sá de Miranda: *Poesias* (Carolina Michaëlis de Vasconcelos, ed.; fac-simile do exemplar com data de 1885 da Biblioteca Nacional). Lisboa: Imprensa Nacional-Casa da Moeda 1989, pp. 253–254.
54 See A. Russell Ascoli: Palinode and History in the Oeuvre of Dante. In Amilcare A. Ianucci (ed.): *Dante: Contemporary Perspectives*. Toronto-Buffalo-London: University of Toronto Press 1997, pp. 23–50.
55 Note the song: "Ohime perche non latra / Per me com'io per lei ne 'l caldo borro? / Che tosto griderei io ni soccorro: / E farei uolentier, si come quelli, / Che ne' biondi capelli, / Ch'amor per consumarmi increspa e dora, / Metterei mano; è satiereme alhora. // S'io hauessi le bionde treccie prese, / Che fatte son per me scudiscio e ferza; / Pigliandole anzi terza / Con esse passerei uespro e le squille: / E non sarei pietoso ne cortese; / Anzi farei come orso quando scherza: / E s'amor me ne sferza, / Io mi uendicherei di piu di mille: / E' suoi begli occhi, onde escon le fauille, / Che m'infiammeno il cor ch'io porto anciso, / Guardarei presso e fiso / Per uendicar lo fuggir, che mi face; / E poi le renderei con amor pace." (*Rime di Diversi Antichi Avtori Toscani*, Vinegia: Io. Antonio, e Fratelli da Sabio 1532, f. 27v).

Another possibility is that the 1595 text exposes instead the standards of third parties. Sá de Miranda's elliptical and obscure style did lend itself to changes ("dantes" [before] / "Dantes"), either in typesetting or outside of it. But this alteration, should it result from a reading by a third party, possibly at a later date, reveals an ambivalence: though acclaimed, the Italian poet did raise reservations; the merest sharp commentary was enough to demean or to reduce him to the level of an anti-example.

A critical outlook on Dante's work can therefore be identified, whose reach or exact incidence escapes us. As an example, while Francisco de Holanda employed aspects of the *Commedia* in order to praise works of painting ("It shows us [...] the torments and perils of the Inferno; it, as much as can be achieved, depicts the glory and peace of the blessed, and that unknowable image of Our Lord [...] and fills us with awe and deepens the spirit and mind beyond the stars, in its figuration of the empire of the beyond."),[56] he was aware that his was not a consensual opinion. In the treatise *Da Pintura Antiga* (1548), regarding the necessary preparation for the 'serious painter' intent on representing the "torments and perils of the Inferno," Holanda advised as follows, as he expatiated on the topic of *ut pictura poesis*:

> I commend the painter [...] not to neglect to read, in the poet Homer, the passage where Ulysses summons souls from hell, among whom are the great Achilles, who claims to prefer being the most ill-fated and destitute of men on earth, than to be a master in hell. And likewise, the entire Book Six in Virgil where, as a Gentile, he wonderfully incites the soul to such spiritual contemplation as is the painting of hell; and do neglect to read Dante, in Tuscan, where the torments of his art are also described, which must not be disdained.[57]

The wording adopted here is not immaterial. At the top, Homer, the founding oracle (early, in the *Republic*,[58] Plato had also recorded the same speech by Achilles). Concerning Virgil, Holanda notes the allegorical tradition centred on the Fourth *Eclogue* and Book VI of the *Aeneid*: there is nothing to prevent the word of a "Gentile" from prompting "spiritual contemplation." Last in this ranking, Dante is the one figure that requires particular argumentative scrupulousness: "do not neglect," "must not be disdained." As if the leap from the Classics to the later poet might require persuasive justification or apology; as if there might be some resistance to be overcome; as if the pertinence of this choice might not be self-ev-

---

56 Francisco de Holanda: *Diálogos em Roma*. Introdução, notas e comentários de José da Felicidade Alves. Lisboa: Livros Horizonte 1984, p. 34.
57 Francisco de Holanda: *Da Pintura Antiga*. Introdução, notas e comentários de José da Felicidade Alves. Lisboa: Livros Horizonte 1984, p. 69.
58 See Plato: *The Republic*. Translated by Benjamin Jowett. New York, NY: Cosimo Classics 2008, p. 56.

ident. In effect, it was not, neither in Italy[59] nor in Portugal. Where is Dante in the letters of *O Lima* (XXI and XXVIII), where Diogo Bernardes dedicated himself to sing the praises of ancient and new authors?[60]

In the same period, however, multiple points of view, multiple discourses coexisted. Jorge Ferreira de Vasconcelos devised, in his comedy *Aulegrafia*, a scene in which two noblemen, Dom Ricardo and Dom Galindo, shared their poetic tastes and raised questions regarding emulation and the affections. Among the various examples brought into the anthology, one derives from the *Commedia* (III, v. 9):

> D. Gal. Do you know, my lord, what I find most wondrous? That fellow Dante's inscription on the gates of Hell: Voi ch'intrate lasciate sperasse. D. Ric. How sublime![61]

As Aníbal Pinto de Castro has pointed out, this is an imprecise quotation.[62] Intentionally so? There is no way to find out. What is undeniable is that this catalogue of prized *excerpta*, committed to memory (and savoured) by the two courtiers, does incorporate a fragment from "that fellow Dante." Devoid of scruples or hierarchies, and serving to add to the *varietas*, the verse from the *Inferno* is released into the dialogue, in among Latin texts, *redondillas* from the *Cancioneiros*, fragments by Petrarca, and decasyllabics by Garcilaso de la Vega. It was not the only example of its kind. Equal enthusiasm can be found in a sonnet addressed to André Falcão de Resende by a "friend" ("full bold, you forsook the royal eagles, / Petrarca, Sanazzaro, Dante, Tasso, / ... Boscán, and Garcilaso / you tamed and pinioned the Muse to the sacred laws.")[63] and another, in which

---

[59] Holanda seems to have in mind the introduction by Bernardo Giunta of the *Rime di Diversi Antichi Autori Toscani*, where the poetry of *Vita Nuova* had been included and where "Così ne 'l mio parlar voglio esser aspro" opened a "Libro" of "Canzoni Amorose e Morali": "se bene a uoi forse parra douere da 'l Petrarca uostro solamente tutto cio riconoscere, Et a quello solo senza alcuno altro eternamente essere obligati: Che se cio bene è uero, che il Petrarca molto piu che ciascuno altro Toscano autore, lucido, e terso sia da giudicare: non dimeno, ne qual de duoi ui uogliate, ò Cino, ò Guido degni saràno giamai di dispregio tenuti; Ne il Diuino Dante ne le sue amorose Canzoni indegno sia in parte alcuna riputato di essere insieme con il Petrarca p[er] l'uno de duoi lucidissimi occhi de la nostra lingua annouerato..."
[60] See Aníbal Pinto de Castro: Boscán e Garcilaso no lirismo português do Renascimento e do Maneirismo. In *Península: Revista de Estudos Ibéricos* 1 (2004), pp. 68–70.
[61] "D. Gal. Sabeys senhor que me mata? a letra do Dante sobre a porta do inferno: Voi ch'intrate lasciate sperasse. D. Ric. Està fidalga." In *Comedia Aulegrafia*, f. 126v (Act IV, scene II).
[62] Aníbal Pinto de Castro: Boscán e Garcilaso no lirismo português do Renascimento e do Maneirismo, p. 71. According to the Italian text, this should read: "Lasciate ogni speranza, voi ch'intrate." (*Inferno* III, 9).
[63] "ousado agui]as reaes atraz deixaste, / Petrarca,] Sanazaro, Dante, Tasso, / [........Bosc]am, e Garcilasso / a Musa às] leis sagradas branda ataste." In André Falcão de Resende, *Obras*. Edição crítica de Barbara Spaggiari, vols. I–II. Lisboa: Edições Colibri 2009, p. 60.

Resende retorts by lauding this same "friend" for "demeaning Xanthos, Mincio, the Arno, and the Nile."[64]

Would the mention of Dante bring distinction, as an element of rarity, to those who employed it? An anonymous commentator of Petrarca's *Triumphs*, in the mid-16th century (post-1560), found it convenient to specify: "in addition to his celebrated COMMEDIA, he wrote sonnets and love songs."[65] This anonymous personage resorted to the "celebrated" *Commedia* in order to declare (*i.e.*, to explicate), for example, an excerpt as the "Arimino copy" ("la coppia d'Arimino," Francesca e Paolo Malatesta).[66] Would this be evidence of widespread consultation of the work? Or instead, of restricted familiarity, confined to passages favoured by literary tradition?

The examples presented above belong to texts of an introductory or metaliterary nature, where a particular name abounds, with its attendant symbolic energy: "Dante." The azorean priest Gaspar Frutuoso, in order to highlight Camões, would say that he was not inferior to "Dante or to Petrarca or to Ariosto".[67] It is much harder to find, either through assimilation or metamorphosis, the poet's text itself. When Sá de Miranda maintains the paradox "Lightens, and cools not, the water such a flame!",[68] is he emulating "Come aqua per chiarezza foco accende"?[69] Does the character of Arima, whose "words" and "deeds" "were not those of a mere mortal,"[70] as well as other details from the love narrative by Bernardim Ribeiro, *Menina e Moça*, derive from the *Vita Nuova*, where about Beatrice "si potea dire quella parola del poeta Omero, 'Ella non parea figliuola d'uomo mortale, ma

---

[64] *Ibidem*, p. 281 ("Soneto a hum livro, que fez hum seu amigo, André da Fons[eca]").

[65] Giacinto Manuppella: Uma anónima versão quinhentista dos *Triunfos* de Petrarca e o seu *Comentário*. In *Revista da Universidade de Coimbra*, XXV (1974), p. 140.

[66] *Ibidem*, p. 132 (see "Triumphus Cupidinis", III, v. 83). Manuppella sought to correct the text (which he explains in an annotation, p. 242), spelling it 'copla d'Arímino'. Vasco Graça Moura (Vasco Graça Moura: Introdução. In A Divina Comédia *de Dante Alighieri*, 2.ª ed. Venda Nova: Bertrand 1996, pp. 9–27. Reed.: Traduzir Dante: uma aproximação. In Daniela Di Pasquale / Tiago Guerreiro da Silva (eds.): *Estudos Dantescos. Tradução e Recepção das Obras de Dante em Portugal e no Mundo*. Lisboa: Cosmos 2014, p. 23) had already noted that at pp. 134, 140, 147 and 216 there are traces of the reading of the *Commedia*.

[67] Gaspar Frutuoso, *Livro Quinto das Saudades da Terra*. Ponta Delgada: Instituto Cultural de Ponta Delgada 1964, p. 145.

[68] "Acende i no resfria agua tal llama!" In *Poesias de Francisco de Sá de Miranda*, p. 332.

[69] *Rime di Diversi Antichi Autori Toscani*, p. 28 ("Amor che muovi tua vertu da 'l cielo", v. 27).

[70] Bernardim Ribeiro: *História de Menina e Moça*. Edição de texto, introdução, nota biobibliográfica, glossário e notas de Marta Marecos Duarte. Lisboa: Imprensa Nacional–Casa da Moeda 2015 p. 137.

di deo'"?[71] Is the disenchantment in the Camonian elegy "O Poeta Simónides, falando" ("what does it serve that men burden / their minds with what's past, given all / passes, unless to regret and know pain?"[72]) likely to contain, somewhere in its genesis, traces of the maxim spoken by Francesca da Rimini (". . . Nessun maggior dolore / che ricordarsi del tempo felice / ne la miseria.")?

Camões

In 16th-century Italy, Petrarca became a consecrated author. This led to a twofold and contradictory repercussion: on the one hand, this canonisation overshadowed (or virtually eclipsed) Dante; on the other, it made room for Dante's poetry to be evoked, as the link to the tradition that flourished in the *Rerum Vulgarium Fragmenta* and the *Triomphi*. The widespread dissemination of anthologies contributed to further this remembrance.

Dante, however, had not simply written the *Vita Nuova* and the "Rime Petrose"; he had been, in addition, the "divine" author of the masterpiece that earned the title of *Divina Commedia* in 1555. Throughout the 16th century, usually through Florentine patronage, this "sacred poem" was reissued, commented on and debated. Dante therefore attained the accolade he had longed for, through his depiction by painters and sculptors, namely Raphael, Bronzino and Zuccaro, among others. And yet this classicising poetical context was unfavourable to him. Pietro Bembo, while acknowledging that there was room for discussion,[73] had dismissed Dante in his *Prose della Volgar Lingua* (1525). Bembo instituted a narrow canon and selected models for which he allowed no alternative: for poetry, the emulation of

---

[71] Dante: *Vita Nuova*. Introduzione di Edoardo Sanguinetti. Note di Alfonso Berardinelli. Milano: Garzanti 1994, pp. 2–3.

[72] Luís de Camões, *The Collected Lyric Poems of Luís de Camões*. Translated by Landeg White. Princeton: Princeton University Press 2008, p. 149.

[73] Pietro Bembo was editor of the *Commedia* in 1502. In his *Prose*, however, he chose to either remain silent on or to be critical of Dante's work, only infrequently moderating his tone. To this point, one of the speakers in the dialogue in Book II states: "Se a queste cose tutte, che messer Federigo e il Bembo v'hanno raccolte, risguardo avessero coloro che vogliono, messer Ercole, sopra Dante e sopra il Petrarca dar giudicio, quale è di loro miglior poeta, essi non sarebbono tra loro discordanti sì come sono. Ché quantunque infinita sia la moltitudine di quelli, da' quali molto più è lodato messer Francesco, nondimeno non sono pochi quegli altri, a' quali Dante più sodisfà, tratti, come io stimo, dalla grandezza e varietà del suggetto, più che da altro." (Pietro Bembo: *Prose Della Volgar Lingua. Gli Asolani. Rime*. A cura di Carlo Dionisotti. Milano: TEA 1989, pp. 175–176).

Petrarca was imperative; and for prose, Boccaccio and his *Decameron*. Faced with Bembo's preeminence, those who dared to stray from this doctrine generally did so discretely and mildly. This was the case, for example, of the compilers of the *Rime di Diversi Antichi Autori Toscani* (1st ed.: 1527); Baldassare Castiglione, in *Il Libro del Cortegiano* (1528); or Sperone Speroni, in the "Dialogo delle Lingue" and in the "Dialogo della Retorica" (*Dialoghi*, 1542). As for more conspicuous dissent, as exercised by Gian Giorgio Trissino, in *La Italia Liberata da Gotthi* (1547), or Anton Francesco Doni, in his compilation of the *Lettioni d'Academici Fiorentini sopra Dante. Libro Primo* (1547), this was at first infrequent,[74] but took on the proportions of a *querelle*[75] mid-century. Four decades after the death of Bembo, the sizeable *Diffesa della Commedia di Dante* (1587), by Jacopo Mazzoni, was printed.

As such, and in view of this rift, which very likely would have been felt in Portugal, how may we interpret, in Ode VI by Camões, the double reference to "Beatrice" and "Laura"?

> Something, I don't know what,
> that emanates, I don't know how,
> emerges invisibly, touching the sight,
> though understanding it's not my purview;
> something poetry of the Tuscan era,
> most favored by Apollo,
> never saw in Beatrice nor in Laura;
>
> in you, Lady, in our own age
> it can be on display . . .[76]

Would both be a gentle allusion to the "duoi lucidissimi occhi" of the "poetry of the Tuscan era," much as Bernardo Giunta tried to assert in his introduction to the *Rime di Diversi Antichi Autori Toscani*? Or did they put forward a subtle distinction between a poetics of *dolcezza* and a poetics of *asperità*, as discussed in the second half of the 16th-century?[77]

---

[74] Gian Giorgio Trissino ostensibly expanded the canon established by Pietro Bembo. To Petrarca and Boccaccio he added – and foregrounded – Dante, "mastro della lingua, / Ch'allhor l'Italia nomerà materna. / Questi dipingerà con le sue rime / Divinamente tutta quella etade." (*La Italia Liberata da Gotthi del Trissino*. Roma: Valerio e Luigi Dorici 1547, f. 173v).

[75] See Francesco Ciabattoni: Dante Alighieri. In Marco Sgarbi (ed.): *Encyclopedia of Renaissance Philosophy*. Springer: Cham 2017 (Online: https://doi.org/10.1007/978-3-319-02848-4_849-1); Claudio Gigante: Per un'edizione critica della *Difesa della Commedia di Dante* di Jacopo Mazzoni. In *Studi Danteschi*, I (2001), pp. 75–79.

[76] Luís de Camões, *The Collected Lyric Poems of Luís de Camões*, p. 140.

[77] See Thomas Hunkeler: Dante à Lyon: des 'rime petrose' aux 'durs épigrammes'. In *Italique*, XI (2008), pp. 9–27.

Camões seems to differ considerably from Dante. He does not follow, in his poetry, the *dolce stil novo*, nor does he trace an *ad Deum* itinerary. Far from devising (assuming he ever attempted to) a book of poetry, a *prosimetrum* or a *Cancioneiro* whose structure spoke for itself, Camões left in his wake texts whose very scatteredness emphasises a "continual zig-zag"[78] and a typically Petrarchist dissent.[79] Conversely, like Dante, he audaciously constructed an immense body of work; like Dante, he metaphorised writing into a journey of adventure;[80] like Dante – pilgrim, poet, pedagogue, and prophet –, he was unafraid to impart his knowledge and wisdom, using an impressive "libertad del dezir."[81] However, a meticulous examination will throw up profound differences, even within these affinities: Dante keeps for himself a "seggio" among the blessed, in Paradiso;[82] whereas Camões describes himself as a suicidal outsider or a figure beset by melancholy,[83] split between fury and despondency. Dante attains the ineffable and "l'amor che move il sole e l'altre stelle" (*Paradiso* XXXIII, 145); while Camões does not liberate himself from the frustrations that pull him, like a tormented Sisyphus, towards the black abyss from which only love for the "paternal ... nest,"[84] momentarily releases him.

In *The Lusiads* (IX, 78, 8), Camões introduces a direct quotation from Petrarca, which is the only occurrence of a foreign language making an appearance in this poem. Dante is not accorded the same measure of protagonism. Is it possible to trace his presence in several passages from different cantos, as averred by Vincenzo Cioffari[85] and noted by some commentators?[86] This is difficult to determine

---

78 Octavio Paz: *The Double Flame: Love and Eroticism*. Translated by Helen Lane. New York: Harcourt Brace 1995, p. 120.
79 See Rita Marnoto: *O Petrarquismo Português do* Cancioneiro Geral *a Camões*.
80 See Luís de Camões: *Os Lusíadas*, 2.ª ed., Lisboa: Ministério da Educação 1989, p. 194 (VII, 79); *Purgatorio* I, 1–3; *Paradiso* II, 1–3.
81 Manuel de Faria e Sousa: *Lusiadas de Luis de Camões Comentadas*. Reprodução fac-similada pela edição de 1639, 2 vols. Lisboa: Imprensa Nacional-Casa da Moeda 1972, I, Vol. I, coll. 53.
82 See *Paradiso* XXX, 133–138.
83 Note the comparison at the end of Canto VII (79, 7) of *The Lusiads* ("like Canace condemned herself to death") or stanzas 8–9 of Canto X. See João R. Figueiredo: Reading through the Sound of Trumpets: Camões's Political Opinions and the Pattern of Allusion in *Os Lusíadas*. In Colin Burrow et al. (eds.): *Imitative Series and Clusters from Classical to Early Modern Literature*. Berlin / Munich / Boston: de Gruyter 2020, pp. 254–255; Isabel Almeida: Poesia, Furor e Melancolia: Notas sobre Ariosto e Camões. In Maria das Graças Moreira de Sá et al. (eds.): Magnum Miraculum est Homo: *José Vitorino de Pina Martins e o Humanismo*. Lisboa: Faculdade de Letras / Universidade de Lisboa 2008, pp. 102–104.
84 Luís de Camões: *Os Lusíadas*, I, 10, 4. (Literal translation from the Portuguese – T / n).
85 Cf. Vincenzo Cioffari: Camões and Dante: a Source Study. In *Italica*, vol. 25, n.º 4 (1948), pp. 282–295.
86 See below, footnote 335.

with any degree of certainty, given the density of the intertextual fabric. Indeed, in the Camonian epic, many of the conceivable Dantean reverberations may result either from the shared connection to Classical authors such as Virgil or Ovid, or from the reading of imitational texts, or texts which (as is the case with Ariosto's *Orlando Furioso*) emulate Dante himself.

One episode in *The Lusiads*, however, that of the Machine of the World, does display particular closeness to the *Commedia*, in its desire to expose "wrongheaded and pitiful mortals" to essential "science."[87] Setting the scene for this initiation, Camões creates "a meadow" "studded / with emeralds and rubies,"[88] much in the same way as the gleam of "rubin" (*Paradiso* XXX, 66) and "topazi" (*Paradiso* XXX, 76) had permeated the landscape of Dante's *Paradiso*. As a corollary to this cosmological structure, lies the heaven of theologians, or Empyrean, the motionless "sphere," which, after Dante, Camões peoples with "unblemished / divine Souls."[89] This harmony, previously examined by Maria Lucília Pires,[90] seduces both poets, unanimous in their celebration of the flawlessness of divine order.

Should these consonances be deliberate, there is a further reason to highlight them. The extraordinary passage of the Machine of the World is not only a meeting point, much like the *Commedia*, of a heterogeneous plurality of sources (from Lucan's *Pharsalia* to Cicero's "Dream of Scipio," and its commentary by Macrobius, as well as the teachings of geographers and astronomers,[91] and Juan de Mena's "Laberinto de Fortuna") but it also signals a willingness to embrace, in full epic mode, that which would have been relegated to the margins in a poetics based exclusively on the deference towards the more Classical among ancient and modern authors.

Epilogue

Although the *Commedia* was targeted by the inquisitional *Indices* of 1581 and 1624,[92] a few 17th-century commentators of Camões, such as Manuel de Faria e

---

87 Luís de Camões: *Os Lusíadas*, p. 266 (X. 76, 3–4). (Literal translation from the Portuguese – T / n).
88 Luís de Camões: *Os Lusíadas*, p. 266 (X. 77, 2–3). (Literal translation from the Portuguese – T / n).
89 Luís de Camões: *Os Lusíadas*, p. 268 (X. 85, 5–6). (Literal translation from the Portuguese – T / n).
90 Maria Lucília Gonçalves Pires: *Harmonia Mundi*: a descrição camoniana da máquina do mundo. In *Arquivos do Centro Cultural Calouste Gulbenkian. Homenagem a Maria de Lourdes Belchior*, vol. XXXVII (1998), pp. 201–210.
91 See Luciano A. Pereira da Silva: *A Astronomia dos Lusíadas*. Coimbra: Imprensa da Universidade 1915 (particularly "A Astronomia em Dante e Camões", pp. 175–226).
92 In the 16th century, the treatise *De monarchia* was part of the list of forbidden works since c. 1559 (see A. Moreira de Sá (ed.): *Indices dos Livros Proibidos em Portugal no Século XVI*. Lisboa:

Sousa and Manuel Pires de Almeida,[93] refused to consign it to oblivion. Others followed in rallying around this work, such as João Soares de Brito, in the *Apologia em que defende* [. . .] *a Poesia do Principe dos Poetas d'Hespanha Luis de Camoens* [. . .] (1641).[94]

The Baroque fondness for the mixing of genres and languages, the taste for obscurity and wonderment, and the fascination, particularly prevalent in the 17th century, with the figure of the Four Last Things greatly contributed to the advancement of Dante. Moreover, those who invoke Dante do so, to a large extent, driven by a desire for erudition, as is the case of Luís Marinho de Azevedo, in the *Primeira Parte da Fundação, Antiguidades e Grandezas da Mui Insigne Cidade de Lisboa* (1652), where this author compares Ulysses's journey to that of Vasco da Gama, and likens passages from Canto XXVI of the *Inferno* to Canto V of *The Lusiads*.[95]

There is more, however. To the original text of Canto XXVI of the *Inferno*, Azevedo appends the translation by "Dom Pedro Fernandes de Vilhegas, Archdeacon of Burgos," "for being a source of delight, in its variety, for those who might

---

Instituto Nacional de Investigação Científica 1983, p. 196). As for the *Commedia*, it only joined the 1581 *Index* under the section "Cautions and reminders, for the purpose of the trade and improvement of books." Censorship targeted the "Commentaries of Cristoforo Landino", because of "some of its propositions," using the example of "its pronouncements" on cantos II and X of the "Inferno" ("First Matter & the Angels & the Heavens are eternal beings, erroneously described by a few gentile philosophers"; "heretics should not be put to death but merely imprisoned: they should be purged of their false opinions"). However, in addition to Landino's (dangerously topical?) commentary, it was "[Dante's] own text" that inspired the Inquisitors' reservations: "there are passages that must perforce be crossed out, which will be shown when presented before the Holy Office." (*Ibidem*, pp. 634–635). In 1624, this sentence was aggravated: "Florentine Dante, *de Monarchia*, which is prohibited in the Roman Index [. . .], as well as his *Commedia* of the Inferno, &c, in addition to the Commentaries or exposition by Cristoforo Landino, & Alexandro Vellutello; over these there is full prohibition, without emendations, as noted in the Expurgatory Catalogue." (*Index Avctorvm Dãnatæ memoriæ*, p. 112). Further on, between pp. 450–452, the censorship is detailed.

93 Manuel Correa and Pedro de Mariz, in *Os Lusiadas do Grande Luis de Camoens. Principe da Poesia Heroica*. Lisboa: Pedro Crasbeeck 1613, do not mention Dante; nor does Dom Marcos de S. Lourenço (see *Os Lusíadas Comentados*. Coimbra: Centro Interuniversitário de Estudos Camonianos 2014), whose work encompasses the dates between 1631–1633. Manuel de Faria e Sousa printed the *Lusiadas* [. . .] *Comentadas* in Madrid, in 1639; Manuel Pires de Almeida's commentaries, which he probably began writing *c*. 1642, remained unpublished.

94 João Soares de Brito: *Apologia em que defende* [. . .] *a Poesia do Principe dos Poetas d'Hespanha Luis de Camoens* [. . .] Lisboa: Lourenço de Anveres 1641, f. 37v.

95 Luís Marinho de Azevedo, *Primeira Parte da Fundação, Antiguidades, e Grandezas da Mui Insigne Cidade de Lisboa*. Lisboa: Officina Craesbeckiana 1652, pp. 159–160.

not know Italian."[96] Additionally, he recalls information obtained in "Christoforo Landino, & Alexandre Vellutelo," "in their glosses of the poet Dante." This reveals that, mindful of the drawn-out exegetical labour developed concerning Dante, Luís Marinho de Azevedo acknowledges Dante as an author, i.e., a figure who holds an established position in the literary sphere.

This is perhaps the main reason why Manuel de Faria e Sousa and Manuel Pires de Almeida gave prominence to the Florentine poet, despite alluding to some of his defects.[97] Faria e Sousa and Pires de Almeida were each, in their own way, involved in the canonisation of Camões, and both take delight in invoking Dante. Better yet, they were invested in learning both from the commentaries produced on the *Commedia* and from the poem itself. Oftentimes, there is no pretention, on their part, to defend the existence of an imitation that directly links Camões to Dante;[98] rather, they are devoted to expanding and enriching their own referential field, guided by the certainty of the *Divine Comedy*'s canonical status, which could not be denied when it came to appreciating another work of comparable quality.

In the 16th century, Dante's presence in Portugal is somewhat doubtful: firstly, due to a lack of openness to dialogue with *modern* Italy; secondly, due to the predominance of a classicizing poetics and the supremacy of Petrarca. In the 17th century, this outlook changed: while Alighieri's presence declined in Italy, it was preserved among a limited group in Portugal. Their attention fixed on 16th-century works, their vast curiosity about all things Italian and their commitment to displaying their learnedness often led scholarly admirers of Camões to keep Dante's memory alive. Faria e Sousa, in the *Lusiadas* [. . .] *Comentadas* (a vast work of commentary printed in Madrid, in 1639), referred to "the great Dante"[99] and lavished noble epithets on this author: "divine in Poetical spirit, and insight-

---

[96] *Ibidem*, p. 159.
[97] Faria e Sousa avers: "his Poem is little more than sacred Theology" (*Lusiadas de Luis de Camões Comentadas*, I, tome I, coll. 77). Or, regarding "proportion", he writes: "Dante, who is the foremost among the vernacular authors, although he greatly resembles Homer, mostly limits himself to passable turns of phrase". (*Ibidem*, I, 83) Also regarding the "teachings" contained in the text, he observes that Dante is one of those authors whose writing "contains little more than what is immediately apparent" (*Ibidem*, I, 87).
[98] Numerous examples can be found in the *Lusiadas de Luis de Camões Comentadas* by Faria e Sousa: *cf.*, tome I, colls. 155, 397, 402, 403, 406, 410, 434, 454; tome II, colls. 94, 98, 141, 275, 308, 361, 376, 387, 424, 473, 484, 608, 630. . . Manuel Pires de Almeida, who was sparing in his identification of Camões's direct imitations of Dante, connects, for example, the ending of Canto I with the verse "Non v'accorgete voi che noi siam vermi" (*Purgatorio* X, 124). See Manuel Pires de Almeida: CCDV-3, f. 121v. Similar indications can be found on ff. 453, 480–480v and 516.
[99] Manuel de Faria e Sousa: *Lusiadas de Luis de Camões Comentadas*, I, tome I, coll. 136.

ful in his writings, and an unwavering emulator of Virgil."[100] This praise stands out for its exuberance and leads to a new question in the present *in fieri* examination: is it by happenstance that these words were authored by a polymath who had resided in Spain since 1619?

Bibliographical References

Alighieri, Dante: *Vita Nuova*. Introduzione di Edoardo Sanguinetti. Note di Alfonso Berardinelli. Milano: Garzanti 1994.
[Alighieri, Dante]: *Comedia Dantis Allegerii florentini*. . . Biblioteca Nacional de Espanha, Ms 10186.
Almeida, Manuel Pires de: *Os Lusiadas de Luis de Camões Commentados*. . . Arquivo Nacional da Torre do Tombo, Casa Cadaval – CCDV 3.
Almeida, Isabel: Poesia, Furor e Melancolia: Notas sobre Ariosto e Camões. In Maria das Graças Moreira de Sá et al. (eds.): Magnum Miraculum est Homo: *José Vitorino de Pina Martins e o Humanismo*. Lisboa: Faculdade de Letras / Universidade de Lisboa 2008, pp. 93–108.
Ascoli, Albert Russell: Palinode and History in the Oeuvre of Dante. In Amilcare A. Ianucci (ed.): *Dante: Contemporary Perspectives*. Toronto-Buffalo-London: University of Toronto Press 1997, pp. 23–50.
Asensio, Eugenio: Las Fuentes de las Barcas de Gil Vicente. In *Estudios Portugueses*. Paris: Fundação Calouste Gulbenkian / Centro Cultural Português 1974, pp. 59–77.
Augustine of Hippo: *Confessions*. Translated by J.G. Pilkington. In *Nicene and Post-nicene Fathers*, First Series, vol. 1. Edited by Philip Schaff. Buffalo, NY: Christian Literature Publishing co. 1887.
Azevedo, Luís Marinho de: *Primeira Parte da Fundação, Antiguidades, e Grandezas da Mui Insigne Cidade de Lisboa* . . . Lisboa: Officina Craesbeckiana 1652.
Bayard, Jean: *Comment parler des livres que l'on n'a pas lus?* Paris: Les Éditions de Minuit 2007.
Bembo, Pietro: *Prose della Volgar Lingua. Gli Asolani. Rime*. A cura di Carlo Dionisotti. Milano: TEA 1989.
Braga, Theophilo: *Historia da Universidade de Coimbra nas suas relações com a Instrucção Publica Portugueza*, vol. I. Lisboa: Por Ordem e na Typographia da Academia Real das Sciencias 1892.
Brito, Álvaro de: *Obras de* . . . . Edição, introdução e notas de Isabel Almeida. Lisboa: Comissão Nacional para a Comemoração dos Descobrimentos Portugueses 1997.
Brito, João Soares de: *Apologia em que defende . . . a Poesia do Principe dos Poetas d'Hespanha Luis de Camoens* . . . Lisboa: Lourenço de Anveres 1641.
Camões, Luís de: *The Collected Lyric Poems of Luís de De Camões*. Translated by Landeg White. Princeton: Princeton University Press 2008.
Camões, Luís de: *Os Lusíadas*. Leitura, prefácio e notas de Álvaro Júlio da Costa Pimpão. Apresentação de Aníbal Pinto de Castro. 2.ª ed., Lisboa: Ministério de Educação 1989.

---

100 *Ibidem*, coll. 141.

Camões, Luís de: *Rimas*. Texto estabelecido, revisto e prefaciado por Álvaro J. da Costa Pimpão. Apresentação de Aníbal Pinto de Castro. Coimbra: Livraria Almedina 1994.

Cancionero de Lope de Stúñiga. Códice del Siglo XV. Ahora por vez primera publicado. Madrid: Imprenta y Estereotipia de M. Rivadeneyra 1872.

Cancionero General de Hernando del Castillo segun la edición de 1511 . . . 2 vols. Madrid: La Sociedad de Bibliófilos Españoles 1882.

Castro, Aníbal Pinto de: Boscán e Garcilaso no lirismo português do Renascimento e do Maneirismo. In *Península: Revista de Estudos Ibéricos* 1 (2004), pp. 65–95.

Cepeda, Isabel Vilares: Os Livros da Rainha D. Leonor, segundo o códice 11 352 da Biblioteca Nacional, Lisboa'. In *Revista da Biblioteca Nacional*, série 2, vol. 2, n.º 2 (1987), pp. 51–81.

Ciabattoni, Francesco: Dante Alighieri. In Marco Sgarbi (ed.): *Encyclopedia of Renaissance Philosophy*. Springer: Cham 2017. Online: https://doi.org/10.1007/978-3-319-02848-4_849-1.

Cioffari, Vincenzo: Camões and Dante: a Source Study. In *Italica*, vol. 25, n.º 4 (1948), pp. 282–295.

Correia, Gaspar: *Crónicas de D. Manuel e de D. João III (até 1533)*. Leitura, Introdução, Notas e Índice por José Pereira da Costa. Lisboa: Academia das Ciências 1992.

Curtius, Ernst Robert: *Literatura Europea y Edad Media Latina*, 2 vols. Mexico-Madrid-Buenos Aires: Fondo de Cultura Económica 1984.

Di Pasquale, Daniela: Le prime ricezioni della *Divina Commedia* in Portogallo: Indizi e ipotesi. In *Studi Danteschi*, vol. LXXIII (2008), pp. 145–177.

El Cancionero de Juan Alfonso de Baena. Ed. Francisque Michel. Con las notas y los indices de la edición de Madrid del año 1851, vols. I–II. Leipzig: F. A. Brockhaus 1860.

Farinelli, Arturo: *Dante in Spagna, Francia, Inghilterra, Germania (Dante e Goethe)*. Torino: Fratelli Bocca 1922.

Figueiredo, João R.: Reading through the Sound of Trumpets: Camões's Political Opinions and the Pattern of Allusion in *Os Lusíadas*. In Colin Burrow et al. (eds.): *Imitative Series and Clusters from Classical to Early Modern Literature*. Berlin / Munich / Boston: de Gruyter 2020, pp. 243–256.

Freire, Braamcamp: Inventario da Guarda-Roupa de D. Manuel. In *Archivo Historico Portuguez*, vol. II (1904), pp. 381–417.

Frutuoso, Gaspar, *Livro Quinto das Saudades da Terra*. Ponta Delgada: Instituto Cultural de Ponta Delgada 1964.

Gigante, Claudio: Per un'edizione critica della *Difesa della Commedia di Dante* di Jacopo Mazzoni. In *Studi Danteschi*, I (2001), pp. 75–90.

Holanda, Francisco de: *Da Pintura Antiga*. Introdução, notas e comentários de José da Felicidade Alves. Lisboa: Livros Horizonte 1984.

Holanda, Francisco de: *Diálogos em Roma*. Introdução, notas e comentários de José da Felicidade Alves. Lisboa: Livros Horizonte 1984.

Hunkeler, Thomas: Dante à Lyon: des 'rime petrose' aux 'durs épigrammes'. In *Italique* [online], XI (2008), pp. 9–27.

Index Avctorvm Dānatæ memoriæ . . . Editvs Avctoritate Ill.[mi] Domini D. Ferdinandi Martins Mascaregnas . . .. Lisboa: Pedro Craesbeck 1624.

[López de Mendoza, Iñigo], Marqués de Santillana: *Comedieta de Ponza, Sonetos, Serranillas y Otras Obras*. Edición de Regula Rohland de Langbehn. Estudio preliminar de Vicente Beltrán. Barcelona: Crítica 1997.

Lourenço, D. Marcos de S.: *Os Lusíadas Comentados por* . . . . Transcrição e fixação do texto por Isabel Almeida, Filipa Araújo, Manuel Ferro, Teresa Nascimento, Marcelo Vieira. Notas por Isabel Almeida, Filipa Araújo, Marcelo Vieira. Nota introdutória, índices e revisão por Isabel Almeida. Coimbra: Centro Interuniversitário de Estudos Camonianos 2014.

Lucain (Marcus Annaeus Lucanus): *La Guerre Civile. La Pharsale*. Texte établi et traduit par A. Bourgery et M. Ponchont. vols. I–II. Paris: Les Belles Lettres 2003.

Manuppella, Giacinto: *Dantesca Luso-Brasileira. Subsídios para uma Bibliografia da Obra e do Pensamento de Dante Alighieri*. Coimbra: Por Ordem da Universidade 1966.

Manuppella, Giacinto: Uma anónima versão quinhentista dos *Triunfos* de Petrarca e o seu *Comentário*. No VI centenário da morte do poeta (1374–1974). In *Revista da Universidade de Coimbra*, XXV (1974), pp. 1–324.

Marnoto, Rita: *O Petrarquismo Português do* Cancioneiro Geral *a Camões*. Lisboa: Imprensa Nacional-Casa da Moeda 2015.

Marnoto, Rita: *O Petrarquismo Português do Renascimento e do Maneirismo*. Coimbra: Por Ordem da Universidade 1997.

Mena, Juan de: *Antología de su obra poética*. Ed. José María Azaceta. Barcelona: Plaza & Janés 1986.

Miranda, Francisco de Sá de: *Obras. Edição Fac-Simile da Edição de 1595*. Estudo introdutório de Vítor Aguiar e Silva. Braga: Universidade do Minho 1994.

Miranda, Francisco de Sá de: *Poesias* (Carolina Michaëlis de Vasconcelos, ed.; fac-simile do exemplar com data de 1885 da Biblioteca Nacional). Lisboa: Imprensa Nacional-Casa da Moeda 1989.

Moura, Vasco Graça: Introdução. In A Divina Comédia *de Dante Alighieri*, 2.ª ed. Venda Nova: Bertrand 1996, pp. 9–27. Reed.: Traduzir Dante: uma aproximação. In Daniela Di Pasquale / Tiago Guerreiro da Silva (eds.): *Estudos Dantescos. Tradução e Recepção das Obras de Dante em Portugal e no Mundo*. Lisboa: Cosmos 2014, pp. 21–41.

Paz, Octavio: *The Double Flame: Love and Eroticism*. Translated by Helen Lane. New York: Harcourt Brace 1995.

Pellizzari, Achille: *Portogallo e Italia nel secolo XVI. Studi e Ricerche Storiche e Letterarie*. Napoli: Società Editrice F. Perrella e C. 1914.

Pires, Maria Lucília Gonçalves: *Harmonia Mundi*: a descrição camoniana da máquina do mundo. In *Arquivos do Centro Cultural Calouste Gulbenkian. Homenagem a Maria de Lourdes Belchior*, vol. XXXVII (1998), pp. 201–210.

Plato: *The Republic*. Translated by Benjamin Jowett. New York, NY: Cosimo Classics 2008

Resende, André Falcão de: *Obras*. Edição crítica de Barbara Spaggiari, vols. I–II. Lisboa: Edições Colibri 2009.

Resende, Garcia de: *Cancioneiro Geral*. Nova edição. Introdução e Notas de Andrée Crabbé Rocha, vols. I–V. Lisboa: Centro do Livro Brasileiro 1973.

Ribeiro, Bernardim: *História de Menina e Moça*. Edição de texto, introdução, nota biobibliográfica, glossário e notas de Marta Marecos Duarte. Lisboa: Imprensa Nacional–Casa da Moeda 2015.

Rime di Diversi Antichi Avtori Toscani in Dieci Libri Raccolte. Vinegia: Io. Antonio, e Fratelli da Sabio 1532.

Sá, Artur Moreira de (ed.): *Índices dos Livros Proibidos em Portugal no Século XVI*. Lisboa: Instituto Nacional de Investigação Científica 1983.

Sá, Isabel dos Guimarães: *Leonor de Lencastre. De princesa a rainha-velha*. Lisboa: Temas e Debates 2016.

Sanvisenti, Bernardo: *I primi influssi di Dante, del Petrarca e del Boccaccio sulla Letteratura Spagnuola con appendici di documenti inediti*. Milano: U. Hoepli 1902.
Santo Agostinho: *Confissões*. Tradução de Arnaldo do Espírito Santo, João Beato e Maria Cristina de Castro-Maia de Sousa Pimentel, 2.ª ed. Lisboa: Centro de Literatura e Cultura Portuguesa e Brasileira, Imprensa Nacional-Casa da Moeda 2004.
Silva, Luciano A. Pereira da: *A Astronomia dos Lusíadas*. Coimbra: Imprensa da Universidade 1915.
Sousa, D. António Caetano de: *Provas da História Genealógica da Casa Real Portuguesa*. Nova edição revista por M. Lopes de Almeida e César Pegado, vol. I, l. III. Coimbra: Atlântida Editora 1947.
Sousa, Manuel de Faria: *Lusiadas de Luis de Camões Comentadas por*. . . . Reprodução fac-similada pela edição de 1639, 2 vols. Lisboa: Imprensa Nacional-Casa da Moeda 1972.
Tarrío, Ana María Sánchez: O obscuro fidalgo João Rodrigues de Lucena, tradutor das Heroides. In *Euphrosyne*, 30 (2002), pp. 371–384.
Tarrío, Ana María Sánchez: A tradição dos clássicos e a poética do *Cancioneiro Geral*. In Cristina Almeida Ribeiro e Sara Rodrigues de Sousa (eds.): Cancioneiro Geral *de Garcia de Resende: um livro à luz da história*. Lisboa: Húmus 2012, pp. 61–72.
Tocco, Valeria: Gli Inferni d'Amore Portoghesi e la Tradizione Allegorica Europea. In *Filologia Medievale e Umanistica*, 127 (1993), pp. 297–359.
[Trissino, Gian Giorgio]: *La Italia Liberata da Gotthi del Trissino*. Roma: Valerio e Luigi Dorici 1547.
Vasconcelos, Jorge Ferreira de: *Comedia Aulegrafia* . . ., Lisboa: Pedro Craesbeeck 1619.
Vicente, Gil: *Obras Completas*. Reimpressão 'Fac-similada' da Edição de 1562. Lisboa: Biblioteca Nacional 1928.
Viterbo, Sousa: Dante, o marquez de Santilhana e Bernardim Ribeiro. In *A Revista: Sciencias e Letras*, n.º 11 (1904).Zurara, Gomes Eanes de: *Crónica do Conde Dom Pedro de Menezes*. Reprodução facsimilada com nota de apresentação por José Adriano de Freitas Carvalho. Porto: Comissão Organizadora do Congresso Internacional "Bartolomeu Dias" 1988.
[Zurara, Gomes Eanes de]: *Chronica do Conde D. Duarte de Menezes*. In *Collecçaõ de Livros Ineditos de Historia Portugueza, dos Reinados de D. Joaõ I., D. Duarte, D. Affonso V., e D. Joaõ II*. Publicados de Ordem da Academia Real das Sciencias de Lisboa. Por José Corrêa da Serra, vol. III. Lisboa: [Academia Real das Sciencias de Lisboa] 1793, pp. 3–376.

João R. Figueiredo
Dante and Camões: Epic and the Portrayal of Humanity

Portuguese literature gravitates entirely around one single poem: *The Lusiads*, by Luís de Camões, published in Lisbon in 1572. There has been no successor to Camões who, to this day, has not had to measure himself against this national epic, cast in the Virgilian mould, but so profoundly lyrical to the point of disintegration *qua* epic. The founder of a certain notion of Portugal – providential, chosen by God, heroic and spearheaded spreader of Christianity throughout the world –, *The Lusiads* is also an arena in which two men are confronted: Vasco da Gama, the official hero of the poem, and Camões, its author, who often makes himself heard in crucial moments of the text, to rebuke the Captain's immoral conduct and to set himself against it as a model of virtue. The emergence of such a strong authorial voice within an epic celebrating collective historical deeds is unparalleled in the tradition of the genre and introduces a sharp break with all that came before. However, if non strictly classical or neo-classical models are to be considered, it is legitimate to establish an affinity between *The Lusiads* and other texts, among which Dante's *Comedy* emerges as a propitious frame of reference that, to a considerable extent, allows the redescription of Camões' epic and, in particular, of its major structural components.

It has been a touchstone in some important studies on Camões to establish a parallel with Dante, even if only briefly. A strictly philological approach that looks for echoes, quotes or allusions proves barren, given the hegemony of Petrarca as a literary model for Renaissance poets.[1] In other cases, the parallel is established taking into account categories that exceed the letter of the text. Fernando Pessoa, for example, for whom his activity as a critic could not be isolated, as in the case of every great poet who was also a critic, from the poetry for which he is mostly known, condemns Camões for contenting himself with the factual history he knew first-hand, thus producing mere "transcendent reportage", unlike Dante, who finds ground "in the Beyond".[2] Another decisive poet-critic in twentieth-cen-

---

[1] See, for instance, Fabio Camilletti: Later Reception from 1481 to the Present. In Zygmunt G. Barański and Simon Gilson (eds.): *The Cambridge Companion to Dante's* Commedia. Cambridge: Cambridge University Press, 2019, p. 260: "[I]n the age of classicism – largely corresponding to the sixteenth century – [. . .] the dominant position of Petrarchism prevented any substantial evaluation of Dante and the *Commedia* on a European scale."

[2] Fernando Pessoa: *Crítica: ensaios, artigos e entrevistas*. Fernando Cabral Martins (ed.). Lisboa: Assírio & Alvim 2000, p. 2015.

https://doi.org/10.1515/9783110796049-010

tury Portuguese literature, Jorge de Sena, puts Dante and Camões in confrontation with regard to the relationship between politics and culture, concluding that, unlike the Portuguese poet, "Dante's political glory has a literary root, in the best sense of the word, that is, it came from culture to political life, and not from the latter, by chance of imagination, to literary history."[3] If epic is the genre that most emphatically thematises such tensions, having history at its centre, it may be a salutary exercise to place the *Comedy* and *The Lusiads* side by side as to inquire in which ways history and poetry contaminate or antagonise one another.

About halfway through *The Lusiads*, Vasco da Gama's fleet encounters the giant Adamastor, who unravels a terrible catalogue of future disasters. These misfortunes will afflict all Portuguese sailors who take the so-called Cape route, between Lisbon and the various destinations on the Indian Ocean coast, including the Malabar Coast, the region of India where spices were produced and traded. Adamastor is an unhappy lover. Ugly and disproportionate, he fell in love with the nymph Thetis and tried clumsily to win her by blackmail and force. As a result, he was set up by the nymph, who humiliated him, leading him to flee from human company to spare himself the shame. Being, moreover, one of the giants who participated in the attempt to dethrone the Olympians, he received, from Thetis and the Olympian gods, a joint punishment: he was petrified and transformed into the Cape of Good Hope, in the southernmost tip of Africa.

Metamorphosed into a mountain, Adamastor retains the faculty of speech. Throughout 192 verses, which correspond approximately to the length of one and a half cantos of the *Commedia*, the giant begins his speech by making his doomed prophecy, and it is only when Vasco da Gama interrupts him that he relates what had happened to him before the Portuguese navigator violated his self-imposed seclusion. The abrupt cut that the captain introduces in the prophecy has the form of a question that we often find in the *Comedy*, whenever someone, confronted with a stranger, asks him to reveal his identity:

> The fearful creature was in full spate
> Chanting our destiny when, rising
> I demanded: 'Who are you, whose
> Outlandish shape utterly dumbfounds me?'
> His mouth and black eyes grimaced
> Giving vent to an awesome roar,
> Then answered bitterly, with the heavy voice
> Of one who speaks compelled and not by choice:

---

[3] Jorge de Sena: A Poesia de Camões: ensaio de revelação da dialéctica camoniana. In *Trinta Anos de Camões*, vol. I. Lisboa: Edições 70 1980, p. 18.

> 'I am that vast, secret promontory
> You Portuguese call the Cape of Storms,
> Which neither Ptolemy, Pomponius, Strabo,
> Pliny, nor any authors knew of.
> Here Africa ends. Here its coast
> Concludes in this, my vast inviolate
> Plateau, extending southwards to the Pole
> And, by your daring, struck to my very soul!
>
> (V, 49–50)[4]

Vasco da Gama's encounter with Adamastor is configured in typically Dantean terms and describes a pattern that we find above all in the *Inferno*, in the way the pilgrim Dante is confronted by the damned, or the damned are questioned by Dante: someone wants to know someone else's identity and asks the question "Who are you?" without much circumlocution, in a straightforward way. This is, for example, what, in canto VIII of the *Inferno*, the irate Filippo Argenti asks the pilgrim: "Chi se' tu che vieni anziora?" In both cases, the stranger's arrival is configured as an audacity and an invasion of privacy, something that transgresses the limits of decorum: the unfortunate also feel entitled to reserve and solitude. The effect that da Gama's question has on the giant is therefore one of profound discomfort, and the reply consists of Adamastor's identification of himself by means of an autobiographical narrative. This encounter thus gives rise to a prophecy about the future of Portugal, as it so often happens in the *Comedy*, when Dante learns about his fate and the future of Florence.

To call this passage a dialogue is perhaps excessive. It is practically a monologue interrupted by the question "who are you?", and without the complexity that we find, for example, in Canto X of the *Inferno*, in which Dante meets Farinata and Cavalcante, with the crisscross conversations, the successive rejoinders, the reactions of each interlocutor, and the extraordinary expressive and discursive realism that Auerbach influentially analysed. But like Farinata and the other inhabitants of the first *cantica*, there is little doubt that Adamastor is a convict, suffering a punishment. From this fact, it is worth describing in greater detail the similarities and differences between Dante's canto and Camões' excerpt.

When the pilgrim and Virgil arrive at the place where the Epicureans are tormented, Farinata degli Uberti, an aristocrat who belonged to the faction in Florence that was opposed to Dante's, shares the grave with Cavalcante de' Cavalcanti, the father of the poet Guido Cavalcanti. Parallel and intersecting conversations, between Dante and Farinata on the one hand, and Dante and Cavalcante

---

[4] All quotations are from Luís de Camões: *The Lusíads*. English translation by Landeg White. Oxford: Oxford University Press 1997.

on the other, reveal in a precise way the psychology of these characters. Farinata, unable to know what is happening in the historical present, is dismayed to learn that his partisans will not be soon able to retake Florence. What is important to underline in this episode, and for the purposes of comparison with *The Lusiads*, is that, in retaliation, the reanimated soul prophetically declares that Dante too will be prevented from returning to the city because of the internecine fighting that rages there.

As already noted by many critics, Farinata's suffering is increased by Dante's words – which are true "speech acts" as Teodolinda Barolini notes[5] –, by triggering reactions and determining the course of events. The Dantean singularity of the prophecy as a deliberately aggressive expression of resentment is also a characteristic of *The Lusiads*, where it is hyperbolised in what turns out to be an exact figuration of the sadism resulting from sexual frustration. Adamastor too feels aggravated and offended, not by what da Gama says, but by the mere fact that da Gama appears in what was supposed to be a safe hiding place, involuntarily humiliating him with the simple act of discovering him, and then asking him who he is, finally prompting the giant to relive his pains by means of autobiographical retrospection. To the illocutionary mode of the prophecy as aggression, Camões adds a new particularity, by making the object of the prophecy arise from the encounter, configured as an offence by the one who makes it:

> 'Because you have desecrated nature's
> Secrets and the mysteries of the deep,
> Where no human, however noble
> Or immortal his worth, should trespass,
> Hear from me now what retribution
> Fate prescribes for your insolence,
> Whether ocean-borne, or along the shores
> You will subjugate with your dreadful wars.
>
> No matter how many vessels attempt
> The audacious passage you are plotting,
> My cape will be implacably hostile
> With gales beyond any you have encountered;
> On the next fleet which broaches
> The turbulent waters, I shall impose
> Such retribution and exact such debts
> The destruction will be far worse than my threats!
>   V, 43

---

[5] In https://digitaldante.columbia.edu/dante/divine-comedy/inferno/inferno-10/ (accessed 10.07.2022).

If Dante distorts and creates exceptions to theology so that the degree of suffering of the souls in pain is altered, which is in itself daring enough, Camões has a condemned man, someone who lives in his own personal hell, private to the extreme, determining the punishment of the free man who meets him by chance. Although indebted to Dante's lead, but even more than in the *Comedy*, the prophecy ceases to be, unlike the *Aeneid*, a narrative expedient above all, let alone a simple ornament, used with the aim of making the discourse varied. At the origin of the historical event as represented in *The Lusiads* is thus a story of frustrated love, in which, perhaps for the first time, a punished person inflicts a punishment on someone else by inventing the facts that will cause pain. This mechanism – the abused becoming the abuser – is well illustrated in the refined cruelty that the giant reserves for Manuel de Sousa Sepúlveda and his wife, Leonor de Sá. At the hands of the African natives, she will suffer horrors that Camões decorously refrains from describing, and both

> [. . .] will watch their dear children,
> Fruits of such love, perish in hunger.
> V, 47

Such cruelty, such a high degree of sadism, that befalls those who had children generated out of love, is the reverse of the incontinent one who failed to consummate his desire for Thetis. By means of the abused one's self-fashioning himself as the abuser, the very notion of *contrapasso* suffers an ironic inversion, for at the moment he himself is prevented from generating children out of love, Adamastor wishes to stop the generation of other human beings – an appropriation, also abusive to the extent that it is perverse and distorted, of the judicative yardstick that one sees applied throughout the *Comedy*. Since Adamastor's prophecies are not merely the description of future events but have a performative force, like the replicas of Dante and Farinata but of a much greater scope, the difference that separates Camões' excerpt from *Inferno* X is that the future events are created at the moment of enunciation: the tragedies that will follow da Gama's journey are, in a way, improvised. Paradoxically, because one cannot do something as easy and undemanding from an intellectual point of view as uniting with Thetis and making children, Adamastor will give himself over to the far more complex task of killing the children of those to come by means of imagination, a kind of poetic fury that stems from narcissistic rage. The giant becomes a prophet, in short, because he is offended, and prophecy generates the very facts it narrates – a discursive, factitious fertility that underlines the inability to generate nature *stricto sensu*. In this sense, Adamastor is a sublime, self-conscious figuration of poetry.

Just as in the petrification of the giant we see nature being created – a case of *natura naturans*, as in the Italian Mannerist grottoes, according to the art historian Philippe Morel[6] –, in prophesying doom we see a narrative being constructed in real time. What in an ordinary prophecy would be acquired knowledge, is here constructed fact. The narcissistic flaw gives rise to prophecy and the making of stories, even if they are disastrous, like the history of Portugal. Like Vico's giants, but in spite of himself, Adamastor moves from a state of sexual unruliness to a kind of restraint of impulses that foreshadows a civilizing process. In the case of *The Lusiads*, and unlike Vico, the god who forces the civilizational process is no Jove that manifests itself by means of lightning, but remains a giant greater than the giants: Love.

The Farinata and Cavalcante canto shows precisely that, for better or for worse, Love is the cause of all human actions. It is Barolini who suggests this, reading canto X in the wider context of the inter-poetic relations between Dante and Guido Cavalcanti, to remind us that the latter sees love not as something salvific, the bearer of beatitude, but as a destructive force. The complex personal relations between the two friends and the subsequent break-up are only part of Dante's personal investment in this concrete step. Not only is at stake his share of responsibility in what was Guido Cavalcanti's fate, but Dante's exile is here prophesied for the second time, this time in a more explicit way.

At this point, it is worth asking: is not the exiled Adamastor, as has already been suggested, a portrait of Camões himself, a poet at once epic and lyric, an exile who wants to intervene in the political life of the kingdom, as he suffers the hardships of love? Is there not in the episode of the petrified giant, which Thetis perpetually tantalises in the form of the sea, the same kind of personal investment that we find in *Inferno* X and that stems from the same deleterious force of certain types of Love that cause so much misfortune, both in the *Comedy* and in *The Lusiads*?

It is not suggested here that Camões had Dante's passage in mind when he composed the Adamastor episode. Nor is it the concern of this interpretative and comparative effort to find a source, or a text that may have been the object of imitation or emulation. What matters is to recognise in the Camões episode an atmosphere, a communicational dynamic, a performativity, which, although in different directions, with very different characters, and in different cultural contexts, gains from being brought closer to certain atmospheres, communicational dynamics and types of performativity that we find in the *Comedy*. Once again, it is not about identifying a relation of ascendancy and descent between the texts, tracing their family tree, describing modalities of imitation or emulation. Rather, it is a matter of imagining that Dante can help us read Camões, that a classic can

---

6 See Philippe Morel: *Les grottes maniéristes en Italie au XVIe siècle*. Paris: Macula 1998.

be placed alongside another classic, and that vicinity has hermeneutic virtues; and of realizing that Dante provides the reader of Camões with a point of view and a vocabulary that allow them to advance their understanding of other texts with which they do not necessarily have intertextual relations in the strict sense.

Unfortunately, unlike in the *Comedy*, da Gama's encounter with Adamastor does not produce any kind of knowledge. The Captain's only concern is to ask God to eliminate the giant's prophecies, even after the latter has stated that "no hand [raised in prayer] can prevail against the heaven" (V, 58). The monster, on the other hand, has learned, and has been able to extract lessons and moral maxims from his life experience, and this is one of the reasons why the reader is led to sympathise with him, but not with Vasco da Gama, whose behaviour is uniform and invariable throughout the poem. The Captain is manifestly incapable of learning from his mistakes or from what happens to him. To some extent, and to use vocabulary we would use to speak of the *Comedy*, he never goes beyond Hell and the state of illusion and ignorance that such a domain entails. The distinction between Dante-poet and Dante-pilgrim is equally operative here, for in *The Lusiads* too a poet acquires the experience that enables him to write new epic poems. The problem lies in the Portuguese nominal epic hero, who often extols the virtues of empirical knowledge but who, unlike the Comedy's pilgrim, never leaves the prison of shadows into the realm of light.

The great and prolix sixteenth century commentator on Camões, Manuel de Faria e Sousa, identified Adamastor with Mohammed (or Mafoma, as he called him, using the archaic Portuguese word). The justification is that, besides being enemies of the Portuguese, the Muslims historically had such a large presence in Africa.[7] Somewhat similar to what David Quint would defend in the twentieth century, Adamastor would be, for Faria e Sousa, the personification of Africa, a kind of avenging genius who fights alongside the Africans, and on their behalf, against the Portuguese.[8] Although in the end Mafoma stands for the devil, it is, however, perhaps worth considering the similarities with Satan himself – not just the devil in abstract, as a principle of evil, but the same Satan the pilgrim Dante and his guide encounter in *Inferno* XXXIV.

Both are imprisoned in a vertex, immobilised, and represent, in a paradoxical way, a point at once low and culminating (at least, for the time being). In Dante's case, it is the place of the supreme evil, the absolute and fixed centre of the Earth and the Cosmos, the worst, most degraded place in the Universe. For

---

[7] See Sousa, Manuel de Faria: *Lusiadas de Luis de Camões Comentadas por. . ..* Reprodução fac-similada pela edição de 1639, 2 vols. Lisboa: Imprensa Nacional-Casa da Moeda 1972, *passim*.
[8] See David Quint: *Epic and Empire: Politics and Generic Form from Virgil to Milton*. Princeton: Princeton University Press 1993, pp. 99–130.

Camões, the speaking colossus is the result of a process of metamorphosis, of petrification, and is condemned to a life sentence in the far South of the African continent: the penalty of suffering with the constant provocations that Tethis, as the sea personified, inflicts on him for all eternity.

> 'My flesh was moulded to hard clay,
> My bones compressed to rock;
> These limbs you see, and this trunk
> Were stretched out over the waters;
> The gods moulded my great bulk
> Into this remote promontory;
> And of all tortures, the most agonizing
> Is that Tethys surrounds me, tantalizing.
> V, 59

Facing eternal suffering, it is here that Adamastor's personality, exactly like Farinata's and the damned souls in general, as pointed out by Auerbach, becomes all the more tangible in all its earthly characteristics. True, at first, unlike Farinata and the others, the giant doesn't seem so eager to seize the opportunity to speak to a living person – to a person, for that matter –, but the length and the sincerity of his utterance betray a real desire to speak, and, most important, the heightening of his humanity is entirely Dantean.[9] Even if the *Comedy* is a distant reference for Renaissance poets when it comes to echoes and allusions, its enduring influence can be seen in the way human nature is portrayed in some major poems such as Camões' epic. For that matter, Adamastor is a direct descendant of Farinata.

But the Adamastor episode, being the midpoint of the journey, is also the centre of the poem, a coincidence calculated by Camões between the two planes: that of the journey to India and that of the text of *The Lusiads*. The fixity, the immobility of Satan trapped in ice, at the innermost point of the Earth, is, as Giamatti has well noted, a parody of the *primum movens*, which delimits the universe and sets in motion the other spheres, in a poem and a journey set in continuous motion by the momentous chain of transmission described in the *first* two cantos.[10] Now, the antithesis of the divine love that Dante celebrates is, in Camões, the unruly giant consumed by sensual desire, which, also fixed and immobile in a poem that celebrates the voyage, has a nefarious agency, because it gives rise to the tragic counterpart of the Portuguese maritime expansion.

---

9 See Erich Auerbach: *Mimesis: The Representation of Reality in Western Literature* (1946). Princeton: Princeton University Press (1955) 2014 (with a New Introduction by Edward Said), pp. 174–202.
10 A. Bartlett Giamatti: *The Earthly Paradise and Renaissance Epic*. New Haven & London: Yale University Press 1966, pp. 97–98.

The intellectual and moral irrelevance of the nominal hero of *The Lusiads* is matched by the political and commercial disaster that his arrival in India proves to be. Nothing has changed since the skirmish just before the cape; the massacre on the island of Mozambique; the ambush at Mombasa. In short, the fleet has to abandon Calecut to save their own skins, and much of the responsibility for such a resounding failure is attributable to the Portuguese Captain. In this sense, if considered the general structure of the Dantean voyage and the tripartition it entails, the so-called Island of Love occupies, in the economy of the Portuguese epic, the place of Paradise. However, conceived by Venus as a site of rest and recreation, a reward for the sailors who spent a long time deprived of female companionship, it appears much less as a prize for Vasco da Gama than for the readers, for having endured so much political and, above all, moral disaster. Perhaps for this reason, and *pace* Giamatti, the vehicle of the allegory (sexual activity in the idyllic landscape) is so wildly disproportionate to its content (the honours, the laurel and palm, the immortality that the island represents):

> For the ocean nymphs in all their beauty,
> Thetys, and the magic painted island,
> Are nothing more than those delightful
> Honours which make our life sublime.
> Those glorious moments of pre-eminence,
> The triumphs, the forehead crowned
> With palm and laurel – these are what is meant
> And what this island's pleasures represent.
>   IX, 89

It is certainly not a correspondence of the same order as that which, for example, underlies the claim that Beatrice is an allegory of theology. The nymphs industriously employed by Venus to arouse the sexual desire of sailors are hardly free from their corporeal nature. But it cannot be ruled out that such a great disparity is deliberate, and perhaps Camões is suggesting that, in view of da Gama's moral conduct, there is no room here for even a glimpse of Paradise. Da Gama can only keep looking to the centre of the *machina mundi*, to the surface of the earth, "the hostel of humanity" (X, 91), where the countless wars, bloody deaths and massacres prophesied by Tethys will continue. India is not the earthly paradise that Vasco da Gama was looking for. On the contrary, it is a new reiteration of the *selva oscura*, or even Hell. For this reason, the final "paradise" is a prosthesis conceived *in extremis* by the poet – pure fruit of poetry, more an allegory of poetry's capacity to produce facticity than of any reality outside itself.

The critical productivity of canto X of the *Inferno* manifests itself on yet another level. It was in Dante's interaction with Farinata that the Russian poet Osip Mandelstam located the scandalous discovery that Dante is a man of low status, uneducated:

When Farinata stands up in his contempt for Hell like a great nobleman who has landed in prison, the pendulum of the conversation is already measuring the full diameter of the gloomy plain, broken by flames.

The notion of scandal in literature is much older than Dostoevsky, but in the thirteenth century and in Dante's work it was far more powerful.

Dante runs up against Farinata, collides with him, in an undesired and dangerous encounter exactly as the rogues in Dostoevsky are always blundering into their tormentors in the most inopportune places [...]:

O Tuscan who travels alive through this city of fire and speaks so eloquently, do not refuse my request to stop for a moment. By your speech I recognize in you a citizen of that noble region to which I – alas! – was too great a burden.

Dante is a poor man. Dante is an internal *raznochinets* of an ancient Roman line. Not courtesy but something completely opposite is characteristic of him. One has to be a blind mole not to notice that throughout the *Divina Commedia* Dante does not know how to behave, he does not know how to act, what to say, how to make a bow. [...]

If Dante were to be sent out alone, without his *dolce padre*, without Vergil, a scandal would inevitably erupt in the very beginning, and we should not have a journey among torments and remarkable sights but the most grotesque buffoonery.

[...] What for us are an unimpeacheable capuche and a so-called aquiline profile were, from the inside, an awkwardness overcome with tortuous difficulty, a purely Pushkinian, Kammerjunker struggle for the social dignity and social position of the poet.[11]

If this description is true, it mainly corroborates what was already known: the *Comedy* is a private apocalypse, an epic poem out of time, the expression of a personal aspiration, not necessarily social but certainly spiritual, as a way of coping with a politically hostile environment. To that extent, Camões too was an intellectual who was not born with a silver spoon in his mouth, striving for the dignity of his art to be acknowledged by the members of aristocracy; and also *The Lusiads* is a long lament about the dissociation between personal vision and political state of affairs, an attempt to bring comfort to the poet himself, who becomes the real and main subject of his poem.[12] Florence and Portugal are two versions of the same problem: ungrateful homelands that would not possess the bones of their best children; nations that are much closer to the desert than to the city of God that Dante sees in Paradise and that Camões can but dream of in the form of a golden age that only poetry can restore. Both exercise poetic justice while divine justice does not arrive, and both deplore the fact that no one listens to them. To

---

[11] Osip Mandelstam: *Selected Essays*. Edited and translated by Sidney Monas, Clarence Brown & Robert Hughes. Austin, Texas: University of Texas Press 1977, pp. 10–11.
[12] Although one could argue that Camões attributed the qualities of the plebeian to Vasco da Gama, who manifestly causes scandal at every stop he makes on his journey, with his lack of the most elementary tact.

that extent, *The Lusiads* is much closer to the *Comedy* than pertaining to the same poetic genre could suggest at first. It too "[gives] to see, in the realm of timeless being, the history of man's inner life unfolding".[13]

Bibliographical References

Auerbach, Erich: *Mimesis: The Representation of Reality in Western Literature* (1946). Princeton: Princeton University Press (1955) 2014 (with a New Introduction by Edward Said).

Camões, Luís de: *The Lusíads*. Translated by Landeg White. Oxford: Oxford University Press 1997.

Camilletti, Fabio: Later Reception from 1481 to the Present. In Zygmunt G. Barański and Simon Gilson (eds.): *The Cambridge Companion to Dante's* Commedia. Cambridge: Cambridge University Press 2019, pp. 259–270.

Giamatti, A. Bartlett: *The Earthly Paradise and Renaissance Epic*. New Haven & London: Yale University Press 1966.

Mandelstam, Osip: *Selected Essays*. Edited and translated by Sidney Monas, Clarence Brown & Robert Hughes. Austin, Texas: University of Texas Press 1977.

Morel, Philippe: *Les grottes maniéristes en Italie au XVIe siècle*. Paris: Macula 1998.

Pessoa, Fernando: *Crítica: ensaios, artigos e entrevistas*. Fernando Cabral Martins (ed.). Lisboa: Assírio & Alvim 2000.

Quint, David: *Epic and Empire: Politics and Generic Form from Virgil to Milton*. Princeton: Princeton University Press 1993.

Sena, Jorge de: A Poesia de Camões: ensaio de revelação da dialéctica camoniana. In: *Trinta Anos de Camões*, vol. I. Lisboa: Edições 70 1980, pp. 15–39.

Sousa, Manuel de Faria: *Lusiadas de Luis de Camões Comentadas por...* Reprodução fac-similada pela edição de 1639, 2 vols. Lisboa: Imprensa Nacional-Casa da Moeda 1972.

---

13 Erich Auberbach: *Mimesis*, p. 202.

Arnaldo do Espírito Santo
Dante and the Fifth Empire

The starting point for the present inquiry is my own translation of the treatise written in Latin by Dante, which he entitled *De monarchia*.[1] It is an easy and pleasant work to read, with a clear and simple style, and a phrasing and vocabulary similar to those used, at one time, by Thomas Aquinas, Albertus Magnus and other contemporary authors. Quotations from the Bible, the Church Fathers, Greek philosophers, many of which by Aristotle, and a few by Plato, abound, as well as some passages by some of the Latin poets and prosaists, among whom Virgil, Lucan, Livy, Cicero and Seneca are prominent. The discursive exposition is based on scholastic logic and dialectics. Its foundational notions are those of origin and consequence, cause and effect, deduction and induction. The demonstrations, while based on different premises, invariably lead to the same conclusion: "the well-being of the world requires that there be a monarchy or empire."[2] Also very much in the scholastic manner, propositions are confirmed through the *auctoritas* of philosophers (reason or rational thought), of poets and historians, of the Church Fathers (theological thought) and, above all, of the divine authority expressed in both Testaments of the Bible.

In this respect there is absolute coincidence in method between Dante's *De monarchia* and Father António Vieira's writings on the Fifth Empire. This, of course, bears no apodeictic value regarding Dante's vestiges in, influence on, or similarity to Vieira, although it is the purpose of this analysis to demonstrate the same. In effect, what approximates Vieira most closely to Dante are the central concepts in their discussion, such as "Lawfulness," "Predestination," "Universal Empire" and "Universal Peace," among others. These notions, common to both authors, reveal an identical way of thinking on the same topics, and of arriving at the same conclusions via the same means, but for purposes which are not entirely equivalent.

To complete this general framing, I should add that at no point is there any difficulty in understanding the meaning of the occasional expression which, while not particularly commonplace in everyday Latin, becomes perfectly clear when read against Aristotle's Greek text, which Dante most certainly came across through a Latin translation. We refer in particular to Aristotle's *Politics*, *Nicomachean Ethics* and the treatise *On the Soul*. Thomas Aquinas, canonised in the year

---

1 Forthcoming with the title *Sobre a Monarquia*. Lisboa: Imprensa Nacional 2022.
2 *De monarchia*, I, v, p. 15.

Note: Translated from the Portuguese by Cassilda Alcobia-Murphy.

following the death of Dante, and therefore referred to only by his first name, "Thomas," is no less influential to the text of this treatise than was the admiration expressed by Dante towards Aquinas in the *Divine Comedy*. In this regard, we shall never know for certain whether some of the quotations of Aristotle derive directly from the Greek philosopher, or indirectly, from Dante's readings of Aquinas, who employed Aristotle profusely.

Some have interpreted *De monarchia* as a work circumscribed to the internecine political conflicts of the Christian princes as well as against the Holy See in the late 13th and early 14th centuries; others identify a work whose reach extends far beyond the circumstances in which it was written; others still have framed it within the perennial genre of utopias that nourish dreams of a golden age projected into the future. While not denying that, to use Dante's words, "the temporal Monarchy or Universal Empire" is the only means of establishing peace and justice in the world, we must bear in mind that this goal is but one among the many beneficial consequences of the establishment of a universal monarchy. Dante had no intention of outlining a utopian solution for the world of his age. What Dante did intend with this treatise was, very specifically, to present the results of his reflection (he favoured the term "inquiry") on "matters of politics." This inquiry is divided into three parts, each corresponding to the following questions:

a) The first is whether the "temporal Monarchy," understood as "universal Empire," or "single Principality" is necessary for the well-being of humanity;
b) The second is whether the "Roman people," which in the past had instituted a "universal Empire" of sorts, had "rightfully appropriated the office of Monarchy";
c) The third is whether "temporal authority" derives directly from God or whether from the Pope.

With such an outline, and particularly regarding the last item, Dante was staking his position regarding a conflict that had called into question the temporal power of the Pope, which had been forcefully denounced, for some years, by Philip the Fair, king of France (not to mention that Dante had consigned Boniface VIII to the Inferno of his *Divine Comedy*). As such, the outcome was predictable: *De monarchia* was added to the *Index Librorum Prohibitorum* from the outset. In Portugal, in particular, it was added to the *Rol dos Liuros defesos nestes Reinos e Senhorios de Portugal que o Senhor Cardeal Iffante Inquisidor geral mandou fazer no Anno de 1564*.[3] There, on page 284 of the Edition of the *Índices dos Livros Proibidos em*

---

[3] *Roll of prohibited books within in these Realms and Dominions of Portugal which the Cardinal-Infante, General Inquisitor, commissioned in the year 1564.*

Portugal no Século XVI, published by Artur Moreira de Sá, the following indication appears: "Dantis Monarchia" ("Dante's Monarchy"), which also appears in the *Indices* of 1581, 1597, and so forth. In previous centuries, as Moreira de Sá has noted, no similar documentation is known, beyond the occasional mention of the burning of heretical books, since this type of scrutiny and censorship was the purview of the Bishops. This climate of strict surveillance notwithstanding, the Grand Inquisitor discovered "that some people did not abstain from possessing and reading books that were censored and prohibited."[4]

What is the Purpose of the Above Expatiation?

Simply to comment on the fact that, during the process of reading Dante in Latin and translating his *De monarchia*, I kept hearing echoes of a translation I had previously completed of Father António Vieira's *Clavis Prophetarum* [Key of the Prophets]. Echoes of the same expressions, of citations of biblical passages and classical authors, and echoes of the same topics, even though they produced different outcomes. A preliminary survey led me, as I read and translated Dante's *De monarchia*, to entertain the hypothesis that Father António Vieira was one of the covert readers of this work, despite its prohibition, thereby occasionally taking care to disguise any commonalities. However, these commonalities are perfectly apparent, for example, between, on the one hand, Vieira's *imperium temporale*, the *temporalis monarchia* and the *principatus universalis* and, on the other hand, Dante's *temporalis Monarchia, quam dicunt 'Imperium,'* and *unicus principatus*.

In the first remarkable example of these echoes, Dante contends that "it is better for mankind to be ruled by one person than by several, and thus by a monarch who is the only ruler; and if this is better, then it is more acceptable to God, since God always wills what is better."[5] This reasoning is thus concluded: "It follows from this that mankind is in its ideal state when it is ruled by one person."[6] These propositions are close to the principle adopted in Vieira's Fifth Empire: "One fold, and one shepherd." Both speak of a universal and temporal empire in this world. In *História do Futuro* [History of the Future], the proposed Emperor is João IV of Portugal. We also know that Father Vieira had had a change of heart in this regard by the time he wrote the *Clavis Prophetarum*.

---

[4] Artur Moreira de Sá (ed.): *Índices dos Livros Proibidos em Portugal no Século XVI*. Lisboa: Instituto Nacional de Investigação Científica 1983, p. 18.
[5] *De monarchia*, I, xiv, p. 39.
[6] *Ibidem*.

At this point in his defence of a universal Monarchy, Dante abandons political theorization and dives straight into Aristotle's *Metaphysics*, to which title, *De simpliciter ente*, i.e. *concerning Simple Being*, or *on Being as Being*, he refers. From Book I he cites the metaphysical arguments that enable him to state that unity is the root of being and of goodness and that, consequently, unity results in the concordance of wills that finds its foremost expression when one will, that of the Prince, "can control and guide all the other wills,"[7] a statement that alludes to the *Nicomachean Ethics*.[8] At various points in his inquiry, Dante describes the Prince as a person "supremely" prepared for the exercise of power since, by virtue of being universally one, he is above cupidity, much as a Philosopher-King, whose greatest prerogative is to be "supremely one," and therefore qualified, to the highest degree, to provide well-being in the world. "Maxime unus" is reminiscent of Aquinas.[9]

At the end of this deductive process, the necessary conclusion is that "there must be a monarch in the world."[10] This is a purely metaphysical justification of power, but of an exclusively temporal, earthly power. In fact, unlike Father Vieira, Dante insistently affirms that the universal Empire, the object of his reflection and of his philosophical inquiry, is merely a temporal reality. However, the scope of the restriction of the universal Empire to the domain of pure temporality must be refined since, in fact, Dante does not fail to consider the nature of human beings themselves, "born of heaven and fire," i.e., essentially spiritual. In short, we should bear in mind that Dante's statements do not follow on from an anthropology oblivious to theological considerations. Dante firmly believes that the greatest gift bestowed by God on human nature is freedom, and that this defines its condition. The Prince must never forget that, short of ensuring the exercise of freedom, there can be no well-being in the world. Dante's thought is, at heart, essentially biblical, as seen in the epilogue to Book I, which I quote at length:

> All the arguments advanced so far are confirmed by a remarkable historical fact: namely the state of humanity which the Son of God either awaited, or himself chose to bring about, when he was on the point of becoming man for the salvation of mankind. For if we review the ages and the dispositions of men from the fall of our first parents (which was the turning-point at which we went astray), we shall not find that there ever was peace throughout the world except under the immortal Augustus, when a perfect monarchy existed. That mankind was then happy in the calm of universal peace is attested by all historians and by

---

[7] *De monarchia*, I, xv, p. 43.
[8] Aristóteles: *Ética a Nicómaco*, X, 9, 1179b. Cf. Aristóteles: *Ética a Nicómaco*. Edição bilingue, tradução e notas de Dimas de Almeida. Lisboa: Edições Universitárias Lusófonas 2012, p. 481.
[9] Thomas Aquinas: *Summa Theologia*. Madrid: Biblioteca de Autores Cristianos 1994, I q. 11 a. 4.
[10] *De monarchia*, I, xv, p. 43.

> famous poets; even the chronicler of Christ's gentleness[11] deigned to bear witness to it; and finally Paul called that most happy state 'the fulness of time.'[12] Truly, that time was 'full', as were all temporal things, for no ministry to our happiness lacked its minister. What the state of the world has been since that seamless garment[13] was first rent by the talon of cupidity we can read about – would that we might not witness it.[14]

This long quotation shows that Vieira, too, has been here, as I hope to demonstrate. But let us continue, for now. Dante does not hesitate to turn to Paul's *Epistles to the Galatians* and to the *Ephesians*, the latter of which probably postdates Paul,[15] in order to incorporate the Roman Empire and the Emperor Augustus in God's plan and salvation history. No present-day exegete would easily accept the notion that "the fullness of time" mentioned in these two Epistles came about with the arrival of the Roman Empire. Father António Vieira reads it, understandably, as the second coming of Christ, in order to establish His Empire, the Fifth in the succession of Empires of Mediterranean humanity, both temporal and spiritual, both earthly and heavenly. Since the Roman Empire was an instrument of God in salvation history, the sacred texts and the prophecies concerning the resistance of earthly kings and princes to the Messiah, God's anointed, and the Emperor, were applicable, from Dante's perspective: "'Why have the nations raged, and the peoples meditated a vain things? The kings of the earth have arisen, and the princes have gathered together against the Lord and against his Christ. Let us burst their chains and cast their yoke from us.'"[16]

This passage from the *Psalms* is quoted by Dante. It should be noted, once again, that these words, used by Dante in defence of the Roman Empire are the same as those used by Vieira to demonstrate the monarchy or majesty of Christ over all peoples, temporal and spiritual.[17] There is only one difference: for Vieira, when the Fifth Empire, or Monarchy of Christ, shall come to be, the Kings and

---

11 Luke, 2:1.
12 Galatians, 4:4; Ephesians, 1:10.
13 John, 19:23.
14 *De monarchia*, I, xvi, p. 43.
15 Cf. Giuliano Vigini: *Dizionario della Biblia*. Città del Vaticano: Libreria Editrice Vaticana 2016, pp. 246–249.
16 Psalms, 2: 1–3; *De monarchia*, II, i, p. 47.
17 Padre António Vieira: Bk. I, Ch. 11, *ms*. FC 1165/1, fl. 94r (autograph manuscript identified in 2020 by Arnaldo do Espírito Santo and Ana Valdez at the Archivio della Pontificia Università Gregoriana di Roma). Cf. Arnaldo do Espírito Santo, «Pontos de vista sobre o original da *Clavis Prophetarum*», in *Letras, Sinais para David Mourão-Ferreira, Margarida Vieira Mendes e Osório Mateus*, Edições Cosmos e Departamento de Literaturas Românicas da Faculdade de Letras da Universidade de Lisboa 1999, pp. 75–84.

Princes in power will not be deposed, but integrated as allies in the establishment of the Kingdom of Christ on earth, in a truly universal 17th century.

The *Epistle to the Ephesians*, according to Giuliano Vigini, "è forse la lettera che ... ha esercitato il maggior influsso sul pensiero e la spiritualità Cristiana."[18] It bears a latent, but powerful apocalyptic tenor, which reinforces the vision of a cosmos in the process of anacephalaeosis, i.e., of recapitulation of "all things in Christ, both which are in heaven, and which are on earth."[19] It envisages, in addition to Christ's cosmic action, the prospect of universal peace and the divine adoption of all humanity, which will be fulfilled according to a plan already in place since before the creation of the cosmos. The *Epistle to the Ephesians* is yet another text shared by Dante and Vieira.

But while the same texts are cited by both authors, Dante was engaged in a different, politicised struggle. His main objective was to demonstrate that the Roman Empire was and remained, qua Holy Roman Germanic Empire, an Empire that was governed legitimately and not by usurpation; and that the Kings and Princes "usurp control of public affairs to themselves,"[20] and that "all men [will] understand that they are free of the yoke of usurpers of this kind."[21]

Nonetheless, both Dante and Vieira anticipate that universal peace will follow closely behind this Empire: for Dante, this would be "universal peace and liberty," and for Vieira, "messianic peace," the subject of his treatise *Sobre a Paz do Messias*, in Latin *De Pace Messiae* [Treatise Concerning the Peace of the Messiah], included in the *Clavis Prophetarum*. This is another shared idea, justified using the same biblical passages, although the "Lord," the Messiah, the "Anointed," was, in Dante's case, the "Roman prince."[22]

It became necessary to augment biblical argumentation, of little credence when it came to the advocacy of the providential role of an empire which, in the early centuries, persecuted Christians and did its utmost to prevent the establishment of Christianity. This is achieved through the implication of reason, provided by theodicy and rational philosophy. In effect, two crucial premises required demonstration: that the "empire existed by Right" and that "the Roman people appropriated the dignity of empire by Right." As to the first, Dante resorts to deductive syllogism: A is in B, B is in C, therefore A is in C. From Book II onwards, this remains the most frequent method of proof in the exposition. In this particular case, and in more explicit terms, it is stated that Right is good, and that all

---

18 Giuliano Vigini: *Dizionario della Biblia*, p. 246.
19 *Ephesians*, 1:10.
20 *De monarchia*, II, i, p. 49.
21 *Ibidem*.
22 *De monarchia*, II, i, p. 47.

that is good is in the mind of God, and that therefore Right is in God. But in a less coldly dialectical and more profound manner, Dante refines the expression of his thought, adding thus to the conclusion of the syllogism:

> and since everything which is in the mind of God *is* God (in conformity with that saying 'Whatever was made was life in him,'[23]), and since God principally wills himself, it follows that right is willed by God as being something which is in him. And since in God will and what is willed are one and the same thing, it further follows that divine will *is* right itself.[24]

It would seem, however, that the philosophical, cultural, and political assumptions underpinning Dante's thought might encounter some resistance, in particular to the outright acceptance of the conclusion "that what God wills in human society must be considered true and pure right."[25] But, as Dante acknowledges, "the will of God in itself is indeed invisible."[26] It is necessary, therefore, to remain attuned to the signs through which it manifests itself. And therefore, Dante resorts to the authority of the *Nicomachean Ethics*, vaguely pointing the reader in the direction of "the beginning," to assert that "certainty is not to be sought in the same way in every subject, but according as the nature of the subject allows."[27] As such, the principle according to which partial certainty is sufficient prevails.

In short, the signs from Roman history would indicate that the Empire enforced over the subdued peoples was the will of God, so as to pave the way for the Son's incarnation. And once again Aristotelian philosophy meets providential history through allegorical interpretation, where the things signified by the words acquire further signification, as defended by Aquinas.[28]

This mode of reading represents, particularly in this case, another coincidence between Dante and Vieira. Dante then moves to demonstrate that the Roman people was, by divine providence, the supreme guide of all the peoples it subdued. Interestingly, the arguments employed point to the nobility of its origins and historical condition, as illustrated in laudatory literature, particularly of the Augustan era. Such arguments are literary and textual, and therefore not always real. But, as in the discussion in defence of the right of the Temporal Empire to exist, here there is equally a level of parallelism with Vieira's considerably more developed argumentation. While Dante does not venture beyond the Roman people's right of *nobilitas*, Vieira frames the issue in multiple ways in the section

---

[23] John, 1:3–4.
[24] *De monarchia*, II, ii, p. 51.
[25] *Ibidem*.
[26] *Ibidem*.
[27] *Ibidem*.
[28] "ipsae res significatae per voces etiam significant aliquid" (Aquinas: *Summa Theologiae*, Prima pars, p. 13, 1. q.1 to 10).

entitled "Presentation and corroboration of the opinion that advocates Christ's Temporal Reign."[29] This opinion rests on a threefold authority, as is the case with Dante and the whole of scholasticism: the Sacred Scriptures, the Church Fathers, and Reason; in other words, the revealed word of God, the comments of the exegetes of the patristic era, and rational reflection, or philosophy.[30] And what this opinion affirms is that "Christ, in His capacity as man, even as He lived His mortal life, possessed perfect, proper and absolute dominion over all things, and the perfect, proper and universal Reign over the entire World."[31] In this capacity He could, as "Supreme King and Absolute Master, dispose of all things, alter kingdoms and kings, and moderate all things according to His will."[32] For support, Vieira clearly employs the *auctoritates* of theologians (about twenty in number), presided over by Thomas Aquinas.

Although Aquinas is quoted by Dante before his canonization, revealing him to be one of the poet's intellectual models, it is also true that the setting in which Vieira invokes Aquinas in his defence of the future existence of a fully legitimated Temporal Kingdom of Christ (much in the same way as the Roman Empire was, for Dante, fully legitimated) is different from the reality theorised and proposed in *De monarchia* as a political solution to the problems of a Europe divided and beset by wars and permanent conflict. Notwithstanding the differences between both proposals for the unification of peoples under a universal empire, it must be noted, once again, that the theme of peace is dominant in *De monarchia* and the *Clavis Prophetarum*. If, in Dante, universal peace can be viewed as a claim made within a political thesis, in Vieira it takes on a wide-ranging scope, as evinced in the length of its development, since it occupies a complete chapter, or is even, perhaps, an independent treatise, as Father Antonio Casnedi seems to suggest in his report on the original manuscript.[33]

Regardless of any conceivable reservations, it is impossible to avoid foregrounding the commonalities between these two authors. One must not, however,

---

29 "Sententia defendens temporale Christi Regnum proponitur et roboratur" (*ms.* FC 1165/1, fl. 36v. *Cf.* Silvano Peloso: *La* Clavis Prophetarum *di Antonio Vieira*. Viterbo: CISCAV, Sette Città 2011, p. 111).
30 "ex Scriptura, ex Patribus et ratione multiplici probare curabimus" (*ms.* FC 1165/1, fl. 37r).
31 "Christum, quatenus Hominem, etiam cum adhuc mortalem vitam agebat, perfectum, proprium et absolutum rerum omnium dominium, et totius Orbis perfectum, proprium et universale Regnum habuisse." (*ms.* FC 1165/1, fl. 36v).
32 "de rebus omnibus disponere, Regna et Reges mutare, et cuncta suo arbitrio moderari, tanquam supremus Rex et absolutus Dominus, potuerit." (*ms.* FC 1165/1, fl. 36v).
33 Cf. Arnaldo do Espírito Santo: Censuras da *Clavis Prophetarum* do Padre António Vieira. In Manuela Domínguez García et al.i (eds.): *Sub luce florentis calami: Homenaje a Manuel C. Díaz y Díaz*. Santiago de Compostela: Universidade de Santiago de Compostela 2002, pp. 620–635.

ignore the differences that characterise the eras in which they lived. When António Vieira speaks of the universality of the Kingdom of Christ, he is thinking of the entire globe: Europe, Africa, Asia, America and Oceania; while Dante could only have had Europe, part of Africa and part of Asia in mind. But Dante finds justification for this universality in the hereditary right of possession and rule conferred by the *nobilitas* of his ascendants, beginning with Aeneas, founder of Rome, whose ancestry dated back to Assaracus, king of Phrygia, granting him the hereditary right of dominion over Asia. This lineage also derived from other early ancestors in Africa and Europe. As such, on the one hand, the conquest of Europe, Asia Minor, Egypt, Carthage and the whole of North Africa is justified by right of succession. On the other hand, Dante states that "the three regions into which the world is divided,"[34] i.e., the entirety of the known world, comprise the territory of the temporal Empire. What is somewhat unexpected is that Dante would conclude his enumeration of evidence from the *Aeneid* regarding the mythological ancestry of the Romans by moving from mythology to allegorical biblical exegesis. He rhetorically deduces: "who will fail to recognise divine predestination in that double confluence of blood from every part of the world into a single man?"[35] One might expect this from Vieira, following an exegetic analysis of the biblical evidence regarding Christ's claim to universal kingship.

As already mentioned, when alluding to the concept of "predestination," both Dante and Vieira have in mind biblical passages from the *Epistle to the Romans*, *Galatians* and *Ephesians*, particularly the verse: "sicut electit nos in ipso ante mundi constitutionem . . ., qui praedestinavit nos in adoptem filiorum per Iesum Christum."[36] Or does Dante perhaps place the Virgil of *De monarchia* on the same level as the psychopomp Virgil of the *Divine Comedy*? In fact, it is not necessary to resort to this device, since it is clear that Dante interprets as miracles those facts and events that the Roman writers and poets described as inexplicable or unexpected wonders, concluding with yet another theological reflection that underlines, from his viewpoint, the biblical source: "It was utterly fitting that he who ordained all things from eternity in harmonious order should operate in this manner: that just as he would, when visible, perform miracles as testimony for invisible things, so he should, while still invisible, perform them as testimony for visible things."[37]

---

[34] *De monarchia*, II, iii, p. 55.
[35] *De monarchia*, II, iii, pp. 57 and 59.
[36] Ephesians, 1:4–5: "According as he hath chosen us in him before the foundation of the world . . . . Having predestinated us unto the adoption of children by Jesus Christ to himself".
[37] *De monarchia*, II, iv, p. 61.

Nonetheless, it might be worth delving a little deeper into Dante's perspective on the sacralization of certain events in Roman history or mythology. One such miraculous event occurred during a sacrifice, an offering to the gods in accordance with pagan rites. It would seem that, for Dante, pagan religions and cults are accepted by God, the one true God of the Faith, qua recipient of all worship and veneration. Father Vieira resolves the dilemma of false religions and their acceptance by the one true God,[38] by stating that God established two peoples on earth: that of revelation and that of nature; in other words, the one of the Law of Moses and the other of Natural law. But God exercises His providence over both by directing them to unity, "in unum," as Dante states, a concept widely debated by Thomas Aquinas.[39] The journey towards the constitution of a single people has thus been slow work, since God "provided for [the pagan peoples] by not providing."[40] Vieira's superb paradox served to explain why the Indians of Brazil, for example, had waited fifteen centuries for the annunciation of the Gospel, this being the only way to assimilate them into the unity that would make them members of the Kingdom of Christ on earth. There would have been a time when Vieira would have phrased this as "members of the Fifth Empire." But in the *Clavis*, and as he found himself in Rome when he wrote these pages, Vieira opted to replace the designation of "Fifth Empire," given its associations with the resurrection of King João IV of Portugal, with that of the *Consummation of the Kingdom of Christ on earth*. What is important, however, is that this is both an earthly, temporal kingdom, much like Dante's imperial *Monarchy*, as well as a spiritual kingdom. Dante praises the Roman Empire for its organisational model and its respect for Right and the rule of law. But despite looking to the past, he is keenly alive to the present moment and views the successor to the Roman Empire as the remedy to the evils of his time. Three and a half centuries later, around 1660, Father Vieira cautioned his contemporaries that "by simply looking at the world of the present day, we know it to encompass a much greater number of empires."[41] After mentioning the empires of the Turks and Tartars, of China, Persia, and the Mughal and Ethiopian empires, he focuses on the Holy Roman

---

38 Cf. Luís de Camões: *The Lusiads*. Translated by Landeg White. Oxford: Oxford University Press 1997: "the false god was worshipping the true" (II, 12, 8).
39 *Aquinas: Summa Theologiae*, I q. 11 a. 1–4.
40 "Since it is, therefore, a sacrilege to believe they have been denied Divine Providence and, withal, since I found myself unable to perceive a reason or mode for such a providence, I arrived at the conceit that I am justified in believing that God provided for them, but that He provided by not providing." (T / n: Translated from the Portuguese version in Padre António Vieira, *Clavis Prophetarum*, *Chave dos Profetas*, Livro III, p. 463.)
41 Antônio Vieira, SJ: *História do Futuro*. José Carlos Brandi Aleixo, SJ, (ed.). Brasília: Universidade de Brasília 2005, p. 347.

Empire of the German nation: "that of Germany which, while lacking its greatness, retains the name [of empire], and that of Spain, which, while lacking the name . . ., retains its greatness." Vieira's outlook, despite the temporal distance, is analogous to Dante's. Vieira, like Dante, considered that the Roman Empire lived on in Germany, since once "Charlemagne was appointed Emperor of the West, the head of the Church [in the figure] of the Pontiff being apportioned to Rome, the seat of Empire was thus transferred to Germany."[42] For Vieira, therefore, as for Dante, this is the Empire that succeeded the Roman Empire, i.e., that identifies itself with the Roman Empire. As such, in Vieira's tally, it corresponds to the Fourth Empire. Both Dante and Vieira theorise a new form of government, a new "politia," a word and concept borrowed from Aristotle, universally based on the authority of one single figure, who alone is able to ensure peace and well-being for all humanity. Dante eventually translated the concept of "politia" into better-known forms of political terminology, and used "monarchia" and "monarcha," "imperium" and "imperator" almost interchangeably. Vieira, for his part, in the *História do Futuro*, names this new form of government "Empire," or the "Fifth," which corresponds to the consummation of the exercise of perfect governance, as was the "Monarchy" for Dante. Dante and Vieira's touchstone was therefore the same. But while Dante envisages a temporal empire in the Roman mode, both civic and secular, for Vieira this empire shall be theocratic, spiritual and temporal, and universal on a global earthly scale, in keeping with the outlook of a European thinker after the age of discoveries. It is also Roman in nature insofar as its head, the Pontiff, the Pope, governs this theocratic empire vicariously, holding power over all the princes of the earth.

In short, for Dante, the temporal empire is due, through human and divine right, to the emperor, regardless of the religious sphere: "Thus it is evident," Dante maintains, "that the authority of the temporal monarch flows down into him

---

42 Antônio Vieira, SJ, *História do Futuro*, p. 349. This passage was written to explain that, in the division of the Empire between Pope Leo III and Charlemagne, Rome came into the possession of the Pontiff as head of the Church, while the seat of Empire passed from Rome to Germany, more precisely, to Aachen (Aix-la-Chapelle). The text that appears in several Portuguese editions of the *História do Futuro* – 'Rome remaining as head of the Church, to the Pontiff was transferred the seat of Empire – Germany', is an erroneous reading of what Vieira wrote. In fact, other editorial mistakes can be found: neither was 'Charlemagne . . . appointed Emperor of the West,' during the papacy of Lucius III (1181–1185), but during that of Leo III (795–816); nor did the Eastern Roman Empire last 'for a period of four thousand years.' This chronology would be historically nonsensical. What Father Antônio Vieira actually wrote was 'for a period of almost a thousand years.' [The word 'quase', meaning 'almost' may have been mistaken for the word 'quatro', meaning 'four', in the original Portuguese-language manuscript. (T / n)]

without any intermediary from the Fountainhead of universal authority."[43] The subject matter of *De monarchia* is "politics," that is, "the source and starting-point of just forms of government."[44] This not from a speculative, but theoretical perspective, because politics entails mostly actions in the exercise of power. Therefore, in his examples of figures who lent dignity to Empire, Dante includes those citizens who resisted corruption, ambition, who fought "for the deliverance of their fatherland"[45] and who cherished above all the "love of freedom."[46]

Dante devotes an entire chapter (II, vi) to an apology of the legitimacy of Empire to exercise the right of conquest and domination over all peoples. The principal source used for this purpose is neither biblical nor patristic, but purely literary, namely Virgil, who becomes a veritable guide for this chapter. From his interpretation of the famous passage in the *Aeneid*:

> Roman, remember to rule over nations [with the empire].
> Your arts shall be: to impose the rule of law,
> Spare subject peoples, and subdue the proud.[47]

and of another, no less significant:

> Not such a son did his fair mother promise,
> Nor for this saved him twice from Grecian arms;
> But that he might rule over Italy,
> Pregnant with empire, clamouring for war.[48]

Dante draws the following conclusion: "These arguments are sufficient evidence to convince us that the Roman people were ordained by nature to rule; therefore the Roman people by conquering the world came to empire by right."[49]

And to corroborate the notion that "nature ordained a place and a nation to exercise universal rule in the world: otherwise she would have failed in her provisions, which is impossible,"[50] Dante resorts to the authority of Philosophy, quoting a passage from Aristotle's *Politics*: "It is manifest therefore that there are

---

[43] *De monarchia*, III, xvi. p. 149.
[44] *De monarchia*, I, ii, p. 7.
[45] *De monarchia*, II, v, p. 67.
[46] Ibidem.
[47] Virgil, *The Aeneid*, VI, 851–853. The translation of this and following passages from the *Aeneid* is taken from Prue Shaw's translation of Dante's *De monarchia*, so as to attend to the context in which they were inserted. (*De monarchia*, II, vi, p. 75.)
[48] Virgil, *The Aeneid*, IV, 227–230; *De monarchia*, Ibidem.
[49] *De monarchia*, Ibidem.
[50] *De monarchia*, II, vi, p. 73.

cases of people of whom some are freemen and the others slaves by nature, and for these slavery is an institution both expedient and just."[51]

By following this sequence of ideas, I mean to point out that in Vieira's thought there is, as in Dante, one people born to subjugate and govern; and this not by nature, but by divine disposition, i.e., by predestination. And it is here, in this notion that recurs in both authors, that the great difference lies regarding the source of the argumentation – not in the idea itself. This difference, however, unfolds in several respects.

The first is that the Fifth Empire had been conceived, early on, as the "Esperanças de Portugal," ["Hopes of Portugal"] that is, it would be an empire triumphantly led by Portugal. Portugal was, at the time, entangled in a historical crisis which it would overcome with difficulty, given the already lengthy war with Spain, a situation furthermore worsened by the death of King João IV on 6 November, 1656, since the king of Portugal had been singled out to become the future emperor of this Empire. When, about two and a half years later, on 29 April, 1659, Vieira wrote to Father André Fernandes imparting some of the ideas he had been entertaining "on the future resurrection of our good Lord and Master," his initial outlook was, at that point, inspired by the Sebastianism which he subsequently negated entirely. It would no longer be King Sebastião who would return from captivity to restore past glories, but rather the resurrected João IV. What are the grounds for this assertion? The same as argued by Paul when he stated that, had Isaac been sacrificed by Abraham, he would have had to be resurrected in order to fulfil God's promise. And God cannot "fail," much in the same way as, for Dante, nature cannot "be deficient in herself." The fallacy in this reasoning notwithstanding, one should note that Father Vieira had repeatedly stated and preached (since 1654 at least, i.e., before the death of the king) that, should João IV die, he would be resurrected, to "fulfil those things Bandarra[52] had prophesied of him."[53] But what were these things?

The first to be mentioned "is the war that the King shall wage on the Turks, and the victory he shall attain over them."[54] The second is that "the King shall

---

[51] Aristotle: *Politics*, I, 5, 1255a1; (Aristotle: *The Politics*. Translated by H. Rackham. Cambridge, MA: Harvard University Press; London: William Heinemann Ltd. 1944.) Cf. *De monarchia*, II, vi, p. 73: "This is why we see that not just certain individuals, bit certain peoples are born fitted to rule, and certain others to be ruled and to serve, as [the Philosopher] affirms in the *Politics*."
[52] Gonçalo Annes Bandarra (c. 1500–1556), a Portuguese cobbler by trade, and author of the prophetical *Trovas* (c. 1541) relating to the Fifth Empire and Sebastianism (T / n).
[53] Padre António Vieira: *Cartas*. Coordenadas e anotadas por J. Lúcio de Azevedo, vol. I. Lisboa: Imprensa Nacional, 1970, p. 469.
[54] Padre António Vieira: *Cartas*, I, p. 477.

depart for the conquest of the Holy Land and become master thereof."[55] The third is that King João IV "shall deliver the peoples of Italy, who are under the martial yoke of the Turks."[56] The fourth is that King John IV would lead an army against the Turks and would personally defeat them; he would divide the conquered lands and ports among the princes who followed him on his expedition, and keep for himself the city of Constantinople when the spoils were divided. Lastly, King João IV would be elected emperor of Constantinople by the kings who followed him in the war against the Turks. In conclusion, Vieira restates that: "Once anointed emperor, . . . the King will return, victorious, bearing two pennants, which must be those of King of Portugal and of Emperor of Constantinople."[57] This leads us to a definition of António Vieira's initial concept of Empire, which is apocalyptic in nature, and whose emperor, elected by four kings, his peers, thus reproduces the historical procedures of the Diet of Augsburg. As an additional note, to mark the conversion of all peoples to the Gospel (another apocalyptic element), the emperor of the Eastern Roman Empire, the King of Portugal, "shall present to the Supreme Pontiff the ten tribes of Israel, who will, at such time, reveal themselves and come forth, to the wonderment of all the world."[58]

The geography of empire is therefore delineated within this quadrate of cities – Lisbon, Rome, Constantinople, and Jerusalem. By this we mean not its physical geography but, as yet, a very generic framework: the seat of empire in the reconquered Constantinople; the defeat of the Turkish Empire, which was the main threat to Christianity in the 16th–17th centuries; and the preservation of Rome's religious supremacy. These elements form a political framework that bears some similarity to Dante's *Monarchy*, while being devoid of its theoretical, legal and civic foundation. By 1659, when he wrote to the Bishop of Japan, André Fernandes, Vieira had already travelled through Italy, including Rome and a lengthy sojourn in Naples. He had travelled through France and Flanders. Might he have read or heard of Dante's *Monarchy*? Vieira's work is notable for its marked originality in the use of apocalyptic thought that is, in this sense, an awkward fit with Dante's. We refer to the integration of the Jews within the Church, and the possible reinstatement of Jewish rites and temples, an idea that was developed at length in the *Clavis Prophetarum*.[59] However, we will now attempt to look for a

---

55 Padre António Vieira: *Cartas*, I, p. 483.
56 Padre António Vieira: *Cartas*, I, p. 485.
57 Padre António Vieira: *Cartas*, I, p. 491.
58 Padre António Vieira: *Cartas*, I, p. 492.
59 *Cf.* Arnaldo do Espírito Santo: O Corpo e a Sombra, a Figura e o Figurado. A Restauração do Templo de Ezequiel, das Cerimónias e dos Ritos Judaicos. In Ana Paula Banza e Manuel Cândi-

broader answer to our main issue, namely that of "Vieira and Dante," by analysing some fragmentary information from *História do Futuro*.

As for the letter *Esperanças de Portugal*, this contains no solid biblical or philosophical argumentation that might associate it with Dante's writing. The sole source of authority invoked throughout is Bandarra, except for the matter of the emergence of the ten tribes of Israel, whose restoration to Jerusalem from millenary exile is invoked in the prophecies of Isaiah. But for many, as Father Vieira notes, the resurgence of the ten tribes and the conversion of the Jews is a sign of the end of times and of the presence of the Antichrist. This is therefore an apocalyptic proposition, in the sense of prophetic revelation, after Bandarra, and also in the sense of eschatological hope, assured, in part, in the *Epistle to the Romans* (chapter 11). Vieira declares this openly when he points "inquiring"[60] readers to the visions in the first three chapters of *Ezekiel*. There, as in Bandarra, are listed the conversion of the Jews, their subjugation to the King of Portugal, victory over the Turks and the eradication of heresies, "through this glorious prince."[61] However, is it plausible that Vieira's assertion that all this "will be followed ... by the universal peace of the world, ... under ... a single monarch" is in fact a formulation that reveals Vieira's reading of Dante? An absolute denial seems impossible, since the idea and the words used by Vieira are the same as Dante's. Can it be a coincidence? Or a reminiscence? The concordance is glaring in another regard, namely the use of syllogism as a method of proof in Vieira, as in Dante. One of these possibilities is highly likely.

However, when Vieira specifies the "other future things that have not yet come to pass"[62] and that João IV will bring about, namely the taking of Jerusalem; the defeat and surrender of the Turks; dominion and rule over "the city and empire of Constantinople";[63] and the presentation of the tribes of Israel to the Pontiff, it is clear that there is no coincidence between Vieira and Dante, other than the notion of the alliance of the Emperor with the Pontiff, or rather, of temporal power with spiritual power, each in its own sphere. Vieira is particularly forceful in this regard when he discloses Bandarra's prophecy: "Shechem stands for the Turk; Dinah, for the Church; Levi, for the Pope, and Simeon, for the King; and just as Levi united with Simeon to avenge Dinah for the injury she had

---

do Pimentel (eds.): *Uma Jornada Vieirina em Évora*. Lisboa: Universidade Católica Editora 2011, pp. 9–20.
60 Padre António Vieira: *Cartas*, I, p. 497.
61 Padre António Vieira: *Cartas*, I, p. 498.
62 Padre António Vieira: *Cartas*, I, p. 498.
63 Padre António Vieira: *Cartas*, I, p. 499.

received from Shechem, so will the Pope unite with the King to avenge the Church for the injury she has received from the Turk."[64]

This is, in short, the expression of Vieira's thought from 1643 (the year Vieira indicates marked the beginning of his reflection on Bandarra's prophecies) until 1659 (the year in which he wrote the Letter *Esperanças de Portugal*). In effect, some aspects here deserve particular notice, since they indicate a possible coincidence with certain views in *De monarchia*. Namely, when Dante, after asserting that the power of the Emperor derives directly from God, without the mediation of the Pope, concludes his work as follows: "Let Caesar therefore show that reverence towards Peter which a firstborn son should show his father, so that, illumined by the light of paternal grace, he may the more effectively light up the world, over which he has been placed by Him alone who is ruler over all things spiritual and temporal."[65]

In fact, Dante's recommendation to the caesar that he manifest filial reverence towards the Pope is very alike the attitude of cooperation that the pope must show the future monarch, according to Vieira. The only difference is that Dante's thought emanates from a recognised and accepted political culture and practice, notwithstanding the circumstances of actual conflict during his era, while Vieira bases his entire argument on prophecies peppered with Sebastianism, or messianic ideologies, some of which are Judaizing in nature, and that yearn for a better world of peace and happiness.[66]

The letter *Esperanças de Portugal* was burdened by a tangle of predictions for the 1660s that never took place. Neither was João IV resurrected; nor was Castile defeated and dominated by the Portuguese; nor the Ottoman Empire destroyed; nor the King of Portugal anointed emperor of Constantinople; nor was the Holy Land reclaimed; nor did the ten tribes of Israel 'suddenly reveal themselves'; nor were the Jews converted to Christianity or welcomed into the Church.

Nonetheless, this did not lead Vieira to abandon an essential part of his vision for the future of the world: a vision formulated without resorting to the prophecies of Bandarra nor to texts of debatable and doctrinally unreliable foundations. A Christology solidly based on the New Testament, particularly Paul, gave way to a further vision for the future, one gleaned from the canonical prophets of the Old Testament, and which was further strengthened, after *História do Futuro*, in the *Clavis Prophetarum*. The third book of the latter work alone includes about 160 cited authors, most of whom precede Dante's death. There is a steady array of

---

[64] Padre António Vieira: *Cartas*, I, p. 499.
[65] *De monarchia*, III, xvi, p. 149.
[66] Such as, for example, Bandarra, St. Methodius, St. Isidore of Seville, Juan de Rocacelsa, and Pedro de Frias, referred to in Padre António Vieira: *Cartas*, I, p. 515.

authors quoted by both: the Bible, both the New and Old Testaments, which both authors would have read and heard, a significant amount of the Church Fathers, and Thomas Aquinas, whose echoes can often be felt. Prudence demands, however, that we note that many of the common references may be the result of scholarship within a culture shared by Dante and Vieira, despite the distance of centuries, namely the Graeco-Latin literary and philosophical, as well as the patristic and scholastic, heritage.

Since, as already stated previously, a simple quotation does not constitute apodeictic proof that Vieira was inspired by Dante, we shall continue our analysis, turning now to *História do Futuro* and the *Clavis*, hopefully with the same exactitude and openness to possibilities employed in the preceding pages, dedicated mostly to the letter *Esperanças de Portugal*. As for the *Clavis*, one cannot disregard that the majority of it was written in Rome. Vieira expressly states that he is writing the text corresponding to page 194 of manuscript 359 of the Pontifical Gregorian University Library, in Rome on April 12, 1671, the day of the canonization of St. Louis Bertrand.[67] This text and that of page 355, also written in 1671, belong in Book I.[68] Another note by Vieira refers to page 505 of the same manuscript, which corresponds to Book II. These annotations lead us to the conclusion that Vieira wrote at least approximately two-thirds of the *Clavis* in Rome.[69] In view of the above, we believe that it is very likely that Vieira read Dante's *Monarchy* around this time, if he had not done so already.[70] This is an important detail to consider in the analysis of possible traces of Dante in Vieira, as is possibly the use of the same passages (by Aristotle, Virgil, the Bible, Aquinas, etc.) to illustrate identical ideas or justify identical arguments.

Thus, when Dante cites Paul's exclamation "O the depth of the riches both of the wisdom and knowledge of God!",[71] he does so to express his wonderment that Alexander the Great should have been removed by Providence from the contest to

---

[67] "praestantissimum Dominicanae militiae ducem Ludovicum Bertrandum, quem ipsa die qua haec scribimus, Aprilis duodecima anni 1671, doctrina et miraculis illustrem, magno totius Orbis Christiani desiderio et Romanae Vrbis plausu, Sanctorum albo adscripsit Clemens X".

[68] "Nonne hic est praesens status Iudaeorum a multis annis, et hoc ipso 1671 quo haec Romae scribo; quando tot eorum Olysippone et Conimbricae cremati sunt".

[69] Cf. Arnaldo do Espírito Santo: A *Clavis Prophetarum* à Luz das Referências Cronológicas Intratextuais. In José Cândido de Oliveira Martins (ed.): *Padre António Vieira: Colóquio*. Braga: Universidade Católica Portuguesa, Publicações da Faculdade de Filosofia 2008, pp. 35–49.

[70] Regarding Father António Vieira as a compulsive and voracious reader, see: Arnaldo do Espírito Santo: Livros de uso do padre António Vieira. In *Leituras: O Livro Antigo em Portugal e Espanha (séculos XVI–XVIII), Jornadas da Biblioteca Nacional*. Lisboa: Biblioteca Nacional 2001, pp. 177–190.

[71] *Romans*, 11:33.

create a universal empire, in order to enable the historical circumstances that led to the first steps taken by Rome in the equally providential creation of its empire. Additionally, and for the same purpose, Virgil's prophecy is cited:

> Surely you promised that from them some time,
> With passing years, the Romans were to come;
> From Teucer's line restored leaders should come
> To hold the sea and all lands in their sway.[72]

This is an undeniable point of contact between Dante and Vieira, for whom the *Aeneid* is equally a source of prophecy, which leads Vieira to state that his *História do Futuro* is to the formation of the Fifth Empire as the shield of Aeneas, forged by Vulcan at Venus's request, was to the formation of the Roman Empire:

> And that loftiest and most judicious spirit of any who wrote in the poetic style saw that, to overcome the most arduous of enterprises, . . . and to found the mightiest and most extended Empire, there could be no weapon sturdier, nor more impenetrable, . . . than a shield fashioned through art and divine wisdom, in which were cast and announced the very same future feats that would be accomplished in that enterprise.[73]

In sum, Dante and Vieira share the belief that poets are prophets and that "the office and bond of poets is not to state things as they have been, but to depict them as they might to be, or as it is meet they should be."[74] This is another documented consonance (which may emanate from Aristotle's *Poetics*) between them, whatever meaning may be attributed to it. What seems incontrovertible is that there is a set of texts in Dante and Vieira which, we venture to restate, constitute a common field of reference, which was read and cited to support their argument and to demonstrate identical perspectives, even if they do not coincide at all times.

A case in point is Dante's use of *Luke* (2:1) to corroborate the argument of "[universal] jurisdiction"[75] promulgated by Virgil, Lucan, and Boethius, among others. Luke or, in Dante's words, the "Christ's chronicler,"[76] refers to the Empire's census of the population to imply that, at the time Christ was born, the "Roman people won the race against all its rivals competing for world [empire]."[77] Dante's conclusion from the above would have been the most forceful of his arguments for the readers of his time, namely the ability to state that "therefore they won by

---

72 Virgil, *The Aeneid*, I, 234–236; *De monarchia*, II, viii, p. 83.
73 Padre António Vieira: *História do Futuro* 2005, p. 179.
74 *Ibidem*.
75 *De monarchia*, II, viii, p. 85.
76 *De monarchia*, II, viii, p. 83.
77 *De monarchia*, II, viii, p. 85.

divine judgment, and consequently they obtained [the Empire] by divine judgment; which means they obtained it by right."[78]

Let us now turn to Vieira, who also paid particular attention to this passage from *Luke*, whom he described as "Historicus," a designation equivalent to that of Dante's "chronicler [*scriba*]." Admittedly, these are different words. But this difference, given the synonymy, in effect approximates rather than separates Vieira from Dante, since it may evince a concern to obfuscate the source for the concept. Moreover, Vieira's emphasis on this passage leads him to resort to the indisputable authority of Aquinas, according to whom the universal census occurred "by divine decree": "In this census, according to St. Thomas, a tax or tribute was paid, in recognition of due servitude, not devoid of wonder, for He who had been born was the true Lord of the world and Monarch, in whose turn Augustus was acting, unbeknownst to him, but by the will of God."[79] For Dante, as for Vieira, the birth of Christ, at the very point in history when Augustus ordered the census of "all the world," *universus orbis*, according to Luke, was the work of divine Providence and the Roman Empire a monumental chapter thereof. In Vieira's view, the Fifth Empire, the successor to the Roman Empire, is the culmination of a plan of salvation for all mankind, which had been predetermined since "the creation of the world." The difference being that Dante concludes his reasoning by claiming equivalence between "divine decree" and the "right of subjugation," which will result in a political order, namely the lawful Empire or Monarchy.

The same dichotomy is found in the reference to the "prophecy of Caiaphas," who was equally ignorant of what he did, "when spoke the truth [about] the heavenly decree".[80] For Dante, this confirms the legitimacy of Pilate's jurisdiction in condemning Christ to death. Vieira interprets the words of Caiaphas, "that one man should die for the people,"[81] as well as the commentary that follows, "[a]nd not for that nation only, but that also he should gather together in one the children of God that were scattered abroad"[82] as proof that all peoples will be gathered together in the Consummation of the Kingdom of Christ on earth, in other words, in the Temporal and Spiritual Empire, in one fold and under one shepherd.

---

78 *Ibidem*.
79 "et in hac descriptione solvebatur census, sive tributum, ut Historiae tradunt, in recognitionem debitae servitutis, non sine mysterio, quia ille natus erat, qui verus erat mundi Dominus et Monarcha, cujus vices gerebat Augustus, licet non intelligens, sed nutu Dei." (Padre António Vieira, *Clavis Prophetarum*, I, caput IV, Probatur ex Patribus, *ms*. FC 1165/1, fl. 39). Cf. Silvano Peloso: *La* Clavis Prophetarum *di Antonio Vieira*, p. 116.
80 *De monarchia* II, xi, p. 97.
81 *John*, 11:50.
82 *John*, 11:52.

There are obvious differences, but the texts, the words, the concepts and the type of argumentation are identical, as is their purpose: universal peace.

While Dante displays reticence regarding the transfer of temporal power from the Empire to the Pope, he acknowledges, as would Vieira later, that Constantine's conversion and the consequent decree granting the right to religious freedom opened the gates to the universal preaching of Christianity. And although their views do not entirely coincide, in essence, Constantine's Empire, despite surrendering some of its rights, according to tradition, is acknowledged by Dante as being predestined by God (and not by nature, as he affirms elsewhere) in his rebuke of the opponents of the Empire of his age: "So let those who pass themselves off as sons of the church stop attacking the Roman empire, seeing that Christ the bridegroom sanctioned it in this way at the beginning and at the end of his earthly campaign."[83] In other words, by submitting to the census when He was born and by submitting to the decree of a lawful judge, an imperial legate, who could not "be authorised unless he had jurisdiction over the whole of mankind, since the whole of mankind was punished in that flesh of Christ 'who bore our sorrows,' as the prophet says."[84] And even the Emperor, Dante adds, "would not have had jurisdiction over the whole of mankind unless the Roman empire had existed by right."[85] Vieira, while not embracing the theology of salvation professed by Dante in the above-mentioned passages, is lavish in his praise for and recognition of this same Empire, for throwing open "very wide and secure gates, throughout the Roman world, for the preaching of the Gospel; not by imposing the obligation to believe in the Gospel, but by granting it the possibility of being preached."[86]

This consonance, some divergences notwithstanding, reveals the latency of a complex issue, namely the relationship, in the monarchy to come as conceived by Dante, between the (Roman) Emperor and the (Roman) Prince during and after Dante's time. On Vieira's part, what is the sensitivity to this and other issues related to the coexistence of the religious sphere and political power, in his time and for the future? Are there any points of convergence or divergence between Dante and Vieira that might be indicative, despite everything, of common points of departure?

Book III of *De monarchia* opens with the figure of King Solomon. For Vieira, Solomon is the quintessential symbol of the cooperation between political and religious power; in other words, between temporal and spiritual power. Solomon was entrusted with the building of the Temple, which the high priest Abiathar had not been able to carry out.

---

83 *De monarchia*, II, xi, p. 97.
84 *Ibidem*.
85 *Ibidem*.
86 Padre António Vieira: *Clavis Prophetarum, Chave dos Profetas*, III, p. 111.

This is a theme on which Dante and Vieira coincide completely. Kingship and the priesthood are two separate instances of power, as were Solomon and Abiathar, but political and religious power must be wielded as they were by the two brothers, Moses and Aaron. Vieira concludes his reasoning thus: "so that power, united and, therefore, in kinship, might lend mutual help."[87] Dante states the same, opting for the simile of the Emperor's filial relationship with the Pope, as seen in the passage mentioned above. We return to this topic because it was precisely the insistence on the separation of powers, emphasised in the statement that Caesar was entrusted with the command of the entire world "by the one alone," i.e., God, the supreme ruler, that was the main cause for the ecclesiastical censorship that consigned the *Dantis monarchia* to the *Index librorum prohibitorum* until the end of the 19th century. Vieira, who would have been well aware of this, attributed the separation of powers, which resulted in their mutual independence, to God, the author of the Sacred Scriptures, and to "Divine Providence." Moses and Aaron, despite being brothers, are two different people, whereby, in symbolic terms, one is committed to secular power and the other to ecclesiastical power. Unsurprisingly, this view, while censored in Dante, was not remarked on by the censors who examined the *Clavis* at the beginning of the 18th century in Lisbon and in Rome. Conversely, Dante's passionate and sincere protestations of innocence and piety towards Christ, the Church and the Pope were to no avail. Dante declares that he prizes the truth above all things: "showing that reverence which a dutiful son owes his father, a dutiful son owes his mother, devout towards Christ, devout towards the Church, devout towards the Shepherd, and devout towards all who profess the Christian religion [. . .], I engage in battle in this book in the cause of truth."[88] Objectively, the censorship of Dante's *De monarchia* was due not only to its denial of the legitimacy of the temporal power of the Church, but also because it questioned the patristic exegesis of the texts on which this power rested. Referred to by Dante, so that he might best challenge them, are the traditional interpretations of the creation, at the beginning of the world, of the Sun and the Moon; the Sun, endowed with its own light, stands for the power of the Papacy, while the Moon, with no light other than the Sun's, stands for the power of Empire. Dante refutes, point by point, the exegesis of this figuration of papal supremacy.

Similarly, he questions the interpretation regarding the birth of the sons of Jacob, whereby the power of the priesthood is vested in Levi, while secular power is vested in Judah. Levi had the advantage of being the first-born, which

---

[87] Padre António Vieira: *Clavis Prophetarum, Chave dos Profetas*, III, p. 583.
[88] *De monarchia*, III, iii, p. 107.

grants him the right of primogeniture, i.e., of primacy. This interpretation leant the Priesthood, the Pope, and the Church supremacy over the Empire by virtue of birthright. Of particular interest is the fact that Vieira resorts to the same texts as Dante, but conferring them the opposite meaning: namely that Christ holds royal power and the power of priesthood by birthright, by primogeniture, by natural right. Vieira dedicates a considerable number of pages to laying out the proof of the right of Christ to wield both powers. We shall confine ourselves to the following passage: "We have, therefore, in Christ's dual genealogy, his dual empire: spiritual through the line of Nathan, as traced by Luke; temporal through the line of Solomon, as traced by Matthew; . . . . Both, however, establish that Christ himself was predestined and born, through his own ancestry, to the crown and, in like manner, to the tiara."[89] Vieira's use of "tiara" is enlightening. He is in fact thinking not of Christ, but of his Vicar on earth; and thereby inserting himself at the centre of a heated controversy which is not of his, but of Dante's time. It is worth noting that Dante was keen to insist that the Pope was not the vicar of Christ, but of Peter. The conclusion to be drawn from the above is that Dante underlies Vieira's discourse, for the purpose of contradiction. In our view, intertextual connections are not always shaped by the convergence of convictions, since differences are sometimes equally or more significant. In Vieira's text cited above, the divergence is sharply expressed in the word "tiara," whose association with Christ might sound strange, as a symbol of profligate power that is harmful, according to Dante, to the peace of the world, and even to the dignity of the Church and her mission.

Dante would undoubtedly agree with the words of Thomas Aquinas quoted by Vieira: "When the Kingdom and Priesthood ceased in Judea, Christ was born, who was a true King and Priest and a true monarch. And this fifth monarchy, which succeeded the Romans, is verily superior to all."[90] This is a case where the context in which the quotation is inserted is more telling than the actual literal content of the cited text. Dante clearly disagrees with Aquinas's assertion that the Fifth Empire is the spiritual and temporal power of the Church, but he would agree with Vieira, who views the Fifth Empire as a new, universal entity, where

---

[89] "Habes igitur in duplici genealogia Christi duplex ejus Imperium: spirituale per lineam Nathan, quam deduxit Lucas; temporale per lineam Salomonis, quam deduxit Matthaeus; . . . uterque vero Christum ipsum ex ipsa generationis serie ad coronam simul et tiaram destinatum natumque demonstrantes." (Padre António Vieira: *Clavis Prophetarum*, I, caput 4, *ms.* FC 1165/1, fl. 45v).

[90] "Cessante, inquit, Regno et Sacerdotio in Judaeanascitur Christus, qui fuit verus Rex et Sacerdos et verus Monarcha. Et haec quinta Monarchia, quae successit Romanis, secundum veritatem omnibus praecellit." (Padre António Vieira: *Clavis Prophetarum*, I, caput 3, *ms.* FC 1165/1, fl. 35r).

tolerance will prevail and the Jews will be welcomed instead of persecuted and burned at the stake, and where fraternity among men, well-being, full existence, happiness and peace will rule. It is here that Vieira's utopia converges with Dante's civic monarchy.

But let us return to Dante and his contradiction of the biblical arguments with which traditional exegesis justified the temporal power of the Church, or rather, of the Vicar of Peter. At issue is the interpretation of the fact that King Saul was anointed through religious power, in this case, by the Prophet Samuel. Dante notes the episode narrated in the first *Book of Kings*, whose contents he refers to explicitly and summarises. What Dante disputes is the conclusion that, just as Samuel, "as God's vicar, had the authority to give and take away temporal power and transfer it to someone else, so now too God's vicar, the head of the universal church, has the authority to give and to take away and even to transfer the sceptre of temporal power; from which it would undoubtedly follow that imperial authority would be dependent in the way they claim."[91]

For Dante, it is not a question of not accepting the authority of the Sacred Scriptures, but of gainsaying what a particular traditional exegesis aims to extract from their literal meaning through abusive processes of allegorical interpretation; the same is the case with the gold and incense brought by the Magi to the newborn Christ. The disagreement lies in the legitimacy of the reasoning. Indeed, it is not legitimate to infer, from the fact that Christ accepted incense and gold "to signify that he was lord and ruler of spiritual and temporal things," that "Christ's vicar is the lord and ruler of the same things, and thus has authority over both of them."[92]

Once again, it is significant that Vieira chooses to comment at length on the episode of the adoration of the Magi, but draws no conclusion from it other than that "Christ intended to reveal, in his childhood, as explained by St. Thomas, his power and his dominion."[93]

Father Vieira's caution in these words, his appeal to the authority of Aquinas, implies that this passage contains a controversial discussion, which he seeks to distance from his own purpose, by insisting that Christ, as an adult, shielded himself in the silence of humility and poverty: "Magno prodigio Magi Christum, majori miraculo divitiae paupertatem adorant";[94] "humili tamen loco iacuit vilibus

---

[91] *De monarchia*, III, vi, p. 115.
[92] *De monarchia*, III, vii, p. 117.
[93] "Itaque ex sententia Divi Thomae, voluit Christus in infantia potestatem et dominium suum probare". (Padre António Vieira: *Clavis Prophetarum*, I, caput IX, *ms.* FC 1165/1, fl. 74r).
[94] Padre António Vieira: *Clavis Prophetarum*, I, caput IV, *ms.* FC 1165/1, fl. 22r.

involutus pannis, qua quidem via Homines melius ad virtutem trahuntur."[95] The picture he paints, in his commentary on the adoration of the Magi, and sheltering behind the words of a homily by St. John Chrysostom, is totally opposed to the pomp of the court and of the Curia: "Neither soldiers weaponed with shields and spears, nor richly decked steeds; nor refulgent chariots of gold and purple."[96] Thus, otherwise, but in the same spirit as Dante, Vieira does not use this passage to align his Kingdom of Christ consummated on earth with ecclesiastical pomp or symbols of temporal power, which Dante refutes and condemns.

The third argument used to defend the temporal power of the Church and of the Pope is difficult to circumvent, since Christ stated very clearly to Peter, that whatever he bound or loosed on earth would be equally bound or loosed in heaven. Faced with an exegesis of this passage, conceived to corroborate the spiritual power of the vicar of Christ, the successor to Peter, Dante begins with the addendum that "this was also said to all the apostles."[97] But to reason, from this, that they "can 'loose' the laws and decrees of the empire, and 'bind' laws and decrees in the place of the temporal power"[98] would take such a logical leap as to render such a conclusion absurd. One of the techniques of Dante's dialectics is precisely the reductio ad absurdum of opposing arguments. But as the process of reduction to absurdity may contain an element of subjectivity, he immediately moves to the foremost method of demonstration, i.e., syllogism. But in this case, what can the premises be, other than Christ's own words? This difficulty is resolved with Dante's use of this method of analysis on the extension of the key concepts in the terms of the propositions. Thus, Dante clarifies that the extension of the term "all" should not be taken absolutely, "but in relation to something."[99] Otherwise, this would entail veering from sophism to sophism, without ever attaining truth or refuting falsehood.

Father António Vieira's argumentation mirrors Dante's, precisely in a work that may be considered extraordinarily symmetrical to Dante's. Vieira cites exactly the same passage; in Latin, in both cases, with no textual differences. But where one might expect Vieira's conclusion to differ, the following can be read: "By this,

---

[95] Padre António Vieira: *Clavis Prophetarum*, I, caput IV, *ms*. FC 1165/1, fl. 39v.
[96] 'Neque enim hastas neque clypeatas ostendit militum catervas, non equos regalibus phaleris insignes, non currus auro ostroque fulgentes.' (Padre António Vieira: *Clavis Prophetarum*, I, caput IV, *ms*. FC 1165/1, fl. 41r).
[97] *De monarchia*, III, viii. pp. 119.
[98] *Ibidem*.
[99] *De monarchia*, III, viii, p. 121.

it is my understanding that Christ transferred his ordinary powers to the Apostles, while keeping for himself his extraordinary powers."[100]

In the distinction between "ordinary power" and "extraordinary power" there is a delimitation of the universal term "all power," which Dante had already postulated. There is an undeniable coincidence in the way both authors regard the scope of "whatsoever thou shalt bind."

The fourth argument employed to confirm the legitimacy of the Pope's temporal power are Peter's words to Christ: "behold, here are two swords."[101] Dante refutes the interpretation that "those two swords" signify the two ruling powers vested in the Pope. On this occasion he disputes the argument through the elimination of the allegorical meaning[102] attributed to them. Vieira, on the other hand, cites the same passage, "Ecce duo gladii hic,"[103] but his meaning differs somewhat from Dante's, and his purpose is predominantly to reformulate the issue. This is, in fact, a dialectical exercise in which Father Vieira reminds us, after St. Bernard, that Christ also said to Peter: "put up thy sword into the scabbard."[104] With this return to the initial quotation, Vieira partly takes on Dante's stance, but does so differently. Equally, and in the same context, he restates, with St. Bernard: "[b]oth swords, namely the spiritual and the material, belong to the Church, and that although only the former is to be wielded by her own hand, the two are to be employed in her service." And he further adds, from the same quotation from St. Bernard: "It is for the priest [the Pope] to use the sword of the word, but to strike with the sword of steel belongs to the soldier, yet this must be by the authority and will of the priest and the direct command of the emperor."[105] There is nonetheless a level of nuance that brings Vieira closer to Dante, including Vieira's conclusion: "Christ therefore held and commanded, under his empire, the two swords, both of spiritual and of temporal power."[106]

---

[100] "Sic intelligo Christum ordinariam suam potestatem in Apostolos transtulisse, extraordinariam sibi reservasse." (*De monarchia*, I, 10; Padre António Vieira: *Clavis Prophetarum*, I, caput X, §XI, *ms*. FC 1165/1, fl. 92v).

[101] *De monarchia*, III, ix, p. 123.

[102] *De monarchia*, III, 9, p. 127.

[103] Padre António Vieira: *Clavis Prophetarum*, I, caput IV, *ms*. FC 1165/1, fl. 46r.

[104] "Converte gladium tuum in vaginam". (Padre António Vieira: *Clavis Prophetarum*, I, caput IV, *ms*. FC 1165/1, fl. 46r. Cf. Silvano Peloso: *La* Clavis Prophetarum *di António Vieira*, p. 125)

[105] Bernard of Clairvaux: Treatise on Consideration, 4:3 [English Translation by Brian Tierney. In Brian Tierney (ed.): *The Crisis of Church and State, 1050–1300*. Toronto: University of Toronto Press 1988, pp. 93–94. (T / n)]

[106] «Ergo utrumque gladium, tam spiritualis quam temporalis potestatis, sub suo Christus habebat et regebat imperio.» (Padre António Vieira: *Clavis Prophetarum*, I, caput IV, *ms*. FC 1165/1, fl. 46r).

But this is precisely what Dante calls into question regarding the Church and the Papacy. What we look to emphasise is that, here also, both the debate and the texts on which it is based are common to Dante and Vieira, and it is a matter of substance for both, each in his own way. A mere coincidence? Highly unlikely.

Finally, the fifth argument employed to demonstrate the supremacy of the Papacy over the Empire is the celebrated document in which Constantine abdicates Rome and bestows it on the Pope: "some people maintain that the Emperor Constantine, cured of leprosy by the intercession of Sylvester who was then supreme Pontiff, made a gift to the church of the seat of empire (i.e. Rome), along with many other imperial privileges. From this they argue that since that time no one can take on those imperial privileges unless he receives them from the church...."[107]

A vigorous refutation of this view ensues. But to return to Vieira's Fifth Empire: Constantine is equally referred to, in practically the same words as Dante's: "And the Emperor [Constantine], having been enlightened by both princes of the Apostles and healed by Pope Sylvester of the Leprosy within and without through baptism . . . ."[108] Both authors reference Pope Sylvester and mention the healing of leprosy. But unlike Dante, Vieira avoids entanglement in the controversy surrounding Constantine's legendary bequest of Rome to the Church as a token of gratitude. His purview is distinct, namely, to point to Constantine as the first example of cooperation with the Church, rather than the Emperor's subjugation to the Pope. This difference is, in point of fact, clarified in Dante's unambiguous statement: "the foundation of the church is Christ, . . . but the foundation of the Empire is human right."[109] For Vieira, Christ is the foundation of both the Church and the Fifth Empire. We refer, of course, to the Consummation of the Kingdom of Christ on earth, the fifth in historical succession, according to the interpretation of Daniel's prophecies as conceived and argued in the *Clavis Prophetarum*. Despite this divergence in reasoning, both Dante's Empire and Vieira's Fifth Empire consist "in the unity of universal monarchy."[110]

The last argument in defence of papal supremacy is challenged by Dante with the use of intellectual categories from Aristotelian-Thomistic philosophy. To conclude his reasoning on the demonstration that the dignities of the Papacy and Empire are not mutually reducible, Dante refers to the last books of the *Nicomachean Ethics*, where Aristotle discusses the relationship between activity, happiness, pleasure and virtue. It is in this regard that Dante adheres to the notion

---

[107] *De monarchia*, III, x, p. 127.
[108] Padre António Vieira: *Clavis Prophetarum, Chave dos Profetas*, III, caput III, p. 111.
[109] *De monarchia*, III, x, p. 129.
[110] *Ibidem*.

of the good man or to that of "the perfect man, who is the measure of all the others."[111] This concept has been translated so as to diverge from the Aristotelian realm and towards the semantic sphere of Paul, in the *Epistle to the Colossians*, which reads: ". . . warning every man, and teaching every man in all wisdom; that we may present every man perfect in Christ Jesus."[112] In short, Dante, who would have been perfectly aware of the Pauline expression "hominem perfectum," deliberately used the Aristotelian "optimum hominem." It is in this supremely anthropological and ethically secular expression that Dante's entire argumentation rests. However, judging by the most recent translations into other languages, it is to be believed that many readers over the centuries have sensed in Dante's words a thought that is Pauline, rather than Aristotelian.

In Vieira it is precisely the Pauline expression "virum perfectum," equivalent to "hominem perfectum" that appears, and it is curiously associated with "mensuram," much as in Dante "optimum hominem" is associated with "mensura," "regula" and "ydea." But a reading of Aristotle's *Nicomachean Ethics* or of the Pauline theology of anacephalaeosis and the fullness of time leads us once again to acknowledge that Vieira's words are the same as those used by Dante for the foundation of the Universal Monarchy, or Empire. We should add, however, that of all the quotations used by Dante to refute the thesis that the Empire is dependent on the Church, not one is taken up by Vieira, contrary to form.

There can only be one dependable conclusion to be drawn from the present study. The previous micro-textual analysis allows us to glean correspondences between Dante and Vieira, on the one hand, while on the other there is a further textual layer which is pointedly unaligned in thought and which is as significant as the layer of coincidences. These two cornerstones assert structuring themes (temporality, universality, peace, happiness, well-being in the world. . .) in Vieira's conception of the Fifth Empire, particularly in the Consummation of the Kingdom of Christ on earth and the *Clavis Prophetarum* that support the hypothesis that Father Vieira, a "voracious reader," was certainly one who undertook an exhaustive reading of Dante's *Monarchy*.

---

111 *De monarchia*, III, xii, p 135.
112 *Colossians*, 1:28.

Bibliographical References

Aquinas, Thomas: *Summa Theologiae*, Prima pars. Madrid: Biblioteca de Autores Cristianos 1994.

[Aristotle] Aristóteles: *Ética a Nicómaco*. Edição bilingue, tradução e notas de Dimas de Almeida. Lisboa: Edições Universitárias Lusófonas 2012.

Aristotle: *The Politics*. Translated by H. Rackham. Cambridge, MA: Harvard University Press; London: William Heinemann Ltd. 1944.

Camões, Luís de: *The Lusíads*. Translated by Landeg White. Oxford: Oxford University Press 1997.

Dante Alighieri, *De Monarchia*. Tradução portuguesa de Arnaldo do Espírito Santo. Lisboa: INCM, 2022.

Espírito Santo, Arnaldo do: Censuras da *Clavis Prophetarum* do Padre António Vieira. In Manuela Domínguez García et al. (eds.): *Sub luce florentis calami: Homenaje a Manuel C. Díaz y Díaz*. Santiago de Compostela: Universidade de Santiago de Compostela 2002.

Espírito Santo, Arnaldo do: O Corpo e a Sombra, a Figura e o Figurado. A Restauração do Templo de Ezequiel, das Cerimónias e dos Ritos Judaicos. In Ana Paula Banza e Manuel Cândido Pimentel (eds.): *Uma Jornada Vieirina em Évora*. Lisboa: Universidade Católica Editora 2011.

Espírito Santo, Arnaldo do: A *Clavis Prophetarum* à Luz das Referências Cronológicas Intratextuais. In José Cândido de Oliveira Martins (ed.): *Padre António Vieira: Colóquio*. Braga: Universidade Católica Portuguesa, Publicações da Faculdade de Filosofia 2008.

Espírito Santo, Arnaldo do: Livros de uso do padre António Vieira. In *Leituras: O Livro Antigo em Portugal e Espanha (séculos XVI–XVIII), Jornadas da Biblioteca Nacional*. Lisboa: Biblioteca Nacional 2001, pp. 177–190.

Peloso, Silvano: *La* Clavis Prophetarum *di Antonio Vieira*. Viterbo: CISCAV, Sette Città 2011.

Sá, Artur Moreira de (ed.): *Índices dos Livros Proibidos em Portugal no Século XVI*. Lisboa: Instituto Nacional de Investigação Científica 1983.

Tierney, Brian (ed.): *The Crisis of Church and State, 1050–1300*. Toronto: University of Toronto Press 1988.

Vigini, Giuliano: *Dizionario della Biblia*. Città del Vaticano: Libreria Editrice Vaticana 2016.

Rita Marnoto
Dante in Portugal: An Ethereal Gaze

A simple online search is sufficient to illustrate the expressive use of the qualifier *dantesco* [Dantean] as soon as we open the first Portuguese language pages that populate the internet. In this regard, journalistic language presents indicators that lend themselves to systematic exploration.[1] The use of this word seems to imply, for the most part, a dysphoric sense, associated, in turn, with the pandemic, environmental damage, or economic speculation. It is nonetheless also possible to trace the use of this word in another sense, with reference to the work of Dante Alighieri and the planned celebrations in Portugal, in 2021, of the death of this Italian prodigy.

Conversely, the terms *dantista* and *dantólogo / a*, which designate scholars of Dante Alighieri, seem to have few or no occurrences in current Portuguese, leading search engines to produce bizarre distortions.[2]

These data are an eloquent symptom of the relationship entertained by the Portuguese culture of the past few decades with the poet-symbol of the Italian nation. A vague idea of who Dante was, very focused on the sombre atmosphere of the *Commedia*,[3] coexists with patchy corners of specialised research, thus creating an overall "a macchia di leopard" picture. In general, the *Inferno* tends to be endowed with metonymic valences that render the first *cantica* into an emblem, not only of the entire *Comedy*, but also of the writer's vast and varied body of work. An aesthetics that celebrates the perfection of the cosmos, a theological and political doctrine based on the notion of love and a colossal encyclopaedic knowledge that combines multiple fields of knowledge, alongside historical observation that captures the essence of extraordinarily diverse personalities and

---

[1] We looked into the online pages of the Portuguese newspapers *Público*, *Expresso* and *Diário As Beiras*.
[2] In Portugal, the two most recent monographs on Dante Alighieri date back to 2001 (Rita Marnoto: *A* Vita nova *de Dante Alighieri. Deus, o amor e a palavra*. Lisboa: Colibri 2001) and 2017 (António Mega Ferreira: *O essencial sobre Dante Alighieri*. Lisboa: Imprensa Nacional-Casa da Moeda 2017).
[3] Dante's *opus magnum* tends to be designated, in Portugal, as *Divina comédia*. As is well known, the qualifier *divine* was added by Giovanni Boccaccio in his biography of Dante, and included in the title over two centuries later, by Ludovico Dolce, in the 1555 edition. The original title is *Commedia*, or more precisely, in Dante's Italian, *Comedía*. This encapsulated the composite character of a work that eluded the standards of the medieval canon in its combination of varied themes, points of view, stylistic levels and imagic planes.

Note: Translated from the Portuguese by Cassilda Alcobia-Murphy.

environments, as well as their potential correlations, are thus watered down in this foregrounding of darkness and dysphoria.

The beginnings of the creative reception of Dante in Portuguese literature occurred, it is well known, within an Iberian setting that dates back to Garcia de Resende's *Cancioneiro geral*, published in 1516, in whose pages is assembled the courtly poetry produced from the middle of the 15th century.[4] In the historiographical field, Gomes Eanes de Zurara refers to Dante in the *Crónica do conde D. Pedro de Meneses* and in the *Crónica do conde D. Duarte de Meneses*.[5] Within the great arc of Classicism that characterised the centuries to follow, the poet remained a reference to be modelled by the greatest among Portuguese writers, to which may be added references and critical commentary, which increased with the advent of the Neoclassical period.

It is from these origins that a 19th-century groundswell arose, which made Dante a prominent figure in the relations between Portugal and Italy, a topic deserving of further in-depth study.[6] The field of translation clearly demonstrates the terms in which this groundswell propagated. It is dominated by the *Comedy*, with particular emphasis on the *Inferno*. Portuguese translations of excerpts from the Dantean poem appeared in the pages of newspapers and gazettes of varying reach until, in 1886 and 1887, two full translations of the *Inferno* were published, by Joaquim Pinto de Campos and Domingos Ennes, the latter including engravings by Gustave Doré and commentary by Xavier da Cunha. If the primacy conferred on the first *cantica* of the poem is revealed in the emotional filtering entailed in this translational work, the publication, in serial form, of the first ten cantos, translated by Domingos Ennes, is a good reflection of their popularity among a large audience of readers. They appeared in *Diário Ilustrado*, *Diário da Manhã* and *Jornal da Noite*.[7] The resulting reception was therefore enthusiastic but, in equal measure, partial and scattered.

High-brow cultural circles lavished copious praise on Dante Alighieri, who was the object of such heartfelt veneration as to remain above any differences in currents of thought or dissent.

---

[4] Mario Casella produced a broad summary of this topic in a review published in *Bulletino della Società Dantesca Italiana* in 1914, which can be read in Giacinto Manuppella: *Dantesca luso-brasileira: Subsídios para uma bibliografia da obra e do pensamento de Dante Alighieri*. Coimbra: Universidade de Coimbra 1966, pp. 156–174.
[5] Detailed bibliographic information in Giacinto Manuppella: *Dantesca luso-brasileira*, pp. 60–61.
[6] To this may be added the lack of partial studies on the presence of Dante in works by Almeida Garrett, Alexandre Herculano, Camilo Castelo Branco, Eça de Queirós and by the intellectuals of the generation of 1870 ("Geração de 70"), as well as in Portuguese Ultra-romanticism, etc.
[7] Detailed bibliographic information in Giacinto Manuppella: *Dantesca luso-brasileira*, pp. 27–28.

A case in point is the thesis submitted by Manuel Pinheiro Chagas for admission to a lectureship in Literary Studies. This is devoted to the high points of European literature, and pride of place is reserved for Dante Alighieri. The first words he dedicates to the poet set the tone for the pages that follow:

> But lo! The great man stands before me, that colossal figure, that pensive Homer in whose mind simmers the entire world of the Middle ages, as I have sought to describe, with its disorienting tumultuousness, its sublime ecstasies, its bold satire – children all of the fevered stirrings of his intellect. I refer to the immortal figure of Dante, that thoughtful Florentine who closes the chapter on the Middle Ages, which he captures in his great book; who builds, with his *Inferno*, the immense bonfire into which he flings his age, then pours it, in torrents of bronze, into the sublime moulds that render the *Divine Comedy* a deathless statue.[8]

This glowing depiction of an *Inferno* whose molten matter pours onto the mould from which the perennial sculpture of the *Commedia* arises undoubtedly played a major part in the success garnered by Pinheiro Chagas's dissertation.

He was aligned with the conservative faction of one of the most heated controversies that raged in literary circles in Portugal, namely the "Questão Coimbrã" [the Coimbra Question], although this faction in no way clashed with the plaudits heard, from the other side of the barricades, in praise of the poet.[9] The progressive wing was headed by another profound admirer of Dante, Antero de Quental.

Antero writes thus on what he considers to be the "quintessential lyrical form", i.e., the sonnet:

> Dante, Michelangelo, Shakespeare, and Camões are admired for the great, for the immense manifestations of their intellect: the Inferno, St. Peter, Othello, the Lusiads; but to truly know these, to truly love them, this beautiful and pure form is necessary, which lent them a mould through which the most intimate sentiments of the soul might flow. There, we admire the Artist, but here, we love the Poet: there, we are swept by excitement, but here, we are moved to tears.[10]

---

[8] Manuel Pinheiro Chagas: *Da origem e caracter do movimento litterario da Renascença principalmente na Itália*, p. 15. The lectureship in Literary Studies ("Curso Superior de Letras"), founded by a decree issued in 1858 by King Pedro V of Portugal, was the first higher education degree in the country dedicated to the teaching of literature. Its third "Chai", of which Pinheiro Chagas was Reader, was initially designated Modern European (with an Emphasis on Portuguese) Literature and, subsequently, Comparative Philology. Chagas had family ties to Italy through his wife. He was one of nine members of the Executive Committee for the commemoration of the tricentenary of the death of Camões, and the only conservative among their ranks.

[9] The controversy was triggered by Antero de Quental, in his 1865 pamphlet *Bom senso e bom gosto* [Good sense and good taste], aimed at António Feliciano de Castilho, in reply to his afterword to *Poema da mocidade* and *Anjo do lar*, by Manuel Pinheiro Chagas.

[10] Antero de Quental: *Prosas*, vol. 1, pp. 134–135.

The terms with which Chagas and Antero proclaimed their veneration indicate evidently vast differences. While Chagas displays heady enthusiasm for the metal poured onto the mould to fix an immortal twilight, Antero illuminates his reading with the absolutization of a dialectic that filters Hegelian panlogism.[11] The spiral where form and fantastical vision, concrete mould and sentiment, in sum, where Artist and Poet meet, finds its supreme craftsmen, for Antero, in Dante Alighieri, Michelangelo, Shakespeare or, in an addition that is almost unheard of at the time, Luís de Camões. These are the divine custodians of the symbiosis between genius and intelligence that sustained the work of one of the greatest sonnetists in the whole of Portuguese literature.[12]

The enthusiastic welcome received by Dante in 19th-century Portugal, visible in a wide-ranging prominence that permeated cultural strata, ways of thinking and diverse intellectual groups, is closely linked to the harmonious atmosphere then experienced in Portugal and Italy. The question of Italian unification propelled the revitalization of the bonds that had, since ancient times, connected the two nations, fostering the circulation of ideas, contacts between intellectuals and a flow of exiles that Portugal welcomed, as always, with open arms, beginning with the King of Sardinia, Charles Albert of Savoy, deposed in 1849.[13] This consonance was sealed, in an 1862 compact, by yet another marriage between a member of the House of Savoy and a Portuguese monarch: Maria Pia, the youngest daughter of Vittorio Emanuele II, and King Luís I.

The history of the political formation of the two countries presents a very disparate chronology. Italy was then one of the countries whose unity, proclaimed in 1861, was one of the most recent in Europe, while Portugal was one of the oldest,

---

[11] Through the mediation of Augusto Vera, as noted by Paulo Archer de Carvalho: "While questioning the route, Catroga credits the suggestion, placing the 'significance of Italian culture in Antero de Quental's deepening of the issues of history, a theme that greatly preoccupied his generation, much of which showed great enthusiasm for the experience of the Risorgimento.' Quental viewed the history of philosophy and historiosophy as the process of overcoming Kantian transcendentalism, by welcoming the Fichtean *I / not-I* antithesis and the lessons from Schelling's subjective idealism – in Hegel's examination, openness to history and to all forms of existence, as read in *Introduction à la Philosophie d'Hégel* (1855), by Vera, a disciple of Cousin in France." (Risorgimento, insorgimento, Antero [ingressos à felicitação a Umberto de Itália]. In *Estudos Italianos em Portugal*, n. s., 6 (2011), pp. 153–175), pp. 167–168. This article examines the Italian roots of Quental's thought, as well as the seed the Risorgimento sowed on his ideology.

[12] "Like Dante's *agens*, the 'I' of the *Sonetos Completos* follows an ascending itinerary, from darkness to light, from the 'ignorant' god to the 'liberated heart,' from the 'bewitched palace of Illusion' to sleep, rest and golden peace," observes Andrea Ragusa (*Como exilados*, p. 130) regarding Dante's presence in Antero's sonnets.

[13] Applicable to all citations of the set of texts edited by Rita Marnoto, *Estudos Italianos em Portugal*, n. s., 6 (2011).

dating back to 1143. Both, however, went through periods in which the hopes for the future stood in stark contrast with the troublesome present.

Italian unification was carried out in the face of conflicts which remained unresolved after the establishment of a national government. The young state was slow to build road and transport networks and an educational and administrative system common to the entire territory. Meanwhile, rural areas and the south were relegated to hopeless oblivion. Revolutionary hopes were therefore a far cry from a present moment that was, in many ways, oppressive. In turn, the series of misfortunes that beset the history of 19th-century Portugal had brought this country to a state of relentless dejection. The French invasions were followed by a troubled period of internecine struggles, in tandem with repeated popular rebellions, within a very unfavourable international context, which culminated in the attempt, by the British Crown, to annex the African territories between Angola and Mozambique. The glories of the nation most definitely belonged to a distant past, recoverable only through memory.

As such, the two nations converged in their equal need to sustain hopes and aspirations through an identitarian and liberating iconology, able to redeem the misfortunes of the present through the projection of past triumphs over these blemishes. In both cases, the divine custodians of the national literatures took on the role of guides, by virtue of their ability to illuminate the present with an identitarian symbology strengthened through their rootedness in times past. In this regard, Dante Alighieri and Luís de Camões were kindred spirits.

The determined and heroic impetus embodied by both was the model that old Portugal and young Italy lacked: strong poets, authors of vigorous poetry, who never stooped to compromise, and who loudly proclaimed their devotion for their homeland, which they loved above all else, but from which they lived far apart. In effect, the dates for their national celebrations took place within the span of a decade and a half. The birth of Dante Alighieri was commemorated in 1865 and the death of Luís de Camões in 1880.[14]

"Dante was proscribed and exiled, but this did not stop him writing; he skewered with gusto the enemies of freedom in his homeland. O for a battalion of such poets on our shores!", exclaimed Almeida Garrett, the writer who introduced Romanticism to Portugal, in *Viagens na minha terra*.[15] An intrepid fighter for the liberal cause, Garrett knew himself the bitter taste of exile. This was, in effect, the same fate as that of prominent figures of the Italian Risorgimento, such as Carlo Cat-

---

[14] For Dante, see Amedeo Quondam: *Petrarca, l'Italiano dimenticato*. Milano: Rizzoli 2004, and for Camões see Fernando Catroga: Ritualizações da história. In *Histórias da história de Portugal. Séculos xix – xx*. Lisboa: Círculo de Leitores 1996, pp. 551–562.
[15] Almeida Garrett: *Viagens na minha terra*, pp. 129–130.

taneo, Giuseppe Ferarri and Giuseppe Mazzini, among many others. Before them, Dante himself had been relegated to an existence embittered by the impossibility of a return to his Florentine homeland, far from which he came to die. Camões, in turn, undertook an even more extensive journey, across distant and inhospitable seas and continents. An outline was thus sketched, which needed only colouring in by the fantasy of Romanticism and Portuguese Ultra-Romanticism.

The connection between Dante and Camões is a leitmotiv of Portuguese literary criticism of the second half of the century. Teófilo Braga was one of the essayists who most extensively wrote on the subject. The parallel lent itself to the exploration of Braga's adopted ideals (via Schlegel and Humboldt) of national belonging:

> Virgil, Dante and Camões synthesise nationalities, it is almost banal to state it; but through this poetic form, for those who have felt the pulsing of the Roman, Italian and Portuguese Fatherlands in these three beautiful Epics, the philosophical critique of our day identifies sublime affirmations of the Unity of Western Civilization, and the most prodigious work and manifestation of the human species, where Humanity shines through as a consciousness of physical nature, thereby founding, through their solidarity, the definitive moral empire and a new subjective or rational order.[16]

This set of ideas rests on a universal theory of what Braga conceived of as Western civilization, especially as represented by the three poets who had guided humanity towards a renewed historical impetus, namely Virgil, Dante, and Camões. As such, the terms in which Braga conceives the connection between the universal and the national planes pertain to a general and comprehensive ideology that does not lend itself to a reading of the specificities of Dante's work.

Conversely, the terms in which the Viscount of Juromenha conceives the parallels between Luís de Camões and Dante Alighieri are considerably more concrete and precise. The impossibility of identifying the mortal remains of Camões with any clear certainty was deeply wounding and demanded solace. An initial commission, appointed for this purpose in 1836, had been to no avail, and a second, in 1854, had reached barely tolerable conclusions:

> While the Commission was unable to assemble and set apart the mortal remains of our Poet, it managed, nonetheless, given the certainty as to location and to the fact that they had not been disturbed, to collect these remains, although together with those of other compatriots, thus preferring, for the sake of loyalty, to commit a measure of fraud, albeit for the best of reasons. The Poet would not bemoan such company: he finds himself among his dear Portuguese; a further caution, for the faithful who visit his tomb, to remember that, alongside the poet, lie his brothers, for whose souls the Church requests divine intercession; and while

---

16 Teófilo Braga: *Camões e o sentimento nacional*. Porto: Ernesto Chardron 1891, pp. 78–79.

in Florence an empty grave awaits Dante's remains, this one, overfull, does not elicit any less respect for the precious spoils that, together with those of other citizens, are enclosed there.[17]

Dante lends comfort and solace for the sorrows caused by the impossibility of identifying the remains of Camões. The difference between the excess of materiality and the excess of emptiness is stark, indeed. On the one hand, the remains of Camões, in the company of those of his beloved compatriots, united in kinship through their shared belonging to the Portuguese fatherland and through the appeal for prayers from the faithful; on the other hand, Dante, and the absence of any concrete trace of his remains that might redeem the distance that separated him from the Florentine homeland. On this occasion, the emptiness that had separated and continued to separate the poet from his native Florence assuaged the reality of the company in which Camões found himself.

The astute way in which the Viscount of Juromenha solved the conflict between these two excesses was not always shared by other critics. However high the esteem in which Luís de Camões was held, the veneration of Dante in Portugal during the 19th century was such that the Italian bard prevailed, more often than not, in comparisons between the two poets.[18] So much so that the recognition of the preeminence of Camões necessitated support from more distant perspectives. In effect, when Francisco Freire de Carvalho, in his commented edition of *Os Lusíadas*, refers to the Adamastor episode in order to uphold the supremacy of the Portuguese epic in relation to the poet of the *Commedia*, he supports his claim by resorting to the assessment by Alexandre-Marie Sané, the French translator of Filinto Elísio: "Homère, Virgile, le Dante et Milton n'ont rien de plus grandiose, de plus fier, de plus original, et la poésie est divine."[19]

The kinship between Dante Alighieri and Luís de Camões signals a truly extraordinary cultural and anthropological harmony between two nations, which can only exceptionally find a parallel with other processes of relationship between nations. It clearly displays reverberations which, based on the corela-

---

[17] Luís de Camões: *Obras. Precedidas de um ensaio biográfico pelo Visconde de Juromenha*. Lisboa: Imprensa Nacional, vol. 1, 1860, p. 154.

[18] Almeida Garrett expressed his well-known reservations as follows: "So now, then: our Camoens, the creator of the epic and – after Dante – of modern poetry, found himself in a quandary: he mixed his religious beliefs with his poetic creed and committed, *tranchons le mot*, a lapse of taste." [Almeida Garrett: *Travels in My Homeland*. English translation by J. M Parker. London: P. Owen, 1987, p. 45].

[19] A. M. Sané (trad.): Francisco Manuel [do Nascimento]: *Poésie lyrique portugaise, ou choix des odes de Francisco Manuel*. traduites en français, avec le texte en regard. Paris: Cérioux 1808, p. 291; Francisco Freire de Carvalho (ed.): Luís de Camões: *Os Lusíadas*. Lisboa: Rollandiana 1843, p. 322.

tion between the eccentric and the polycentric, are sustained through the powerful and constant dynamics that, over time, shaped the relationship between Portugal and Italy.[20]

The incisiveness and breadth of the iconology that equally surrounded the poets, and its attendant excesses, led to the creation of gaps that have remained irreparably vacant. The referral to Dante as the poet of the *Commedia*, when not merely of the *Inferno*, or even of one or two of its episodes, consigned to oblivion essential aspects of his work, which critics from all over Europe had in the meantime been devotedly scrutinizing. What prevailed, in the end, was the generic and reductive image of the aggrieved artist, the herald of the fatherland, the intrepid hero, or the universal poet. Dante's ethereal tonalities evanesced with a degree of volatility that is still felt today.

This can be witnessed, in our time, by any traveller who, perhaps wielding the app containing the ticket for a journey in the northern rail line, travels through Coimbra or descends at the station. Equally fluid and discreet, a Dantean eye watches over this earthly landscape. It belongs to the sculpted figure that towers over the hill of Conchada and the cemetery at its summit – Beatrice.

Suspended on a ridge over a steep gorge, the Cemetery of Conchada faces the west, towards the woods of Choupal and the Mondego river.[21] The statue of Beatrice crowns the apex of what is commonly referred to as the mausoleum of the Condes do Ameal [Counts of Ameal]. It was commissioned by João Maria Correia Aires de Campos (Coimbra, 1847–1920), the 1st Count of Ameal, in 1901, to house the remains of his father, João Correia Aires de Campos (Lisbon, 1818-Coimbra,

---

[20] Rita Marnoto: Relações culturais Portugal Itália: excentralidade, policentralidade. In Monica Lupetti et al. (eds.): *Giochi di specchi. Modelli, tradizioni, contaminazioni e dinamiche interculturali nei e tra i paesi di lingua portoghese*. Pisa: ETS 2016, pp. 15–31.

[21] Its placement outside the city gates and in a steep location was a response to the hygienic programme by physician Augusto Costa Simões, who designed an orthogonal layout, subsequently replaced by the irregular polyhedron devised by mathematician Venâncio Rodrigues, in emulation of the Cemetery of Prazeres, in Lisbon. Following the 1835 decree for the creation of public cemeteries, the Cemetery of Conchada officially opened in 1860. For historical and architectural information, see Elisa Rosendo de Carvalho e Silva: *Evolução identitária de um lugar: A Conchada de Coimbra*. Dissertação de Mestrado Integrado em Arquitectura apresentada ao Departamento de Arquitectura da FCTUC 2012, pp. 47–81; Marta Alexandra Soares Espírito Santo: *O espaço cemiterial moderno. Um estudo comparativo entre Abney Park e Conchada*. Dissertação de Mestrado Integrado em Arquitectura apresentada ao Departamento de Arquitectura da FCTUC, 2020, pp. 105–120.

1885). The purchase of the plot and an initial project date back to 1895, although the corresponding works were interrupted and resumed in 1902.[22]

The mausoleum holds a privileged position. Entirely surrounded by pathways that define the cemetery's road network, it occupies an undivided plot, located at the intersection of the cemetery's main thoroughfares. Its neo-historicist style mirrors the taste of the age, with a profusion of spires, arches, buttresses, gargoyles, and other Gothic motifs. The polyhedral structure is topped by a steeple, over which rises the statue of Beatrice. Carved from the region's limestone, the statue holds a book in which are engraved the Roman numerals from I to X.[23]

The placement of neo-Gothic centrepieces in dominant positions within cemeteries was a common occurrence in the 19th century, particularly in Britain.[24] It was the area customarily reserved for the church building. In the Cemetery of Conchada, instead, the centrality of the church is replaced by the mausoleum with the spire of Beatrice, which towers above its crest.

João Correia Aires de Campos, father of the Count of Ameal, was a politician and a representative for Coimbra in Parliament. He distinguished himself as an archaeologist, art collector and bibliophile. A visionary and an intellectual, he founded the Portuguese Institute of Archaeology, the precursor to the Machado de Castro Museum, edited several Portuguese medieval manuscripts and pub-

---

[22] The purchase of the plot was recorded in a City Council session on 16 May 1895: "We hereby approve a proposal to cede, for a total of one thousand réis, with regret that it could not be done free of charge, the land necessary to place the vault of João Correia Aires de Campos, in recognition of the services he rendered to the municipality." Then, on 26 June, 1902: "The councillor in charge of the cemetery shall meet with the Count of Ameal regarding the construction of a vault begun many years ago and whose works were interrupted." Information available in José Pinto Loureiro: *Anais do município de Coimbra 1890–1903*. Coimbra: Biblioteca Municipal 1939, p. 108, no. 163; p. 246, no. 246. The research conducted at the city's Historical Office, the archive at the Cemetery of Conchada and the Health and Environment Department at Coimbra City Hall bore no fruits regarding this construction project. It was only possible to identify Beatrice due to Clara Moura Soares: A coleção de arte do Conde do Ameal: o leilão de 1921 e as aquisições do estado português para os museus nacionais. In Denise Corrêa, Daverson Guimarães (eds.): *Histórias da arte em coleções: Modos de ver e exibir em Brasil e Portugal*. Rio de Janeiro: Rio Books 2016, a study that includes extremely useful information on João Maria Correia Aires de Campos, the Count's father, as well as the family and the art collection in question.

[23] Readable only through magnification, given its height, and one cannot exclude the possibility that a simple generic effect was intended. These echo, however, the biblical and patristic symbology associated with the *Commedia* and modelled by the *incipit* of the *Vita nova*: "In quella parte del libro della mia memoria dinanzi alla quale poco si potrebbe leggere, si trova una rubrica la quale dice *Incipit Vita Nova*.", etc. See Rita Marnoto: *A Vita nova de Dante Alighieri*, pp. 91–101. The initial "I" is shared by "In quella parte", *Incipit Vita Nova* and the Roman numeral I.

[24] This is the case, for example, of Abney Park Cemetery; see Marta Alexandra Soares Espírito Santo: *O espaço cemeterial moderno*.

lished several works of research. His son, João Maria Correia Aires de Campos, who was equally a Law graduate from the University of Coimbra, followed in his footsteps. In politics, he led the Coimbra Regenerator Party ('Partido Regenerador de Coimbra') and held several government positions, as well as serving as mayor for the city of Coimbra. He was a member of the Geographical Society and was awarded several titles of cultural merit. In addition, he expanded the family's already remarkable art collection, which was, at the time, one of the most discerning privately owned collections in Portugal.

This was housed at the Palace of Colégio de São Tomás, located in Rua da Sofia. The palace was designed by architect Diogo de Castilho and was acquired by Aires de Campos in 1892. It was refurbished three years later, under the direction of Augusto de Carvalho da Silva Pinto (Lisbon, 1865–1938), who endowed it with his neo-historicist inclinations. Silva Pinto was also the author of the project for the Mausoleum of Conchada, whose statuary is authored by António Augusto da Costa Mota, tio [the uncle] (Coimbra, 1862-Lisbon, 1930).

For Costa Mota, tio, already a renowned sculptor at the time, the author of the commission for the mausoleum would have been a very special patron.[25] Among the various areas in which Aires de Campos followed in his father's footsteps was social work, since both men were directors of Coimbra's Asilo de Mendicidade [Poorhouse]. The son of a carpenter, Costa Mota, tio, was an impoverished youth who took all available opportunities to study the arts, such as the lessons offered at the Artists' Association to the children of craftsmen, and the António Augusto Gonçalves Escola Livre de Desenho [Free School for the Pictorial Arts]. Aires de Campos was quick to recognise Costa Mota, tio's potential, and in 1883 sponsored his studies at the Academy of Fine Arts in Lisbon.

After the death of the Count of Ameal, his collection was sold at public auction, resulting in the production of several sale catalogues. The *Catalogue for the noteworthy and exquisite book collection owned by illustrious bibliophile Count of Ameal, of Coimbra (João Correia de Campos)* includes three items relating to Dante:

> 764 – *Dante Alighieri* – Opere di Dante Alighieri, Con varie Annotazioni (di Pomp. Venturi e di Giov. Ant. Volpi), e copiosi Rami adornata. Dedicata alla sagra imperial maestà di Elisabetta Petrona [Petrowna] Imperatrice di tutte le Russie ec. ec. ec., dal conte Don Cristoforo Zapata de Cisneros. *In Venezia, MDCCLVII. Presso Antonio Zatta*. . . In-4.° gr., 4 Tomos em 5 vols. de XIV-CCCCIV; CCCCXIII; CCCCLII-IV-103-I; xii-408, e IV-264-LXXIV-II págs. [. . .]

---

25 For information on the biography and artistic career of Costa Mota, tio, see Elsa Belo: António Augusto da Costa Mota tio. In *Arte e Teoria* 4 (2003), pp. 151–164.

765 – La || divina comedia [commedia] || di || Dante Allighieri [Alighieri] || illustrata || – || dedicata al municipio di Firenze || Inferno (e Purg.) || *Le illustrazioni furono disegnate dal Professor Cav.* || Francesco Scaramuzza || *Ditectore* [Direttore] *della R. Academia* [Accademia] *di Parma* || *e fotografate da* Carlo Saccani || – || Parma || Carlo Saccani Fotografo Editore || 1878. – In-4.º gr. ou fól. peq. de frontispício (ornado) e 72 belas fotografias assentes sôbre igual núm. de ff. de cartão branco. E. [. . .]

766 – La Divine Comédie traduite en français et annoté [annotée] par Artaud de Montor. Nouvelle édition, précédée d'une Préface par M. Louis Moland. Illustrations de Yan,['] Dargent. Paris: Garnier. Frères Libraires-Éditeurs. . . 1879. (*Typ. Charles Unsinger*). In-8.º gr. de IV-xij-XXIII-592 págs. E. [. . .][26]

In Italian, the Count of Ameal owned not only the *Commedia*, but an edition of Dante's complete works, printed in Venice in 1757. He additionally possessed a French translation. A common feature of the volumes in this collection is the fact that they contain illustrations by some of the most famous engravers of Dante's work. Of particular note is the work by the Parma painter Francesco Scaramuzza, considered a masterpiece of Italian engraving.[27]

This Dantean bibliographical collection reflects not only the Count of Ameal's admiration for Dante, but also the refined means through which this was cultivated, clearly privileging the intersection between literature and the fine arts. One can only imagine the artists who would have gathered around these engravings, in the drawing rooms at the Palace of the Colégio de São Tomás, among them Aires de Campos, the architect Silva Pinto and the sculptor Costa Mota, tio, the Count's protegé.

In effect, Costa Mota, tio, was the author of a prolific body of work in addition to the little-known statue of Beatrice which towers over the crest at Conchada. He also sculpted, in 1908, the statue of Pinheiro Chagas, located in Avenida da Liberdade in Lisbon – the very same Pinheiro Chagas who was so enthralled by Dante as to cause the indignation of Antero de Quental. Previously, in 1894, Costa Mota, tio, had also carved two of his greatest masterpieces, namely the funerary monuments to Luís de Camões and Vasco da Gama, housed at the Jerónimos Monastery.

The same hand that sculpted the vault holding the remains that, as the Viscount of Juromenha stated, placed Camões in the fellowship of his beloved Por-

---

[26] José dos Santos: *Catálogo da notável e preciosa livraria que foi do ilustre bibliófilo conimbricense Conde do Ameal (João Correia Aires de Campos)*. Intr. Gustavo de Matos Sequeira. Porto: [Tipografia da Sociedade de Papelaria] 1924, pp. 186–197. I consulted the copy belonging to the collection of the Viscount of Trindade at the Biblioteca Geral, University of Coimbra, on whose margins were noted the values of some of these books. Next to item 765, with engravings by Scaramuzza, the astronomical figure of 751$00 (751 escudos) was noted.
[27] On the occasion of the Dantean celebrations of 2021, Scaramuzza's engravings were the subject of a series of exhibitions.

tuguese brothers, seeking the intercession of the Church, equally fixed the form of an ethereal Beatrice, almost imperceptible from the heights of its supreme distance, watching over all those who have travelled and who continue to travel through the landscape. Between excess of materiality and evanescence into the distance, an ethereal gaze continues to watch over the memory of Dante Alighieri in Portugal.

Bibliographical References

Belo, Elsa: António Augusto da Costa Mota, Tio. In *Arte e Teoria* 4 (2003), pp. 151–164.
Braga, Teófilo: *Camões e o sentimento nacional*. Porto: Ernesto Chardron 1891.
Carvalho, Francisco Freire de (ed.): Luís de Camões: *Os Lusíadas*. Lisboa: Rollandiana 1843.
Carvalho, Paulo, Archer de: Risorgimento, insorgimento, Antero (ingressos à felicitação a Umberto de Itália). In *Estudos Italianos em Portugal*, n. s., 6 (2011), pp. 153–175.
Catroga, Fernando: Ritualizações da história. In *Histórias da história de Portugal. Séculos xix – xx*. Lisboa: Círculo de Leitores 1996, pp. 551–562.
Chagas, Manuel Pinheiro: *Da origem e caracter do movimento litterario da Renascença principalmente na Itália: Memoria para o concurso à terceira cadeira do Curso Superior de Letras*. Lisboa: Imprensa de Joaquim Germano de Sousa Neves 1867.
Espírito Santo, Marta Alexandra Soares: *O espaço cemiterial moderno. Um estudo comparativo entre Abney Park e Conchada*. Dissertação de Mestrado Integrado em Arquitectura apresentada ao Departamento de Arquitectura da FCTUC, 2020.
Ferreira, António Mega: *O essencial sobre Dante Alighieri*. Lisboa: Imprensa Nacional-Casa da Moeda 2017.
Garrett, João Baptista Leitão de Almeida: *Travels in My Homeland*. Translated by J. M Parker. London: P. Owen 1987.
Garrett, João Baptista Leitão de Almeida, *Viagens na minha terra*. Ofélia Paiva Monteiro (ed.). Lisboa: Imprensa Nacional-Casa da Moeda 2010.
Luís de Camões: *Obras. Precedidas de um ensaio biográfico pelo Visconde de Juromenha*. Lisboa: Imprensa Nacional, vol. 1, 1860.
Loureiro, José Pinto (ed.): *Anais do município de Coimbra 1890–1903*. Coimbra: Biblioteca Municipal 1939.
Manuppella, Giacinto: *Dantesca Luso-Brasileira. Subsídios para uma Bibliografia da Obra e do Pensamento de Dante Alighieri*. Coimbra: Por Ordem da Universidade 1966.
Manuppella, Giacinto: Uma anónima versão quinhentista dos *Triunfos* de Petrarca e o seu Comentário. No VI centenário da morte do poeta (1374–1974). In *Revista da Universidade de Coimbra*, 25 (1974), pp. 1–324.
Marnoto, Rita: *A Vita nova de Dante Alighieri. Deus, o amor e a palavra*. Lisboa: Colibri 2001.
Marnoto, Rita (ed.): Unificação da Itália. 1861–2011, *Estudos Italianos em Portugal*, n. s., 6 (2011).
Marnoto, Rita: Relações culturais Portugal Itália: excentralidade, policentralidade. In Monica Lupetti et al. (eds.): *Giochi di specchi. Modelli, tradizioni, contaminazioni e dinamiche interculturali nei e tra i paesi di lingua portoghese*. Pisa: ETS 2016, pp. 15–31.

Quental, Antero de: *Prosas*. Lisboa: Couto Martins 1923–1931, 3 vols.
Quondam, Amedeo: *Petrarca, l'italiano dimenticato*. Milano: Rizzoli 2004.
Ragusa, Andrea: *Como exilados distantes do céu. Antero de Quental e Giacomo Leopardi*. Vila do Conde: Arranha Céus 2019.
Sané, Antoine Marie (trad.): Francisco Manuel [do Nascimento]: *Poésie lyrique portugaise, ou choix des odes de Francisco Manuel*. Traduites en français, avec le texte en regard. Paris: Cérioux 1808.
Santos, José dos: *Catálogo da notável e preciosa livraria que foi do ilustre bibliófilo conimbricense Conde do Ameal (João Correia Aires de Campos)*. Intr. Gustavo de Matos Sequeira. Porto: [Tipografia da Sociedade de Papelaria] 1924.
Silva, Elisa Rosendo de Carvalho e: *Evolução identitária de um lugar: A Conchada de Coimbra*. Dissertação de Mestrado Integrado em Arquitectura apresentada ao Departamento de Arquitectura da FCTUC 2012.
Soares, Clara Moura: A coleção de arte do Conde do Ameal: o leilão de 1921 e as aquisições do estado português para os museus nacionais. In Denise Corrêa, Daverson Guimarães (eds.): *Histórias da arte em coleções: Modos de ver e exibir em Brasil e Portugal*. Rio de Janeiro: Rio Books 2016, pp. 89–105.

Figure

Figure 1: Mausoleum of the Counts of Ameal. Cemetery of Conchada, Coimbra. Photograph by Rita Marnoto.

Jorge Vaz de Carvalho
Dante: Poetry and Translation

In the first Book of the *Convivio* (VII, xiv), Dante states that "nothing harmonised according to the rules of poetry can be translated from its native tongue into another without destroying all its sweetness and harmony." Translating the art of the Muses is, for Dante, a transgression that inevitably ruins the poetic qualities of the original. The sacrilege I have committed in translating the *Divine Comedy* is therefore an unrepentant defiance of Dante's axiom. That Dante himself failed to adhere to his words should be reason enough. Dante, who often cites, in his *Comedy*, religious hymns or scholastic terms in Latin, did nonetheless transpose into his Italian *terza rima* Virgil's dactylic hexameter from the *Eclogues* (IV, 5–7) which had, since the early Christians, been interpreted as a prophecy of the advent of the Messiah:

> magnus ab integro saeclorum nascitur ordo
> iam redit et Virgo, redeunt Saturnia regna;
> iam noua progenies caelo demittitur alto.[1]

In Canto XXII of the *Purgatorio* (70–72):

> Secol si rinova;
> torna giustizia e primo tempo umano,
> e progenïe scende dal ciel nova.[2]

Frederico Lourenço, in the "Preface" to his translation of the *Eclogues*, states that these verses are among "the most untranslatable of all poetic texts," adding that the "haunting beauty of Virgilian verse (which, in Latin, produces music comparable to Mozart's) completely evaporates in a different language."[3] And yet, like Dante, he translates. And why shouldn't Dante's translator do as Dante, regardless of his precept?

---

[1] "Now the last age by Cumae's Sibyl sung / Has come and gone, and the majestic roll / Of circling centuries begins anew" (Virgil: *Eclogues and Georgics*. Transl. by James Rhoades. Mineola. NY: Dover Publications 2005, p. 11).
[2] My translation into Portuguese: 'O século renova; / tornam justiça e o tempo humano são / e progénie do céu já desce nova.' (Dante Alighieri: *Divina Comédia*. Trad. Jorge Vaz de Carvalho. Lisboa: Imprensa Nacional 2021, p. 537).
[3] Virgílio: *Bucólicas*. Trad. Frederico Lourenço. Lisboa: Quetzal 2021, p. 11.

Note: Translated from the Portuguese by Cassilda Alcobia-Murphy.

https://doi.org/10.1515/9783110796049-013

In his epistle to Can Grande della Scala, Dante elucidates the purpose of the *Comedy*: "the end of the whole as well as of the part is to remove those living here from a state of misery and to guide them to a state of bliss" (XV, 39). Now, by translating his lived experience into poetry, in a journey along the three conditions of Christian eternity, with the mission of revealing, or better yet, of reminding conflicting humanity of the path to redemption, Dante would surely not have wished to be read by the speakers of his language alone, thereby excluding from this ecumenical message all those who did not command it. By discarding Latin, which was not only the lingua franca of the age, but the link that connected European cultural identity, and in doing so precisely because the poem was not intended simply for a handful of scholars, but for the universe of all those who lacked a moral pedagogy, Dante was of a mind with painters such as his friend, Giotto di Bondone, who transposed into the images of church frescoes what the majority was unable to read in the Latin of sacred texts. Two centuries later, Martin Luther did the same, by translating the Bible into the German vernacular. However, by writing in his *vernacular* tongue, the poet limited the linguistic understanding of the *Comedy* to the populations of the Italian peninsula. Therefore, to fully accomplish the divine mission in service of the well-being and salvation of all mankind, Dante would have to agree that his poem cannot dispense with translators.

The intention of the present translator is not, it should be noted, to contribute to the redemption of Portuguese souls. My ambition was, however, to render intelligible to those receptive minds who speak the language of my homeland one of the most brilliant creations of the human spirit. To this end, I chiefly followed the principles I set out in the "Introduction" to my translation of the *Vita Nuova*:[4] once the work had been studied to the point of extreme familiarity, I endeavoured to understand Dante's personal mode of expression within his historical-cultural space-time, with the intention of allowing the author's poetic diction to shine through by reproducing the text that I believe he would have written had he employed the Portuguese language. There is no originality in this: Jorge de Sena stated as much in his "Introduction" to *80 Poemas de Emily Dickinson*: "To translate is not to create our own poetry using the poetry of others, but to create, with our language, what Emily Dickinson would have said and done had she attempted an identical poem in Portuguese."[5]

One hundred years after Dante, his biographer, Leonardo Bruni (1374–1444), produced the most clear-sighted text on translation of the European Renais-

---

4 Cf. Dante Alighieri: *Vida Nova*. Tradução e introdução de Jorge Vaz de Carvalho. Lisboa: Relógio d'Água 2010, pp. 13–16.
5 Jorge de Sena (trad.): *80 poemas de Emily Dickinson*. Lisboa: Guimarães 2010, p. 29.

sance, *De interpretatione recta*. To avoid inept, inelegant and damaging translations, this notable humanist called for a profound, experienced and judicious mastery of the language of origin, as well as full proficiency in the language into which one translates; he prescribed a good understanding of style, and the preservation of both signification and ornamentation which, according to Bruni, lent brilliance to words and thoughts, so that the original style may be emulated in "mind, spirit and will"; additionally, knowledge of the culture and of the writer's preferences was essential; as was a good ear, so as not to distort the rhythm and the harmony of speech (the very same poetic musicality that Dante believes to be unattainable).

In addition to Bruni's precepts, and at the risk of self-quotation, I should repeat that aesthetic criteria do not preclude ethical criteria, and that the translator must honour a *triple pact of fidelity*: to the author, to the reader, and to his own language.

The author and his creative act, I cannot stress this enough, are absolutely sacred to me. The original truth and personality of a text and its creator are unbetrayable. Translation is not a mercenary and predatory adventure, where one appropriates another's creation in order to make it one's own. Any pretence on the part of the translator of using a masterpiece such as the *Comedy* as a steppingstone to appropriate the inventiveness of a genius of Dante's stature would be altogether laughable, as no rewriting could ever live up to the original. The good translator is one who blends into the background of the linguistic exchange in order to carry across the *authority* which, as Dante writes in the *Convivio* (IV, 6, iii), "is nothing but 'the pronouncement of an author.'" In Dante's case, linguistic authority derives precisely from a moral authority since, against the backdrop of a daunting crisis of Christianity, the vacancy of the Emperor's throne and the usurpation of Peter's throne; that is, in the absence of figures of political and religious authority that might direct the temporal and the spiritual,[6] the poet was compelled to become, as I noted in the "Preface" to my own translation, "a divine messenger, while the writing of the *Comedy*, and the truth it bears, take on the apostolic value of a new Revelation and a new Testament."[7]

From the respect and fidelity accorded to the original creation ensues the respect and fidelity towards the reader. I have stated elsewhere that I consider the noble role of the translator to be akin to that of the musical performer. While the composer and the listeners rely on the musician and his skill to hear the score, so do the literary

---

[6] Dante Alighieri: *Divina Comédia*, Purgatorio XVI, 106–108: "Rome, which made the world good, used to have / two suns; and they made visible two paths— / the world's path and the pathway that is God's".

[7] Cf. Prefácio. In Dante Alighieri: *Divina Comédia*. Lisboa: Imprensa Nacional 2021, p. 14.

author and the readers who do not know the original language depend on the translator to access what was truly written. The role of the performer is essential, but a pianist does not have the right to add musical notes not written by the composer, or to eschew style, by performing, for example, a baroque piece in the romantic mode: the listener would obviously feel defrauded. Much like the music performer, the translator cannot help but lend the text his own personality, but does so in the knowledge that he is not the creator (as the pianist or the vocalist are not the composer) and that his honourable mission is one of *medium* between the work he is bound to serve and the recipients, who have placed their trust in the translator and who have the right to the meticulousness of a text that follows the intentions and effects of the original. Which in the case of Dante's *Comedy* is, in and of itself, the highest of privileges. The translator's creativity is measured in the strictest faithfulness.

The translator also owes fidelity to the native language, to the extent that his expressiveness must be worthy of the original language, in the richness of the invention and suggestive energy of the verses, and in the thematic, imagic and linguistic coinages, which are prodigiously innovative in the *Comedy*. It is not simply a matter of finding the most apt lexical, syntactic, prosodic and rhythmic equivalents, rhetorical processes, and figures of speech, but also of examining what Umberto Eco has called the *intention* of the text, namely what it "states or suggests in relation to the language in which it is expressed and the cultural context in which it was created."[8] This is what I call the *text's identitarian specificity*. One must acknowledge "the cultural, intellectual, sentimental and emotional matter that goes into an extraordinary vision of human beings, in the immanence of their diminutive and ephemeral earthly actions, when compared with the transcendental immensity of eternity."[9] One must render the precise terms in which Dante rewrote biblical, mystical, philosophical and literary texts of eminent authority, and transpose with absolute rigour the words and expressions from scholastic theology, Aristotelian-Thomistic philosophy, technology and science (Astronomy, Physics, Optics, Geometry, Medical Physiology, etc.). Translation is an embrace of identities.

To achieve the best approximation of European Portuguese to the vernacular which Dante raised to the level of literary dignity worthy of a cultured Italian language, the first task is, of course, the repeated, careful, and thoughtful reading of the work. In the case of the *Comedy*, since we have not been handed down a sole manuscript of Dante's, nor his signature, it is necessary to study and contrast

---

[8] Cf. Umberto Eco: *Dizer Quase a Mesma Coisa: Sobre a Tradução*. Trad. Port. Lisboa: Difel 2005, p. 14.
[9] Cf. Prefácio. In Dante Alighieri: *Divina Comédia*. Lisboa: Imprensa Nacional 2021, p. 24.

several editions from the most erudite among his curators and to settle, with the help of commentators and scholars, on the text to be translated (and more so, given that this is a bilingual edition). I studied the versions set down by Giorgio Petrocchi, Natalino Sapegno, Giuseppe Vandelli, Umberto Bosco and Giovanni Reggio, Anna Maria Chiavacci Leonardi, and Giorgio Inglese.

I necessarily retained, in the translation, the formal structure of Dante's *terza rima* to lend rhythmic unity and cohesion to the poem and, likewise, the rhyme scheme and metric of the Portuguese decasyllable, which corresponds to the Italian hendecasyllable. I observed and respected a further essential element of the *Comedy*, namely its stylistic plurality, in the poetic ascent from the first to the third *cantica*, and similarly within each of the *cantiche*, coherently suiting the speech to different themes, situations and characters, so that "my tale would not differ from the fact" (*Inferno* XXXII, 12).

I offer an example of exceptional luminosity and delicacy in the *Inferno* (II, 55–72). Virgil explains that a lady, Beatrice, moved by the power of love (divine compassion), had descended from heaven to entrust him with the mission of aiding Dante and leading him to salvation. These verses are reminiscent of the *dolce stil novo* (in Dante's famous description in *Purgatorio*, XXIV, 57) and of the poetry of the youthful *Vida Nuova*:

> Lucevan li occhi suoi più che la stella;
> e cominciommi a dir soave e piana,
> con angelica voce, in sua favella:
>
> 'O anima cortese mantoana,
> di cui la fama ancor nel mondo dura,
> e durerà quanto 'l mondo lontana,
>
> l'amico mio, e non de la ventura,
> ne la diserta piaggia è impedito
> sì nel cammin, che vòlt' è per paura;
>
> e temo che non sia già sì smarrito,
> ch'io mi sia tardi al soccorso levata,
> per quel ch'i' ho di lui nel cielo udito.
>
> Or movi, e con la tua parola ornata
> e con ciò c' ha mestieri al suo campare,
> l'aiuta sì ch'i' ne sia consolata.
>
> I' son Beatrice che ti faccio andare;
> vegno del loco ove tornar disio;
> amor mi mosse, che mi fa parlare.

In the Portuguese translation:

> Luziam os seus olhos mais que a estrela;
> começou-me a dizer, suave e lhana,
> com voz angélica, em sua loquela:
>
> 'Ó alma tão cortês e mantuana,
> de quem no mundo a fama ainda dura,
> e durará quanto ele se alontana,
>
> o amigo meu, e o não é da ventura,
> tão na deserta praia é impedido
> no andar, que atrás voltou pela tremura;
>
> e temo que já esteja tão perdido,
> que ao seu socorro tarde eu vá levada,
> p'lo que no céu eu dele tenho ouvido.
>
> Vai, pois, e co' a palavra tua ornada
> e com o que é mister p'ra se salvar,
> o ajuda, tal que eu seja consolada.
>
> Eu sou Beatriz, a que te faço andar;
> vim do lugar onde tornar desejo;
> amor moveu-me, que me faz falar.

The translation sought the greatest possible approximation in terms of lexical choice, so as not to lose the precision and relevance of the original, as well as the sounds and the rhythm of the verses, in their musical sweetness.

A different tone can be read in the strong language used by St. Peter in his harsh invective against Boniface VIII, the pope who, in 1300, unworthily occupied Peter's throne, to such an extent as to assuage Satan's perverse desires (*Paradiso*, XXVII, 22–27):

> Quelli ch'usurpa in terra il luogo mio,
> il luogo mio, il luogo mio che vaca
> ne la presenza del Figluol di Dio,
>
> fat' ha del cimitero mio cloaca
> del sangue e de la puzza; onde 'l perverso
> che cadde di qua sù, là giù si placa.

Translated thus into Portuguese:

> O que na terra usurpa o lugar meu,
> o lugar meu, o lugar meu que vaca
> ante o Filho de Deus por seu labéu,

fez lá do cemitério meu cloaca
do sangue e do fedor; donde o perverso
daqui caído em baixo lá se aplaca.

The main translational concerns were to preserve the greatest possible lexical proximity, to transpose the anaphoric repetition, remarkable in its emotional effect, and to add, by necessity of rhyme, the expression "por seu labéu" ['to his discredit'], which is perfectly in keeping with the meaning of the verse.

The greatest difficulty in translating the *Comedy* does not lie in the knowledge and transposition of Dante's lexicon. T. S. Eliot, in his essay "Dante"(1929), deemed that Dante's poetry was "in one sense, extremely easy to read," not because he wrote plain content in a plain manner, but because he was "the most *universal* of poets in the modern languages," since he dealt with what is universally human and did so in an Italian vernacular that was still close to a Latin unaffected by the separation of the various national languages, and common to an entire European culture that still reasoned collectively. While this is not the venue to address Eliot's debatable arguments, I must agree that "[t]he style of Dante has a peculiar lucidity – a *poetic* as distinguished from an *intellectual* lucidity. The thought may be obscure, but the word is lucid, or rather translucent."[10] And a powerful reason behind the intelligibility of Dantean poetry, as signalled by Eliot, is the use of the allegorical method which, unlike the rhetoric of obscuring figures like metaphor or metonymy, is a process of elucidation, through *clear visual images*, which allow the reader to see what the poet claims to have seen. Another of Dante's dominant figures is simile, with its appeal to the reader's lived experience, all in service of a clear understanding of the universal message that the poet is tasked with transmitting.

For example, in the last canto of *Paradiso* (58–66), Dante emphasises the inadequacy of human words to express what he has seen, and compares himself to someone who, waking from a dream, retains an imprint of the experienced feeling, while the image has already faded in the mind:

Qual è colüi che sognando vede,
che dopo 'l sogno la passione impressa
rimane, e l'altro a la mente non riede,

cotal son io, ché quasi tutta cessa
mia visïone, e ancor mi distilla
nel core il dolce che nacque da essa.

Così la neve al sol si disigilla;
così al vento ne le foglie levi
si perdea la sentenza di Sibilla.

---

10 Cf. Thomas S. Eliot: Dante (1929). In *Essays*. London: Faber and Faber 1934, pp. 234–277.

In the Portuguese translation:

> Como esse ao qual sonhando ver sucede,
> e após o sonho a paixão impressa
> resta, e nada mais à mente acede,
>
> assim sou eu, que quase toda cessa
> minha visão, e ainda me destila
> no coração dulçor nascido dessa.
>
> Assim a neve ao sol se dessigila;
> e ao vento em folhas leves já perdida
> assim era a sentença de Sibila.

The lexicon, in its wide-ranging diversity and ability to express all human and divine realities, is not, I repeat, the translator's greatest difficulty. Simple, sonorous, and lucid in its eloquence, it must be studied and interpreted until the correct correspondences are found, through "the long study and ... intense love" (*Inferno*, I, 83) that Dante the disciple declares he has dedicated to the master and author, Virgil. There are words, sentences and passages whose interpretation may be controversial or obscure, allegorical meanings which would have been obvious to Dante's contemporaries but which are no longer so to us. Nonetheless, for example, the still debated identity of the providential figure of the Greyhound (*veltro*), which, it is prophesied, will be sent by God to restore order and harmony in the world (*Inferno* I, 101), constitutes an exegetical, rather than a translational, problem.

Most important of all is that the translator does not resort to processes extraneous to Dantean aesthetics. Since they are typical of Dante's discourse, I did not shy away from employing archaisms ("cor" for *coração* [heart], "bosco" for *bosque* [woods or forest], "foco" for *fogo* [fire], "loco" and "logo" for *lugar* [place], "mençonha" for *mentira* [lie, falsehood], and "aspeito" for *aspecto* [aspect]) and Latinisms ("despecto" for *despeito* [spite], "audace" for *audaz* [audacious])[11] which were present in medieval Portuguese, as attested to by glossaries and dictionaries. For the same reason, I translated literally the neologisms coined by Dante ("dislaga,"[12] in the sense of emerging from the waters; the verb "trasumanar,"[13]

---

[11] Archaic Portuguese words used in the Portuguese translation have been signaled in inverted commas, with the modern Portuguese correspondence in italics (T / n).
[12] Dante Alighieri: *Divina Comédia, Purgatorio* III, 15: "que para o céu mais alto se deslaga". (In the source text: "che 'nverso 'l ciel più alto si dislaga.")
[13] *Paradiso* I, 70–71: "Transumanar *per verba* não observa / significado". (In the source text: "Trasumanar significar per verba / non si poria.")

in the sense of overcoming human nature; "intuassi" and "inmii,"[14] meaning to "enter you, as you enter in me" "s'insempra," in the sense of becoming perpetual[15]; "s'indraca,"[16] to become a dragon; "inmilla,"[17] to exceed the thousands).

Most difficult of all, in this translation, is to achieve the exact rhyme-word, which is crucial, since the tension in the verses converges towards it, both in the phonic and the semantic aspects. The greatest care was taken to avoid forced rhymes or rhymes obtained at any cost, by corrupting or abandoning meaning. Equally, care was taken not to alter verbal tenses, distort verses or introduce spurious words, or to overuse the same rhyme within the same canto. The question is one, therefore, as defended by Leonardo Bruni, of a profound understanding of ways of saying and of figures of diction, and of a refusal to resort (due to haste or indolence, lack of research or of application) to processes extraneous to those practised by Dante.

I sought to share a table with Dante, as if partaking in a conversation between faithful friends who exchange experiences of beauty. I would have liked to persuade him that he is not entirely right in his pronouncement regarding translation, by embracing his poetry, in its wealth of virtues and values, and in order to lend further dignity to the Portuguese language. As a translator, within my humble means (and never will the adjective "humble" be more apt than in the face of this poem), I believe that I have done my utmost to be spared the frozen destiny of the innermost of all infernal circles, that of the "melancholy hole" of traitors. I know that I have proffered, in service to this mission, my most loving fidelity.

Bibliographical References

Dante Alighieri: *Vida Nova*. Tradução portuguesa e introdução de Jorge Vaz de Carvalho. Lisboa: Relógio d'Água 2010.
Dante Alighieri: *Divina Comédia*. Tradução portuguesa e prefácio de Jorge Vaz de Carvalho. Lisboa: Imprensa Nacional 2021.

---

14 *Paradiso* IX, 81: "se eu me intuasse, como tu te inmias". (In the source text: "s'io m'intuassi, come tu t'inmii")
15 *Paradiso* X, 148: "salvo onde se ensempra a alegria". (In the source text: "se non colà dove gioir s'insempra.")
16 *Paradiso*. XVI, 115: "A arrogante estirpe que se endraga". (In the source text: "L'oltracotata schiatta che s'indraca".)
17 *Paradiso*. XXVIII, 93: "mais que em xadrez o duplicar se inmila". (In the source text: "più che 'l doppiar de li scacchi s'inmilla.")

Eco, Umberto: *Dizer Quase a Mesma Coisa: Sobre a Tradução*. Trad. Port. Lisboa: Difel 2005.
Eliot, T. S.: Dante (1929). In *Essays*. London: Faber and Faber 1934, pp. 234–277.
Sena, Jorge de (trad.): *80 poemas de Emily Dickinson*. Lisboa: Guimarães 2010.
Virgil (Publius Vergilius Maro): *Eclogues and Georgics*. Transl. by James Rhoades. Mineola, NY: Dover Publications 2005.
[Virgil] Virgílio: *Bucólicas*. Portuguese translation by Frederico Lourenço. Lisboa: Quetzal 2021.

Epilogue

Alberto Manguel
Dante the Geographer

> *O God! I could be bounded in a nutshell,*
> *and count myself a king of infinite space...*
> Hamlet, II:2

Spaces don't exist: we create them. The universe is blind to its own measures, its dimensions, its speed and duration, and like Pascal's definition of the godhead (which medieval philosophers had long before invented), the universe is a circle whose centre is everywhere and whose circumference is nowhere. We, however, carry our centre within us and from our dusty corner call out to the world and say: "You orbit around me." Home patch, township, province, fatherland, continent, hemisphere are our necessary inventions, like the unicorn and the basilisk. Within this invented perimeter, we draw squares and circles, and trace paths from one place to another in order to have the illusion of being somewhere and someone. Northrop Frye tells the story of a doctor friend who, travelling on the Arctic tundra with an Inuit guide, was caught in a blizzard. In the icy dark, outside the boundaries he knew, the doctor cried out: "We are lost!" His Inuit guide looked at him thoughtfully and answered: "We are not lost. We are here."

Up to the discoveries of Copernicus, we had dreamed up a universe that was a comfortable place. Sitting at the heart of everything, we enjoyed the circling of Plato's musical heavens above our heads and if, like Lucian, we had to travel upwards, it was in the safe knowledge that we belonged to the divinely-chosen unmovable core around which circled the sun and all the other stars. In the good old days, travelling through outer space required neither time nor physical displacement. As Beatrice reminds Dante, in Heaven everything is always here and now.

Then, long after Dante's death in Ravenna, the universal centre shifted. First to a subservient ring of the solar system, then to cloudy patch of a minor galaxy, finally to a distant corner of the expanding universe. While we still felt that everything revolved around us, we realised at the same time that the Earth on which we stood was the Siberia of the cosmos. The realization did not diminish our desire to travel. "Everyone in Siberia wants to leave," Joseph Brodsky once said. Perhaps not everyone on Earth dreams of leaving it, but over and over, throughout the generations, we have imagined ways of going out there, beyond the constellations, into the unknown darkness, just to see what it's like.

Dante dreamed up for his otherworldly travels simple methods: forced marches, arduous mountain-climbing, crossing infernal rivers in demon-ferried crafts, being flown down a chasm by the Monster of Fraud or being lifted and set down by one of the giants of Genesis. Other methods involved anesthetic sleep and tele-transportation in which the pilgrim dreams of being carried away as Lucy's beloved or as Jupiter's Ganymede. Later travellers sought the lesser magic of mechanical devices. From the mechanical wings invented by Da Vinci to the bird-drawn chariots imagined by Cyrano de Bergerac, from Astolfo's aerodynamic hippogriff to Don Quixote's wooden horse, from the spaceships of Jules Verne and H. G. Wells to the toy rocket Meliès sinks into the eye of a disgruntled moon, we have designed countless contraptions to go beyond our sky, into the ocean of space in which we find ourselves marooned. Modern science-fiction inherited the daring cartography of theology and peopled the distant galaxies with rewards and punishments in the shape of benevolent heroes and green-scaled monsters, hunky paladins like Luke Skywalker and evil threats like Darth Vader. Mainly threats, of course, because, like all our imaginary places, outer space ends up resembling life on Earth. Whether on Stanislav Lem's Solaris or Ray Bradbury's Mars, away from our home Eden, we relive our earthly nightmares over and over again.

Since the days of Dante, what attracts us to the Great Beyond? Why seek beyond the stars a setting for what we can do equally badly back on Earth? Ulysses called it *"ardore"*. If the gateposts of our house are a sort of domestic Columns of Hercules, then the sky above our roof is like the forbidden ocean, endlessly tempting us to cross it. We are seldom satisfied with staying home. Like readers enthralled by an adventure story, we want never to reach the last page. Space seems to promise us always a new chapter.

This is the paradox: our earthly world (like Dante's dark forest) is terrible but is capable of defining itself and its limits, and in doing so frames everything that lies beyond it, allowing us, its sleepy inhabitants, to discern that which we might want to attain, whether a mountain's peak ahead or the *cose belle* in the fathomless cosmos above. But once we leave that world (or that forest), once we enter the space of constellations being born and galaxies dying, we enter a realm without borders. Everything out there is simultaneously limited and expanding, not boundless (scientists tell us) but of boundaries impossible to conceive. Out there we want to travel from our familiar here, there the dreams of astrophysicists and theologians and science-fiction writers blend. Out there (as on Ariosto's moon) are all the things we've lost or think we've lost: the trust in wisdom, the chance for happiness, the hope for a better future. Down here we live.

We are cartographers at heart and we parcel and label our "down here" and believe that we move about, towards alien territory, perhaps merely in order to shift our grounding and our sense of identity. And so we believe that in one place we are alone and look out onto the world, and in another we are among our brethren and look back upon our self, lost somewhere in the past. We pretend to travel from home to foreign grounds, from a singular experience to a communal one, from whom we once were towards who we'll one day be, living in a constant state of exile. We forget that, wherever we find ourselves, we are always "here".

The Beyond is a "here" particularly rich for imaginary travel, as Ulysses proved in his descent to the Underworld. When visiting the souls in the Kingdom of the Dead, Homer has Ulysses meet Tiresias the seer who tells him that if he surmounts the difficulties set out for him and does not disturb the cattle of Apollo, he and his crew may all return home safely. However, Tiresias prophesises, once back in Ithaca, Ulysses will burn with the urge "to go forth once more." Tiresias's words, as Dante understood, add depth and a tragic aspect to the story of return, rendering it somehow infinite with the promise of "once more". Ulysses, whom Dante places in Hell for lying, recounts in the *Commedia* this final voyage less as a new enterprise than as a summary of all the previous ones. Addressing his fellow men, he says:

"O frati", dissi, "che per cento milia	'Brothers,' I said, 'o you, who having crossed
perigli siete giunti a l'occidente,	a hundred thousand dangers, reach the west,
a questa tanto picciola vigilia	to this brief waking – time that still is left
d'i nostri sensi ch'è del rimanente	unto your senses, *you must not deny*
non vogliate negar l'esperïenza,	*experience* of that which lies beyond
di retro al sol, del mondo sanza gente.	the sun, and of the world that is unpeopled.
Considerate la vostra semenza:	Consider well the seed that gave you birth:
fatti non foste a viver come bruti,	you were not made to live your lives as brutes,
ma per seguir virtute e canoscenza".	but to be followers of worth and knowledge.'

(*Inferno* XXVI, 112–120) (m.e.)

Putting down anchor in some sleepy port; mimicking the routine of animals who are born, eat, procreate and die; ignoring virtue and rejecting knowledge: a return to Ithaca would, it seems, amount to this. To escape such a miserable destiny, Ulysses and his men set sail on what Dante calls a *"folle volo"*, a "mad flight"; heading west, they see a mountain rise up from the sea and are heartened, but their good cheer soon turns to tears when a storm rages over them, a whirlpool opens up in front of the prow and – *"com'altrui piacque"* – "as pleased Another" – they are plunged into unknown waters. That is how the Dantesque Ulysses' story ends.

However, before *"che 'l mar fu sovra noi richiuso,"* "the sea closed over us" – and Poseidon (or God, or Providence) has his triumphant revenge, let us remember that none of these threats has diminished the curiosity of our hero. Rather than let himself by frightened by danger, Ulysses never stops wanting to know what's *"retro al sol"* – he yearns to see what lies beyond the world known to humans, *"il mondo sanza gente"*. Ulysses, like Dante, wants to keep exploring.

In the Christian realm, the hierarchical realms of Heaven and Hell and the intermezzo of Purgatory, developed from timid roots in the countries of the dead of Greece and Rome. Saint Paul was said to have travelled to the Beyond following the footsteps of Ulysses' disciple, Aeneas, and dozens of other mystics assured their readers of the truth of their otherworldly excursions. The Christian imagination, like that of a real-estate developer, crowded the ancient otherworldly universe with gardens and wastelands, gated neighbourhoods, and slums, in an imagistic effusion that scandalised St. Augustine. Mountains, rivers, and valleys were implanted, both under and above the Earth, to house the dead, and in those landscapes were erected mansions and palaces with their walls, moats, and towers, such as the Celestial Jerusalem and the infernal city of Dis. During his travels in the ninth century, Saint Brendan thought he had found the Garden of Eden somewhere in the East, behind a wall of fog.

Chronicles of travel to these imaginary places fill the medieval libraries both in the East and the West, and to design their larger-than-human geography, writers gave the everyday elements of the world of clay and stone impossible and marvelous characteristics. Medieval eschatology provides superb examples of their inventions: floors so low that they sink into a bottomless pit (in the *Apocalypse of Paul*), doors that are not meant to be used (in the *Apocalypse of Ezra*), walls with no windows (in the *Book of Enoch*) or with too many (according to the *Vita Ludovici regis* of the Abbé Suger), roofs through which the eye can see but through which no light can enter (in the *Passion of Perpetua and Felicitas*), houses of boundless space with many rooms (in the *Gospel According to John*).

But it was Dante who, more than anyone else, conceived and planned his otherworldly realms with geological, architectural and theological precision. Unlike his predecessors, who described the Hells and Heavens they saw with a somewhat careless ambiguity, Dante's travel diaries to the Other World are meticulous records of these imaginary realms. Banished forever from his native Florence, burdened with the cares of exile, living in a shifting landscape of cities and rooms that he could never call his own, Dante built in his mind something more solid, more lasting and more intimate than the place to which he was bound by political sentimentality, angry nostalgia and a baptismal document. With the care of a meticulous travel guide, Dante notes throughout his journey details of colour and touch, height and width and breadth; he gives instructions for crossing a river of blood or a stream of crystal-clear water; he tells the reader when to travel by day and when by night; he explains how to cross through the heavenly spheres.

On the morning of Easter Friday of 1300, the year of Christendom's first jubilee, Dante tells us that he emerged from a dark forest where the straight path was lost. Attempting to describe it renews in him the fear he felt: it was *"selvag-*

gia ed aspra e forte" ("wild and rough and strong") and so "*amara*" ("bitter") that death is scarcely worse. He can't remember how he entered, because he was so full of sleep then, but as he finally comes out from the darkness he sees before him a mountain rising where the valley ended, and above the mountain the rays of the Easter sun. The exact location of the forest is not given: it is everywhere and nowhere, the place into which we enter when our senses are blurred, and the place from which we emerge when the rays of the sun wakes us, what Saint Augustine (whom Dante had so carefully read) called "the bitter forest of the world." Dark things happen in the darkness, as our fairy tales tell us, but it may be that since our expulsion from the forest that was also a garden, the path through the other terrible forest is almost certainly our promised path into the light. It is only once Dante has crossed the forest where "*la notte, ch' i' passai con tanta pieta*" ("I spent the night so piteously") that he begins the journey that will lead him to an understanding of his own humanity.

The entire *Commedia* can be read as an exodus from the forest and as a pilgrimage towards the human condition. And not only towards a perception of the pilgrim's singularity: also, and most important, towards his condition as a member of the human fold, both contaminated and redeemed by what others have done and what others are. During the whole of the voyage Dante is never alone. Guided by Virgil or by Beatrice, speaking with souls condemned or saved, Dante's progress is one of a constant dialogue with others. This is the reason why the dead have not lost the gift of language, so that they may communicate with the living, and why their physical form, shuffled off on this Earth, is apparent when Dante meets them, so that he might know it is with humans that he speaks and interacts, and not merely with intangible spirits. In the dark forest he was alone, but after that, never again.

Dante's forlorn forest comes at the present end of a long succession of forests, far older than that of Dante, older perhaps than the demon forest through which Gilgamesh must journey at the beginning of our literatures, forests that include the one first Ulysses and then Aeneas must cross on their quest, the live forest that advances to defeat Macbeth the butcher, the black forest in which Red Riding Hood and Tom Thumb and Hänsel and Gretel lose their innocent way, the bloodsoaked forest of Sade's unfortunate heroines, the adventurous forests of the heroes of Kipling and Edgar Rice Burroughs, the gentler, subtle forests of Jean Giono and Julien Gracq. These are all forests on the edge of other worlds, forests of the night of the soul, of erotic agony, of visionary threat, of the final totterings of old age, of the unfolding of adolescent longing. It is of such forests that Henry James's father wrote in a terrible letter to his adolescent sons:

> Every man who has reached even his intellectual teens begins to suspect that life is no farce;
> that it is not genteel comedy even; that it flowers and fructifies on the contrary out of the
> profoundest tragic depths of the essential dearth in which its subject's roots are plunged.
> The natural inheritance of everyone who is capable of spiritual life is an unsubdued forest
> where the wolf howls and the obscene bird of night chatters.

These unsubdued forests are always double: they lend us the illusion that it is "here," in the darkness, that the action takes place, and yet we know the forests exist not only through the trees and filtered light, but within the greater land that frames them and lends them context. Into Dante's forest we too are lured, but he never allows us to forget that there is also another space outside. Inside may be darkness ("visible darkness", as Milton described the darkness of Hell) and yet a web of shapes and shadows outline the promise of a twilight sky. The truth is that our literary spaces, like the realms of the *Commedia*, are places in which, as spectators or readers, we must stand each alone, is a preparatory stage, an initiation ground for that which is still to come: the encounter with the other, "*mon semblable, mon frère.*"

At the end of Dante's descent into Hell, twenty-two cantos away from the shadows of the forest, after following Virgil down through the various infernal circles, Dante reaches the frozen lake where the souls of traitors are trapped up to the neck in ice. Among the dreadful heads that shout and curse, Dante hits his foot against one and then thinks he recognises in the shivering features a certain Bocca degli Abati who, in Florence, betrayed his party and took arms on the side of the enemy. Dante asks the angry head to tell him his name and, as has been his custom throughout the magical journey, promises to bring the sinner posthumous fame by writing about him when he returns among the living. Bocca answers back that he wishes for the exact opposite, and tells Dante leave him to his unrepentance. Furious at the insult, Dante grabs hold of Bocca by the scruff and tells him that, if he doesn't give him his name, he'll tear out every hair on his head. "*Perché tu mi dischiomi, / né ti dirò ch'io sia, né mostrerolti, / se mille fiate in sul capo tomi.*" "Even if you leave me bald," Bocca replies, "I will not tell you my name, nor show you my face, even if you pound my head a thousand times." Dante then pulls "*più d'una ciocca,*" "more than one fistful," making the tortured sinner howls in pain. All the while, Virgil, Dante's heavenly appointed guide, remains silent.

Virgil's silence can be read as approval. Several circles earlier, in Canto VIII, as both poets are ferried across the River Styx, Dante sees one of the souls condemned for the sin of wrath rise from the filthy waters, and, as usual, he asks him who he is. The soul doesn't give his name but says that he is merely one who weeps, for which Dante, unmoved, curses him horribly. Delighted, Virgil takes Dante in his arms and fulsomely praises his ward ("*benedetta colei che in te s'incinse*," "blessed be she who bore you") with the same words Saint Luke uses in his Gospel in praise of Christ Himself. Dante, taking advantage of Virgil's encouragement, says that nothing would give him greater pleasure than to see the sinner plunged back into the ghastly swill. Virgil agrees, and the episode ends with Dante giving thanks to God for granting his wish. Outside the forest, the rules of engagement are not exclusively our own.

Over the centuries, commentators have tried to justify Dante's actions as instances of "noble indignation" or "just anger," not a sin like wrath (as one of Dante's intellectual masters, St Thomas Aquinas, maintained) but the virtue of being roused by the right cause. The problem, of course, resides in the reading of "right." In the case of Dante, "right" refers to his understanding of the unquestionable justice of God: to feel compassion for the damned is "wrong" because it means setting oneself against God's imponderable will. Only three cantos earlier, Dante was able to faint with pity when the soul of Francesca, condemned to whirl forever in the wind that punishes the lustful, tells him her sad story. But now, advanced in his progress through Hell, he is less of a sentimentalist and more of a believer in the higher authority. According to Dante's faith, the legal system decreed by God cannot be mistaken or wicked; therefore, whatever it determines must be just, even if human understanding cannot grasp its full validity. Dante's deliberate infliction of pain to the prisoner tortured in the ice, and his prurient desire to see the other prisoner tortured in the mire, must be understood (these critics say) as humble obedience to the Law and acceptance of Superior Judgment.

The stories we tell put into words our experience. An argument similar to that of Aquinas is put forward today by those rallying against the investigation and prosecution of official murderers and torturers. And yet, as almost any reader of Dante will admit, however cogent the theological (or political) arguments may be, these infernal passages leave a very bad taste in the mouth. Perhaps the reason is that, if Dante's justification lies in the nature of divine will, then, instead of Dante's actions being redeemed by faith, faith is undermined by Dante's actions, the human debased, not elevated, by the divine. Much the same way, the implicit condoning of torturers, merely because their abuses took place in the unchangeable past and under the superior judgment and law of another administration, instead of encouraging faith in the present administration's politics, undermines that faith and those politics. And worse still: left unchallenged, the old excuse of "I merely obeyed orders," tacitly accepted, will acquire new prestige and serve as precedent for future exculpations.

There are, however, other possible explanations. One is that sin is contagious and in the presence of sinners, Dante becomes contaminated by their faults: among the lustful he pities the weak flesh, among the wrathful he is filled with bestial anger, among the traitors he betrays even his own human condition, because no one, certainly not Dante, is incapable of sinning like others have sinned. Our fault lies not in the possibility of evil but in our consent to do evil.

Another explanation lies in the nature of language. Coming out of the dark forest Dante's pilgrim is confronted by his fellow men and women, sinners like himself, whose stories he wishes to know, perhaps because of prurient curiosity (for which Virgil chides him) or to mirror his own condition (for which Virgil praises him.) Some of the souls want to be remembered on earth and tell their story so that Dante may retell it; others, like Bocca, scorn the idea of posthumous fame. All this happens through speech, through the weak and inefficient instrument of language which is, alas, the only one we possess. We recount, describe, explain, judge, demand, beg, affirm, allude, deny – but in every case we must rely on our interlocutor's intelligence and generosity to hear in the sounds we make and the sense and meaning we wish to convey. The abstract language of images helps us no further: something in our constitution makes us want to translate into words even that which is given as untranslatable: the immanent, the ineffable. Semantic innocence is beyond us.

At long last, having descended into the abyss of Hell and climbed the summit of Purgatory to the Garden of Eden, Dante enters Paradise and sees Beatrice gazing at the Sun of God. Comparing himself to the fisherman Glaucus who, according to Ovid, having tasted magic grass that grew on the shore was seized with a longing for plunging into the deep, Dante is filled with longings of the divine and says to the reader:

Trasumanar significar per verba	To pass beyond what is human in words
non si poria; però l'esemplo basti	may not be told, so the example must be enough
a cui esperienza grazia serba.	for him to whom grace granted the experience.

Paradiso I, 70–72

This is the paradox: after the unspeakable experience of suffering the world alone, narrating that experience to ourselves consciously and unconsciously, we enter the world of things shared and of common language, but here the communication, full communication, is no longer possible. The dark forest is terrible, but it defines itself and its limits, and in doing so frames the world outside, allows us to discern that which we want to attain, whether the sea's shore or the mountain's peak. But past the forest, the world of experience has no such borders. Everything outside, like the universe, is simultaneously limited and expanding, not boundless but of boundaries impossible to conceive, utterly unconscious of itself. Here we set ourselves up as witnesses. And here we live.

Editions and Translations

Unless otherwise stated, editions and translations of Dante's works are the following:

Commedia
La *Commedia secondo l'antica vulgata*. Giorgio Petrocchi (ed.). 2nd edn, 4 vols. Florence: Le Lettere, 1994. (Società Dantesca Italiana Edizione Nazionale. Mondadori 1966–1975, 4 vols.)
The *Divine Comedy*. Trans. by Allen Mandelbaum and Peter Armour. New York: Knopf. Distributed by Random House 1995 – sometimes adapted.

Convivio
Il Convivio (ridotto a miglior lezione e commentato da G. Busnelli e G. Vandelli. Con introduzione di Michele Barbi. Seconda edizione con appendice di aggiornamento a cura di Antonio Enzo Quaglio). (1964). Series: *Opere di Dante*, Vol. V. Edizione Nazionale. Florence: Le Lettere 1995.
Dante's Convivio (The Banquet). Trans. by Richard H. Lansing. New York: Garland 1990.

De vulgari eloquentia
De vulgari eloquentia. Edited by Pier Vincenzo Mengaldo. In: Dante Alighieri: *Opere Minori*. 2 vols. Milan and Naples: Ricciardi, 1979–1988. ii, pp. 1–237.
De vulgari eloquentia. Trans. by Steven Botterill. Cambridge: Cambridge University Press 1996.

Epistole
Epistole. Testo critico della Società Dantesca Italiana. Edited by Ermenegildo Pistelli. Florence: Società Dantesca Italiana 1960.
Dante Alagherii epistolae = The Letters of Dante. Trans. by Paget Toynbee, 2nd edn. Oxford: Clarendon Press 1966.

Monarchia
Monarchia. Edited by Prue Shaw. Florence: Le Lettere 2009.
Monarchia. Trans. by Prue Shaw. Cambridge: Cambridge University Press 1996.

Vita nuova
Vita nuova, in Idem: *Opere minori*, tomo 1, parte 1. Edited by Domenico De Robertis and Gianfranco Contini. Milan and Naples: Ricciardi 1984.
Vita Nova. Trans. by Andrew Frisardi. Evanston IL: Northwestern University Press 2012.

∗ ∗ ∗

The biblical passages are quoted according to *The Niv Study Bible: New International Version*. Edited by Kenneth Baker. Grand Rapids (Michigan): Zondervan, Anniversary ed. 1985.

The Psalms are numbered in accordance with the Septuagint system, with Masoretic numbering in brackets.

∗ ∗ ∗

The following **Databases** are used throughout:

Biblehub.com: https://biblehub.com
Corpus Corporum – repositorium operum latinorum apud Universitatem Turicensem:
    https://www.mlat.uzh.ch
Corpus Thomisticum: https://www.corpusthomisticum.org
Dartmouth Dante Project (DDP): dante.dartmouth.edu
Documenta Catholica Omnia: http://www.documentacatholicaomnia.eu/a_1020_Conspectus_
    Alphabeticus_Secundum_Sermones_Qui_Innati_Sunt_LT.html
Glossae Scripturae Sacrae-electronicae (Gloss-e): https://gloss-e.irht.cnrs.fr
The Latin Library: http://www.thelatinlibrary.com
Patrologia Latina (Jacques Paul Migne. *Patrologiae Cursus Completus*. Series Latina):
    https://patristica.net/latina/
Perseus Digital Library: perseus.tufts.edu
Theoi Texts Library: https://www.theoi.com/Library.html

Notes on Contributors

Isabel Almeida is Associate Professor in the Department of Romance Literatures, School of Arts and Humanities, at the University of Lisbon, where she teaches Portuguese Literature of the Renaissance and the Baroque, and Italian Literature (13th–16th centuries). She is the author of several articles and books on Gil Vicente, Jorge Ferreira de Vasconcelos, Fernão Mendes Pinto, Padre António Vieira, and Camões, among others. Recently, she integrated the team that edited and profusely annotated a hitherto not published 17th-century manuscript: Os Lusíadas comentados por D. Marcos de S. Lourenço.

Albert Russell Ascoli, Ph.D. Cornell University 1983. He taught for 14 years at Northwestern University, and for another 22 at the University of California, Berkeley, where he now holds the title of Terrill Distinguished Professor Emeritus. His principal field of research is Medieval and Early Modern Italian culture from the 13th to the 16th centuries. He is the author of *Ariosto's Bitter Harmony. Crisis and Evasion in the Italian Renaissance* (Princeton: Princeton U.P. 1987); *Dante and the Making of a Modern Author* (Cambridge: Cambridge U.P. 2008) and *A Local Habitation, and a Name: Imagining Histories in the Italian Renaissance* (Fordham: New York 2011). He has edited several essay collections, including *Machiavelli and the Discourse of Literature* (with Victoria Kahn, Cornell University Press: Ithaca NY 1993); *Making and Remaking Italy: The Cultivation of National Identity around the Risorgimento* (with Krystyna von Henneberg; Berg: Oxford 2001); a double issue of *Renaissance Drama* titled "Italy and the Drama of Europe" (with William West, 2010); *Italian Futures*, an issue of the electronic journal *California Italian Studies* (with Randolph Starn, 2011); and, most recently, *The Cambridge Companion to Petrarch* (Cambridge | New York: Cambridge U.P. 2015). He has held several fellowships and visiting appointments, including the NEH-Mellon Rome Prize at the American Academy in Rome (2004–2005), Visiting Professor at the Center for Advanced Studies in Munich (Spring 2011), and Visiting Professor at the Villa I Tatti (spring 2017). He has been elected "membro straniero" of the Academy of Arts and Science of the Istituto Lombardo and "socio" of the Accademia dell'Arcadia. From 2014–2020 he served as President of the Dante Society of America. His current research projects include a study of Boccaccio's *Decameron* and an essay on *Hamlet* and St. Augustine's *Soliloquies*.

Teresa Bartolomei is CITER (Research Centre for Theology and Religious Studies, UCP) full Member and Lecturer at the Faculty of Theology, Catholic University of Portugal. Her main recent publications are *Radix Matrix* (Lisbon: Universidade Católica Editora 2018), *Dove abita la luce?* (Milan: Vita e Pensiero 2019); *The Poet in Hell. From Dante to Jorie Graham* (Lisbon: Universidade Católica Editora 2021).

Lina Bolzoni is Professor Emeritus of Italian Literature at the Scuola Normale Superiore in Pisa and Global Distinguished Professor at New York University. She has taught in France (Collège de France, École Normale Supérieure) and in the United States (UCLA, Princeton, Harvard University). She has been a fellow of All Souls College and Christ Church at Oxford and Robert Lehman Visiting Professor at Villa I Tatti. She is a member of the scientific council of the Istituto dell'Enciclopedia Italiana, a member of the national committee for Dante's 7th centenary, a national member of the Accademia dei Lincei, a fellow of the British Academy, a foreign member of the Académie des Inscriptions et Belles Lettres, and a member of the American Philosophical

Society. Her studies have focused on the relationship between literature and philosophy in the sixteenth and seventeenth centuries; sacred and profane rhetoric; chivalric poetry; the utopian tradition; the art of memory and its relationship with literature and the figurative arts; the experience of reading. Her books, translated into several languages, include: *La stanza della memoria* (Torino: Einaudi 1995); *La rete delle immagini. Predicazione in volgare dalle origini a Bernardino da Siena* (Torino: Einaudi 2002, Viareggio Prize); *Poesia e ritratto nel Rinascimento* (Roma|Bari: Laterza 2008); *Il cuore di cristallo. Ragionamenti d'amore, poesia e ritratto nel Rinascimento* (Torino: Einaudi 2010); *Il lettore creativo. Percorsi cinquecenteschi fra memoria, gioco, scrittura* (Napoli: Guida 2012); *Una meravigliosa solitudine. L'arte di leggere nell'Europa moderna* (Torino: Einaudi 2019, De Sanctis Prize for an innovative essay). She edited *L'idea del theatro* by Giulio Camillo for Adelphi and for the Istituto della Enciclopedia Italiana *La* Commedia *di Dante nello specchio delle immagini* (Roma: Treccani 2021). She curated the following exhibitions: "La fabbrica del pensiero. Dall'arte della memoria alle neuroscienze" (Florence, Forte di Belvedere, 1990); "Donne e cavalieri, incanti, follia. Viaggio attraverso le immagini dell'*Orlando Furioso*", Pisa, San Michele degli Scalzi Exhibition Centre, 15 December 2012–15 February 2013; "Orlando Furioso e le arti", Accademia Nazionale dei Lincei, Rome, 1 September-28 November 2015. She contributes to the Sunday Book Supplement of *Il Sole 24 Ore*.

José Tolentino Calaça de Mendonça is a Portuguese prelate of the Roman Catholic Church. A theologian and university professor, he is also a renewed poet. His work includes poetry, essays, and plays that he signs José Tolentino Mendonça. An archbishop since July 2018, he has served as Archivist and Librarian of the Holy Roman Church from September 2018 to September 2022, when he was appointed Prefect of the Dicastery for Culture and Education of the Holy See. Pope Francis created him cardinal on 5 October 2019. In February 2020 he was made a member of the Pontifical Council for Culture. The relationship between Christianity and culture is at the heart of his writings. He has received numerous literary prizes and awards. His poems are collected in the volume *A noite abre os meus olhos* (Lisboa: Assírio & Alvim 2006 / 2021⁴). In 2021 he published a new book of poetry: *Introdução à pintura rupestre* (Lisboa: Assírio & Alvim). His main essays include: *A construção de Jesus: uma leitura narrativa de Lucas 7,36–50* (Lisboa: Assírio & Alvim 2004); *A leitura infinita. Bíblia e interpretação* (Prior Velho: Paulinas Editora, 2008); *A mística do instante* (Prior Velho: Paulinas Editora 2014); *Elogio da sede* (Lisboa: Quetzal 2018); *Metamorfose necessária: Reler São Paulo* (Lisbon: Quetzal 2022).

Arnaldo do Espírito Santo is Emeritus Professor of Latin Language and Literature, at the School of Arts and Humanities at the University of Lisbon, specialised in critical editing; Portuguese and Neolatin Literature (XVI–XVIII century); reception of classical authors in Portuguese Literature. Since 2012 he has been Director of the Institute of Portuguese Language and Culture; since 2008 he has been Vice-President of the Portuguese Association of Neo-Latin Studies – APENEL. His main publications include numerous translations (c / aliis, Santo Agostinho, *Confissões*, Lisbon: INCM 2001, 3.ª ed. rev. 2021; Saint Augustine, *De Trinitate* / Trindade, Lisboa: Paulus 2007; Leon Battista Alberti, *Da arte edificatória*, Lisbon: Fundação Calouste Gulbenkian 2011; Fr. Tomás Pereira, *Cartas*, vol. I e II, Lisbon: CCCM 2011); essays ("Leituras de Terêncio na Literatura Latina Medieval", in *Estudios sobre Terencio*, Granada: Editorial Universidad de Granada 2006, 403–429; "A Clavis prophetarum à luz das referências chronológicas intratextuais", in *Padre António Vieira. Colóquio*, Braga: UCE 2009, 35–49; "Os Lusíadas à luz da teorização da epopeia nos tratados latinos do Cinquecento", in *Camões e os Contemporâneos*, Ponta Delgada: CIEC 2012, 43–54; critical editions (Pe. António Vieira, *Clavis*

Prophetarum / Chave dos Profetas, Book III, Lisbon: Biblioteca Nacional 2000; Pe. António Vieira, *Sermões I e II*, Lisbon: INCM 2008 and 2010).

In 2022, together with the researcher Ana Travassos Valdez, he rediscovered in the Gregorian Library in Rome the original manuscript of the work *Clavis Prophetarum*, written by Father António Vieira, which had been missing for 300 years.

Giulio Ferroni is an Italian literary critic, literature historian, essayist and academic. From 1982 to 2013 he was full professor of Italian literature at the University of Rome "La Sapienza"; he regularly contributes to the cultural pages of Italian newspapers such as *L'Unità* and *Il Corriere della sera*. He has devoted himself to studies on the theatre and the Renaissance (focusing on Machiavelli, Ariosto, and Aretino). He has also worked on the theory of literature and contemporary literary production. His most important works include: *Mutazione e riscontro nel teatro di Machiavelli e altri saggi sulla commedia del Cinquecento* (1972); *Il comico nelle teorie contemporanee* (1974); *Le voci dell'istrione: Pietro Aretino e la dissoluzione del teatro* (1977); *Il testo e la scena: saggi sul teatro del Cinquecento* (1980); *Una Storia della letteratura italiana* (4 voll., 1991); *Dopo la fine: sulla condizione postuma della letteratura* (1996); *Passioni del Novecento* (1999). His most recent publications include: *I confini della critica* (2005); *La passione predominante. Perché la letteratura* e *Prima lezione di letteratura italiana* (both published in 2009); *Scritture a perdere. La letteratura negli anni zero* (2010); *Gli ultimi poeti. Giovanni Giudici e Andrea Zanzotto* (2013); *La fedeltà della ragione* (2014). In 2019 he published *L'Italia di Dante. Viaggio nel paese della Commedia*, Viareggio-Rèpaci 2020 Prize for Nonfiction.

João R. Figueiredo is Assistant Professor at the University of Lisbon, where he teaches Portuguese Renaissance Literature, Visual Culture and Literary Theory. He is the author of *A Autocomplacência da Mimese* (Coimbra: Angelus Novus, 2003) and of several essays, mainly on Camões. He guest-edited the volume *Post-Imperial Camões*, in the *Portuguese Literary and Cultural Studies* series (Dartmouth, Mass.: Tagus Press, 2002), and, with António M. Feijó and Miguel Tamen, *O Cânone* (Lisboa: Fundação Cupertino de Miranda and Tinta-da-China, 2020), a collection of revisionary essays on Portuguese authors. He is the chair of the post-graduate Program in Literary Theory (School of Arts and Humanities at the University of Lisbon).

Alberto Manguel is an Argentine Canadian anthologist, translator, essayist, novelist, and editor. He is the author of several novels and non-fiction books dedicated to film and literary criticism such as *The Dictionary of Imaginary Places* (with Gianni Guadalupi. Toronto: Lester & Orpen Dennys 1980 |1987); *Into the Looking Glass Wood* (Toronto: Knopf Canada 1998); *The Traveller, the Tower and the Worm: The Reader as Metaphor* (Philadelphia: University of Pennsylvania Press, 2013); *Monsieur Bovary et d'autres personnages* (Montmorillon: L'Escampette, 2014); *Curiosity* (New Haven | London: Yale U. P., 2015); *Fabulous Monsters: Dracula, Alice, Superman, and Other Literary Friends* (New Haven | London: Yale U. P., 2019). He edited numerous literary anthologies on a variety of themes or genres ranging from erotica and gay stories to fantastic literature and mysteries. Passionate bibliophile, Manguel is also the author of several books on the art and history of reading, as well as on libraries as a figure of the spirit, such as *A History of Reading* (Toronto: Knopf Canada 1996); *The Library at Night* (Knopf, Toronto, 2006); *Packing My Library: An Elegy and Ten Digressions* (New Haven | London: Yale U. P., 2018). He has received numerous awards, among others the Gutenberg Prize, the

Formentor Prize, the Premio Grinzane Cavour, and the Prix Médicis Essai. He is Officier de l'Ordre des Arts et des Lettres (France) and Doctor honoris causa of the universities of Liège (Belgium) and Poitiers (France). In 2021, he gave the Roger Lancelyn Green lecture to the Lewis Carroll Society on his love of the 'Alice' stories. Until August of 2018 he was the director of the National Library of Argentina. He is now the director of the Centro de Estudos da História da Leitura (CEHL) in Lisbon, Portugal, and occupies the Chair of "Europe: languages and literatures" at the Collège de France.

Rita Marnoto is a Professor at the Faculty of Arts and the College of Arts of the University of Coimbra, where she teaches Italian Studies, Translation and Literature and Arts. She is Director of the PhD Course in Modern Languages – Cultures, Literatures and Translation, Coordinator of the Italian Studies Section and Vice-President of the "Centre International d'Études Portugaises de Genève". She has devoted her studies to contemporary Italian literature (historical avant-garde, modern theatre, neo-realism, post-modernism), the Portuguese avant-garde of the early 20th century and the reception of Pirandello and other contemporary writers in Portugal; the relationship between Portugal and Italy during the Risorgimento; the history of 18th century Portuguese literature and Roman Arcadia; baroque Portuguese poetry; Luís de Camões, coordinating a project on his commentary; court society and 16th century Portuguese Petrarchism. She has translated Goldoni and Pirandello into Portuguese and translated Carolina Michaëlis into Italian. She has edited the text of Fernando Távora's diary. She has also been active in the field of dramaturgy and reflection on the fine arts. She has received several distinctions, including the "Grande Ufficiale della Repubblica" of the "Ordine della Stella della Solidarietà Italiana", awarded by the President of the Italian Republic Carlo Azeglio Ciampi. She is Commissioner for the Commemorations of the 5th Centenary of the Birth of Luís Vaz de Camões (2024–2025).

Paola Nasti is Associate Professor of Italian and Director of Undergraduate Studies in Italian at the Weinberg College of Art and Sciences, Northwestern University (Evanston, Illinois). Her research focuses on medieval Italian literature and religious culture, textual and intellectual history. She studied at the University of Naples (IT) and the University of Reading (UK). Trained as a Dante scholar and medievalist, she holds a Ph.D. in Italian Studies from the University of Reading. Her doctoral research and her first book explored Dante's appropriation of the biblical books attributed to King Solomon (*Favole d'amore e "saver profondo": la tradizione salomonica in Dante*. Ravenna: Angelo Longo Editore 2007). She has also contributed to chapters on Dante's religious and scriptural culture in *The Cambridge Companion to the Divine Comedy* and the first Italian companion to Dante. Further research on Dante's indebtedness to religious culture will form the core of a forthcoming monograph on Dante and the medieval mendicant friars. The reception of texts and modes of interpretation is at the heart of her work on the early commentary tradition of the *Comedy*. She co-edited the first volume on the Dante commentaries in the Anglophone world (Paola Nasti and Claudia Rossignoli (eds.): *Interpreting Dante: Essays on the Traditions of Dante Commentary* (Chicago: Notre Dame University Press 2013).

Carlo Ossola has been a Professor at Collège de France since 2000 where he has been the Chair of Modern Literatures of Romance Europe until 2020. He has previously taught at the University of Geneva (CH), University of Padua, and University of Turin (Italy). From 2007 to 2017 he was Director of the Institute of Italian Studies, USI (CH). He is co-editor of the journals *Lettere Italiane* and *Rivista di Storia e Letteratura Religiosa*; a member of the Accademia dei Lincei since 1995; a corresponding fellow of the British Academy; a member of the Scientific Council of the Istituto dell'Enciclopedia Italiana. For twenty years he directed the "Corsi di Alta Cultura" organised by the Giorgio Cini Foundation, publishing, with Vittore Branca, volumes of broad cultural interest. In 2017, he was elected President of the Italian National Committee for the celebrations of the 700th anniversary of Dante Alighieri's death, remaining in office until 2022.

He has worked and published extensively on Renaissance civilisation and on court culture in Europe; on the topoi of texts and ideas; on contemporary authors (among whom a privileged place is reserved for Ungaretti). Dante's work, which has accompanied him since his university studies, has become increasingly prominent in his research in recent years, resulting in a series of important publications that include, in addition to countless essays, the following monographs and critical editions of the *Commedia*: *Introduzione alla* Divina Commedia (Venezia: Marsilio 2012); *Personaggi della* Divina Commedia (Venezia: Marsilio 2021); *Dante* (Paris: PUF 2021); introduction and new critical edition of the *Divina Commedia* for "Pléiade" (Paris: Gallimard 2021) and for Marsilio (Venezia 2021).

Jorge Vaz de Carvalho is Assistant Professor at the Faculty of Human Sciences of the Catholic University of Portugal, where he gained his doctorate in Cultural Studies. His academic activity combines an outstanding musical career as a professional lyric singer and a significant literary production in the field of poetry and short fiction. In the field of essayistic, Jorge Vaz de Carvalho is the author of several publications, namely *Jorge de Sena:* Sinais de Fogo *como romance de formação*, PEN Club Prize 2010 and Jorge de Sena Prize 2011; *Why read the classics*, Lisbon: UCE 2020. Passionate about translation, he has translated a remarkable series of British and Italian classics (Giambattista Vico's *Scienza Nuova*, FCT / União Latina Scientific and Technical Translation Award 2006; William Blake's *Songs of Innocence and of Experience*; *Emma* by Jane Austen; *Tolstoy or Dostoevsky* by George Steiner; *Ulysses* by James Joyce, APT / SPA Literary Translation Grand Prize 2015; *Diaries and Travels* by Virginia Woolf; works by Umberto Eco; *The Book of the Courtier* by Baldassarre Castiglione). He stands out as the most renowned Portuguese translator of Dante today, with published translations of the *Vita nuova* (Lisbon: Imprensa Nacional 2020) and of the *Divine Comedy* (Lisbon: Imprensa Nacional 2021), as well as the ongoing translation of the *Convivio* (Lisbon: Imprensa Nacional 2022).

Supported by:

ADFLUL – Associação para o Desenvolvimento da Faculdade de Letras da Universidade de Lisboa

BAV – Vatican Apostolic Library

CECC (Research Centre for Communication and Culture | Catholic University of Portugal)

CITER (Research Centre for Theology and Religious Studies | Catholic University of Portugal)

Embassy of Italy in Portugal

Embassy of Italy
Lisbon

FLUL – School of Arts and Humanities | University of Lisbon

Calouste Gulbenkian Foundation

FCT – Foundation for Science and Technology Portugal

UIDB/00126/2020
UIDP/00126/2020

Fundação para a Ciência e a Tecnologia
MINISTÉRIO DA CIÊNCIA, TECNOLOGIA E ENSINO SUPERIOR

IIC – Italian Cultural Institute of Lisbon

General Index

Aachen (Aix-la-Chapelle) 225
Aaron, Biblical prophet 235
Abiathar, Biblical priest 234
Abies, arbor alta (Cistercian manuscript, pre-1230) 68, 73
Abraham, Biblical patriarch 227
Achilles, Greek Hero 138, 190
Adam 53–54, 76
Adam Scotus (Adam of Dryburgh) 33
– *De tripartito tabernaculo* 33, 43
Aeneas, Troyan Hero 112, 126–127, 129, 223, 232, 272–273
Africa 7–8, 173, 204–205, 209–210, 223, 247
Alan of Lille (Alanus de Insulis) 184
– *In Distinctionibus Dictionum Theologicalium* 49, 71, 72, 73
– *Summa de arte praedicatoria* 67, 73
Alberti, Leon Battista 40, 280
Albertus Magnus (Albert the Great),
– *De animalibus* 67–70, 73, 151, 215
Alexander III the Great, king of Macedonia 231
Alfonso V, king of Naples 149
allegory 46–47, 48, 59, 74, 76, 78, 80, 82, 124, 139, 147, 211
– poetic allegory, *in verbis*; theological allegory, *in factis* 111–112, 115–116, 130–131
– *littera, res gestae*; litteral vs. allegorical 5, 71, 90–91, 115, 131–132, 137
Almeida, Isabel 6, 13, 179, 182, 195, 199, 201, 279
Almeida, Manuel Pires de 197–199
Álvares de Villasandino, Alfonso 184–185
Ambrosius, Saint 32
– *Expositio in psalmum David CXVIII* 32, 43
Ameal, Counts of 250–253, 255–256
America 223
anacephalaeosis 220, 241
angels 70, 88–89, 99, 102–103, 108, 133–134, 161, 174, 197
Anselm, Saint 53–54, 56, 77, 79
Antichrist 229
antomata, entomata, anulosa 66, 69–70, 78

Antonius Patavinus (Antonius Olisiponensis)
– *Sermo in dominica I post nativitatem Domini* 68, 73
Apocalypse of Ezra 272
Apocalypse of Paul 272
Apollo 271
Apostolic Letter "Candor Lucis Aeternae" 12, 27
Aquinas, Thomas 36–37, 52, 57, 59, 66, 71, 77, 87, 151, 215–216, 218, 222, 231, 233, 236–237, 275
– *Expositio super Isaiam ad litteram* 65, 73
– *In psalmos Davidis expositio* 37, 39, 43
– *Quodlibet* 72–73
– *Sententia libri Metaphysicae* 41, 43
– *Summa contra Gentiles* 43, 67, 73
– *Summa theologiae* 37, 43, 218, 221, 224, 242
– *Super Evangelium S. Matthaei lectura* 57, 73
Ariosto, Ludovico 106, 188, 192, 195–196, 199, 270, 279, 281
– Astolfo 270
Aristotle 41, 72, 86–87, 185, 215–216, 225, 231
– *De anima* 215
– *De animalibus* 64, 68–70, 80, 88
– *Metaphysics* 218, 226–227
– *Nicomachean Ethics* 215, 218, 240–241, 242
– *Poetics* 231
– *Politics* 215
Arius, Cyrenaic presbyter, theologian 57
Arnaut Daniel (Arnaldum Danielem), Occitanic troubadour 123
Arno, Tuscan River 157, 192
Ars praedicandi 48–49, 67, 73–74, 79
– Sermons 48–49, 55, 68, 74
art 8, 12–13, 16, 40–41, 52, 75, 80, 90–94, 104, 114, 133–144, 149, 160, 172, 184, 190, 232, 251–254, 257
Ascoli, Albert Russell 4–5, 13, 81–83, 85–87, 89–94, 96, 98, 99, 101, 105–106, 130, 146, 167, 176, 199, 189, 279
Asia, Asia Phrygia, Asia Minor 173, 223

https://doi.org/10.1515/9783110796049-017

288 — General Index

Assaracus, Trojan hero 173, 223
Athanasius of Alexandria, Coptic Church Father 54
Atlas, giant 173
auctor, auctores 87, 92–93, 100, 102, 103, 158
auctoritas 87, 94, 158, 215
auctoritates 48, 71, 103, 183, 222
Auerbach, Erich 12, 59, 74, 100–101, 107, 115, 146, 168, 205, 210, 213
Augsburg 228
Augustine, Saint 36, 38, 54–55, 66–67, 78, 122, 124–126, 136, 186–187, 199, 27, 273, 279, 289
– *Confessiones* 122, 187, 199
– *Enarrationes in Psalmos* 55, 73
Augustus, Roman emperor 173, 218–219, 233
autobiography 109–111, 118–119, 130, 133, 146–147
– autofiction 109, 113, 147
– life writing 110–115, 130, 147
– self-testimonial fallacy 5, 109–110, 121, 126, 130
automata 69
Averroes 174
Avicenna
– *Canon* 67
Azevedo, Luís Marinho de 197–199

Bakhtin Mikhail 169, 176
Bandarra, Gonçalo Anes 227, 229–230
Barolini, Teodolinda 12, 82, 97, 107, 115, 125, 128, 133, 136, 146, 156, 160, 206, 208
Bartholomaeus Anglicus
– *De proprietatibus rerum* 64, 67, 73
Bartolomei, Teresa 1, 6, 8, 109–110, 146, 279
Battaglia, Salvatore 169, 176
Baxandall, Michael 153, 160
Bayard, Jean 179, 199
Bede, the Venerable, Saint 45, 75
– *In cantica canticorum allegorica expositio* 62, 73
Bembo, Pietro 188, 193–194, 199
Benedict, Saint 4, 33–34, 37–38
Benivieni, Benedetto Gerolamo 153
Benvenuto da Imola
– Commentary on the *Comedy* 35, 39, 43

Bernard of Clairvaux, Saint 26, 62, 78, 149, 161, 175
– *Sermones super Cantica Canticorum* 61, 73
– *Treatise on Consideration* 239
Bernardes, Diogo
Bible
– I Book of Kings 237
– Book of Revelation 98
– Deuteronomy 31
– Ezekiel, book of 98, 229
– Genesis 68, 133, 270
– Hosea, book of 59
– Isaiah, book of 65
– Jeremiah, book of 59
– Job, book of 53
– John, Gospel of 219, 221, 233, 272
– Luke, Gospel of 129, 219, 232–233, 236, 275
– Mark, Gospel of 52, 65
– Matthew, Gospel of 32, 52, 54–55, 57, 236
– New Testament 32, 46–47, 54, 57, 59, 65, 75, 78, 128, 215, 230–231
– Old Testament 45, 47, 57, 65, 78, 215, 230–231
– Psalms 37, 39, 43, 54, 57, 59, 73, 277
– Psalm 2 219
– Psalm 4 36–37
– Psalm 5 51, 76
– Psalm 8 174
– Psalm 17 (18) 34, 36–37
– Psalm 21 (22) 52, 54–58
– Psalm 39 (40) 143
– Psalm 50 (51) 39, 51
– Psalm 51 (52)
– Psalm 91 (92) 35
– Psalm 113 (114) 92, 96, 98
– Psalm 118 (119) 32, 43, 91, 96–97
– Song of Songs 54, 59–62, 74, 78–80
Biblical intertextuality IX, 4, 45–48, 51–52, 58, 61–62, 65, 75–78
Blake, William 14, 283
Boccaccio, Giovanni 187, 188, 202, 243
– *Decameron* 194, 279
– *Rime*, "Prosopopea di Dante" 132, 146
Boethius 88, 122–123, 126, 184, 186, 232
– *De consolatione philosophiae* 128
Boiardo, Matteo Maria 183

Bolzoni, Lina 5, 13, 149–154, 160–161, 272
Bonaventure, Saint 62, 76, 152
– *Itinerarium mentis in Deum* 32, 43
Boncompagno da Signa
– *Rhetorica novissima* 153, 160
Bonvesin da la Riva 65
Book of Enoch 272
Boscán, Juan 191, 200
Botticelli, Sandro V, 14
Bouguereau, William-Adolphe 14
Braga, Teófilo 8, 180, 199, 248, 254
Brandão, Diogo 182
Brazil 234
Brendan, Saint 128–129, 272
British Library 149, 161
Brito, Álvaro de 181–182, 199
Brito, João Soares de 197
Brodsky, Joseph 269
Bronzino (Agnolo di Cosimo, said Bronzino) 193
Bruni, Leonardo
– *De interpretatione recta* 258–259, 265
Bruno di Segni
– *Expositio in Psalmos* 39, 43
Buonarroti, Michelangelo 154, 160
Burgos, Diego de 184

Caiaphas, Jewish high priest 234
Camões, Luís de IX–X, 7–8, 179, 183, 192, 193–194, 246–249, 253, 254, 279–280, 281–282
– Ode VI 194–195
– *Os Lusíadas / The Lusiads* 7, 195–213, 224, 242, 245, 249, 254, 279–280
– Adamastor 7, 204–210, 249
– Vasco da Gama 7, 197, 203–205, 209, 211–212, 253
Campos, Joaquim Pinto de 244
Can Grande della Scala 12, 72, 82, 85, 106, 112, 258
Caritas 37, 57–58, 60, 62, 78–79
Carrai, Stefano 116, 128, 146
Carthage 223
Carruthers, Mary 45, 150–152, 160
Carvalho, Francisco Freire de 249, 254
Casa di Dante (Roma) 154, 161, 166

Casaliano 184
Casella, Mario 244
Casnedi, Padre António 222
Castelo Branco, Camilo 244
Castiglione, Baldassare 194, 283
Castile 182–183, 230
Castilho, António Feliciano de 245
Castilho, Diogo de 252
Castillo, Hernando del 183–184, 200
Castro, Aníbal Pinto de 191, 199–200
Catalonia 183
Catholic kings (Fernando and Isabel) 182
Catroga, Fernando 246–247, 254
Cattaneo, Carlo 248
Cavalcanti, Guido 78, 85, 205, 208
Chagas, Manuel Pinheiro 245–246, 253–254
Charlemagne 225
Charles Albert of Savoy, king of Sardinia 246
China 224
Christ 14, 39, 42, 51–63, 68, 75–77, 80, 91–92, 99, 139, 181, 219–220, 222–224, 232–241, 275
– Christ as fulfilment 52, 77
– Christ-*patiens* 57
– 'joyful' Christ (*Cristo lieto*) 56–57, 76–77
– kingdom of 55
chronos 127, 220, 222–224, 233, 236, 238, 240–241
Church 2, 13, 45–46, 53, 55, 59–60, 62, 63, 73, 80, 82, 173, 175, 225, 228–230, 234–242, 248, 254, 280
Church Fathers 32, 49, 54, 62, 80, 187, 199, 215, 222, 231
Cicero 72, 88, 151, 184, 187, 215
– *Dream of Scipio* 196
Cino da Pistoia 12, 188, 191
Cioffari, Vincenzo 179, 195, 200
Clement X, Pope 231
Coimbra 180, 199, 245, 250–256, 282
Commendatore (*Don Giovanni*, W.A. Mozart) 113
Concordantiae, Distinctiones 4, 48–49, 63, 76, 79–80
– Hugh of Saint-Cher
 – *Concordantiae sacrorum bibliorum* 48

- Jerome, Saint
  - *Interpretationem hebraicorum nominum motti, verba theologica, significationes* 48
- Peter Cantor (Petrus Cantor)
  - *Distinctiones Abel* 49, 74
- Petrus Comestor (Pierre le Mangeur)
  - *Historia scolastica* 66, 73
  - *Summarium bibliae* 49
- Waleys, Thomas
  - *De Modo Componendi Sermones* 48–49
- William Brito (William the Breton)
  - *Expositio prologorum Biblie* 49
  - *Expositiones vocabulorum Biblie* 49
Constantine, Roman emperor 234, 240
Constantinople 228–230
Contini, Gianfranco 101, 107, 113, 147, 151, 160, 167, 277
Conversio, metanoia 17, 82, 88, 96, 101, 107, 112, 156, 160, 228–229, 234
Copernicus, Nicolaus 269
Cornish, Alison 95, 107
Cortonese, Codex 35
Croce, Benedetto 12
Cunha, Xavier da 244
Curtius, Ernst Robert 6
- *European Literature and the Latin Middle Ages* 167–168, 176, 185, 200
Cyrano de Bergerac 270

Damnatio 54, 103
Daniello, Bernardino
  - Commentary on the *Comedy* 154
Dante Alighieri
- as *exemplum salutis* 112
- as *exul immeritus* 5, 117
- as *histor / chronicler* 218–219, 233
- as pilgrim, *homo viator* 32, 36, 113, 116–117
- as *scriba Dei* 46, 72, 104, 113, 115
- as *theologus-poeta* 52, 72, 78, 82, 107
- Dante and reading, Dante and his readers IX, 5, 11–12, 14, 17, 27, 55, 63, 67, 72, 81–83, 85–108, 149, 153, 155, 158–159, 170, 259, 263, 274–276
- Dante as narrator/*auctor*, character/*agens*, historical *persona* 51, 94, 112–113, 158, 246
Divina Commedia
- *Inferno* V, 7, 14, 15, 18, 21–22, 63–65, 67, 74, 93–95, 98, 100, 116, 130, 146–147, 153–154, 156–157, 165–166, 185, 190–191, 197, 205, 207–209, 211, 216, 243–245, 250
- *Purgatorio* 18, 22, 36, 39–40, 53–54, 56, 63, 76, 80, 88–89, 96–100, 107, 139–145, 149–150, 155, 160, 168, 189
- *Paradiso* 25–26, 35, 37–39, 42, 47, 53, 57–59, 61–62, 76, 79, 93, 100, 102–106, 108, 149, 155–156, 159, 161, 172, 195–196
- CHARACTERS
  - Adrian V, Pope 116
  - Aeneas 157
  - Apollo 102, 194
  - Arachne 133, 136
  - Beatrice 20, 23, 25–26, 36–38, 59, 85–86, 99, 104, 117, 127–128, 133, 140, 155–156, 175, 188–189, 192, 194, 211, 250–251, 253–254, 261, 269, 273, 276
  - Bertran de Born 123, 156
  - Bocca degli Abati 116, 274, 276
  - Boniface VIII 216, 262
  - Brunetto Latini 116–117, 140
  - Cacciaguida 117, 126
  - Casella 88, 96, 107
  - Cavalcante de' Cavalcanti 205, 208
  - Cerberus 63, 64–65, 67–68, 70, 129
  - Charles Martel 116
  - Ciacco 116–117
  - David 51–52
  - Dido, queen of Carthage 157
  - Eve 54, 68, 142
  - Farinata degli Uberti 7, 21, 116–117, 205–208, 210–212
  - Forese Donati 53, 56, 77
  - Frederic II, Holy Roman emperor 95
  - Geryon 95
  - Guinizelli, Guido 42
  - Henry III, the Young King 156
  - Henry VII of Luxembourg, Holy Roman emperor 172–173, 175
  - Hugh Capet, first king of the House of Capet 172
  - James, Saint 99
  - John, Saint 98–99
  - Judas Iscariot 129

General Index

- Lucifer 64, 67–68, 70, 136, 154, 184
- Lucy, Saint 270
- Malaspina, Corrado 117
- Malaspina family 170
- Manfredi, king of Sicily 116
- Mary, Virgin 26, 134, 155, 161, 187
- Master Adam 157
- Moses 99, 155, 161
- Oderisi da Gubbio 117, 140, 143, 145
- Paolo Malatesta and Francesca da Rimini 1, 157, 192–193, 275
- Peter, Saint 17, 99, 105, 262
- Petrus Hispanus, Pope John XXI 172
- Pia de' Tolomei 116
- Pier della Vigna 116
- Samuel, Biblical prophet 129, 155, 237
- Satan 7, 209–210, 262
- Solomon, Biblical king 59, 61–62, 282
- Tiresias 271
- Trajan, Roman emperor 42, 136
- Ugolino della Gherardesca 157
- Ulysses 41, 112, 126, 129, 170–171, 190, 197, 270–273
- Vanni Fucci 117
- Virgil 18, 20, 21, 23, 32, 51, 94, 97, 105, 116–117, 125, 132, 143–144, 149, 157, 168, 182, 205, 261, 264, 273–276
- TOPOGRAPHY
  - Earth
    - Brenta 171
    - Cadiz 170–171
    - Carinthia, *Carentana* 171
    - Columns of Hercules 170–171, 270
    - Jerusalem 85, 170, 228–229
    - North Sea 171
    - Ocean 173, 270
    - Padua Plains 171
    - Phoenicia 170
  - Afterlife
    - Caina 158
    - Celestial Jerusalem 272
    - Celestial Rose 161
    - City of Dis 272
    - Dark / shadowed forest 3, 17, 20, 51, 157–158, 270, 272–276
    - Earthly Paradise, Garden of Eden 24, 34, 98, 210–211, 213, 270, 272, 276
    - Heaven of the Moon, Heaven of the Sun 58, 62, 78, 105, 155
    - Hell 18, 24, 41, 64, 66–67, 70, 129, 136, 140, 152–154, 158, 171, 180, 190–191, 209, 211–212, 271–272, 274–276, 279
    - Mountain of Purgatory 34
    - Paradise 15, 25, 38, 41, 53, 79, 108, 112, 129, 149, 152–153, 156, 211–212, 276
    - Purgatory 14–15, 21, 23–24, 56, 132, 136–137, 143–144, 152–155, 272, 276
    - River Eunoe 36
    - River Lethe 36, 39
    - River Styx 274
- GLOSSARY
  - *Contrapasso* 139–140, 142–144, 156–159, 207
  - *Delectatio*, *Dilatatio* 4, 33–39, 44, 86, 107
  - experience 25, 33, 40–42, 271, 276
  - Light 15–18, 20–27, 33–35, 58, 89, 209, 273
  - *Pan degli angeli* (Bread of the Angels) 88–90, 102–103
  - *Trasumanar* (Passing beyond the human) 3, 25, 33, 42, 117, 186, 264, 276
  - *Visibile parlare* (*Visible speech*) 6, 132, 136–137, 141, 146, 149, 150, 160
  - Vision, visions IX, 3, 6, 11, 14–15, 17–18, 20–27, 36–40, 57, 65–67, 82, 100, 108, 127, 134, 136, 137–138, 145, 149, 159
  - Words-*Citations*: Eli 4, 51–58
  - Words-*Monads*: Worms 4, 54, 63–69
  - Words-*Pericopes*: *Diletto* (Beloved) 4, 58–64, 78
- OTHER WORKS
  - "Amor che nella mente mi ragiona", canzone 96
  - "Io son venuto al punto de la rota", canzone 170
  - *Convivio* 1, 13, 60, 75, 85–93, 96, 99, 101–104, 106–108, 111, 115, 121–127, 133, 140, 189, 257, 259, 277, 283
  - *De Monarchia* 1, 6–7, 13, 31, 50, 172–175, 196–197, 215–223, 225–227, 230, 232–242, 277

- *De vulgari eloquentia* 1, 13, 102, 123–124, 127, 170, 277
- *Epistolae* 66, 13, 277
  - *Epistle* VII 173
  - *Epistle to Can Grande della Scala* 12, 85, 112, 258
- *La Vita Nuova* 1, 60, 78, 82, 83, 85, 87, 88–89, 97, 101, 106, 124, 126, 130, 142, 167, 189, 191–193, 199, 243, 251, 254, 258, 277, 283

Dante Society of America 95, 279
Dardanus, progenitor of the Trojans 173
Davidic *imitatio* 51–52, 75, 77
de Man, Paul 109–11, 113–114, 118–119, 130, 137, 143, 146–147
De Sanctis, Gaetano 168, 280
Del Popolo, Concetto 43
Derrida, Jacques 111, 119, 146
Dickinson, Emily 110, 146, 258, 266
Dinah, Biblical matriarch 229
Dionysius the Aeropagite 72
dissimilitudo (dissimilarity) 69–70
Divine providence 59, 61, 221, 224, 231, 271
Dolce, Ludovico 243
Domenico di Michelino 153, 164
Dominic, Saint 170
Don Quixote (Miguel de Cervantes) 270
Donatus 70
Doni, Anton Francesco 194
Doré, Gustave 14, 244
Draelants, Isabelle 64, 66–68, 75
Durling, Robert 86, 105

Earth, Earthly 3, 4, 7, 24, 34, 36, 39, 60, 62, 63, 98, 99, 117, 120, 127, 129–131, 133–134, 136–140, 143–144, 158–159, 170, 172, 175, 190, 209, 210, 211, 213, 218–220, 224–225, 233–234, 236, 238, 240–241, 250, 260, 269–270, 272–273, 276
Easter Friday 272
Eastern Roman Empire 225, 228
Egypt 55, 91–92, 223
Electra, Dardanus' mother 173
Eliot, Thomas S. 12, 167, 263, 266
Elísio, Filinto 240
empire, emperor X, 7, 33, 95, 172–175, 181, 209, 213–230, 232–236, 238–241, 259

Empyrium 175
epitaph 116–121, 124, 126, 131–132, 139, 145, 147
Espírito Santo, Arnaldo do 7, 13, 202, 215, 219, 222, 228, 231, 242, 280
Euclid 185
Exegesis, Biblical 46, 48–51, 58–59, 78–79, 83, 92, 108, 152, 223, 235, 237, 238
- four senses of Scripture 91–92, 114
- *lectio, meditatio, ruminatio* 32, 45, 81, 105, 150–151, 160
- *littera, commentum* 5, 45–46, 49, 51, 54, 57, 60–61, 71, 73, 76, 80, 86, 108, 131–132, 137
Ethiopian Empire 224
Europa, abduction of 170–171
Europe, European III, IX, 6, 12, 152, 161, 167–176, 182, 185, 200, 202–203, 222–223, 225, 245–246, 250, 258, 260, 263, 279, 283
Eurydice, Greek heroine 127, 129, 140, 142
exile 88, 106, 115, 117, 122–123, 125, 208, 229, 247, 271–272
expiatory, atonement 39, 53, 56, 80, 144
Ezekiel, Biblical prophet 98

faith 12, 23, 38, 56, 86, 89, 94–97, 104–105, 132, 224, 275
- faith of the reader IX, 5, 81–82, 87–89, 92–99, 101–103, 105–106
Faria e Sousa, Manuel de 195–198, 202, 209, 213
Fernandes, Padre André 227–228
Fernández de Villegas, Pedro 197
Ferrari, Giuseppe 248
Ferreira de Vasconcelos, Jorge 6, 19, 202, 279
Ferroni, Giulio 6, 13, 167, 168, 281
Fifth Empire X, 7, 215, 217, 219, 224–225, 227, 232–233, 236, 240–241
Figueiredo, João R. IX–X, 1, 7, 13, 195, 200, 203, 281
figura, typological-figural 5, 69–72, 84, 92, 109–110, 113–116, 128, 130–132, 135–136, 138–140, 143, 146
Flamano, João/Flaminio, Giovanni 180

Florence 85–86, 88, 125, 152, 153, 164, 205–206, 212, 249, 274
fontaine de Jouvence 40
Francis of Assisi, Saint 4, 34, 38, 62
– as an *alter-Christus* 63
Francis, Pope 12, 27
Freccero, John 82, 88–89, 107, 133, 146, 156, 160
Frederick III, Holy Roman emperor and wife Dona Leonor 181
Frias, Pedro de 230
Frye, Northrop 269
Fulgentius, Fabius Planciades 184

Gadamer, Hans-Georg 5
Galilei, Galileo 41, 153
Gama, Vasco da 7, 197, 203–207, 209, 211, 212, 253
Ganymede 270
Garrett, Almeida 244, 247, 249
Genette, Gérard 114
Germany 225
Gilson, Étienne 12
Giotto di Bondone 137, 258
Giovanni di Paolo 149, 161
Giovanni Pico della Mirandola 4, 34
– *De hominis dignitate* 4, 34
Giraut de Bornelh (Gerardum de Bornello) 123
Giunta, Bernardo 191, 194
Glossa ordinaria 54, 60, 66
Gmelin, Herman 100
God 4, 17, 21, 31–34, 45, 50–52, 56, 59, 61–63, 70, 72, 82, 93, 95, 97, 98, 100, 101, 103–105, 107, 115, 127, 131, 132, 136–139, 142, 144, 149, 151, 155, 156, 159, 173, 186, 203, 209, 212, 216–219, 221, 222, 224, 227, 230, 231, 233–235, 237, 259, 264, 269, 271, 275
Gregory the Great (Pope Gregory I), Saint 33, 34, 38
– *Dialogues* 34
Grifo, Antonio 154, 166

Hegel, Georg Wilhelm Friedrich 246
Herculano, Alexandre 244
Hercules 112, 129

history 5, 6, 12, 13, 26, 51, 62, 63, 98, 115, 124, 126–128, 130, 135–137, 139, 143, 168, 175, 187, 203, 204, 208, 213, 219, 221, 224, 233, 246, 247, 281, 282
Holanda, Francisco de 190, 191
Hollander, Robert 82, 88, 89, 93
Holy Land 228, 230
Holy Roman Germanic Empire 220, 224
Homer 85, 138, 185, 186, 190, 198, 245, 249, 271
Horace 85, 96, 131, 185
– *Ars Poetica* 96
Hugo, Victor 138
Humanism 2, 4, 9, 13, 34, 40–42
– Biblical 4, 31, 33, 39
Humboldt, Alexander von 248

Imperial, Francisco 185, 186
Index Librorum Prohibitorum 216, 235
Inglese, Giorgio 261
invisibilium, invisibilia 72, 104
Isaiah, Biblical prophet 65, 66, 229
Isidore of Seville 64, 66
– *Etymologies* 64
Israel 90–92, 228–230
Italy 6, 7, 123, 171–173, 175, 181, 187, 191, 193, 198, 226, 228, 244–247, 250, 282

Jacob 235
James, Henry 273
Jerusalem 85, 170, 228, 229, 272
João IV, king of Portugal 217, 224, 227–230
John Climacus, Saint
– *Scala Paradisi* 32, 43, 65
John Chrysostom, Saint 238
Journey V, 2, 3, 5, 12, 13, 15–17, 20, 21, 23–27, 36, 41, 42, 51, 94, 96, 97, 104, 105, 111, 112, 115–118, 126, 127, 129, 131, 149, 153–155, 159, 168–170, 188, 195, 197, 207, 210, 212, 224, 248, 250, 258, 272–274
Juan de Rocacelsa 230
Judah 235
Judea 91, 236
Jupiter, Jove 172, 208, 270
Juromenha, Viscount of 248, 249, 253
Justice 6, 31, 93, 121, 122, 138, 156, 157, 173, 175, 212, 216, 275
Juvenal 184

Kipling, Rudyard 273

Lamennais, Félicité de 31
Landiano 190 (Codex Beccario) 35
Landino, Cristoforo 153, 197, 198
– Commentary on the *Comedy* 153, 197
Latin Urbinate, Codex 35
Latini, Brunetto 12, 116, 117, 140, 170
– *Trésor* 12, 170
Laurentian Library, Florence 152, 162, 163
Lejeune, Philippe 118
Leo III 225
Leonardi, Anna Maria Chiavacci 261
Leonardo 40, 41
– *Treatise on Painting* 40
Leonor (queen of Portugal) 181
Leonor (empress) 181
Levi 229, 235
Liber scalae Machometi (Kitab al Miraj: The Book of Muhammad's Ladder) 65
Lignum vitae 152
Lisbon V, 2, 3, 8, 12, 81, 181, 203, 204, 228, 235, 250, 252, 253
Liturgy, liturgical 51–53, 55, 73, 74, 77, 79
Livy 180, 184, 215
Longfellow, Henry Wadsworth 81
López de Mendoza, Íñigo (Marquis of Santillana) 183
Louis Bertrand, Saint 231
Lourenço, Frederico 257
Lucan 84, 85, 131, 184, 186, 196, 215, 232
Lucca 154, 181
Lucius III, Pope 225
Luís I, king of Portugal 246
Luther, Martin 258

MacIntyre, Alasdair 110
Macrobius 184, 196
Magi 237, 238
Magnentius (v. Lucan) 184
Mandelstam Osip 11, 13, 27, 211
– *Conversation about Dante* 13
Manetti, Antonio 153, 154
– *Sito, forma e misura dello Inferno* 153
Manguel, Alberto 2, 3, 13, 153, 269, 281
Manuel I (king of Portugal) 181

Manuel de Faria e Sousa 198, 209
– *Lusíadas comentadas* 198
manuscripts (of *Commedia*) V, 153
Marcolini, Francesco, typographer 154
Maria Pia of Savoy, queen of Portugal 246
Marnoto, Rita 7, 13, 179, 188, 243, 282
Martinez, Ronald 82, 98
Martínez de Medina, Diego 185
Maximus, Valerius 180, 184
– *Facta et Dicta Memorabilia* 180
Mazzini, Giuseppe 248
Mazzoni, Jacopo 194
Mazzotta, Giuseppe 82
memory
– *loci* 6, 151, 153–155
– *imagines agentes* 6, 151–153, 156–158
– memory, art of 5, 150–151, 153, 161
Mena, Juan de 183, 185, 196
Mendonça, José Tolentino de 2, 3, 149, 280
metalepsis (typological-figural) 5, 109, 113–116, 130, 138
metamorphosis 192, 210
metaphor 59, 62, 66, 104, 114, 152, 156, 157, 263
Methodius, Saint 230
Middle Ages 4, 5, 45, 46, 52, 59, 64, 66, 67, 87, 150, 151, 167, 170, 245
Milton, John 120, 249, 274
mimesis 133, 135–138, 140–142, 144, 145, 156
Mincio 192
miniatures 149, 154, 161–163, 166
Miranda, Francisco de Sá de 6, 188, 190, 192
Miserere 39, 51, 52
Mnemosyne 150
Montemor, Jorge de 188
monarchy 174, 215–219, 224, 225, 233, 234, 236, 237, 240, 241
Moore, Edward 58
Moses 224, 235
Mota, António Augusto da Costa (the uncle) 252, 253
myth 150, 170

Nardi, Bruno 12, 88
Nasti, Paola 4, 13, 45, 282
Nathan 236
Nekyia 112, 129

Nestorius 57
Nile 192

Oaths of Strasbourg (842 AD) 33
Ocean (Indian) 173, 204, 206, 211
Oceania 223
Onorius di Autun 62
– *Expositio Super Cantica canticorum* 62
Orpheus 91, 92, 112, 128, 129, 133, 139, 140
Ossola, Carlo 4, 12, 13, 31, 282
Ovid 33, 84, 85, 90, 91, 131, 185–187, 196, 276
– *Heroides* 33

palinode 89, 103, 133
Pascal, Blaise 269
Passion, of Jesus Christ 52, 53, 54–58
Passion of Perpetua and Felicitas 272
Paul, Saint 130, 144, 219, 227, 230, 231, 241, 272
– *Colossians* 241
– *Ephesians* 219, 220, 223
– *Galatians* 173, 219, 223
– *Romans* 223, 229
Pedro V, king of Portugal 245
Persephone 129
Persia 224
Peter, Saint 230, 236–239, 259
Petrarca, Francesco 7, 184, 187, 188, 189, 191–195, 198, 203
– Laura 188, 194
– *Rerum Vulgarium Fragmenta* 193
– *Triomphi* 193
– *Triumphus Cupidinis* 188
Petrocchi, Giorgio 35, 261
Philip the Fair, king of France 216
philosophy 40, 87, 88, 220–222, 226, 240, 246, 260, 280
Pilate, Pontius 233
Pinto, Augusto da Silva 252, 253
Pires, Maria Lucília 196
Pistoia, Cino da 123, 188
Plato 111, 185, 187, 190, 215, 269
– *Phaedrus* 111
– *Republic* 190
plenitudo temporis 173
Plutarch 150
– *De gloria Atheniensium* 150

poetry
– of integrity 123
– of passion 127, 128
– of virtue 123, 124, 127, 128
Politia 225
Pope, Papacy 216, 225, 229, 230, 234–236, 238–240
Pope, Alexander 118
Pound, Ezra 33
– *Spirit of Romance* 33
Portugal 3, 6, 7, 13, 172, 179, 180, 183, 187, 191, 194, 198, 203, 205, 208, 212, 216, 217, 224, 227–230, 243–247, 249, 250, 252, 254
predestination 7, 129, 130, 215, 223, 227
prosopopoeia 5, 109–113, 115, 118–119, 130, 132, 136, 143
– personification 130, 209, 83

Quaglio, Antonio Enzo 36
Quental, Antero de 245, 246, 253
Queirós, Eça de 244
Quintilian 184

Rabanus Maurus 32, 55
– *Opusculum de Passione Domini* 55
Raphael (Raffaello Sanzio) 193
Rauschenberg, Robert 14
Ravenna 269
Resende, André Falcão de 191
Resende, Garcia de 244
– *Cancioneiro Geral* 180–183, 187, 244
Rhetorica ad Herennium 151
Ribeiro, Bernardim 6, 182, 192
Rice Burroughs, Edgar 273
Ricoeur, Paul 110
Riffaterre, Michael 137, 143
Risorgimento (Italian unification) 8, 246, 247, 282
Rodin, Auguste 14
Rodrigues, Venâncio 259
Roiz del Padrón, Juan 183
Roman Empire 33, 219, 220, 22, 224, 225, 228, 232–234
Roman de la rose 130
Rome 85, 125, 154, 173, 175, 188, 223–225, 228, 231, 232, 235, 240, 259, 272, 281

Rupert of Deutz 39
– *De divinis officiis* 39

Sá, Artur Moreira de 217
Sallust 184
salvation 5, 17, 52–54, 96, 98, 103, 113, 115, 123, 124, 127–129, 132, 138, 140, 175, 218, 219, 233, 234, 258, 261
Samuel 129, 155, 237
Sané, Alexandre-Marie 249
Sanguineti, Federico 36
Sannazzaro, Jacopo 188
Sapegno, Natalino 261
Saul, Biblical king 129, 237
Scaramuzza, Francesco 253
Schlegel, August Wilhelm 248
Shechem 229, 230
Scholasticism 40, 222
– philosophy of 'universals' 40
Sebastianism 227, 230
Sebastião, king of Portugal 227
Sena, Jorge de 258, 204
Seneca, L. Annaeus 184, 184, 215
Sermo, Res 71, 72
Servius 113
– Commentary on Vergil's *Aeneid* 113
Seville 185, 186
Shakespeare, William 120, 129, 245, 246
– *Hamlet* 269, 279
– *Macbeth* 129
Shklovsky, Viktor B. 16
Siberia 269
Simeon 229
Simões, Augusto Costa 250
Simonides of Ceos 193, 150
Singleton, Charles S. 12, 82, 100, 101
sins 54, 154
Solomon, Biblical King 185, 234–236
Spain 182, 186, 199, 225, 227
Speroni, Sperone 194
Spitzer, Leo 100, 101
Statius 96, 97, 184
Suger of Saint Denis, French abbot 272
– *Vita Ludovici regis* 272
Summarium bibliae 49

Tasso, [Bernardo] 191
Terence 184
theology 2, 62, 63, 87, 105, 198, 207, 211, 234, 241, 260, 270
Theseus, Greek Hero 112, 129
Tolstoy, Leo 16
Torre, Andrea 154
translation 8, 13, 58, 143, 215, 217, 241, 244, 253, 257–265
Tree of virtues, Tree of vices (*Arbor virtutum, Arbor vitiorum*) 152
Tribes of Israel 228–230
Trinity 56, 104, 105
Trissino, Gian Giorgio 194
Turkish Empire 228
Turris sapientiae 152, 163

Valencia 183
Vasconcelos, Carolina Michaëlis de 188
Vasconcelos, Jorge Ferreira de 6, 191, 279
Vaz de Carvalho, Jorge 8, 13, 283
Vega, Garcilaso de la 191
Vellutello, Alessandro 154
– *La Comedia di Dante Alighieri con la nova esposizione* 165, 197
Venus 211, 232
Vicente, Gil 6, 181, 279
Vieira, Padre António 7, 215, 217–225, 227–241, 279–281
– *Clavis Prophetarum* 7, 217, 220, 222, 224, 228, 230, 231, 235, 240, 241
– *De Pace Messiae* 220
– *História do Futuro* 217, 225, 229–232
Vigini, Giuliano 220
Villena, Enrique de 182–184
Vinsauf, Galfredo de 184
Virgil 84–85, 112, 128, 131, 184–186, 190, 196, 199, 203, 209, 213, 215, 233, 226, 231, 232, 248, 249, 257, 266
– *Eclogue* IV 106, 128, 190, 257
– *Aeneid* 85, 93, 95, 113, 127–128, 157, 173, 190, 207, 223, 226, 232
Visio Pauli 65
volgare (vernacular) 2, 83–85, 88–90, 93, 105, 123, 130, 131, 142, 170, 198, 258, 260, 263

Volkmann, Ludovico 154
Vulcan 232
Vulgate 35, 58

Weinrich, Harald 156
witch of Endor 129
Wordsworth, William 118–120, 132
– *Essays Upon Epitaphs* 118

Xanthos 192

Yates, Frances 151

Zanzotto, Andrea 170
Zuccaro, Federico 193
Zurara, Gomes Eanes de 180, 181, 244

Printed in the USA
CPSIA information can be obtained
at www.ICGtesting.com
JSHW021305141024
71656JS00017B/94

9 783111 627427